LARS HARTMAN

Prophecy interpreted

THE FORMATION

OF SOME JEWISH APOCALYPTIC TEXTS AND

OF THE ESCHATOLOGICAL DISCOURSE

MARK 13 PAR.

CWK GLEERUP LUND SWEDEN

Translated by Neil Tomkinson, B.A., F.I.L.,
with the assistance of Jean Gray, B.A.

Almqvist & Wiksells
BOKTRYCKERI AKTIEBOLAG
UPPSALA 1966

To Ulla

Contents

PART ONE
Construction in Jewish Apocalyptic Texts

PART TWO

Traditio-Historical Analyses of the Eschatological Discourse

Introduction

A. The aims and methods of the investigation

"Instead of a quagmire, one feels solid ground under one's feet ... here the land is open." It was with metaphors like these that Albert Schweitzer would describe the feelings of the person who came to read Johannes Weiss's book about Jesus' preaching of God's kingdom,[1] after having studied Weiss's precursors.[2] Schweitzer's own contribution ("consistent eschatology") was, of course, intended to offer an equally open field, in which there would be even solider ground under one's feet. The three-quarters of a century which have now elapsed since Weiss's book appeared have, however, seen this open field converted, if not into a battlefield, at any rate into a kind of thicket, and the firm ground has been industriously undermined. The solutions which to Schweitzer appeared exhilarating and well established have had several successors which are largely in radical contradiction both with Schweitzer's theses and with each other.

I shall not make any attempt here to describe the discussions on eschatology which have been carried on in this century, as they have been summarized and analysed in various special works.[3] However, two things which form part of the background of the present work should be noted about these discussions. One is the part played by the intertestamental Jewish apocalyptic literature on the different sides taken in them, and the other is the neglected position occupied by the eschatological discourse in expositions of the eschatology.

The fact that the Jewish apocalyptic literature found its way onto the

---

[1] J. WEISS, *Die Predigt Jesu vom Reiche Gottes* (1892).

[2] A. SCHWEITZER, *Geschichte der Leben-Jesu-Forschung* (2nd ed. 1913), 232.

[3] F. HOLMSTRÖM, *Das eschatologische Denken der Gegenwart* (1936); F. M. BRAUN, *Neues Licht auf die Kirche* (1946), 103–32; A. N. WILDER, The Eschatology of Jesus in Recent Criticism and Interpretation, *J. Rel.* 28 (1948), 177–87; G. R. BEASLEY-MURRAY, A Century of Eschatological Discussion, *Exp. Times* 64 (1952/53), 312–16; N. Q. HAMILTON, The Last Things in the Last Decade, *Interpr.* 14 (1960), 131–42; J. RICHTER, Die "konsequente Eschatologie" im Feuer der Kritik, *Zschr. Rel.- u. Geistesgesch.* 12 (1960), 147–66; O. KNOCH, Die eschatologische Frage, ihre Entwicklung und ihr gegenwärtiger Stand, *Bibl. Zschr.* 6 (1962), 112–20; G. LUNDSTRÖM, *The Kingdom of God in the Teaching of Jesus* (1963); N. PERRIN, *The Kingdom of God in the Teaching of Jesus* (1963).

scholars' desks[4] gave rise to a vital impulse which contributed both to the "eschatological solution" (J. Weiss) and to the whole of the subsequent discussion, an impulse which has been reinforced in recent years by the finds in the Qumran caves. This Jewish apocalyptic constitutes a world of ideas which calls to mind a good deal of the material in the Gospels. Thus the discussions carried on and the standpoints adopted as regards the NT eschatology have in many respects been characterized by the way in which the protagonists adjudged the relations between, on the one hand, Jewish apocalyptic and, on the other, Jesus' preaching and teaching and the faith of the early Church. These three quantities—Jewish apocalyptic, the teaching of Jesus and the faith of the early Church—are thus related to each other in different ways by the protagonists in the exegetical discussion, such as Schweitzer, Bultmann, Werner, Otto, Dodd, Cullmann and Kümmel.[5]

Thus, while eschatology has been allotted a place in the foreground by both exegetical and systematical scholars,[6] one of the Gospel texts which deals with τὰ ἔσχατα most thoroughly, viz. Mk 13 par., has fallen into some obscurity. This is connected with the fact that the majority of the exegetes have assumed that the main part of this chapter of Mark's Gospel is purely Jewish, possibly a miniature Jewish apocalypse incorporated (by Mark).[7] Thus it is supposed that this chapter tells us

[4] The texts were made known by, inter alia, A. DILLMANN's editions and translations of 1 Enoch (ed. 1851, trans. 1853) and Jubilees (ed. 1859, trans. 1849–50), by A. HILGENFELD's works, such as Messias Judaeorum (1869), and later, above all, by the two great editions by E. KAUTZSCH (1900) and R. H. CHARLES (1913). Systematizing works in the history of religion which have helped to make these texts known were written by E. SCHÜRER (Geschichte des jüdischen Volkes II, 2nd ed. 1886, 417 ff.), H. GUNKEL (Schöpfung und Chaos in Urzeit und Endzeit, 1895), W. BOUSSET (Der Antichrist, 1895), P. VOLZ (Jüdische Eschatologie von Daniel bis Akiba, 1903) and H. GRESSMANN (Der Ursprung der israelitisch-jüdischen Eschatologie, 1905).

[5] SCHWEITZER, op. cit.; here might also be mentioned W. MICHAELIS, Täufer, Jesus, Urgemeinde (1928); H. D. WENDLAND, Die Eschatologie des Reiches Gottes bei Jesus (1931); F. BURI, Die Bedeutung der neutestamentlichen Eschatologie für die neuere protestantische Theologie (1935), and later works, such as those of R. SCHNACKENBURG and H. CONZELMANN. See moreover the Bibliography.

[6] Especially perhaps P. ALTHAUS (e.g. Die letzten Dinge, 4th ed. 1933), K. BARTH (e.g. Der Römerbrief, 2nd ed. [1922]; Die kirchliche Dogmatik II:1, 2nd ed. 1946, 712 ff.; IV:1, 1960) and M. SCHMAUS (Katholische Dogmatik IV:2: Von den letzten Dingen, 3rd and 4th eds. 1953). In Sweden E. BILLING (De etiska tankarne i urkristendomen I–II, 1907), G. AULÉN (Den allmänneliga kristna tron, 1923, 5th ed. 1957; trans. The Faith of the Christian Church, 1960), A. NYGREN (Commentary on Romans, 1952), and HJ. LINDROTH (Tankar om kyrkan och sakramenten, 1948).

[7] See on this point the exhaustive survey by G. R. BEASLEY-MURRAY, Jesus and the Future. An Examination of the Criticism of the Eschatological Discourse, Mark 13, with Special Reference to the Little Apocalypse Theory (1954).

12

little of Jesus' own view. However, interest in this "discourse" has increased to some extent since *Redaktionsgeschichte* came on the scene.[8] In this connection the intention is to trace, by analysing the redactional history of the discourse, how the religious views and intellectual proclivities of the evangelist (and his milieu) are reflected in the way in which he selected his material from the mass of traditions, re-worded and re-arranged it, inserted interpretative framework, etc. But the majority of these scholars share the usual view of the origin of the discourse and thus allow it to testify to the early Church's way of thinking, but they do not reckon that it is particularly reliable as a witness to what Jesus meant.

I have subjected this problematical discourse to a fresh critical scrutiny. My aim was to try and shed light on the history of the tradition of these texts, i.e. I wished to disclose, by analyzing these texts, some of the phases—not necessarily all of them—in the development the traditions underwent up to the period when they were written down in the Synoptic Gospels. Part II of this book is devoted to these analyses. This is a limited literary aim and the discussion is mainly carried on on the literary plane. But in so far as firm conclusions are reached there, they are relevant to greater problems which I cannot enter upon now to any appreciable extent, such as the exegesis of the discourse, the assessment of the shifting views of the early Church as regarded eschatology and apocalyptic, and questions concerning the original character and history of the Gospel material. To analyse literary structures in this way means to get tolerably firm ground under one's feet with regard to the controversial situation just indicated, which is also complicated by the arguments of the form critics and by the disputes concerning the de-mythologization of the Gospels.

These literary analyses show that the OT plays an essential part in the structure of the eschatological discourse. Taken together with the hypotheses as to the Jewish origin of the discourse, this fact forms the starting-point for Part I, which has to supply the necessary background for the analyses in Part II. The purpose of Part I is, then, to elucidate certain structures in Jewish apocalyptic texts whose contents resemble that of Mk 13 par., and a principal consideration is the part played by the OT in the building of these structures.[9] The structures I am refer-

---

[8] Represented, for example, by G. BORNKAMM, H. CONZELMANN, W. MARXSEN and W. TRILLING.

[9] In the last few decades, scholars have increasingly realized the importance of the OT in influencing thought both in Judaism around the beginning of the Christian era and in the early Church. This is, of course, not a new discovery, but the last few years have seen the appearance of a rapidly growing stream of special studies in this sphere. See below, 103 f., notes 5 and 7.

13

ring to are, on the one hand, patterns of thought or conceptual frameworks which seem to have played a part in the formation of individual portions of text (they seem to function somewhat like the *Gestalten* in psychology). Attention will be directed, on the other hand, to the detailed structure of some portions of apocalyptic text, and I shall try to make clear the way in which the motif threads are woven together. Here I shall analyse the texts by methods which are in part new and I flatter myself that I shall be able to present some fresh conclusions in the sphere of Jewish apocalyptic, although this field has already been so well examined.[10]

For the investigation in Part I, I have included, if not all, certainly the majority of passages in Jewish intertestamental apocalyptic literature which describe directly and in any detail what is to happen immediately before and in connection with the commencement of the time of salvation.[11] This meant that I had to draw a borderline excluding the large parts of this apocalyptic literature which deal with other matters. This borderline also excluded rabbinic texts and the Qumran texts, at least those published and reported so far. For the evil time which is to precede the coming of the Messiah is certainly discussed in M Sot. IX, but this text is not an apocalypse and is moreover of somewhat too late a date. The Qumran texts certainly contain an abundance of apocalyptic and eschatological motifs,[12] but no text from Qumran has yet been published which describes the last days directly and in detail, in the form of an apocalypse. This limitation is justified by the fact that the investigation is concerned with literary structures in the available Jewish apocalyptic texts and not the origin or history of the ideas, motifs and concepts. The results of the literary analyses debouching in these problems must consequently be compared with and supplemented by researches in the history of ideas, culture and religion, if they are to have conclusive force in these spheres.

It is scarcely necessary to point out that I use the method of historical criticism. However, on account of the hermeneutic discussions of the last few years, I would call attention to the fact that I discuss the Biblical

---

[10] The literature on the subjects I refer to in the two parts of this book is also enormous, and only a selection from it is quoted in the notes.

[11] The portions of text are enumerated below, Chap. II, note 13.

[12] See, for example, F. NÖTSCHER, *Zur theologischen Terminologie der Qumran-Texte* (1956), 149–93; P. GRELOT, L'eschatologie des Esséniens et le livre d'Hénoch, *Rev. Qumr.* 1 (1958/59), 113–31; I. HAHN, Josephus und die Eschatologie von Qumrān, in *Qumran-Probleme* (1963), 167–91; A. S. KAPELRUD, Die aktuellen und die eschatologischen Behörden der Qumrangemeinde, ibid., 259–68; L. STEFANIAK, Messianische oder eschatologische Erwartungen in der Qumransekte?, in *Neutest. Aufsätze, Festschrift für J. Schmid* (1963), 294–302.

14

texts in what is in principle the same fashion as the Jewish texts and thus have no reason to change my point of departure when I pass on from the study of the Jewish texts in Part I to the dissection of the NT texts in Part II. In this respect I adopt the same view as Professor Bultmann,[13] though I do not share his philosophical approach, when, after requiring that the scholar shall "understand" (in the sense of "be unprejudiced about") the object of his research and its historical setting, he goes on to demand that he must have an "existential encounter" (*existentielle Begegnung*) with it, in order to be able to interpret it correctly.[14] Here we touch upon the fundamental questions of historical research (which we need not enter into in detail here), questions such as the possibility of objectivity and how a complicated combination of personal and environmental influences and conscious and unconscious factors enters into the individual scholar's work on his material.[15]

It is self-evident, then, that I have used the method of historical criticism and it is equally self-evident that my method of investigation has been to *analyse* my material. Nevertheless I have unfortunately to emphasize this, as scholars sometimes talk as if the "analytic" method was only really practised by Professor Bultmann and his students of the first and second generations, while other scholars use a "synthetic" method.[16] In order that the reader may be kept constantly informed as to how my results are gained, I have made my account analytic also, instead of presenting the results of the analyses in a synthetic form. This may have made the book more difficult to read, but, on the other hand, the reader is always in a position to check my arguments.

B. A couple of definitions

The controversial situation to which I have already referred makes it necessary to define briefly in what senses I use the two main terms "escha-

---

[13] R. BULTMANN, Das Problem der Hermeneutik, in *Glauben und Verstehen* II (1952), 231.

[14] BULTMANN, op. cit., 217 ff.; id., Wissenschaft und Existenz, in *Glauben und Verstehen* III (1960), 112 ff., and Ist voraussetzungslose Exegese möglich?, ibid., 147 f.

[15] See, for example, L.-E. HALKIN, *Eléments de critique historique* (1960), 25 ff., 101 ff., and cf. also I. S. KON, *Die Geschichtsphilosophie des 20. Jahrhunderts* II (1964), 1–135 (and the references there).

[16] Thus H. CONZELMANN, Jesu självmedvetande, *Svensk Exeg. Årsbok* 28–29 (1963–64), 39 f., in which he does Swedish exegetes the favour of classifying them as taking the middle way between the "synthetic" and the "analytic" methods. The question is whether "analytic" has not sometimes been used as more or less synonymous with "form-critical", including not only the objective isolation of form-elements, but also the philosophy which Bultmann, Dibelius and their pupils have associated with it.

tology" and "apocalyptic".[17] "Eschatology", which is derived from τὸ
ἔσχατον, τὰ ἔσχατα ("the last things"), has been traditionally used, on
the one hand, of "individual" eschatology and, on the other, of "general"
or "collective" eschatology. Individual eschatology refers to the fate
of the individual after death, while general or collective eschatology
refers to the fate of the whole world before and in connection with "the
end", for example, the destruction of the world, the general resurrection
and judgement, and often also the establishment of a divine kingdom,
and so on.

This traditional meaning of the word has faded under the influence of
the existentialist philosophy, so that "eschatology" is no longer used to
describe a saying on the "last things" in the way mentioned above but
is used instead of what is characterized by the existential decision (*Entscheidung*). In this process the time aspect disappears. I propose to
use the word in its traditional sense, though in most cases I refer only to
"general" eschatology.[18]

The word "apocalyptic" is not used altogether unambiguously in
modern exegetical literature either.[19] This word was formed from the
Greek ἀποκάλυψις ("revelation"), and is used, on the one hand, to denote
a form of literature in which secrets are revealed to selected persons.
These secrets may be concerned with history or parts of history, particularly the final phase, with the cosmos, its origin and characteristics
or with divine mysteries. On the other hand, the word may be used of
the content of this kind of literature, which is sometimes quite imaginative and often gives detailed descriptions, especially of catastrophes
which are to occur at the end of time. A similar content may also be
found in texts which are not apocalypses in the formal sense. On account
of these imaginative features, such literature has been adjudged to consist of sterile speculations and to be the expression of unseemly curio-
sity, which has resulted in the word "apocalyptic" being given a dis-
paraging connotation.[20]

---

[17] See on the following paragraphs G. WIDENGREN, *Religionens värld* (2nd ed·
1953), 333 f.; C.-M. EDSMAN, Eschatologie I, *Rel. in Gesch. u. Geg.* II (3rd ed. 1958)·
650 f.; O. CULLMANN, *Heil als Geschichte* (1965), 60 ff. Also A. STROBEL's booklet
Die apokalyptische Sendung Jesu (1962), 7 ff.

[18] Similarly N. A. DAHL, Eschatologie und Geschichte im Lichte der Qumrantexte,
in *Zeit und Geschichte, Festschrift R. Bultmann* (1964), 3 f.

[19] See on the following paragraph H. RINGGREN, Apokalyptik I, II, *Rel. in
Gesch. u. Geg.* I (3rd ed. 1957), 463–66.

[20] Thus, for example, J. B. FREY, Apocalyptique, *Dict. de la Bible, Suppl.* I
(1928), 350 f.; G. EBELING, Der Grund christlicher Theologie, *Zschr. Theol. Ki.*
58 (1961), 230 ff.; E. FUCHS, Über die Aufgabe einer christlichen Theologie, ibid.,
245 ff.; R. BULTMANN, Ist die Apokalyptik die Mutter der christlichen Theologie?,

16

I propose to use the word in a neutral sense, with reference to a number of texts in which secrets are "revealed" *and* with particular reference to the contents of those texts which allude to the last things. Sometimes, in the interests of clarity, I use the combination "eschatological and apocalyptic".

Finally I would point out that I have tried to avoid such expressions as "late Judaism" or similar equivalents of the German *Spätjudentum* and its derivatives. Instead I use the term "Judaism" and its derivatives, sometimes supplemented with expressions which describe more precisely the epoch in the long history of Judaism to which I am referring—the epoch a couple of centuries before and a century or so after the beginning of the Christian era.

C. The texts: versions, dates, etc.

We unfortunately know little of the history of the tradition behind the Jewish apocalyptic texts to be dealt with in Part I, i.e. of the milieu in which they came into existence, the work and functions of their authors and editors, the dates at which they were written and edited, the function of the texts in their original milieux and in the contexts in which they were afterwards transmitted. However, we are not entirely in the dark on these points. Here and there traces of editorial activity may be discerned. Thus the Apocalypse of Weeks was incorporated in a context that was completely new to it (with the result that it acquired fresh nuances of meaning). But it must be acknowledged that a good deal of the history of the texts under consideration is enwrapped in a somewhat embarrassing obscurity.[21]

One of the first subsidiary problems we are faced with in a detailed study of the Jewish apocalyptic texts is their language. Of the texts I shall devote my attention to here, only Or Sib is extant in the original language. (The Qumran finds which have been published or reported do

---

in *Apophoreta, Festschrift für E. Haenchen* (1964), 64–69. Those who are opposed to a negative assessment include G. E. LADD, Why not Prophetic-Apocalyptic?, *J. Bibl. Lit.* 76 (1957), 192–200; STROBEL, op. cit.; E. KÄSEMANN, Die Anfänge christlicher Theologie, *Zschr. Theol. Ki.* 57 (1960), 179 ff. (this article gave rise to the articles by Fuchs and Ebeling just cited, and, together with the following one, to that by Bultmann); id., Zum Thema der urchristlichen Apokalyptik, ibid., 59 (1962), 257 ff.; D. RÖSSLER, *Gesetz und Geschichte* (1960), 43 ff.; B. VAWTER, "And He Shall Come Again with Glory", *Analecta Bibl.* 17 (1963), 143–50.

[21] See on this problem the introductions to the editions of the texts in the Bibliography; also S. ZEITLIN, The Apocrypha, *Jew. Quart. Rev.* 37 (1946/47), 219–48; D. S. RUSSELL, *The Method and Message of Jewish Apocalyptic* (1964), 51 ff.; for Jubilees, see M. TESTUZ, *Les idées religieuses du Livre des Jubilés* (1960), 16 ff., and for Test XII Patr, see the literature mentioned in notes 26 and 27.

not include any of the portions of text which are to be discussed here.)
The rest have reached us only in translations, in several cases in translations of translations.[22] Much may, of course, happen to a text during a
process of translation like this. When different translations of a text
exist and they coincide fairly well, this may be an indication that no
serious changes have resulted from the translations in these cases.[23]
Thus the different Greek and the Ethiopic versions of 1 En agree pretty
well. Here and there the different versions of 4 Ez also give a fairly uniform picture but it often seems very difficult to establish a reliable text
for extracts from this book.

Most of the texts under consideration have several MSS. behind them,
as a mainstay for the scholar who wishes to establish as good a text as
possible, but in a couple of cases the position is not so satisfactory.
Thus, for Ass Mos, for example, there is only a single (Latin) MS.[24]

The last part of the history of these texts was enacted on Christian
ground. This involved their being given an *interpretatio christiana*, which
may also have been reflected in the christianizing of passages by re-
wording and interpolating. Thus, for example, the Latin version of 4
Ez 7,28 reads "my son Jesus", instead of the probably more original
"my son the Messiah".[25]

Recently there has been a heated discussion regarding the possible
Christian interpolations in the Testaments of the Twelve Patriarchs.
On the one hand, A. Dupont-Sommer has asserted that this book is pre-
Christian and purely Jewish and that its original milieu was the Qumran

---

[22] Cf. the previous note and for 4 Ez F. ZIMMERMANN, Underlying Documents
of IV Ezra, *Jew. Quart. Rev.* 51 (1960/61), 107–34. I have no knowledge whatever
of Ethiopic (1 En Sim, Jub), nor of Old Slavonic (Apc Abr), and my acquaintance
with Syriac (2 Bar) is very slight. I have had recourse as often as possible to texts
containing versions that I could understand and have otherwise compared several
modern translations (see the Bibliography). Dr. R. A. Carlson has kindly scrutinized
the sections which deal with texts transmitted in Ethiopic only and has collated
the translations.

[23] Of course, one has to enter a reservation for the possibility that a poor version
may have formed the basis of other versions, which then inherited the poor quality
of their prototype.

[24] Other texts that have a meagre textual basis and are to be considered here are
Jubilees and 2 Baruch. See, for example, R. H. CHARLES in *Pseudepigrapha* (1913),
2 f., 471, and O. EISSFELDT, *Einleitung in das AT* (3rd ed. 1964), 824, 853.

[25] Perhaps this also is secondary in relation to an even more original "my Messiah". See G. H. Box, *The Ezra-Apocalypse* (1912), ad loc., and J. BLOCH, Some
Christological Interpolations in the Ezra-Apocalypse, *Harv. Theol. Rev.* 51 (1958),
89 ff. According to the summary in *Harv. Theol. Rev.* 58 (1965), 463, M. STONE
would read "servant" in the passages in which the "Son" of God is spoken of
(*Features of the Eschatology of Ezra* (1965?)).

community.[26] On the other hand, a directly opposite view has been presented by M. de Jonge, who thinks that the Testaments are a Jewish-Christian work, dating from about the beginning of the third century.[27] I have adopted the view that it was pre-Christian and Jewish in origin but contains Christian interpolations.[28]

This brings us to the question of the dating of these texts. Though there is in most cases a far-reaching consensus of opinion on this point, it is advantageous to recall that the dating often rests upon a rather flimsy basis. On these questions I have adopted the views presented by O. Eissfeldt in his introduction to the OT,[29] i.e. assumed that all the texts under consideration came into existence before the beginning of the Christian era, except Ass Mos (whose author seems to have been a contemporary of Jesus), 4 Ez, 2 Bar and Apc Abr, which can be dated after 70 A.D. (in the last two cases at the beginning of the second century). Thus I also assume a pre-Christian date for the origin of 1 En Sim. As regards these parables, J. T. Milik has presented a view similar to that of de Jonge on the Testaments of the Twelve Patriarchs, that they were written during the second century by a Jewish Christian. One of his principal reasons is that fragments of other parts of 1 En have been found at Qumran but no fragments of 1 En Sim.[30] This *argumentum e silentio*

---

[26] A. DUPONT-SOMMER, *Aperçus préliminaires sur les manuscrits de la Mer Morte* (1950), 116; E. J. BICKERMAN, The Date of the Testaments of the Twelve Patriarchs, *J. Bibl. Lit.* 69 (1950), 245–60; M. PHILONENKO, *Les interpolations chrétiennes des Testaments des Douze Patriarches et les manuscrits de Qoumrân* (1960). Cf. for Philonenko's book E. LARSSON, Qumranlitteraturen och De tolv patriarkernas testamenten, *Svensk Exeg. Årsbok* 25 (1960), 109–18.

[27] M. DE JONGE, *The Testaments of the Twelve Patriarchs* (1953); id., The Testaments of the Twelve Patriarchs and the NT, in *Studia Evangelica* (1959), 546–56; id., Christian Influence in the Testaments of the Twelve Patriarchs, *Nov. Test.* 4 (1960), 182–235 (against Philonenko, op. cit.); id., Once More: Christian Influence in the Testaments of the Twelve Patriarchs, *Nov. Test.* 5 (1962), 311–19.

[28] For the representatives of this view (J. E. GRABE, F. SCHNAPP, W. BOUSSET, R. H. CHARLES and others), see EISSFELDT, *Einleitung*, 859 f., and RUSSELL, *Method and Message*, 55 ff.

[29] EISSFELDT, op. cit., 821 ff. On Apc Abr, see, however, R. MEYER, Abraham-Apokalypse, *Rel. in Gesch. u. Geg.* I (3rd ed. 1957), 72.

[30] J. T. MILIK, [a communication in] Le travail d'édition des fragments manuscrits de Qumrân, *Rev. Bibl.* 63 (1956), 60; id., *Ten Years of Discovery in the Wilderness of Judaea* (1959), 33 f. Cf. G. BEER, in KAUTZSCH, *Apokryphen* II (1900), 230 ff.; E. SCHÜRER, *Die Geschichte des jüdischen Volkes* III (4th ed. 1909), 272 ff.; R. H. CHARLES, *The Book of Enoch* (2nd ed. 1912), lii ff.; W. BOUSSET, *Die Religion des Judentums* (3rd ed. 1926, ed. H. GRESSMANN), 12 f.; C. KAPLAN, The Pharisaic Character and the Date of the Book of Enoch, *Angl. Theol. Rev.* 12 (1929–30), 531–37; M.-J. LAGRANGE, Le Judaïsme avant Jésus-Christ (1931), 112 ff.; E. SJÖBERG, *Der Menschensohn im äthiopischen Henochbuch* (1946), 1 ff.; H. H. ROWLEY, *The Relevance of Apocalyptic* (3rd ed. 1963), 93 ff.; RUSSELL, op. cit., 51 ff.

seems scarcely conclusive, even in combination with the thesis that the idea of the Son of Man which can be read in 1 En Sim is so advanced that it must point to a later period.[31]

Finally I should mention that I give the Jewish apocalyptic texts in translations which largely, though not always, follow those in R. H. Charles's *Pseudepigrapha*. The quotations from the Bible are as a rule from the Revised Standard Version, but I have sometimes—without mentioning it explicitly on each occasion—given a translation which follows the basic text more closely.

---

[31] See also A. DUPONT-SOMMER, *Les écrits esséniens découverts près de la mer Morte* (1959), 311 ff.

PART ONE

Construction in Jewish Apocalyptic Texts

CHAPTER I

The Raw Material

1. *Introduction*

IN THIS chapter I shall give a brief account of the themes of the texts which are to be dealt with later on. Attention will be concentrated on some portions of Jewish texts of an apocalyptic and eschatological nature, dating approximately from the period between the Old and the New Testaments.[1] These texts include extracts on the last things from 1 En, Jub, Ps Sal, Test XII Patr, Ass Mos, 4 Ez, Apc Abr, 2 Bar and Or Sib 3–4.[2]

To designate the content of these texts as "apocalyptic and eschatological" is almost the same as saying that they are pervaded by a comprehensive view of history. For what is "revealed" is in most cases large or small portions of past history, current affairs and future events.[3] This revealed history is regarded in these texts in a special perspective, viz. how God guides the course of history in one way or another towards a goal which He has determined upon—that His kingdom shall be established.[4] The God in whom these authors believe is not a God who leaves

---

[1] In its latest parts Daniel is practically contemporary with some of this literature, but I have nevertheless kept it separate from the texts for discussion, since, as a more or less canonical writing, it very soon came to be directly inspiratory and indeed authoritative for other texts of this kind. See O. EISSFELDT, *Einleitung in das AT* (3rd ed. 1964), 705 ff., 765; *Discoveries in the Judaean Desert* III (ed. M. BAILLET etc., 1962), 107, 114; Josephus, *Ant.* 10,11,7, and below, 63, 97.

[2] A more detailed account of the texts is given below in Chapter II, note 13. The principles of selection are stated above in the Introduction, 14.

[3] Cf. G. WIDENGREN, *Religionens värld* (2nd ed. 1953), 333 f., and G. ÖSTBORN, *Yahweh's Words and Deeds* (1951), 53 f.

[4] On this and the following paragraphs see F. C. BURKITT, *Jewish and Christian Apocalypses* (1914), 30 ff.; W. KÜPPERS, *Das Messiasbild der spätjüdischen Apokalyptik* (1933), 66 ff.; I. L. SEELIGMANN, Phasen uit de Geschiedenis van het Joodsch historische bewustzijn, *Ex Oriente Lux* 7 (1947), 49–73; M. A. BEEK, *Inleiding in de Joodse apocalyptiek* (1950), 66 ff.; W. MANSON, Eschatology in the NT, *Scot. J. Theol., Occ. Pap.* 2 [1953], 1 f.; R. BULTMANN, History and Eschatology in the NT, *NT Stud.* 1 (1954/55), 5 ff.; M. NOTH, Das Geschichtsverständnis der alttestamentlichen Apokalyptik, in *Gesammelte Studien* (1957), 248–73; O. PLÖGER, *Theokratie und Eschatologie* (1959), particularly 37 ff.; D. RÖSSLER, *Gesetz und Geschichte* (1960), 43 ff.; H. H. ROWLEY, *The Relevance of Apocalyptic* (3rd ed. 1963), 166 ff.; D. S. RUSSELL, *The Method and Message of Jewish Apocalyptic* (1964), 205 ff. Cf. E. FASCHER, Antike Geschichtsschreibung als Beitrag zum Verständnis der Geschichte, *Theol. Lit.-Zeit.* 77 (1952), 641–52; O. PLÖGER, Geschichte und Geschichtsschreibung, *Rel. in Gesch. u. Geg.* II (3rd ed. 1958), 1473–76 (refs.).

His elect in the lurch. He will therefore strike down those who are the enemies of His righteous ones and consequently His enemies also. He is a just God, who avenges wrong and punishes sinners. On the other hand, the elect (the righteous) may look forward to a bright future in the new age that will soon commence. Thus, in the last resort what determines these authors' view of history is their idea of God.

A teleological and linear view of history like this is rightly thought to be antithetical to the cyclical view of history, such as is found in the Hellenistic world.[5] An important reason why this view may be said to be teleological is that these authors hold that history has a *telos*, which is contained in divine promises that have not yet been fulfilled.[6] The fact that they believe in a righteous God and that He has promised to intervene and to set up His kingdom, into which His faithful servants may enter, means that history, of necessity, has a goal.

The God who has announced this luminous goal has, however, also laid down the path by which it must be reached. "Let not your spirit be troubled on account of the times; for the Holy and Great One has appointed days for all things" (1 En 92,2). Certain elect ones may already have insight into this path and may catch a glimpse of the goal. This is indeed all prescribed in God's eternal decree, which He has revealed to a few initiates. One of these initiates expresses himself as follows: "I know a mystery and have read the heavenly tablets, and have seen the holy books"[7] (1 En 103,2). This revelation is now accessible in the present apocalypse.

The revelations are ascribed to the great men of the past, such as Enoch, the patriarchs, Moses, Ezra and others, and so they are made to prophesy concerning historical events which occurred before the real author's time and give intimations and consolatory promises concerning

---

[5] G. HÖLSCHER, *Die Ursprünge der jüdischen Eschatologie* (1925), 6; O. CULLMANN, *Christ and Time* (3rd ed. 1962), 51 ff. "Cyclic" has a different meaning in ÖSTBORN's book: see, for example, 54 and 65. Cf. S. H. HOOKE, The Myth and Ritual Pattern in Jewish and Christian Apocalyptic (in *The Labyrinth*, 1935), 221, and RUSSELL, op. cit., 213 ff.

[6] See, for example, R. H. CHARLES, *A Critical History of the Doctrine of a Future Life* (1899), 168 f., and T. W. MANSON, Some Reflections on Apocalyptic, in *Mélanges M. Goguel* (1950), 139–45.

[7] 1 En 81,1 f.; 93,2; 106,19; Jub 5,13. Cf. Dn 10,21 and 1 QH I. 24. The concept of heavenly tablets is not only used in this way: see R. H. CHARLES, *The Book of Enoch* (2nd ed. 1912), 91 f.; P. BILLERBECK, *Kommentar zum NT aus Talmud und Midrasch* II (1924), 169–76; G. WIDENGREN, *The Ascension of the Apostle and the Heavenly Book* (1950), particularly 27 ff.; L. KOEP, Buch IV, *Reallex. Ant. u. Christ.* II (1954), 725–31, particularly 726 f., and F. NÖTSCHER, Himmlische Bücher und Schicksalsglaube in Qumran, *Rev. Qumr.* 1 (1958/59), 405 ff.

what is to come. In this way the author gets authority for what he writes.[8]

But this pseudonymity may also be connected with the author's view of history. For example, when an author has Enoch "foretell" the history of Israel up to the time of the Maccabees, he is in reality relating what he knows from the OT, other sources or his own experience. But may not this narrative technique also incorporate a belief that, if the hero concerned had really prophesied concerning the history of Israel and if he had seen the heavenly tablets, then the content of his prophecy would be precisely what is now being put into his mouth? For God has ordained that these "prophecies" shall come to pass, just as much as that which is in the future from the author's point of time. This view results in a kind of determinism. In spite of God's having alone written and directed this drama, these authors seem nevertheless to count on the existence of an interplay between divine activity and human actions. They do not go so far as to deny human free will and individual responsibility.[9]

This history, which is irresistibly guided by God towards its predetermined goal, is also a continued struggle between God and the powers of evil.[10] This evil resistance to God comes from Satan, fallen angels,[11] evil men, heathens, and apostates and may culminate in a Satanic world empire, which will set itself in opposition to God and all that is sacred. As the struggle approaches its final and decisive phase, the powers of evil will increase their efforts. Nature herself may at that time fall into disorder and suffer from the revolt of the powers of chaos, until at last God, in fulfilment of His promises, finally strikes down the enemy and sets up His kingdom.

The view of history here described in brief is based on the OT. If we compare it very briefly with the OT view of history (in so far as we can speak of an OT view of history that is anything like uniform),[12] we find a

---

[8] RUSSELL (op. cit., 135 ff.) would explain this pseudonomity by the idea of "corporate personality" and of "contemporaneity".

[9] Jub 5,13 versus 41,24 ff.; Ps Sal 14,5 versus 9,7; Apc Abr 22 versus 26; 2 Bar 48,40; 85,7. See ROWLEY, op. cit., 168 ff., and RUSSELL, op. cit., 230 ff. Cf. Ab. III.16; 1 QS III.15 ff.; IV.25; V.1; XI.17; 1 QpH VII.13 f.; Si 33,10 ff. versus 15,11 ff.; Josephus, *Ant.* 13,5, 9. See NÖTSCHER, op. cit., and E. F. SUTCLIFFE, *The Monks of Qumran* (1960), 70 ff.

[10] This conception of a struggle between God and the evil powers is especially stressed by E. STAUFFER, *NT Theology* (1955), for example, 19.

[11] See B. NOACK, *Satanás und Soteria* (1948), 24 ff.

[12] For the theme, see J. PEDERSEN, *Israel* III–IV (1940), 567, 574, 596 ff., 653 ff.; C. R. NORTH, *The OT Interpretation of History* (1946); G. VON RAD, Theologische Geschichtsschreibung im AT, *Theol. Zschr.* 4 (1948), 161–74; G. HÖLSCHER, *Geschichtsschreibung in Israel* (1952), 130 ff., 243 ff.; ÖSTBORN, op. cit.; M. BURROWS,

similar teleological outlook. Thus, in the Deuteronomic[13] and Chronist historical books, we see that what is described has an internal coherence, characterized by the fact that God has sin and idolatry punished and rewards godliness with blessing. All things, however, lead on to the glorification of God's people. The same perspective is to be found in the prophetic literature; the goal is the salvation of God's people, a salvation which is often connected with a Messianic figure. This history is characterized in the OT also by the struggle between God and the powers of evil, a description which covers all kinds of resistance to God, including national enemies.[14]

The differences between the OT view of history and the later apocalyptic view are largely to be found in the shifts of emphasis. Some of these shifts are obviously connected with the changed political circumstances: the Jews had become a small and oppressed people, squeezed in between great powers. The centre of interest has moved forward to the last days, when there will be judgement and salvation. The superiority of the enemies and the evil powers over the people of God has grown greater: the enemy is great, while the people of God are powerless. We discern a tendency to despair of the present state of the world, a tendency which may be intensified into a kind of dualism. According to the OT, God certainly guides the nations of the earth (Ps 67,5), but here this view is heightened into the determinism mentioned above, one manifestation of which is probably the desire to arrange the history of the world in periods.[15]

At the same time we must be quite clear that it is unrealistic to distinguish the apocalyptic view too sharply from the OT view.[16] Even in

Ancient Israel, *Amer. Orient. Series* 38 (1955), 99–131; H. GESE, Geschichtliches Denken im Alten Orient und im AT, *Zschr. Theol. Ki.* 55 (1958), 127–45; G. FOHRER, Die Struktur der alttestamentlichen Eschatologie, *Theol. Lit.-Zeit.* 85 (1960), 401–20; I. ENGNELL, Historieskrivning, *Svenskt Bibl. Uppslagsverk* I (2nd ed. 1962), 970 f.

[13] See M. NOTH, *Überlieferungsgeschichtliche Studien* I (1943), 87 ff.; I. ENGNELL, *Gamla Testamentet* I (1945), 210; R. A. CARLSON, *David, the Chosen King* (1964), 22 ff. and passim.

[14] I. ENGNELL, Motståndare, *Svenskt Bibl. Uppslagsverk* II (2nd ed. 1963), 169–71.

[15] Cf. CHARLES, *Critical History*, 173 ff.; E. STAUFFER, Das theologische Weltbild der Apokalyptik, *Zschr. System. Theol.* 8 (1930/31), 203–15., especially 207 ff.; N. N. GLATZER, *Untersuchungen zur Geschichtslehre der Tannaiten* (1933), 14 ff., 20 ff.; P. VOLZ, *Die Eschatologie der jüdischen Gemeinde* (2nd ed. 1934), 4 ff.; E. SJÖBERG, *Gott und die Sünder im palästinischen Judentum* (1938), 235 f.; E. C. RUST, *The Christian Understanding of History* (1947), 119 ff.; J. BLOCH, *On the Apocalyptic in Judaism* (1952), 15 ff.; PLÖGER, *Theokratie*, 39 f.

[16] See, for example, R. OTTO, *Reich Gottes und Menschensohn* (1934), 28, and BLOCH, op. cit., 28.

the OT, and not only in Daniel, there are sections which are closely related to the later apocalyptic writings (for example, Is 24–27, Ezekiel
and Joel)[17] and the transition appears to be even more fluid if we consider that there is a great probability that even the non-apocalyptic
texts of the OT became apocalyptic *de facto*, in so far as they were considered to have something to say to later generations about their present
and their future. In this respect the old prophecies were obscure, but, if
understood aright, they also contained instruction as to what was to
happen in the future. [18] The statement on the Teacher of Righteousness
in the Habakkuk commentary of the Qumran sect would seem to be
significant: the sect may hear of "all the things that are to co[me upon]
the last generation from the mouth of the priest whom God has placed
in [the congregation] to expound all the words of his servants the prophets, [by whom] God has related all which is to come upon his people".[19]
It is not surprising that the apocalyptic texts to be discussed are also
leavened with such "topical" and eschatological expositions of the
Bible: how this came about we shall see in more detail later on.

This view of history and its deep roots in the OT have contributed to
the creation of a certain harmony in all the different formulations of
Jewish eschatological expectation in relation to the future, as they are
depicted in the apocalyptic writings. But the details in these formulations
vary considerably, even as regards such relatively essential matters as
whether *one* Messiah or two or no Messiah at all will inaugurate the time
of salvation (or a Messianic kingdom for a limited period of time).[20]

[17] Cf. S. B. FROST, *OT Apocalyptic* (1952). Is 24–27 is generally held to be a later
addition. See, for example, L. AUBERT, Une première Apocalypse (Esaie 24–27),
Et. Théol. Rel. 11 (1936), 280–96, 12 (1937), 54–67; J. LINDBLOM, *Die Jesaja-
Apokalypse, Jes. 24–27* (1938); E. S. MULDER, *Die Teologie van die Jesaja-Apoka-
lipse (Jesaja 24–27)* (1954). On the other hand, see I. ENGNELL, Jesajas bok, *Svenskt
Bibl. Uppslagsverk* I, 1143–47.

[18] See J. KAUFMANN, Apokalyptik, *Enc. Jud.* II (1928), 1144; R. T. HERFORD,
Talmud and Apocrypha (1933), 181; H. W. HERTZBERG, Die Nachgeschichte alttesta-
mentlicher Texte innerhalb des AT, *Zschr. At. Wiss., Beih.* 66 (1936), 110–21;
G. E. LADD, The Kingdom of God in the Jewish Apocryphal Literature, *Biblioth.
Sacra* 109 (1952), 322 f.; E. JANSSEN, *Juda in der Exilszeit* (1956), 89 ff., 105 ff.;
R. BLOCH, Midrash, *Dict. de la Bible, Suppl.* V (1957), 1267 ff. This "topical"
interpretation can be seen also in the LXX: see I. L. SEELIGMANN, *The Septuagint
Version of Isaiah* (1948), 70 ff. Cf. G. HÖLSCHER, Problèmes de la littérature apo-
calyptique juive, *Rev. Hist. Phil. Rel.* 9 (1929), 101 f.

[19] 1 QpH II.7–10. Cf. Si 39,1 ff.

[20] One Messiah in, for example, Ps Sal 17,23 ff.; two Messiahs in 1 QS IX.11,
CD XII. 23 (probably); no Messiah in 1 En 1–36, Ass Mos. And cf. G. R. BEASLEY-
MURRAY, The Two Messiahs in the Testaments of the Twelve Patriarchs, *J. Theol.
Stud.* 48 (1947), 1–12; K. G. KUHN, Die beiden Messias Aarons und Israels, *NT
Stud.* 1 (1954/55), 168–79; M. SMITH, What is Implied by the Variety of Messianic

Just as it is now regarded as erroneous, as far as the primitive Church is concerned, to freely mix together evidence from the Gospels of Mark and Luke, the Epistles of Paul and the Book of Revelation, for example, so we should be aware of the risks and the uncertainty involved in supplementing statements from, say, 1 En 1–36 with features from 2 Bar or Ass Mos, with the conscious or unconscious assumption that there was an eschatological dogma in the Jewish apocalyptic.

In presenting the raw material (the elements from which the thought patterns of the different texts were formed) against the background of this view of history, I shall divide this raw material into five groups of constituents:[21]

A. The description of the background of the divine intervention, evil times, moral evil, catastrophes, etc.

B. A divine intervention (by God or the Messiah).

C. The passing of judgement.

D. The fate of sinners, their punishment, etc.

E. The time of salvation, the blessed state of the elect, etc.

These themes do not always appear in this order in the texts. It may happen that they are interlaced, so that, as in 1 En 99 f., the woes over the sinners cover both their future punishment (D) and their misdeeds in the present (A), which will result in this punishment.

2. *The Preliminary Time of Evil (A)*

The texts to be considered often give the divine intervention a dark background, characterized by all kinds of evil, oppressions and irregularities.[22] These descriptions of the background may include material from the author's own period, for example, the persecution of the faithful in Ass Mos 8,1 ff.,[23] and also motifs from the OT, for example, the family conflicts in Is 19,2 or Mi 7,5 f. The essential thing here is that this material has been, as it were, transposed and given a quite definite place in the historical scheme.[24] The sufferings of the righteous man are

---

Figures?, *J. Bibl. Lit.* 78 (1959), 66–72; W. S. LaSor, The Messianic Idea in Qumran, in *Studies in hon. A. A. Neuman* (1962), 343–64.

[21] For a more detailed description and more ample illustration, see Volz, *Eschatologie*. See also L. Gry, La "mort du Messie" en IV Esdras, VII, 29 [III, V, 4], in *Mémorial Lagrange* (1940), 133–39.

[22] This phenomenon is to be met with in several religions: see, for example, Widengren, *Religionens värld*, 347 ff.; A. Olrik, *Om Ragnarok* I–II (1902–14); C. C. McCown, Hebrew and Egyptian Apocalyptic Literature, *Harv. Theol. Rev.* 18 (1925), 371 ff.

[23] See B. Noack, trans. (1963), ad loc.

[24] See Rowley, *Relevance*, 171 ff.

then not anything he happens to be subjected to in some hidden nook of history; they are set in a wider context, like the convulsions going on around him. Through spectacles coloured by the above view of history, all these events are seen to have clear functions. On the one hand, they are an expression of the ever-increasing efforts made by all the powers of evil in their hopeless struggle with God, who will strike when the struggle reaches its approaching culmination. (Here we get an inkling of the deep roots which these ideas have in old cultic and mythical patterns[25].) On the other hand, in acquiring in this way a "meaning", a function in the history of the world in relation to God, these sufferings may also form a basis for consolation and exhortations to faithfulness. Thus a description of this evil time which is used in rabbinic literature is "the pangs of the Messiah" (חבלו של משיח, Aram. חבליה דמשיח): from these pangs the good Messianic era will be born. This term is not to be found in the literature with which we are concerned now.[26]

If we survey the texts under discussion, we see that a description of the evil time which is to precede the divine intervention does not occur in them all. This applies principally to 1 En 1–36 and 37–71 (Sim). The evil of this world is not altogether eliminated on this account,[27] but the difference is striking in comparison with other parts of 1 En, not to mention 4 Ez and 2 Bar which are very thorough in this respect. We may ask ourselves why we do not find in these sections of 1 En the same interest as elsewhere in relating the wickedness of the sinners to the eschatology. It is included here mainly because it is punished. This may be connected with the fact that these two "books" show only a slight desire to fit the evil world into a course of events which moves step by step towards its goal. Thus, what is revealed in 1 En 1–36 is rather how evil came into the world through the fall of the angels (Gn 6) and how these introducers of evil are to be punished.[28] Again, 1 En Sim seems to con-

---

[25] See, for example, S. Mowinckel, *Psalmenstudien* II (1922), 45–77, 244–68.

[26] b Sanh. 98b, Mek. Ex 16,25 (Billerbeck, *Comm.* I, 1922, 950; IV, 1928, 977 ff.) As regards Qumran, the picture of the birth in 1 QH III.6–18 has been the subject of discussion. See A. S. van der Woude, *Die messianischen Vorstellungen der Gemeinde von Qumrân* (1957), who finds that it describes the tribulations of the Qumran sect in the last days. Cf. J. V. Chamberlain, Another Qumran Thanksgiving Psalm, *J. Near East. Stud.* 14 (1955), 32–41; id., Further Elucidation of a Messianic Thanksgiving Psalm from Qumran, ibid., 181 f.; G. Hinson, Hodayoth III, 6–18: in what sense messianic?, *Rev. Qumr.* 2 (1959/60), 183–204 (refs.); H. Ringgren, *Tro och liv enligt Döda-havsrullarna* (1961), 153 ff. (refs.).

[27] 1 En 46,7 f.; 47,2.

[28] L. Jung, *Fallen Angels in Jewish, Christian, and Mohammedan Literature* (1926), 90 ff.; A. Lods, La chute des anges, *Rev. Hist. Phil. Rel.* 7 (1927), 301 ff. T. F. Glasson, *Greek Influence in Jewish Eschatology* (1961), 62 ff., finds a parallel between these fallen angels and the Titans. O. Cullmann, *Die Christologie des NT*

centrate so completely on the transcendental—the Son of Man and his kingdom—that the events of this world seem to pale into insignificance: the righteous "have hated and despised this world of unrighteousness" (1 En 48,7) much more than they have fitted it into a view of history.

Otherwise these texts give us a multitude of details in their descriptions of this evil background. By simplifying them somewhat we may classify their motifs in four groups:

(a) *Errors in religious and moral respects.* False prophets arise and men devote themselves to idolatry (especially according to Or Sib [29]). Men are evil and immoral in all sorts of ways[30] and do not let bonds of friendship or family ties prevent them from committing evil deeds against persons closely related to them.[31] As wisdom and genuine faith in God are often combined, we may also include here, as a related phenomenon, the circumstance that wisdom is rare among men.[32]

(b) Sometimes the preceding group is quite closely related to motifs of *confusion and suffering caused by external circumstances.* People fall into a panic[33] or suffer tribulations.[34] The righteous are oppressed or persecuted by unjust persons in authority or by heathens.[35]

(c) The *political misfortunes* take up a great deal of space. Evil rulers or empires arise.[36] Peoples and cities go to war or raise revolts.[37] The

---

(2nd ed. 1958), 147 f., attempts, from the fact that in 1 En the blame for the Fall is not laid on Adam, to draw the conclusion *e silentio* that this was because the Son of Man was regarded as the Primordial Man coming again. This conclusion seems too uncertain to me. Cf. moreover below, 39, note 27.

[29] 1 En 80,7; 99,7; Test Levi 17,11; Test Jud 21,9; 23,1; Test Is 6,1 (Belial); Test Napht 4,4; Or Sib 3,29 ff.; 3,63 ff. (Belial); 3,275 ff.; 3,604 ff., 5,74 ff. Of course, this is connected with the environment and propagandist aim of Or Sib. For the connection between Belial, false prophets and idolatry, cf. Dt 13.

[30] 1 En 91,6 f., 93,9; 99,1 ff., 8 ff.; 106,19–107,1; Jub 23,14, 17 ff.; Ps Sal 17,22; Test Levi 4,1; 14,1; Test Jud 21,8; Test Iss 6,1; Test Zeb 9,9; Ass Mos 7,4 ff.; 4 Ez 5,2, 11; Apc Abr 29,2; 2 Bar 27,12; 48,37 f.; Or Sib 3,568 f.; 4,152 ff. See also M Sot. IX.15 and 1 QH III.25 ff.

[31] 1 En 99,5, 15; Jub 23,19; 4 Ez 5,9; 6,24. See also M Sot. IX.15. Cf. Philo, *De execrat.* 134 ff.

[32] 4 Ez 5,10; 2 Bar 48,33, 36. See also M Sot. IX.15, and cf., e.g., Dn 11,33, 35; 12,3.

[33] 4 Ez 5,1; 6,23 f.; 13,30; 2 Bar 25,3; 70,2, 6; Or Sib 3,566.

[34] Jub 23,12 f.; Apc Abr 29,15 f.; 2 Bar 25,3 f.; Or Sib. 3,602. Cf. 3 Q5 I–II.

[35] Jub 23,23 ff.; Ps Sal 17,15 ff.; Test Jud 21,9; Ass Mos 8,1 ff.; 4 Ez 11,42; 2 Bar 27,11.

[36] Ass Mos 7,3 ff.; 8,1 ff.; 4 Ez 5,6; 11,40 ff.; 2 Bar 39,5 f.; 70,3 f.; 82,3 ff.; Or Sib 3,75 ff. And cf. M Sot. IX.15.

[37] 1 En 99,4; Jub 23,13; 4 Ez 5,5; 9,3; 13,31; Apc Abr 30,6; 2 Bar 72,2; Or Sib 3,632 ff. Furthermore, 2 Bar 48,32, with CHARLES' conjectural amendment of ܢܘܫܠܬ "shall rest" to ܢܘܚܙܠܬ "shall be moved". For the interchange of ע and ח, cf. P. WERNBERG-MØLLER, Observations on the Interchange of ע and ח in the Manual of Discipline (DSD), *Vet. Test.* 3 (1953), 104–107.

Jews are attacked and their country is devastated by their enemies.[38] Sieges take place and are accompanied by starvation, plague, massacres,[39] and imprisonment or dispersion.[40]

(d) *Accidents or abnormal phenomena in the natural creation.* Mention is made of earthquakes,[41] strange events in the heavens,[42] the falling of fire and the like[43] and drought and failure of crops.[44] Man's labour is in vain.[45] The animal world is also affected.[46] Ghosts are seen and omens occur.[47]

A glance at the notes on the preceding paragraphs will show that these details are not spread evenly over the eschatological portions of these writings. This fact may once more serve to emphasize that it is inadvisable to draw conclusions as to the content of Jewish apocalyptic expectation mainly on the basis of 2 Bar and 4 Ez,[48] which have the most abundant motifs in this respect.

The belief that evil times would precede the end was probably favoured by two factors in the Jewish milieu in the period under discus-

---

[38] Jub 23,23; Test Jud 23,3 f. (cf. 22,2); Apc Abr 27,1 ff. The motif of the last assault of the heathen occupies an intermediate position between, on the one hand, the motifs I have grouped together as the "background" of the divine intervention (A) and, on the other, the group of motifs which includes the fate of sinners, their punishment and the like (D), to which we shall return later on. In so far as the present texts relate the appearance of these enemies and their destruction *seriatim*, I include them under (D). I also assign 2 Bar 70,7 to (A), though with a certain hesitation: ("then the Most High will reveal those peoples which He has prepared before. And they shall come and make war with the leaders that shall then be left"). I do so because the earthquake, fire and famine mentioned in 70,8 do not seem to refer to these assailants. Doubt may be raised by 71,1, in which the holy land is said to have mercy on its own and to protect its inhabitants (cf. 1 En 56,7). Volz (*Eschatologie*, 149) denies the possibility of this "Dogma" in 2 Bar on grounds that are a little too systematic (cf. 48,37, which I assign to (D)). R. H. Charles (*Pseudepigrapha*, 1913, 517) is doubtful.

[39] Jub 23,13, 23; Test Jud 23,3; Apc Abr 30,6 f.; 2 Bar 27,3 ff.; 70,6 ff.; Or Sib 3,265 f., 566 f., 601 ff.

[40] Jub 23,13; Ps Sal 17,20; Test Jud 23,3; Test Napht 4,2; Or Sib 3,265 ff. Cf. Philo, *De execrat.* 137 ff.

[41] Test Levi 4,1; 4 Ez 5,8; 9,3; Apc Abr 30,6; 2 Bar 27,7; 70,8. Cf. 1 QH III.29 ff.

[42] 1 En 80,4 ff.; Test Levi 4,1; 4 Ez 5,4; Or Sib 3,65 (Belial's "signs"), 798 ff.; 4,174.

[43] Test Levi 4,1; 4 Ez 5,8; 2 Bar 27,10; 70,8; Or Sib 4,173 ff.

[44] 1 En 80,2 f.; Jub 23,18; Ps Sal 17,20 f.; Apc Abr 30,5; 2 Bar 27,6. Cf. Philo, *De execrat.* 127 ff.

[45] Jub 23,18; 4 Ez 5,12. Cf. Philo, *De execrat.* 141 f., and 1 QpMi XVII–XIX.2 ff.

[46] Jub 23,18; 4 Ez 5,6, 8; Apc Abr 30,6.

[47] 4 Ez 5,5 ff.; 6,21 f., 24; 2 Bar 27,9; 48,34; Or Sib 3,798 ff.

[48] E. Schürer, *Geschichte des jüdischen Volkes* II (4th ed. 1907), 609, may be misunderstood in this way.

sion.[49] On the one hand, there was the interpretation of history and the contemporary world inspired by the OT along the lines indicated above and, on the other, there were the statements in the OT which were interpreted as prophecies of increasing evil. At this point I would only indicate one passage from the OT which would seem to have played a certain part, viz. the account of the increasing evil before the Flood (Gn 6,5). The Flood was now interpreted as a *typos* of God's visitation at the end of time.[50] We find this first in the "Book of Noah"[51] and later in other parts of 1 En. This increasing evil then became a *topos* in the subsequent apocalyptic,[52] which was underpinned by the dramatic view of history and expanded by the addition of details which were often taken from the OT.

In its different variations this evil time is not now presented soberly, as simple notes concerning facts in the future but is coloured in different ways by the view of history just described. Most of the phenomena in the (*b*) and (*c*) groups of motifs, together with the drought and the vain labour in the (*d*) group, were thus considered to be divine punishments inflicted on mankind on account of its wickedness, a wickedness which was often described in terms of the (*a*) group. (However, both wickedness and punishment are predicted: there is still this dualism of determinism and freedom of choice with responsibility.[53])

We may take as an example Ps Sal 17,21: "The heavens withheld the rain from dropping upon the earth, springs were stopped (that sprang) perennial(ly) out of the deeps, (that ran down) from lofty mountains, for there was none among them that wrought righteousness and justice".[54] This is the old way of regarding the matter, well known from

---

[49] This is not to say that I reject the possibility that the contacts with Iran may have been stimulating in these respects too, but anyhow the ideas are essentially cast in the Jewish mould. See G. WIDENGREN, Quelques rapports entre Juifs et Iraniens à l'époque des Parthes, *Suppl. Vet. Test.* 4 (1957), 197–241, esp. 223 ff., and RUSSELL, *Method and Message*, 270 f.

[50] 1 En 91,5 ff.; 93,4: the Flood = "the first end". Cf. 1 En 10; Jub 5,9 ff.; Vit Ad 49,3. Moreover Mek. Ex 18,1; Gn R. 49 (ad 18,25); Mt 24,37 par.; 2 Pt 3,6 f. See VOLZ, *Eschatologie*, 160, 336, and J. DANIÉLOU, *Sacramentum futuri* (1950), 55–85. Cf. E. LÖVESTAM, En problematisk eskatologisk utsaga: Mark. 13:30 par., *Svensk Exeg. Årsbok* 28–29 (1963–64), 64–80, esp. 73, 78 f.

[51] 1 En 6–11; 39,1–2*a*; 54,7–55,2; 60; 65,1–69,25; 106–107. See, for example, CHARLES, *Pseudepigrapha*, 168, and HAMMERSHAIMB, trans., 71.

[52] 1 En 91,6; 93,4 ff. (the Apocalypse of Weeks); Jub 23,9 ff.; 4 Ez 5,2.

[53] Consider, for example, how 1 En 106,13 ff. prophesies the Fall of the Angels (Gn 6), divine judgement in the form of the Flood and then still greater iniquity on the earth. All this the prophet can say, because he knows "the mysteries of the holy ones" and has "read in the heavenly tablets" (106,19).

[54] See also Jub 23,11 ff.; Test Jud 21,6–22,3; Test Zeb 9,5 ff.; Or Sib 4,152–179.

the OT, where the Deuteronomic books especially apply it almost mechanically.[55]

We find exactly the same tradition when in some texts the authors have punishment in the form of exile followed by divine intervention. This involves the people being re-assembled in the Holy Land, with which the restoration is connected.[56]

In some texts—although none of those with which we are concerned here—the authors also consider the enemy's devastation of the country and the conquest of Jerusalem as punishment for the sins of the people.[57] But when the author of a portion of 4 Ez has to adopt an attitude to the events around the year 70 A.D., he refuses to follow this line.[58] The destruction of the City and the Temple was not only felt by him as a national and religious insult but also disturbed his faith in God and posed the question of whether there is any divine justice: "I have seen how you suffer the sinners and spare the ungodly and have destroyed your people and preserved your enemies; and you have not made known at all to any one how your way may be comprehended[59]" (4 Ez 3,30 f.). A reference to the inscrutability of God's plans does not suffice: "I have not desired to ask about the ways of what is above, but about those things which pass over us daily: why is Israel given up to the heathen? ... The Law of our fathers is set at nought ... We indeed are not worthy to obtain mercy, but what will He do for His name, which is called upon us?" (4 Ez 4,23–5). The final solution is the bright future which is depicted in the continuation of the apocalypse.

In the mind of the author of these lines from 4 Ez we glimpse an intense struggle, resulting from his inherited view of God as the leader of history. We have to regard the prospect of a bright future not only as a projection of desires arising from resentment but also as the consequence of the author's belief in a just God who has promised this time of salvation to the faithful.[60]

---

[55] Cf. above, note 13, and see, for example, Lv 26; Dt 28; Jdc 6,1 ff.; Is 9,8–10,34; Jr 13,22 ff.; 16,10 ff.; 32,26 ff.; Thr 4,13; Ez 35. For the relation between the Deuteronomic work and Jr, see J. BRIGHT, The Date of the Prose Sermons of Jeremiah, *J. Bibl. Lit.* 70 (1951), 15–35, and S. HERRMANN, *Die prophetischen Heilserwartungen im AT* (1965), 157, 163–95.

[56] See Ps Sal 17,28; Test Jud 23,5; Test Iss 6,4.

[57] Ps Sal 2,1 ff.; Josephus, *Bell.* 4,3,12; 5,13,6; 7,8,1; b Shab. 119b, b Taan. 29a, b Yoma 9a, b BM. 30b. Cf. 2 Bar 10,18.

[58] For the theme, see W. MUNDLE, Das religiöse Problem des IV. Esrabuches, *Zschr. At. Wiss.* 47 (1929), 235 ff.; W. WICHMANN, *Die Leidenstheologie* (1930), 32 ff., 43 ff.; SJÖBERG, *Gott und die Sünder*, 228 ff.; M. SIMON, *Verus Israel* (1948), 19 ff.

[59] Thus with the Syr. Lat. *derelinqui*. Cf. 2 Bar 14.

[60] Cf. how the author wrestles with similar problems in Ps Sal 2. See H. L. JANSEN, *Die spätjüdische Psalmendichtung* (1937), 110 f.

One expression of the same theocratic view is the way in which an evil ruler or a world empire in the last days is transposed so as to epitomize the Satanic resistance to God. In Christian texts this phenomenon was developed into "Antichrist".[61] To speak "great things" against God, to lay claim to divine honours, to profane the Temple of the one God with idols—these things were regarded as manifestations of a purely superhuman and Satanic will to power *vis-à-vis* God. In apocalyptic contexts we first meet with this phenomenon in Daniel, where in 8,11 we read of a horn which "magnified himself even to the prince of the host". However, older texts of the OT are behind this: we need only recall the arrogance of Babylon in Is 14: "I will ascend into heaven, I will exalt my throne above the stars of God; ... I will be like 'Aelyon" (v. 13 f.).[62]

A further manifestation of this teleological view of history is that many of the phenomena referred to here are considered to be "signs".[63] This applies to 4 Ez, 2 Bar and Or Sib, and is consequently, judging from the present texts, of relatively late occurrence in Palestinian apocalyptic.[64] In Ps Sal (17,20 f.) drought is a punishment for the sins of the people. But in 2 Bar (27,6) drought and crop failure are included in a series of signs of the end of the world. The things enumerated there are certainly evil things, but at the same time they point to something beyond the objective event. The concept is connected with the belief that these evil things form part of the dramatic struggle in the last days, which will soon end in the victory of God. It is this victory that the signs witness of, as signs.

3. *Divine Intervention (B)*

The divine intervention in the events of the last days is a necessary peripeteia in what these authors regard as the drama of history. Here also they have a long tradition behind them, evidenced for centuries before in the OT, which in different contexts and in different ways relates how the kingdom of God will be set up[1] or how the Day of Yahweh

---

[61] Ass Mos 8,1 ff.; 4 Ez 5,6 (thus G. H. Box, *The Ezra-Apocalypse*, 1912, ad loc.); 11,40 ff.; 2 Bar 39,5; Or Sib 3,63 ff. See B. Rigaux, *L'Antéchrist* (1932), 174 ff.; A. Fridrichsen, Antikrist, *Oikodomé* 1 (1949), 43–57; Rowley, *Relevance*, 33 ff., 172 ff.; V. Maag, Der Antichrist als Symbol des Bösen, in *Das Böse* (1961), 63–89.

[62] Cf. 1 En 46,7; b Ḥag. 13 a.

[63] Cf. H. Schlier, Zum Verständnis der Geschichte nach der Offenbarung Johannis, in *Die Zeit der Kirche* (3rd ed. 1962), 266 ff.

[64] Cf. Sap 8,8; 2 Mcc 5,2 ff.; Josephus, *Bell.* 6,5,3. For the relation with the OT, see below, 76.

[1] See J. Hempel, Königtum Gottes im AT, *Rel. in Gesch. u. Geg.* III (1959), 1706–09, and refs. there.

will dawn with judgement and salvation.[2] The futurist aspect of these ideas has come to be emphasized more than it was at the time of their probable origin in the cult.[3] Proclamations and oracles have become prophecies of the future and promises or threats concerning what is to happen. When we come to consider the Jewish texts under discussion, we find that this futurist aspect has been supplemented to the extent that the divine intervention is thought to be predetermined,[4] in the same way as the evil things that were discussed in the previous section.

While in ancient times "the kingdom of God's anointed" did not differ essentially from "the kingdom of God"—the anointed king sat on the throne of Yahweh (cf. 1 Ch 29,23)[5]—in the present texts there is often a difference between the two, in the sense that some texts refer only to God's intervening in order to set up His kingdom, others describe the intervention of a representative of God and others again (4 Ez, 2 Bar) solve the problem by introducing the Messiah and his kingdom as a preliminary stage to the kingdom of God.[6]

God's own entry upon the scene is expressed by saying that God "comes" down to the earth, God "rises up", God is "revealed", etc.[7] Sometimes this coming is depicted in colours taken from the texts of OT theophanies: all things tremble, the mountains melt like wax, the earth is shattered, etc.[8]

[2] See W. A. HEIDEL, *The Day of Yahweh* (1929); L. ČERNÝ, *The Day of Yahweh* (1948), and G. VON RAD, The Origin of the Concept of the Day of Yahweh, *J. Sem. Stud.* 4 (1959), 97–108.

[3] See MOWINCKEL, *Psalmenstudien* II, 44–145, 229 ff.; id., *He That Cometh* (1956), 138 ff.; A. BENTZEN, *King and Messiah* (1955), 21 ff.; A. R. JOHNSON, *Sacral Kingship in Ancient Israel* (1955), e.g. 124 ff.; G. WIDENGREN, *Sakrales Königtum im AT und im Judentum* (1955), 62 ff.; H. RINGGREN, *The Messiah in the OT* (1956), 21 ff.; I. ENGNELL, Messias 1–2, *Svenskt Bibl. Uppslagsverk* II, 77–92; id., Yttersta dagen, ibid., 1449–52. ENGNELL (op. cit., 1451) rightly cautions against drawing too sharp a distinction between present and future, as regards the cult experience. Cf. the refs. in CARLSON, *David*, 20 f.

[4] See, for example, 1 En 93,2—93,15; 48,6 f.; Ps Sal 17,23.

[5] JOHNSON, op. cit., 110; MOWINCKEL, *He That Cometh*, 169 ff.; WIDENGREN, op. cit., 44 ff.; ENGNELL, *Gamla Testamentet*, 146 f.

[6] It is not obvious that texts, that speak only of God's intervention for that reason reflect an environment in which people did not expect any Messiah. Nevertheless it is not permissible, in the absence of an explicit denial of Messianism, to assume the existence of such a belief. Cf. H. RIESENFELD, *Jésus transfiguré* (1947), 55 f.

[7] 1 En 1,3 f.; 25,3; 90,15; 91,7; 100,4; Test Jud 22,2 (Arm. version *om.*); Ass Mos 10,3; 4 Ez 6,18; 7,33; 2 Bar 48,39. Cf. Test Zeb 9,8. Similarly 1 En 47,3, in which the visionary sees "the Head of Days" sitting upon His Throne: the scene is modelled on Dn 7,9 ff. Cf. J. BOWMAN, Early Samaritan Eschatology, *J. Jew. Stud.* 6 (1955), 63–72 (God's personal intervention on the "Day of Vengeance").

[8] See 1 En 1,3 ff.; 90,18; Ass Mos 10,4 ff. For the OT, see, for example, Ex 19,18 ff. (cf. 4 Ez 3,18); Ps 18,8 ff.; 68,8 f.; Na 1,5; Hb 3,3 ff. 1 En 102 describes the same

When a representative of God is introduced,[9] however, there are as a rule no such magnificent accompaniments, although a couple of passages on the Son of Man (in 4 Ez) have something very like them.[10] This representative is the Messiah (in the narrow sense; Apc Abr, the Elect One;[11] Test Levi, a new priest) or the Son of Man (1 En Sim, 4 Ez).[12]

The terminology used to describe the entry of this divine representative on the scene may be worth noting. Thus, of the Messiah it is sometimes said that God "sends" him or "raises him up".[13] We recognize the phraseology from the OT: God "sends" Moses or the prophets. This not only declares from whom they have received their commission but

---

phenomenon, without any explicit mention of God's revelation, though it is implied. Cf. Or Sib. 3,82 ff., and see below, 71, note 1, There are texts in which these phenomena have been disconnected from the theophany and have become "signs" which foretoken the end (see above, 34, and below, 75 f.).

[9] I gladly refrain from giving any bibliographical references to this enormous subject. See instead the bibliographical sections in RUSSELL, *Method and Message*, 413 ff., and ROWLEY, *Relevance*, 205 ff. They do not mention the important book by W. KÜPPERS, *Das Messiasbild der spätjüdischen Apokalyptik* (1933), which especially elucidates the relation between God and the Son of Man (51 ff.). A recent, sober exposition is to be found in E. DHANIS, De Filio hominis in VT et in Iudaismo, *Gregor.* 45 (1964), 1–59.

[10] *1 En 51,4* says, following Ps 114,4, 6: "In those days shall the mountains leap like rams and the hills also shall skip like lambs satisfied with milk". The motif is linked in Ps 114 with a kind of theophany; here it is used in order to describe the joy felt in the presence of the Elect One. (For this expression, cf. below, note 28.)

1 En 52,2 ff. speaks of seven (actually six) mountains of different metals, which, it is said, are to "serve the dominion of His Anointed" (4). In his presence they will be as wax before the fire (6), and here the text uses the wording of theophany texts in the OT (Ps 97,5; Is 64,1 LXX, and esp. Mi 1,4). In vv. 7–9, however, these metals are given an interpretation, which, using Ez 7,19, Zph 1,18, and Hb 2,18, says that in those days none will be saved by gold and silver, and that there will be no iron for war, etc. Thus it is rather a question of the conditions that will prevail in the reign of the Elect One. Cf. G. KUHN, Beiträge zur Erklärung des Buches Henoch, *Zschr. At. Wiss.* 39 (1921), 265 ff.

4 Ez 13,3 ff. comes closest to the real theophanies: in the sight of the Son of Man all things will tremble, and at the sound of his voice all things will melt like wax before the fire (cf. Ps 46,7; 68,2 f.; 97,5). The aim would seem to be to depict the world's fear of the Man sent by God. Some of the motifs may have been taken over from the earlier tradition about the Son of Man (cf. 1 En 52,2 ff. mentioned above).

[11] Cf. 4 QMess.ar. I.10. (The text in J. A. FITZMYER, The Aramaic "Elect of God" Text from Qumran Cave IV, *Cath. Bibl. Quart.* 27, 1965, 357 f.)

[12] For the Messiah–(Son of) Man in 4 Ez, cf. M. STONE, *Features of the Eschatology of IV Ezra*, summarized in *Harv. Theol. Rev.* 58 (1965), 463.

[13] Ps Sal 17,23 (ἀνάστησον); Test Levi 18,2 (ἐγερεῖ); Apc Abr 31,1 (Box, send; RIESSLER, senden); Or Sib. 3,286 ff., 652 ff. (πέμψει). Cf. KÜPPERS, op. cit., 55.

also the authority by which they may appear in this capacity.[14] Similarly the OT says that God "raises up" a righteous branch for David (Jr 23,5).[15] In both these cases the terminology indicates the divine guidance of coming events and a divine initiative in that direction.

On the other hand, the Son of Man is said to "be revealed" or to "appear". This mode of expression harmonizes with the fact that he is hidden in various ways, partly with God before his appearance (his enthronement)[16] and partly from the sinners, in contrast to the saints, who have already received an insight into the mystery of the Son of Man.[17] When 4 Ez and 2 Bar also say of the Messiah that he is "revealed", this is an expression of a similar idea—that the coming Saviour is hidden before his appearance.[18]

When those of the present texts which are earlier than 4 Ez and 2 Bar speak of the Messiah and his reign, it is an "earthly" kingdom of joy that is depicted. (I put the word "earthly" in quotation marks, as the difference between heavenly and earthly and between transcendent and immanent is often inapplicable to these texts.[19]) We have here a "hea-

---

[14] See K. H. RENGSTORF, ἀποστέλλω κτλ., *Theol. Wörterb.* I (1933), 397–448, esp. 399 ff. (cf. 419 f), and B. GERHARDSSON, Die Boten Gottes und die Apostel Christi, *Svensk Exeg. Årsbok* 27 (1962), 89–131, esp. 105 ff.

[15] Cf. A. OEPKE, ἀνίστημι κτλ., *Theol. Wörterb.* I (1933), 368 f., and ἐγείρω κτλ., ibid. II (1935), 333.

[16] 1 En 38,2 (on the reading, see CHARLES, *Book of Enoch*, ad loc.); 39,6 f.; 48,2 ff.; 52,9; 62,7; 69,26. See E. SJÖBERG, *Der Menschensohn im äthiopischen Henochsbuch* (1946), 102 ff.; id., *Der verborgene Menschensohn in den Evangelien* (1955), 41 ff. 4 Ez 13,3, 26, in which the (Son of) Man comes out of the sea, has a similar meaning: see the interpretation in 4 Ez 13,52 (SJÖBERG, *Der verborgene*, 46 f.).

[17] 1 En 48,7; 62,7. See SJÖBERG, *Menschensohn*, 103 f. He maintains with VOLZ (*Eschatologie*, 208) against CHARLES (op. cit., ad loc.) that here the author is not thinking of the OT Messianic sayings which had come to the knowledge of the elect. I am inclined to agree with them on this point, though doubtless OT Messianic sayings were applied to the Son of Man. See below, 119 ff.

[18] 4 Ez 7,28; 12,32 ("Messiah, whom the Most High has kept unto the end of the days"); 2 Bar 29,3; 39,7. In the last passage CHARLES emends ܐܠܘܝ ("beginning") to ܐܠܘܝ ("principate"). Prof. G. WIDENGREN, in a private communication, has suggested reading ܐܠܘܝ ("principate"), which seems to be a more likely reading; cf. how in the Qumran texts it is often impossible to distinguish *Waw* and *Yod*: see P. WERNBERG-MØLLER, *Waw* and *Yod* in the "Rule of the Community" (1 QS), *Rev. Qumr.* 2 (1959/60), 223–36. On the subject, see SJÖBERG, *Der verborgene*, 48 f. "Revealed" (etc.) is also used of Behemoth in 2 Bar 29,4, of the attacking peoples in 2 Bar 70,7, of the great joy in the new age in 2 Bar 73,1, of the "city" in 4 Ez 7,26 (for textual criticism, see B. VIOLET, ed., 1910–24, ad loc.), of Gehenna and Paradise in 4 Ez 7,36, i.e. of things that God is holding in readiness for the end of the world. The expression is used of the Most High, for example, in 4 Ez 7,33.

[19] KÜPPERS, *Messiasbild*, 42 ff. Cf. W. BOUSSET, Die Religion des Judentums (3rd ed. by H. GRESSMANN 1926), 259 ff., 276 f., and VOLZ, *Eschatologie*, 212. See

venly" joy on earth under a ruler with divine authority, all signifying the time of final salvation.[20]

In 4 Ez and 2 Bar, on the other hand, the period of Messianic rule—in spite of all sorts of paradisical delights and in spite of the new Jerusalem revealed in 4 Ez 7,26—is no longer simply the period of salvation but only an preparatory phase of the kingdom of God, which is the new age (*saeculum futurum*, 4 Ez 8,1) inaugurated by God Himself. The reign of the Messiah will come to an end before then and the Messiah will disappear from the picture in one way or another.[21] The last judgement, which is passed by God, is part of the transition to the new age.[22]

4 Ez and 2 Bar belong to the latest texts which provide our material and it is probable that in the respects under discussion they represent a combination of earlier lines of thought.[23] We have already encountered two components separately: the Messianic "earthly" kingdom and the idea that God Himself will intervene. But we have just found, through the terminology describing their appearance, that the Messiah (the (Son of) Man) whom we encounter in 4 Ez[24] and 2 Bar is regarded as being hidden before his appearance. This feature—a third component—we now find in the texts concerning the Son of Man in 1 En Sim.

Thus, the Son of Man in 1 En Sim is "revealed" after having been hidden with God: he is revealed to the righteous[25] and appears as representing God (52,9; cf. Dn 7,13). He is himself pre-existent[26] and is assigned to the divine sphere with considerably greater emphasis than is

---

also M. A. BEEK, *Nationale en transcendente Motieven in de joodse Apokalyptiek* (1941), and C. STEUERNAGEL, Die Strukturlinien der Entwicklung der jüdischen Eschatologie, *Festschrift A. Bertholet* (1950), 480 ff.

[20] Cf. BILLERBECK, *Comm.* IV:2, 799 ff., and SJÖBERG, op. cit., 41 ff., 51 ff. The Messiah who appears in 1 En 90,37 f. would also seem to rule in the final kingdom of peace.

[21] 4 Ez 7,29 (the Messiah dies); 12,34 (till the end comes); 2 Bar 30,1 (the Messiah "returns in glory" ‎ܠܐܘܣܒܐܠܐ ‎ܝܥܩܘܝܘ); 40,3 ("till the world of corruption is at an end"; cf. 2 Bar 73,1).

[22] 4 Ez 7,33; and cf. 2 Bar 83,2.

[23] Cf. BILLERBECK, loc. cit. The view taken in 4 Ez and 2 Bar largely corresponds to that found in the Rabbinate (see BILLERBECK, op. cit., 815 ff.).

[24] As the texts stand at present, the Messiah and the (Son of) Man in 4 Ez are obviously identical. That 4 Ez 13,3 is clearly connected with Dn 7,13 did not lead the translator of the Latin version to write *filius hominis* (like vg ad Dn 7,13) but only *homo*. Cf. below, 96, note 40.

[25] See notes 16 and 17 above.

[26] 1 En 48,6; 62,7. T. W. MANSON (The Son of Man in Daniel, Enoch, and the Gospels, *Bull. J. Ryl. Libr.* 32, 1949/50, 171 ff.) denies the pre-existence of an individual Son of Man in these texts. For a discussion see SJÖBERG, *Der verborgene*, 45 f.

the case as regards the divine representatives we have mentioned so far.[27] We learn this especially from the descriptions of how this Son of Man sits on the throne of divine majesty (or perhaps on another throne of heavenly glory).[28] A good deal of the colouring in the description of the joy of the Messianic kingdom is missing and the discussion of the joy of the elect under the rule of the Son of Man or, to put it more exactly, together with him is in fairly general terms of light, joy, glory and praise. It is characterized by the chiaroscuro which distinguishes these visions, but it would seem to be clear that not only the divine representative but also his people and their condition have here a marked tendency to be elevated into a transcendent existence.[29]

Both the Messiah (in the narrow sense of the word) and the Son of Man are described in detail in some of these texts.[30] This is done to a very large extent by using OT motifs, which are derived especially from passages which, to all appearances, were interpreted in Messianic senses in the author's environment. We shall return to this point later on.[31]

---

[27] Here I refrain from entering into the relation between, on the one hand, the Son of Man and, on the other, the sacral kingship in ancient Israel and the Near East, and the associated *Urmensch* concepts. Phenomenologically there are similarities, but the difficulty seems to be the historical distance between pre-Israelite Canaan and the earliest period of the kings, on the one hand, and Dn 7 and 1 En Sim, on the other. Cf. I. ENGNELL's review of Sjöberg, Menschensohn, in *Biblioth. Orient.* 8 (1951), 191 f., and id., Människosonen, *Svenskt Bibl. Uppslagsverk* II, 229–32, with SJÖBERG, *Menschensohn*, 190 ff.; G. WIDENGREN, Till det sakrala kungadömets historia i Israel, *Horae Soederbl.* I:3 (1947); id., *Religionens värld*, 363; S. MOWINCKEL, Urmensch und "Königsideologie", *Stud. Theol.* 2 (1948), 71–89, and id., *He That Cometh*, 420 ff. It is clear that the OT ferment must have played a large part (see below, 119 ff.).

[28] 1 En 45,3; 51,3; 61,8; 62,2; 69,27. On the question of what throne the Son of Man sits on, see SJÖBERG, op. cit., 63 ff. Here we stand somewhere on a line between the old ideology about sacral kingship and the fearful meditations of later Jewish mysticism on the mysteries of the Throne and Metatron. Cf., for example, 1 Ch 29,23; Ps 110,1; Ez 1,26; 1 En 14,9 ff.; 71,5 ff.; 2 En 20,1–21,5; M Ḥag. II.1; b Ḥag. 12b–13a, 14a; M Meg. IV.10; T Ḥag. II.1. For the rabbinical treatment of 1 Ch 29,23, see Midr. Cant. ad 1,1. See further H. ODEBERG, *3 Enoch* (1928); id., *Fragen von Metatron, Schekina und Memra* (1942), and G. SCHOLEM, *Jewish Gnosticism, Merkabah Mysticism, and Talmudic Tradition* (1960).

That the Elect One and the Son of Man are identical is wrongly denied by N. MESSEL, *Der Menschensohn in den Bilderreden des Henoch* (1922), and M.-J. LAGRANGE, *Le Judaïsme avant Jésus-Christ* (1931), 242 ff. On the other hand, see N. JOHANSSON, *Parakletoi* (1940), 101 f.; SJÖBERG, op. cit., 17 ff., 95 f.; MOWINCKEL, *He That Cometh*, 354 f.

[29] 1 En 38,2 ff.; 45,3 ff.; 51,1 ff.; 58,2 ff.; 61,4 f.

[30] Ps Sal 17,24 ff.; Test Levi 18,2 ff.; Test Jud 24,1. To some extent Or Sib 3,652 ff; also 1 En 46,3 ff.; 48,2 ff.; 51,3 ff.; 71,14 ff.; 4 Ez 13,3 ff.

[31] See Chap. IV.

We have now dwelt for some time on the person who makes the divine intervention and to some extent on its results (the reign of the Messiah or the new age). But it may also be worth while to give an account in some detail of the activity which is assigned to God or His representative in these descriptions of the divine intervention.

When it is God Himself who "comes" etc., most of the texts say that He does so in order to judge.[32] This judgement comes into force at the beginning of the new era after the end of the Messianic period (4 Ez, 2 Bar) or is associated without any Messianic preliminaries with the destruction of the sinners and the deliverance of the righteous by God Himself (for example, in 1 En 1,3 ff.).

When a text says that the Messiah or the Son of Man will judge, this is often worded in such a way as to make it clear that he will do so on God's behalf and possess extraordinary powers. Thus, we have in 1 En 61,8: "And the Lord of Spirits placed the Elect One on the throne of glory. And he shall judge ..." and in 1 En 69,27: "And he sat on the throne of his glory and the sum of judgement *was given* unto the Son of Man".[33] The passive here probably has the same function as that used at times in Jewish writings and even more in the NT to paraphrase an active sentence in which God was the subject.[34]

4 Ez and 2 Bar are more reserved in delegating judgement to the Messiah or the Son of Man: the last judgement is reserved to God Himself and is removed from the Messianic age.[35] In other (earlier) texts, as has already been mentioned, the state of affairs is somewhat different; we should, however, note that in these texts "to judge" often has almost the sense of "to govern".[36] These distinctions are, of course, connected with the different views of the end of time: the Messianic kingdom belonging to this world and forming only a preparatory phase of the world to come, in the transition to which God will judge mankind (4 Ez, 2 Bar), an

---

[32] 1 En 1,7 ff.; 25,4; 90,20 ff.; 91,7; Ass Mos 10,3 ff.; 4 Ez 7,33; 2 Bar 48,39.

[33] The question is whether CULLMANN (*Christologie*, 160) judges the Son of Man in 1 En too much by NT models, when he says that the real function of the Son of Man, when he comes, will be to judge. In 1 En he neither "comes" nor has judgement as his principal function. Cf. W. STAERK, *Soter* (1933), 76 f.

[34] See J. BOEHMER, *Die neutestamentliche Gottesscheu* (1917), 20 ff.; G. DALMAN, *Die Worte Jesu* (2nd ed. 1930), 183 f.; BILLERBECK, *Comm.* I, 443. Possibly the text has an echo of Dn 7,13 f., 26; cf. K. H. RENGSTORF, Old and New Testament Traces of a Formula of the Judaean Royal Ritual, *Nov. Test.* 5 (1962), 229–44, esp. 239 f.

[35] However, the Messiah (the (Son of) Man) judges, more or less, in the texts in which he is said to accuse his enemies — 4 Ez 11,37 ff.; 12,32; 13,37; 2 Bar 40,1.

[36] Thus Ps Sal 17,28, 48 and Test Levi 18,2. The background of this mode of speaking is, of course, in the OT. See F. BÜCHSEL and V. HERNTRICH, κρίνω κτλ., *Theol. Wörterb.* III (1938), 920 ff., and I. ENGNELL, Dom, *Svenskt Bibl. Uppslagsverk* I, 426–28.

40

"earthly" Messianic kingdom, which is moreover equated with the time of salvation, when God's Messiah will judge (possible meaning "will govern") (for example, Ps Sal), and finally a more transcendent kingdom ruled by the Son of Man, which will be set up when he judges the sinners in connection with his enthronement (1 En Sim).

Considered in relation to the view of history which pervades the minds of the authors, this divine intervention means that the long struggle between God and the powers of evil in different forms will be brought to an end. Thus it is natural that these texts should often relate that this divine intervention will involve the destruction of enemies, sinners, Belial, etc., when either God or His representative has intervened to set up the kingdom of peace.[37]

Conversely, the righteous and the elect will rejoice at this intervention. They will escape the judgement and the frightful punishments that will be meted out to the sinners; they are "saved" and taken into the kingdom, the goal of history to which they looked forward.[38]

4. The Judgement (C)

The relationship between God, on the one hand, and the spiritual powers and mankind, on the other, is a religious and moral one and is determined by the fact that God is the sovereign who demands the obedience of mankind to His will, which He has made known to them. But as far as mankind is concerned, this revelation of God's will has been made within the framework of a "covenant", i.e. God also has taken upon Himself certain obligations, amongst other things, to maintain justice, which, as far as the obedient are concerned, is manifested by God giving them His blessing. We meet with different variations of this idea in the OT and later Jewish writings.[39] Inset in the view of history which I tried to describe briefly above, this means that the struggle between good and evil which is seen in history is not regarded as being carried on between two equal forces. However dualistic this view may be,[40] the fact remains that God will finally uphold justice, judgement will be given and righteousness will prevail.

---

[37] God: 1 En 1,9; 90,26; the Messiah: Test Levi 18,12; 4 Ez 12,33; 2 Bar 40,2; 72,2; the Son of Man 1 En 46,4 ff.; 62,2 ff.

[38] 1 En 48,7; 50,3; 51,2; 99,10; Ps Sal 17,51; 4 Ez 12,34. For a more detailed and differentiated account, see W. FOERSTER, σῴζω κτλ., *Theol. Wörterb.* VII (1964), 984 ff.

[39] On this point, see J. PEDERSEN, *Der Eid bei den Semiten* (1914), 31 ff.; id., *Israel* I–II (1926), for example, 348 ff.; J. BEGRICH, Berit, *Zschr. At. Wiss.* 60 (1944), 1–11; J. HEMPEL, Bund II, *Rel. in Gesch. u. Geg.* I (3rd ed. 1957), 1513–16; A. JAUBERT, *La notion d'alliance dans le Judaïsme* (1963), 43 ff.

[40] Cf. above, 26.

In briefly discussing the motif of judgement in this presentation of the apocalyptic raw material, I shall try to describe somewhat more precisely what the word "judgement" means, who is the judge and who is judged. In what senses are the words "to judge" and "judgement" used in the present texts? Without going into detail, we may distinguish the following features. In most cases judgement means that justice is maintained, in that the judge, often sitting upon his throne,[41] passes judgement. This judgement may be the great last judgement[42] or preliminary decisions[43] (in which, for example, the apostate angels are doomed to stay in purgatory until the great last judgement) or may refer to a more extensive activity, involving a ruler's judicial function[44] (for example, Test Levi 18,2: "Messiah shall execute a righteous judgement upon the earth for a multitude of days").[45]

"Judgement" does not necessarily mean solely conviction here, no more than in the OT. Thus, in 1 En 47,2 the righteous pray to God that "judgement may be done unto them"; that justice is maintained and judgement given is a deliverance and a victory for the righteous.[46]

However, as this judgement is as a rule something that need only be feared by sinners, the authors easily seem to equate "to judge" with "to punish". This is quite natural, if we bear in mind the distinction which these texts make between their own ranks (the righteous) and their oppressive adversaries (the sinners). It is, of course, difficult to be sure of the nuances from case to case, but it seems as if the idea of a court and the maintenance of justice through the judge's acquittal and conviction is not present in some cases, especially in some texts from Or Sib 3. "Judgement" here is directly synonymous with "punishment" and "vengeance" on God's part.[47] From this it is only a short step to the equation of "judgement" with "punishment, visitations, misfortunes".

---

[41] For example, 1 En 61,8; 62,2; 69,27; 4 Ez 7,33 f.; see also 1 En 25,3 f.

[42] God: 1 En 1,7, 9; 25,4; 90,20 ff.; 91,15; 4 Ez 7,33 f., 39; 2 Bar 83,2 f. The Son of Man: 1 En 62,2; 69,27. In Test Levi 4,1 it is uncertain which judgement is being referred to, whether it is visitations in history, like the Flood, or the Last Judgement; cf. R. EPPEL, *Le piétisme juif* (1930), 96 f.

[43] 1 En 10; 61,8 (see SJÖBERG, *Menschensohn*, 67 f.; for 45,3, cf. ibid., 75 ff.).

[44] Ps Sal 17,28, 31, 48 (Messiah). Cf., for example, 1 En 63,8, which describes God's attributes rather than dwells on a special occasion of judgement: "our Lord is true in all His works, and in His judgements and His justice; and His judgements have no respect of persons". See also 1 En 50,4.

[45] Cf. Ps 9,8 f.; Is 2,4; 11,4.

[46] See PEDERSEN, *Israel* I–II, 348; V. HERNTRICH, κρίνω κτλ.B, *Theol. Wörterb.* III (1938), 922–33; O. BOOTH, The Semantic Development of the Term צָפַט in the OT, *J. Bibl. Lit.* 61 (1942), 105–10.

[47] Or Sib 3,287, 670, 689. Also 1 En 45,6; 91,12; 102,5 (cf., however, Chap. II, note 27); 103,6; Jub 23,30 f.; Apc Abr 29,14.

This is the case in the passages just mentioned from Or Sib 3 (for example, "he shall judge every man in blood and blazing fire" (3,287)).[48]

Who passes this judgement? When it is God alone who intervenes, it is also He who passes judgement.[49] In 4 Ez and 2 Bar, as we saw, a Messiah comes into the picture before God's own intervention, but he is not involved in the great last judgement, for which God Himself is responsible.[50] This is not entirely unlike the situation in Or Sib 3, which mentions a Messiah, although it is God who passes judgement.[51] (This should be compared with the circumstance that in Or Sib 3 "judgement", as we saw, was often, though not always,[52] equated with "visitations and misfortunes".)

In some texts (from Test XII and Ps Sal), in which the time of salvation is equivalent to the period of an "earthly" Messianic kingdom, it is the Messiah who judges, as well as intervenes.[53] It is also in these texts that "to judge" often has the secondary meaning of "to rule",[54] but this ruler must, as such, uphold justice against sinners and heathens. However, it is with God's authority that he judges (cf. the "sending" terminology above; he is *God's* Messiah[55]) and it is God's judgements which he passes. Thus, Test Levi 18,2 says that to the Messiah "shall all the words of the Lord be revealed; and he shall execute a righteous judge-

---

[48] See the preceding note. Cf. Test Levi 15,2 (exile).

[49] See, for example, 1 En 1,7, 9; 90,20 ff.; 91,7; 4 Ez 7,33 f.

[50] Some texts move directly to the judgement, without previously presenting a divine intervention. This is the case in the Apocalypse of Weeks in 1 En (93; 91, 12–17), in which 91,14 f. mentions that there will be judgement in the ninth and tenth weeks. Nevertheless it is clear from the context that it is God who judges, here as in other similar cases (Jub 23,30 f.; Test Levi 4,1; (15,2, modelled on the exile); 2 Bar 83,2).

[51] See note 47. The nearest the Messiah comes to judgement is in 3,287, in which God will send a king and will judge every man in blood and blazing fire. Here the Messiah *may* be the subject of κρινεῖ. In the context the exile has been spoken of and the good things which await the people after it, and after the passage quoted an allusion is made to the building of the Temple after the return from exile. The manner of judgement indicates that it is God who is the subject and that "every man" means mankind, except the Chosen People.

[52] See 3,55 f., 91 f., and also 4,183.

[53] See Ps Sal 17,28, 31, 48; Test Levi 18,2; Test Jud 24,6. And cf. Test Levi 4,1 (see note 42).

[54] See above, 42.

[55] The expression is to be found in Ps Sal 17,36, where the MSS actually read χριστὸς κύριος, which is rightly adjudged to be a Christian amendment of χρ. κυρίου. See K. G. KUHN, *Die älteste Textgestalt der Psalmen Salomos* (1937), 73 f. The passage had been advanced as evidence, as regards assessing the value of the Syriac version of Ps Sal. See on this point J. BEGRICH, Der Text der Psalmen Salomos, *Zschr. Nt. Wiss.* 38 (1939), 133 f.

ment". As regards its content, the second sentence has the character of a consecutive clause to the first; it is because the Messiah is instructed by God that he is able to pass judgement.[56]

This intimacy between God and His representative appears even more markedly, as regards the Son of Man, in 1 En Sim. This is illustrated in 61,8 f.: the Lord of Spirits places the Elect One on the throne of glory to judge the angels, and he judges "their path according to the way of the righteous judgement of the Lord of Spirits". The last judgement is also entrusted to the Son of Man.[57]

Finally, who is judged? As a rule, only sinners are mentioned as being subject to judgement, which is, of course, connected with the fact that the negative meaning of the word is often predominant. This in its turn is connected with the opposition between the righteous and the sinners which is so marked in several passages. The righteous look forward to the time when their adversaries will meet their just fate.[58]

In several places the text says that "all" shall be judged, but this probably means in reality "all except the righteous". This would seem to be the case in 1 En 25,4, for example, where it is said of the Tree of Life that no one may touch it "till the great judgement, when there is vengeance on all and consummation for ever; then it shall be given to the righteous and holy".[59] Here the righteous would scarcely seem to be included amongst the "all" on whom vengeance is to fall and thus the wide sense of rewarding both sinners and righteous according to justice would not seem to attach to the word "judgement".

But in a number of passages it really is "all" who are brought before the judge, though the righteous need feel no alarm on that account. For example, in Baruch's letter to the nine and a half tribes (2 Bar 78–86) we read: "He will assuredly judge those who are in this world, and visit in truth all things by means of all their hidden works. And He will assuredly examine the secret thoughts ... Let none therefore of these present things ascend into your hearts" (83,2 ff.).[60]

The "all" who are to be judged, according to 2 Bar, actually means all,

---

[56] We have the same combination in Ps Sal 17,35 f., where the Messiah is taught by God (v. 35), and in v. 36 is king over the people.

[57] On the Son of Man sitting in judgement, see SJÖBERG, *Menschensohn*, 66 ff. and 81 f. To be sure, God's judgements are mentioned in some passages (45,6; 50,4), but this is not to deny that it is the Son of Man who pronounces God's judgements; it only emphasizes the close relation between God and His delegate.

[58] 1 En 38,1, 3; 45,6; 50,4; 53,1; 62,2 f.; 90,25 f.; 91,12; 99,15 f.; 100,4; Test Levi 4,1; cf. 15,2.

[59] I follow here the Greek Gizeh fragment. See also 1 En 1,7 f. (cf. below, 72, note 5); 91,14; Test Levi 4,1 (sons of men); Or Sib 3,287, 689 ff.

[60] Similarly in 4 Ez 7,33 ff., and Or Sib 4,183 ff.

in so far as this text preaches a general resurrection for this judgement. This is also the case in 4 Ez. 1 En 22 (3 f.) is almost alone amongst the earlier texts in presenting a similar belief.[61]

Among the sinners who will be affected by the judgement, the heathen are sometimes specially mentioned,[62] and the same evil generation includes the fallen angels and "Antichrist".[63] The judgement on the heathen is given a slightly different colour in Test Levi 18 and Ps Sal 17, where the judgement of the Messiah, as has already been pointed out, is a function of his rule, and the judgement on the heathen comes principally to mean that the heathen are subject to him. Ps Sal is, however, more hostile to the heathen than Test Levi 18. Not only does it say that "he shall judge peoples and nations in the wisdom of his righteousness" (Ps Sal 17,31) but also that "he shall destroy the godless nations with the word of his mouth" (27).

The last-mentioned judicial function of the Messiah naturally also applies to his own people: "He shall judge the tribes of the people that has been sanctified by the Lord his God" (Ps Sal 17,28).

5. *The Fate of the Sinners (D)*

With a good deal of intensity the texts often describe the fate that will befall the sinful adversaries. Even though some resentment may underlie these passages,[64] we should, on the one hand, be aware that the punishment of sinners has an organic place in these authors' fundamental view of God and the world and, on the other, bear in mind the function which these texts quite likely had, viz. the function of consoling and admonishing. For example, we read in 2 Bar 82,1 f.: "I have written to you, that you may comfort yourselves regarding the multitude of your tribulations. (2) For know that our Maker will assuredly avenge us on all our enemies, according to all that they have done to us; also that the consummation which the Most High will make is very nigh, and His mercy that is coming, and the consummation of His judgement is by no means far off."[65]

---

[61] 4 Ez 5,45; 7,32; 14,35; 2 Bar 42,8; 50,2. And cf. 1 En 51,1; Jub 5,14; Or Sib 4,180 ff. For the resurrection of only the just, see below, 48 f.

[62] 1 En 91,9; Apc Abr 29,14; Or Sib 3,669 ff.; 4 Ez 13,37 (the reproaches of the (Son of) Man, cf. section 3 above, note 35).

[63] 1 En 56,1 ff.; 90,21 ff.; 91,15 (fallen angels); 4 Ez 11,39 ff.; 12,32 f. (the Messiah accuses the fourth beast; cf. section 3 above, notes 35 and 37).

[64] BOUSSET & GRESSMANN, *Religion*, 209 ff.

[65] See W. O. E. OESTERLEY, The Apocalyptic Literature: a Seer among his People, in *Judaism and Christianity* I (1937), 88 ff.

The underlying presupposition is a firm belief in the power of God and in His justice, and not least a steadfast conviction that this God will abide by His promises to crush the evil and bring joy to His own.[66] It is an integral part of the whole view that the misdeeds that the righteous witness and assess in different ways (cf. above in section 2) will also be punished when God's justice is to be maintained.

The punishment of sinners and their like, to which these texts refer, may be arranged in different groups, according to their nature, viz. (a) the sinners perish, are destroyed or are driven away, (b) the sinners are humiliated, covered with shame, afflicted with anguish and find no peace, (c) the sinners are destroyed by fire or undergo punishment in some place of torment. This grouping according to content is also supported by the texts themselves, which often bring the punishments together in similar groups.[67]

The banishment or destruction of the sinners is a very common motif in these texts.[68] The humiliation and anguish of the condemned are mainly to be found in 1 En, combined with the statement that they perish etc.[69] Destruction by fire and torments of various kinds—either or both sometimes in a special place of torment (the Valley of Judgement or Gehenna) —are to be met with in 1 En, also in combination with the statement that they are destroyed etc. But the punishment by fire also recurs in other texts, although not as a rule in combination with statements that the sinners will perish. In Or Sib especially, rivers of fire and the like figure amongst the punishments, and 4 Ez and 2 Bar state that torments await the unfortunate.[70] The fourth beast and Belial are very special sinners, whose punishment will be to perish.[71]

---

[66] Cf. A. MARMORSTEIN, *The Old Rabbinic Doctrine of God* I (1927), 181 ff., and R. MACH, *Der Zaddik in Talmud und Midrasch* (1957), 32 ff.

[67] See the passages quoted in the following notes.

[68] 1 En 1,9; 38,3; 48,9 f.; 50,4; 53,2, 5; 62,2, 10 f.; 63,11; 80,8; 91,11; 99,1, 9, 12, 16; Jub 23,28 ff.; Ps Sal 17,25 ff.; Test Levi 4,6; Test Zeb 10,3; 4 Ez 12,33; 2 Bar 30,4 f.; 51,6; Or Sib 3,51 ff., 670 ff.

[69] 1 En 38,4; 46,4 ff.; 48,8; 62,4 f., 9 f.; 63,11; 99,2, 8, 13, 16; also Apc Abr 31,3. Here we may also include the fact that they are exposed to the delight of the just at their punishment: 1 En 62,12; cf. Jub 23,30. For the combination with the motif of perishing, cf. the previous note.

[70] 1 En 48,9; 53,1, 3; 62,11; 69,28; 90,24 ff.; 91,9; 100,4, 7 ff.; 102,1; 103,8; Test Jud 25,3; 4 Ez 7,36 ff.; 9,9; Apc Abr 31,4; 2 Bar 30,5; 51,6; Or Sib 3,54, 72 ff., 287, 673 f., 689 f.; 4,186 f. For the combination with the motif of perishing, see note 68, above. Cf. R. MAYER, *Die biblische Vorstellung vom Weltenbrand* (1956). Here the Iranian parallels are especially striking: see H. WINDISCH, *Die Orakel des Hystaspes* (1929), 26 ff.

[71] Test Levi 18,12 ("shall be bound"); Test Jud 25,3 (Belial); Ass Mos 10,1 (Satan); 4 Ez 11,45 (the eagle); Or Sib 3,73 f. (Belial).

Here I also include a point which has already been indicated above in section 2, viz. the "last assault of the Gentiles". The theme is to be found in 1 En 56,6 ff.; 99,13 ff.; 4 Ez 13,5; Or Sib 3,660 ff., and more briefly in Test Jos 19,8.[72] The heathen are gathered and sometimes incited to an attack on the Holy Land or on the Son of Man on Sion (4 Ez), but before the attack becomes really dangerous, the attackers are destroyed in a veritable bloodbath or by rivers of fire. The description is often related to Ez 38 f., which very likely inspired this theme.[73]

6. *The Joy of the Elect (E)*

This fearful background to the divine intervention and the terrible fate which afterwards overtakes the unfaithful is in contrast to the bright existence depicted by these apocalyptic writings for the elect. Thus, while we found folly, anxiety, panic, anguish and war under *A* and *D*, we meet here with their opposites; the faithful have wisdom, peace, tranquillity and joy. They are "saved" from suffering and torment.[74] The lot of the ungodly may be darkness and torment in Sheol, while they are banished from the presence of God and excluded from the joy of the faithful. The blessed, on the other hand, have been gathered together and live near to God or in communion with Him, with the Messiah or the Son of Man, in light and glory.[75] Whereas formerly their lives were threate-

---

[72] In my opinion also 2 Bar 48,37, but in a more rudimentary form. For 2 Bar 70,7 ff., see above, section 2, note 38.

[73] Far back in time there was perhaps an original cultic *Sitz im Leben*, the so-called sham fight. See MOWINCKEL, *Psalmenstudien* II, 126 ff.; id., *The Psalms in Israel's Worship* I (1962), 181 ff.; G. W. AHLSTRÖM, *Psalm 89* (1959), 69 ff.

[74] Peace: 1 En 1,8; 11,2; 45,3, 6; 71,17; 90,33 ff.; 103,3; Jub 23,28; Test Levi 18,4, 9; Test Jud 22,2; 4 Ez 11,46; 2 Bar 73,1; Or Sib 3,703, 780. Cf. Philo, *De praem.* 91–97.

Joy: 1 En 10,16; 25,6; 51,5; 103,3 f.; Jub 23,30; Test Levi 18,5, 14; Test Jud 25,5; Ass Mos 10,8; 4 Ez 7,28; 12,34; Apc Abr 29,19; 2 Bar 29,6; 73,1 f.; Or Sib 3,619, 703, 771.

Wisdom: 1 En 48,1; 91,10; Test Levi 18,5; 4 Ez 8,52.

Saved: 1 En 10,17; 48,7; 50,3; 99,10; Jub 23,30; Test Jud 22,2; 4 Ez 9,8; 12,34; Apc Abr 29,17; cf. Ps Sal 17,51.

[75] Gathered: 1 En 57,1 f.; 90,33; Ps Sal 11; 17,28; 4 Ez 13,12, 39 ff.; Apc Abr 31,2.

God's nearness etc.: 1 En 1,8; 25,6; 39,5; 45,6; 62,14; 105,2; Test Levi 5,2; 18,13; Test Jud 24,3; Or Sib 3,703 ff.

With the Messiah or the Son of Man: 1 En 38,2; 45,4; 48,4; 51,3 ff.; 62,8, 14; 71,16; 90,37; Ps Sal 17,23 ff.; Test Levi 18,9 (possibly an interpolation: see CHARLES's ed., ad loc.); 4 Ez 7,28; 2 Bar 40,2 f.

Light and glory: 1 En 1,8; 38,2, 4; 50,1; 58,2 f.; 62,15; 92,4; 103,3; 104,2; 2 Bar 51,3, 10; Or Sib 3,282 ff.; 4,191. See S. AALEN, *Die Begriffe 'Licht' und 'Finsternis'* (1956), 308 ff.

ned with suffering and death, they now have a very long or "eternal" life,[76] a life of pure righteousness, since all evil and transgression have passed away.[77] The heathen, who were previously a danger to the security of God's people and thus enemies to both God and His people are now either subjugated and *hors de combat* or loyal subjects and believers in the true God.[78]

The tribulations which befell mankind as a consequence of the Fall are wiped out in the joy of the elect. The heavy work (Gn 3,17 ff.) which proves to be futile recurs in the themes concerning the agonies of the last days (drought, crop failures and starvation afflict mankind instead): in the time of salvation the earth is again fruitful,[79] and according to 2 Bar, the manna returns,[80] work does itself[81] and the lost Paradise (Gn 3,23 f.) is again accessible,[82] as well as the Tree of Life.[83] 2 Bar provides us with more on this theme: the curse of women's travail in childbirth (Gn 3,16), which is so common as an image of the agony of the last days, is no longer in force.[84] Enmity between men and animals (Gn 3,15) is abolished.[85]

This blessed existence may be located in a new world, in which heaven and earth are transformed[86] and in some cases a new Temple or a new heavenly Jerusalem are mentioned.[87] It is often said that the righteous

---

[76] 1 En 10,17; 25,6; 58,3; Jub 23,27 f.; 2 Bar 51,9; 73,3. They are permitted to eat the fruit of the Tree of Life: 1 En 25,4 f.; Test Levi 18,11. Cf. Test Jud 24,4, which CHARLES holds to be a Christian interpolation (though with some hesitation). Cf. above, 18 f.

[77] 1 En 10,16; 92,5; 91,11, 17; 100,5; Ps Sal 17,28 f.; Test Levi 18,9; Test Jud 25,3; 4 Ez 6,27 f.

[78] The heathen worship God etc.: 1 En 10,21; 48,4 f.; 57,3; 91,14; Test Jud 24,6; Apc Abr 29,11; Or Sib 3,616, 717 ff., 772 ff., 808.

The heathen subdued: 1 En 62,9 f.; 90,30, 37; Ps Sal 17,31 ff.; 4 Ez 13,13; 2 Bar 72,5.

[79] 1 En 10,18 ff.; 2 Bar 29,5; Or Sib. 3,620 ff., 660. Cf. Philo, *De praem.* 101 ff., *De execrat.* 168.

[80] 2 Bar 29,8. Cf. Or Sib Prooem. Frag. 3,49 (ed. A. KURFESS, 1951).

[81] 2 Bar 74,1; cf. 1 En 11,1.

[82] Test Levi 18,10; 4 Ez 7,36; 8,52; 2 Bar 51,11.

[83] 1 En 25,4 f.; Test Levi 18,11; 4 Ez 8,52.

[84] 2 Bar 73,7.

[85] 2 Bar 73,6; Or Sib 3,788 ff. (which uses Is 11,6 ff.). Cf. Gn R. 95,1; S. Lv 26,6; Philo, *De praem.* 85—90.

[86] 1 En 45,5; 91,16. Cf. 4 Ez 6,20: *supersignabitur saeculum quod incipiet pertransire.* I suggest that the image is derived from Is 34,4, in which God rolls up the skies like a scroll. Cf. Box, ed., ad loc. Is 34,4 is alluded to in Or Sib 3,82 too.

[87] 1 En 90,28 f.; 91,13; Or Sib 3,289 ff. (pattern of exile); similarly Or Sib 3,657 ff. See also Or Sib 5,250 ff., 420 ff.; 4 Ez 13,36 (a new Sion).

dead will be resurrected for this time of joy (or alternatively for the time of joy which will follow the Messianic period; 4 Ez, 2 Bar).[88]

Finally, I would like to add a reminder. It should be noted that what has just been described is a systematization of scattered details in a few overlapping points of view. It is not a description of what is to be found even in the majority of the accounts of this period of rejoicing.

---

[88] Test Jud 25,1 ff. (the patriarchs, "the fathers"); 2 Mcc 7 (the martyrs); 1 En 91,10; 92,3; Ps Sal 3,16; Test Jud 25,4 (the just in general). See P. GRELOT, L'eschatologie des Esséniens et le livre d'Hénoch, *Rev. Qumr.* 1 (1958/59), 120 f. Cf., on the general resurrection, above, 49 f.

Patterns of Thought

1. *Introduction*

Now that the raw material has been presented, we may pass on to consider in more detail how it is arranged in the different texts. I would first like to point out that I am not seeking to discover any kind of eschatological dogma, nor to give a systematic account of the eschatological ideas either in Jewish apocalyptic in general or in individual collections of writings, separate "books" or "sources" in that sphere. For such accounts it may be sufficient to refer to the works of W. Bousset–H. Gressmann, R. H. Charles, E. Schürer, P. Volz and others.[1]

I shall concentrate attention here on small portions of text and ask: have these portions of text any distinguishable patterns of thought, as regards the motifs concerning the last days? This is not the same thing as inquiring whether they reflect a definite and elaborate view of the events that are to take place in the last days and of the order in which these events are to take place—a kind of apocalyptic "dogma".[2] One might say that this question about patterns of thought is more an inquiry about phenomena on the intuitive plane than about phenomena on the strictly intellectual plane. This method of asking questions seems to me so much the more justified in that the texts are so closely connected with, and perhaps even partly consist of, hymns, prayers, prophecies, descriptions of visions and the like,[3] that is, material that cannot easily be caught up in the dogmatist's pincers. These apocalyptic texts do not represent a dogmatic system, though behind them there may be one or more modes of reflected thinking on the last things. These texts are not didactic poems, giving us, say, some schemes of the events in the last days in chronological order.

---

[1] CHARLES, *A Critical History*; SCHÜRER, *Geschichte* II, 579–650; BOUSSET & GRESSMAN, *Religion*, 202–301; VOLZ, *Eschatologie*. RUSSELL's *Method and Message* is a modern survey. See also K. SCHUBERT, Die Entwicklung der eschatologischen Naherwartung im Frühjudentum, in *Vom Messias zu Christus* (1964), 1–54. As regards 4 Ez, see also J. KEULERS, *Die eschatologische Lehre des 4 Ez* (1922), 56–193.

[2] Cf. how CHARLES, perhaps a little too easily, finds "eschatological systems" (op. cit., 180, for example), or how Box quite hastily draws literary conclusions from inconsistent contents (*Ezra-Apocalypse*, 108 ff.).

[3] See on this point JANSEN, *Spätjüdische Psalmendichtung*, 124 f., 144 f., and below, Chap. IV.

50

Stylistic considerations already make it clear that it is possible to isolate small portions of text and not only treat them as if they were building-blocks in a dogmatic construction. A hymn or a vision presented in poetic prose may quite easily be something complete in itself, something which, to be meaningful, does not need to be put into its place in a line of thought expounded in a series of texts.

Though stylistic reasons may support the proposition that it is permissible to deal with literary works in this atomistical way, this support is nevertheless not sufficient. Further support is given by the literary fact that some of these units probably lived their own separate lives before they were incorporated in the present writings. The psalms in Ps Sal still show this independent character.[4] Other units that were originally independent are the Apocalypse of Weeks inserted in 1 En and the Book of Noah.[5] It is discoveries like these that have given rise to the fairly general opinion that the apocalyptic authors and editors were compilers, perhaps even uncritical compilers.[6] The accusations of uncriticalness may be due to the fact that their works have been too much regarded as didactic poems or assumed to be systematizations of the ideas concerning the last days which it is not at all certain that the authors made or intended to make. When the editor of an apocalypse with such a relatively fixed and settled eschatological system as 4 Ez is nevertheless accused of inconsistency of doctrine by Box[7], this may be a caution to us. If a controlling hand like his fumbled, what can we expect in the way of uniformity in, say, Test XII Patr, which is more loosely put together?

Of course, earlier material can be discerned in several of these texts but it is a long step from this to regarding them as altogether patchwork. Here we have to put a question of prime importance, a question which has not yet been answered and to which no certain answer can be given here: what was the *Sitz im Leben* of these texts? How did they come into existence and what was their function? Here I can only mention a few brief considerations which are relevant to the problem of whether the "pericopes" can be isolated as units or not.

It cannot be taken for granted that the *Sitz im Leben* was the same for

---

[4] See JANSEN, op. cit., 100 ff.

[5] The Book of Noah: 1 En 6–11; 39,1–2*a*; 54,1–55,2; 60; 65,1–69,25; 106 f. The Apocalypse of Weeks: 1 En 93,1–10; 91,12–17. See CHARLES, *Book of Enoch*, xlvi f., 1 f., and HAMMERSHAIMB, trans., 71.

[6] VOLZ, *Eschatologie*, 5; RUSSELL, *Method and Message*, 118 ff.

[7] Box in CHARLES, *Pseudepigrapha*, ad 4 Ez 7,26 f. Cf. ROWLEY (*Relevance*, 156 ff.), who defends the unity of 4 Ez, *inter alia*, by pointing out how Charles, who argues in favour of different sources on account of the inconsistencies in the books, is not even consistent himself.

all these apocalyptic texts. They cover a long period of time and Or Sib is not of Palestinian origin. However, we may record one circumstance which applies to all these works: though an individual work may form a relatively uniform cycle, it nevertheless to a great extent consists of small units each having a relatively independent and consistent content. Furthermore, here and there in the Palestinian books we catch a glimpse of a group of men in the background[8] and sometimes the apocalypses are mentioned as writings used by this group.[9] For, even though we may be confronted with a literary stereotype,[10] there would seem to be at any rate some reality behind the words, when, for example, we read in 1 En 104,13: "To them (sc. the righteous and wise) shall the books be given, and they shall believe in them and rejoice over them". The statement made in 4 Ez 14,44 ff. would also seem to be relevant to this problem: 24 books are open, so that the worthy and the unworthy may read them, but 70 books are secret and are given to the wise, and in them is the source of wisdom.[11] The parallel with the OT (the 24 books) may perhaps also be transferred to the way in which they are used: just as the Law and the Prophets were read pericope by pericope, so also the present texts may have been used portion by portion[12] at meetings of the group. This might have been an environmental feature connected with the above-mentioned structure of fairly consistent units partly isolated from each other.

My procedure, which I consider as justified by the above-mentioned considerations, will be as follows. I have extracted about 65 pericopes on the last things from 1 En, Jub, Ps Sal, Test XII Patr, Ass Mos, 4 Ez, Apc

---

[8] 1 En 46,8; 53,6; 93,10; Jub 23,16; Apc Abr 29,17; 4 Ez 14,46. On the question of the origin, see CHARLES, *Pseudepigrapha*, vii ff.; F. C. PORTER, *The Messages of the Apocalyptic Writers* (1916), 13 ff.; K. KOHLER, The Essenes and the Apocalyptic Literature, *Jew. Quart. Rev.* 11 (1920), 145–68; HERFORD, *Talmud and Apocrypha*, 193 f.; VOLZ, op. cit., 9 f.; BEEK, *Inleiding*, 55 ff.; BLOCH, *On the Apocalyptic*, 52 ff.; C. P. VAN ANDEL, *De Structuur van de Henoch-Traditie en het NT* (1955), passim; RUSSELL, op. cit., 23 ff.

[9] Dn 12,4, 9 f.; 1 En 82,1 ff.; 100,6; Ass Mos 1,16 ff.; (10,11); 4 Ez 12,37 f.

[10] Cf. Dn 12,4, 9 f.

[11] A. KAMINKA, Beiträge zur Erklärung der Ezra-Apokalypse, *Monatsschr. Gesch. Wiss. Jud.* 76 (1932), 510, thinks that they include the Mishnah.

[12] The Christian interpolations point in the same direction. Those who made these interpolations did not shrink from giving a text a radically new meaning by doing so. They seem to have regarded the "pericopes" of the text as relatively isolated units. It is primarily the Test XII Patr that are involved. See, for example, Test Levi 4 and 18,7; Test Dan 5,13. A phrase was interpolated in Test Zeb 9,8, MSS *bdg*, so as to make a section which clearly concerns the Return from Exile refer to Jesus. Cf. above, 18 f., and note 74 below in this Chap.

Abr, 2 Bar and Or Sib[13] and examined them as to whether it is possible to discern any pattern of thought or any recurrent way of grouping the ideas concerning the last things. The pericopes are not always very sharply delimited in the text. As the history of the tradition of these texts is so difficult of access, it can afford no help in delimiting the pericopes. For this reason, the content has often been allowed to determine the limits of these portions of text rather than their literary form. For the same reason I abide by the available texts and do not attempt to distinguish between earlier traditions and the final redaction of the work.[14]

One example may illustrate how a pericope may be excised. One of my pericopes is Test Jud 23,1–25,5. From the point of view of literary form it is perhaps possible to isolate 24,1–6 and 25,3–5 as more poetic in style; Charles's translation marks them as poetry. In that case the two μετὰ ταῦτα in 24,1 and 25,1 would be framework; 24,1 would introduce a Messianic prophecy on the Star of Jacob and his reign and in 25,3–5 we would have a prophecy about the people's joy in the time of salvation. However, these two "prophecies" are combined with 23,1–5, which deals with Israel's future sins and their punishment, and with the intermediate 25,1–2, which relate that Abraham, Isaac and Jacob will arise and how the twelve patriarchs will become leaders of the Israelite tribes again. Along with this, Test Jud 23,1–25,5 gives an exposition of the events of the last days, partly in a prophetic style. This may seem to point in a different direction from that which I mentioned just now, as regards hymns and visions being in themselves relatively self-contained. But it is far from self-evident that portions of text with varying styles are for that reason compounded of different elements, which can be characterized and distinguished by their style.[15] The whole portion may just as well have been woven in one piece and the "cement" at 24,1 and 25,1 may have been taken over from conventional style.

Thus it is the content which must very often be allowed to indicate

---

[13] 1 En 1,3–9; 10,16–11,2; 25,3–6; 1 En (Sim) 38,1–6; 45,1–6; 46,1–8; 47,1–48,10; 49,1–4; 50,1–51,5; 52,1–53,7; 56,1–57,3; 58,1–6; 61,1–13; 62,1–16; 63,1–12; 69,26–29; 71,14–17; 1 En 80,2–8; 1 En 90,13–19; 90,20–42; 91,6–11; 92,2–5; 93,9 f., 91,12–17; 99,1–16; 100,1–9; 102,1–11; 103,1–15; 104,1–105,2; 1 En 106,18–107,1; Jub 23,11–31; Ps Sal 17,5–51; Test Levi 4,1–4; 14,1–16,5; 17,11–18,14; Test Jud 21,6–22,3; 23,1–25,5; Test Iss 6,1–2; Test Zeb 9,5–9; Test Napht 4,1–5; Ass Mos 7,1–8,5, 10,1–10; 4 Ez 5,1–12; 6,18–28; 7,26–29; 7,31–43; 9,1–12; 11,37–12,3; 12,32–34; 13,1–13 a; 13,25–50; Apc Abr 27–31; 2 Bar 25,2–30,5; 39,1–40,4; 48,31–41; 50,2–52,7; 70,2–71,1; 72,2–74,4; 82,3–83,9; Or Sib 3,29–56; 63–92; 265–294; 562–623; 632–761; 767–807; 4,152–192; 5,74–85. For the choice of pericopes, cf. above, 14.

[14] An exception: I keep the Apocalypse of Weeks together (cf. note 5, above).

[15] See also G. WIDENGREN, *Literary and Psychological Aspects of the Hebrew Prophets* (1948), 82 f.

the limits of these "pericopes". In the example from Test Jud, 23,1 clearly begins afresh as regards content, and the same is the case with 26,1, which follows this portion. In other cases the limits of my portions do not coincide at all with the limits of the ascertainable literary units but begin or end at some distance into the portion, because other parts of it do not contain anything that is of direct significance for the present subject. Thus I have included, for example, only the four last weeks of the ten in the Apocalypse of Weeks.

It now appears that all five of the groups of components which I presented in the previous chapter are represented in approximately every fourth portion, while at least four of them are to be found in approximately three out of four. Yet there are included in the list half a dozen portions which only deal with one main motif, for example, 1 En 58,1–6, which deals solely with the coming felicity of the elect. Thus, to express it in a much simplified way, there is the same basic structure, as regards content, in most of these portions of text, a basic structure which covers the following situation: against the background of a sinful and/or otherwise abnormal period there occurs a divine intervention, which is accompanied by judgement and punishment for the wicked and by joy for the faithful.

I now distinguish between two main variants in this basic structure and in this connection my criterion is whether it is God alone who intervenes or whether the Messiah plays any part. In connection with the presentation of each main form or variant of it, I quote parallels to the pattern in the OT. It would seem not to be altogether without significance if we can find counterparts to the structures of the contents in which these pericopes are embedded, in a collection of texts which was for contemporary Judaism the great source of divine revelation. The parallels will have greater significance in so far as we may assume that the authors or editors of these texts had their ideas of the last things nourished by an OT which they considered to contain instruction also in eschatology. This will be demonstrated in some points in Chapters III and IV.[16] The texts of the OT which are advanced as parallels are not only those which are directly stated to deal with the last days (from Daniel, for instance), but also texts which it must have been natural for a contemporary reader with eschatological interests to interpret eschatologically (for example, portions on the Day of Yahweh or oracles of judgement and salvation), and further texts in which such an interpretation does not seem altogether self-evident to a modern reader, but instances of it occur in the Judaism of the period.

---

[16] As regards the "gap" between these OT parallels and the structural investigations of Chaps. III and IV, see below, 137.

54

2. *The First Main Form (God Intervenes, No Messiah)*

A. The ordinary pattern

This first main form has the following basic pattern:

A. Evil times.

B. God intervenes, rises up, comes, etc.

C. God judges.

D. The sinners are punished.

E. The righteous rejoice.

I find this pattern or parts of it in about 20 of the texts mentioned above.[17]
1 En 100,1–9 may be quoted as an example:

A. (1) And in those days in one place the fathers together with their sons
    shall be smitten
  and brothers one with another shall fall in death
  until there flows a stream of their blood.
  (2) For a man shall not withhold his hand from slaying his sons and his
    sons' sons,
  and the sinner shall not withhold his hand from his honoured brother:
  from dawn till sunset they shall slay one another.
  (3) And the horse shall walk up to the breast in the blood of the sinners,
  and the chariot shall sink down to its height.[18]

B. (4) In those days the angels shall descend into the secret places
  and gather together into one place all those who brought down sin,
  and the Most High will arise on that day of judgement

C.D. to execute great judgement amongst sinners.

E. (5) And over all the righteous and holy he will appoint guardians from
    amongst the holy angels
  to guard them as an apple of an eye,
  until he has made an end of all wickedness and all sin,
  and though the righteous sleep a long sleep they have nought to fear.
  (6) Then the wise men shall see the truth,[19]
  and the children of the earth shall understand all the words of this book,[20]
  and recognize that their riches shall not be able to save them
  in the overthrow of their sins.

D.A. (7) Woe to you, sinners, when you afflict the righteous on the day of
    strong anguish[19]

---

[17] 1 En 10,16–11,2; 80,2–8; 91,6–11; 99,1–16; 100,1–9; 102,1–11; 103,1–15; 104,1–105,2; Jub 23,11–31; Test Levi 4,1–4; 14,1–16,5; Test Jud 21,6–22,3; Ass Mos 7,1–8,5; 10,1–10; 4 Ez 6,18–28; 9,1–12; 2 Bar 48,31–41; 50,2–52,7; 82,3–83,9; Or Sib 3,63–92; 4,152–192. Cf. Test Zeb 9,5–9.

[18] Gr.: "to its axles".

[19] The Greek text argues against CHARLES's emendation of the Ethiopic MSS.

[20] By transferring the whole of v. 6 to *E*, I do not mean to suggest that men's knowing of this book would mean that they would be converted. The sinners' tardy remorse and realisation of their neglected duties is rather an illustration of the triumph of the just. Cf. 1 En 63.

and burn[21] them with fire:
ye shall be requited according to your works.
(8) Woe to you, ye obstinate of heart,
who watch in order to devise wickedness:
fear shall come upon you,
and none shall help you.
(9) Woe to you, ye sinners, on account of the words of your mouth,
and on account of the deeds of your hands which your godlessness has
    wrought:
in blazing flames worse than fire shall ye burn.

In this passage we find all five elements represented, and they are also quite strictly separated from each other. They are however not arranged in a definite chronological order. One rather gets the impression that the text expresses a complex of ideas with a certain structure, in which the bloodshed under A and the wretched state of the sinners under D occupy prominent places, while God's coming (B) and judgement (C) are only lightly touched upon.

The above example is *one* case of the shifting of emphasis within this pattern. Other texts dwell principally on the coming felicity of the just (E) or the future misery of the sinners (D) and others again on the evil background of the divine intervention (A).[22] But even where one or two motifs predominate in the text, they do not squeeze out the others entirely (cf. the above example).

There is often a certain connection between sin and oppression under A, on the one hand, and the punishments under D, on the other,[23] a connection which was related above to the authors' view of history.[24] In the text just quoted this connection is clear in vv. 7 ff.

It was noted that, in 1 En 100,1–9, God's judgement was mentioned rather casually and in the presentation of the raw material in Chap. I it was observed that the concept of "judgement" was often not strictly distinguished from that of "punishment".[25] This explains why the judgement, as a session of a court and a trial, as a rule takes up so little space in these texts. It is the Almighty who judges without discussion and this judgement is manifested in punishments, i.e. we must not let the dis-

---

[21] The Eth. MS q supports a Greek variant reading φυλάξητε. Cf. C. C. TORREY, Notes on the Greek Texts of Enoch, *J. Amer. Orient. Soc.* 62 (1942), 58 f., and G. ZUNTZ, Notes on the Greek Enoch, *J. Bibl. Lit.* 61 (1942), 196.

[22] For example, the stress placed on E: 1 En 10,16–11,2; 104,1–105,2; (cf. 4 Ez 6,18–28); on D and E: 1 En 103,1–15; 2 Bar 50,2–52,7; on A: 1 En 80,2–8; Jub 23,11–31; Test Jud 21,6–22,3; on A and D: 1 En 99,1–16; 4 Ez 9,1–12.

[23] Evil in A is the cause of punishment under D: 1 En 91,6–11; 99,1–16; 102,1–11; 103,1–15; 104,1–105,2; 2 Bar 48,31–41; 82,3–83,9 (slight connection).

[24] See above, 33 and 46.

[25] See above, 42 f.

tinction between C (judgement) and D (punishment) mislead us into assuming that, when C is not mentioned or is rapidly touched upon, no divine judgement is to be imagined as entering into the picture. Because God is the Ruler of all things, He is also the Judge of all things. The misery of the sinners and the joy of the blessed are actually separate aspects of the divine judgement, though the word "judgement" may perhaps not be mentioned.[26]

Ass Mos 10,1 ff. provides another expression of the same complex point of view. This says that God's kingdom will appear through the whole creation (*parebit regnum illius in omni creatura illius*). This appearance is described in theophany categories: (3–7) The earth shall quake, the sun be darkened, the sea fall into the abyss, etc. The implicit consequence of the appearance of God's *regnum* is that the judging activity which appertains to the *Rex* also begins, and this is naturally reported in vv. 7 ff.: The nations are punished and Israel exalted. [27]

Finally it should be noted that, of all the texts I have brought together as representing this main form of the basic pattern, 2 Bar 48,37 perhaps has a variant of the motif of the last great attack on Israel:

And many shall be stirred up in anger to injure many,
and they shall raise up armies in order to shed blood,
and in the end they shall perish together with them.

Here the motif is inserted in connection with the other catastrophes which will occur in the evil time before God's intervention (48,39).[28]

Counterparts to the pattern in the OT

It is not surprising that this pattern A, B, C, D and E, in which B and C refer to God's intervention and judgement respectively, have parallels in the OT. At this stage I content myself with only demonstrating this parallelism as a fact. For parallelism alone would tell us nothing about the relation between the pattern in the OT and its parallel in 1 En, for example.

We may take Dn 7,23–27 as an example of the complete basic pattern:

A. (23–25) The last king (horn) of the fourth kingdom (beast) blasphemes against God, persecutes His saints and changes times and laws.

B, C. (26) Judgement is passed (we have already been told in v. 9 f. how the Ancient of Days will sit upon His throne to give judgement).

---

[26] Cf. BÜCHSEL and HERNTRICH, κρίνω κτλ., *Theol. Wörterb.* III, 920 ff.

[27] Another passage in which God's judgement is not explicitly mentioned, but His intervention is described in terms of a theophany is 1 En 102,1–11. Note that judgement can be spoken of in CHARLES's translation (v. 5) only by making an emendation. The Greek does not support this emendation.

[28] Cf. below, 62.

D. (26) The dominion of the last blasphemous king is taken from him and destroyed.

E. (27) The kingdom and dominion over all other kingdoms are given to the people of the saints of the Most High.[29]

As in the intertestamental texts, we may also find different emphases in the OT texts in which there is this pattern or a major part of it. Some lay stress on the coming time of salvation, others on the judgement and its causes, and others again on the evil times etc.[30]

In the extra-biblical apocalyptic texts we found that the moral wickedness described under *A* was often stated to give rise to the punishments under *D*. This is also the case in the OT. One example which will be important in connection with texts to be mentioned later on is Gn 6, where the fact that the wickedness is great (רבה רעת האדם) is the cause of the Flood. There are many examples of the same way of looking at the matter in the prophetic literature, especially in texts which resemble the apocalyptic ones in the pattern of their thought.[31]

We also found that in the Jewish texts the explicit statements that God will pass judgement were sometimes few and far between and were not specially emphasized, owing to the fact that the authors had, so to say, paid less regard to the trial aspect of the judgement than to the fact that the judicial function is one of the functions of the Ruler, which is expressed by the sinners being punished and the righteous favoured. This detail is also to be found in OT texts with the same structure, as regards content, as the pattern of thought under discussion. Is 59,1–21 may be quoted as an example:

A. (1–15) Israel has sinned and its sins are many.

B. (15*b*–17) Yahweh interposes with His arm and puts on righteousness and vengeance.

D. (18–19) He will requite His enemies; they shall fear Him.

E. (20–21) But He will redeem Sion and His spirit will be upon them.[32] Thus, in this case the text can move naturally from Yahweh's intervention with justice (צדקה) in vv. 15–17 to the execution of the "judgement" in vv. 18–21.

It is almost a truism to say that a description of God's intervention in terms of a theophany has OT parallels. But we also find OT theophany

---

[29] Other examples: Ps 7; 94; Is 3–4; 24; Ez 16; Zph 3; Si 35,14–26; 36,1–19.

[30] Stress on *E*: Is 51; 60; Ez 34; Zch 2–3; 8; on *D* and *E*: Ps 37; Is 37; Ez 11; Ob; on *A*, *D* and *E*: Is 26; 65; on *A*: Ps 12; Is 59; Jr 9; Dn 11–12; on *A* and *D*: Jr 25; Ez 5; 7.

[31] Other examples: Gn 13,13 + 18,20 + 19,1–29; Jr 9; Ez 7; 35; Ho 12; Ob; Mi 1; 3–4; Zph 1.

[32] Other examples: Dt 29,16–30,10; Ps 102; Is 9,8–10,34; Ez 35; Dn 2,37–45; 11–12.

texts which relate that sinners will be punished and the righteous saved
without mentioning God's judgement, which is part of His function as
Ruler, the function which is demonstrated in the theophany. This is the
case in Hb 3, in which God's intervention causes the earth to split, the
peoples to tremble and the sun and moon to stay still in their habitation.[33]
His intervention brings with it salvation to His people but punishment for
the unrighteous.[34]

In the texts under discussion we found a possible example of the motif
of the last great attack of the heathen, which, however, is warded off by
divine help. An almost self-evident parallel is Ez 38 f. If, for the moment,
we restrict ourselves to ch. 39, we find there also the main features
in the pattern of thought: the attack of the heathen: Gog is incited to
attack and is destroyed by God (vv. 1–20); A, vv. 21–24, Israel has been
faithless and has sinned, and has therefore fallen into captivity; B, C,
vv. 21–24, Yahweh's glory shall be revealed, all peoples shall see His
judgements; D, E, vv. 25–29, God's people will be gathered together and
His Spirit will be poured out upon them.[35].

Thus, we find parallels in the OT, both for this main form of the
pattern and for different variants of it, primarily in the Prophets but
also in the Psalms and the Pentateuch.

B. A variant

I include, as a variant of this main type, a couple of cases in which God
is still the only actor, but the evil background (A) is not described. One
example is 1 En 25,3–6;[36] Enoch has seen in a vision seven magnificent
mountains and a delightful tree, a vision which is interpreted as follows:

B. (3) This high mountain (which you have seen[37]), whose summit is like
the throne of God, is His throne, where the Holy Great One, the Lord of
Glory, the Eternal King, will sit, when He shall come down to visit the earth
with goodness.

C, D. (4) And as for this fragrant tree no mortal is permitted to touch it
till the great judgement, when He shall take vengeance on all and bring
(everything)[38] to its consummation for ever.[39]

E. It shall then be given to the righteous and holy. (5) Its fruit shall be
a life-giving food[40] to the elect; it shall be transplanted to the holy place, to

---

[33] Heb. זְבֻלָה.

[34] Other examples: Ps 97; Jr 4,23 ff.; Mi 1.

[35] Other examples: Ps 48; Jl 2,18 ff.; 4,9 ff.; Mi 4,11 ff.

[36] In addition, only 1 En 1,3–9.

[37] The Gr. omits the words in parentheses.

[38] Supplied by CHARLES.

[39] Or with the Gr.: "When there is vengeance on all and consummation for ever".

[40] Gr. εἰς ζωὴν εἰς βοράν. The Eth. text is corrupt, according to CHARLES
(*Book of Enoch*, ad loc.).

the temple of the Lord, the Eternal King. (6) Then shall they rejoice with joy and be glad, and into the holy place shall they enter.[41] And its fragrance shall be in their bones, and they shall live a long life on earth, such as their fathers lived, and in their days shall no (sorrow or[37]) plagues or torments or calamities touch them.

Here, as in 1 En 1,3–9 it is the coming joy of the righteous that is emphasized.

As in the main form discussed above, we find here in its variant a text (1 En 1,3 ff.) which describes God's intervention in terms similar to those in the OT theophany texts. Here also the natural consequence of the theophany is the judgement (although here the judgement is explicitly mentioned):

(7) The earth shall be rent in sunder,
and all that is upon the earth shall perish,
and there shall be a judgement upon all,
(8) and with the righteous he will make peace ...[42]

As regards 4 Ez 7,31–43, we may note, finally, that it uses this pattern for the age of consummation, which will not ensue until after the end of the 400-year period of Messianic rule (7,26–29), i.e. the pattern which in 1 En applied to the whole of the final course of events here refers only to the last transcendental phase.[43]

Counterparts to the pattern in the OT

In this case also there is no difficulty in finding OT texts which show the same pattern, as regards content, as the present variant. Ps 68,2–4 may serve as an example:

B. God rises up and His enemies are scattered.
D. The wicked perish in His presence.
E. The righteous rejoice before God.[44]

3. *The Second Main Form (the Messiah has a Place in the Pattern)*

While the picture in the first main form is relatively easy to fix, in spite of the details varying, the whole thing becomes considerably more complicated when a Messiah has also to be fitted into the picture of

---

[41] Thus the Gr.

[42] For the text, see below, 72, note 5.

[43] There is something similar in 2 Bar 30,2–5. Cf. J. KLAUSNER, *The Messianic Idea in Israel* (1955), 408 ff., and see KÜPPERS, *Messiasbild*, 53 ff., and RIESENFELD, *Jésus transfiguré*, 57 f.

[44] See also, for example, Ps 76; Is 25; Na 1.

the last things. The vital point is how the relation between God's work and that of His Anointed was thought of. In certain cases, however, it is perhaps not advisable to expect to find any reflections on this relation. Thus we find here, on the one hand, an oscillation between God and His representative as the author of the events,[45] an oscillation which to a modern reader may appear confusing. On the other hand, we meet with a considerably more strict distinction between the two: first a Messianic period, then the coming age, in which God alone will be responsible for what is done.

Faced with this kaleidoscope, we must be on our guard against having in mind, consciously or unconsciously, any form of Christian eschatology as a pattern. The traditional Christian expectation that the Son of Man will come down to earth on the clouds of heaven to pass judgement on all men, after which wickedness will be punished and the faithful will be allowed to enter into the kingdom which has been prepared for them— this is not a view for which we should too simply expect to find equivalents in these texts.

I now present four variants of a second main pattern, in which the Messiah occupies different positions in relation to the direct divine activity.

A. The Messiah plays a small part

In one or two texts (1 En 90,11–42 and 104,1–105,2, the latter of which is somewhat doubtful[46]) the Messiah plays a very small part. The pattern is actually that of the first main form discussed above, except that the Messiah crops up at the end of the description of the final happy situation (*E*). Thus we have:

A. Evil times.
B. God intervenes.
C. God judges.
D. Punishment befalls the sinners.
E. The righteous rejoice; the Messiah appears.

1 En 90,11–42, which follows this pattern, describes from v. 28 onwards how after the judgement (vv. 20–27) "a new house" comes from God, how the heathen are subjected, how the scattered are gathered together and how all have good and true knowledge (v. 35). Of the

---

[45] See above, Chap. I, sections 3 and 4.

[46] The other text, 1 En 104,1–105,2 runs in 105,2: "I and My son will be united with them for ever". CHARLES (*Book of Enoch*, ad loc.) doubts the authenticity of the passage, and the Greek papyrus containing the last chapters of 1 En found later confirms his suspicion, inasmuch as it is missing there (*The Last Chapters of Enoch in Greek*, ed. C. BONNER, 1937).

Messiah, it then says: "And I saw that a white bull was born, with large horns, and all the birds of the air feared him and made petition to him all the time" (v. 37), i.e. a ruler arises in the time of salvation brought about by God and subdues the heathen.

This text also contains the motif of the heathen's great final attack on Israel and the destruction of the attackers (90,13–19). Here the motif has its place in connection with *A*, before God's judgement (90,20 ff.).[47]

Counterparts to the pattern in the OT

In the OT there are parallels for the introduction of a Messiah, not as intervening or judging but as coming into the picture only when the joy of the consummation is spoken of. This is the case in Ez 34. In this case we may speak not only of a parallel but also of a direct model, for 1 En 90,11–42 was in all probability inspired by Ez 34.[48]

A. (1–8) Woe over shepherds who scatter the flock. This flock is ravaged by wild beasts.

B, D. (9–10) Yahweh will take action against the shepherds.

E. (11–16) Yahweh will gather the flock together.

C. (17–22) Yahweh will pass judgement.

E. (23–31) David as shepherd in the kingdom of peace.[49]

B. The 1 En Sim form

In the texts on the Son of Man in 1 En Sim we meet with a Messianic figure who has a greater and more prominent place in the pattern of thought, which may be outlined as follows:

A. The wicked oppress the righteous (in most cases this is given as a reason for punishment under *D*).

Bg. God sits enthroned.

Bm. The Son of Man appears for God and/or is enthroned (by God) or is already enthroned.

C. (God judges, or—as a rule—) the Son of Man passes judgement on God's behalf.

D. The wicked are punished by God or the Son of Man.

E. Joy and triumph under the aegis of the Son of Man.

Firstly, it may not be inappropriate to warn the reader once more against the misconception that the above stages are necessarily in chronological order. They should rather be regarded as parts of a complex of

---

[47] Cf. above, 57.

[48] See below, 83 f.

[49] Another example is Jr 23,1–8, which moreover has often been assumed to have served as a pattern for Ez 34. See J. HERRMANN, *Comm. Ez* (1924), ad loc., and W. ZIMMERLI, *Comm. Ez* (1963), ad loc. See also Dn 7,1–14.

ideas, or as different motifs in a stage picture (this particular comparison with a stage picture is a useful one—these pericopes are designed as visions).[50]

We meet with this variant in its entirety in 1 En 47,1–48,10:

A. (47,1–2) The righteous pray for vengeance on the oppressors, and the holy ones in heaven join them in their prayer.

Bg. (3) The Head of Days takes His seat on His throne, surrounded by His court.

Cg. The books of the living are opened.[51]

E. (48,1) The fountain of righteousness, and the fountain of wisdom, of which the thirsty drink.

Bm. (48,2–3) The Son of Man is named before the Head of Days.

Bm, E. (4–7) He is a staff to the righteous and the light of the Gentiles etc.

D. (8–10) The kings of the earth perish ashamed.

Here the main stress is laid on the Son of Man and his reign, and on the fate of the wicked. Both motifs are common (and natural) in pericopes of this variant type.[52] As above under the first main form, we find a marked causal connection between the evil under *A* and the punishment under *D*.[53]

It is evident that the picture in 1 En 47 f. was deliberately painted with Dn 7,9 ff. as a model. It is assuredly precisely this model which gave us what was called *Bg* above. This *Bg* motif is included in only two of the pericopes from Sim which fall in this category of pattern.[54]

This pattern occurs in several texts[55] with no *Bg* motif. However, the Son of Man does not on this account act alone. Thus in 45,4 ff., for ex-

---

[50] Cf. below, Chap. IV, section 1.

[51] That this means judgement is clear from its proximity to Dn 7,9 f. See, for example, A. DILLMANN, *Das Buch Henoch* (1853), ad loc.

[52] Stress on *B* and *D*: 1 En 46,1–8; 50,1–51,5; 52,6–53,7; 62,1–16; 69,26–29; on *D* 1 En 38,1–6; 63,1–12.

[53] Thus 1 En 46,1–8; 52,6–53,7; 63,1–12.

[54] Besides 1 En 47,1–48,10, there is also 1 En 46,1–8, in which particularly the background of Dn makes it probable that He who has a head of days sits enthroned. There is no need here to raise the question of whether these two passages represent the complete pattern and the others are only part of it or whether these two are to be understood as showing an amplified form, with reference to Dn 7 in particular. There is even less need to try and answer this question, since we are at present only trying to trace some actual structures in these texts. The problem is not entirely an academic one, because further on it contains the question of the origin and development of the ideas of the Son of Man and the part played by Dn in this connection.

[55] Thus in 1 En 52,6–53,7; 62,1–16. There is perhaps also a copy of the pattern we then get (with an *A* element but with no *Bg*) in Or Sib 3,29–56. (See also the following note.)

ample, it is God who lets the Son of Man appear and who transforms heaven and earth. We also noted above that the *A* part is in most cases not an independent motif in the picture but instead occurs only in descriptions of the punishment of the wicked, as a justification for it. Consequently it has rather a weak position. It is therefore not surprising that it is entirely absent in several texts.[56] Thus there remain the following motifs in this variant.

Bm. The Son of Man is revealed and/or is seated on a throne.[57]

C. The Son of Man judges on God's behalf.

D. The wicked are punished by God or by the Son of Man.

E. Joy and triumph under the aegis of the Son of Man.

As an example I choose 1 En 69,26–29:

E.   (26) And there was a great joy amongst them (viz. the stars and the spirits of winds and the like),
and they blessed and glorified and extolled,[58]

Bm. because the name of that Son of Man had been revealed unto them. (27) And he sat on the throne of his glory,

C.   and the sum of judgement was given to the Son of Man,

D.   and he caused the sinners to pass away and be destroyed from off the face of the earth ...

E.   (29) And from henceforth there shall be nothing corruptible,

Bm. for that Son of Man has appeared,
and has seated himself on the throne of his glory,
and all evil shall pass away before his face,
and the word of that Son of Man shall go forth
and be strong before the Lord of Spirits.

Here we may note the heavenly public: there is no mention of any righteous men on this occasion.

In one of the texts which fall in this category of variant, viz. 1 En 55,3–57,3, we find the motif of the great attack by the heathen on the elect and the destruction of the attackers. The motif is fitted into the text as follows. The text of 55,4 mentions how the Elect One (the Son of Man)[59] sits on his throne and judges the apostate angels (*Bm, C*). The next few verses (56,1–4) relate that angels of punishment make ready the place of torment for the condemned (*C*), after which the description of the heathen assault follows (6–8). To this is added directly the motif of how the scattered people of God are re-assembled (*E*). Thus, in comparison with the previous cases (2 Bar 48,37 and 1 En 90,13–19),[60] in which the motif

---

[56] 1 En 38,1–6; 45,1–6; 49,1–4; 50,1 – 51,5; 55,3 – 57,3; 61,1–13; 63,1–12; 69,26–29.

[57] 1 En 61,8 is the only passage speaking of an enthronement.

[58] MS *g* omits.

[59] Cf. above, 39, note 28.

[60] See above, 57 and 62.

was connected with *A* and preceded the judgement (*C*), this text brings it nearer the joy of the last days (*E*).

Counterparts to the pattern in the OT

I mentioned earlier Dn 7,9 ff. as not only an OT parallel but also a model for the passage from 1 En 47,1–48,10 reported above. We find a similar pattern in Ps 2:

A. (1–3) The nations conspire and the kings of the earth rise up against Yahweh and His Anointed.

Bg. (4–5) "He who sits in the heavens laughs; Yahweh has them in derision" and will speak to them in wrath and terrify them.

Bm. (6–7) "I have set (actually "cast" נסכתי) my king on Sion". Of this king, Yahweh says: "You are my son; today I have begotten you".

C, D. (8–12*a*) The heathen will be the king's heritage: he will dash them in pieces (or, will pasture them) with a rod of iron (תרעם בשבט ברזל).[61] The kings are exhorted to fear Yahweh.

E. (12*b*) Blessed are they that put their trust in Him.

The stress here is laid on the power of the Son in virtue of his divine authorization and on the subjection of his enemies, i.e. there is a shift of emphasis not unlike that which we found in the example above. As in that case, there would also seem to be a causal connection here between the behaviour of the nations and the kings in vv. 1–3 (*A*) and their fate in vv. 8–12 (*D*).

In the above "pericopes" it was more common for the scheme to lack the *A* and *Bg* motifs and to include instead *Bm* (the Son of Man is revealed and/or is seated on a throne), *C* (the Son of Man judges on God's behalf), *D* (the wicked are punished by God or by the Son of Man) and *E* (joy and triumph under the aegis of the Son of Man).

Here we may quote Ps 110,1–6 as an OT parallel to the pattern:

Bm. (1–4) The king is placed on Yahweh's throne: he shall rule from Sion as priest-king on behalf of Yahweh.[62]

---

[61] TM vocalizes תְּרֹעֵם "you shall break them"; LXX, Pesh. assumes תִּרְעֵם "you shall pasture them", the same reading as lies behind Ap 2,27 and 19,15. The latter metaphor goes back to the image of the king as a shepherd (cf. for example, 2 Sm 5,2; Is 44,28; Ez 34,2 ff.). This image has a similar function in intertestamental literature: see 1 En 89,59; Ps Sal 17,45 f.

[62] V.3 is problematical. As far as I am concerned, it is enough to note that it deals with the attributes of the enthroned one or (TM) with his young warriors. The LXX reading would suit admirably anyone who was looking for OT support for the pre-existence of the enthroned Son of Man: ἐκ γαστρὸς πρὸ ἑωσφόρου ἐξεγέννησά σε. Cf. 1 En 48,3: "before the sun and the signs were created, before the stars of the heaven were made, his name was named before the Lord of Spirits".

C, D. (5–6) The Lord will shatter kings on the day of His wrath: He will pass judgement among the nations.

We may also quote Is 11,1–9:

Bm. (1–2) The Branch of the root of Jesse, on which the Spirit of Yahweh shall rest.

C, D. (3–5) He will judge the meek justly and will slay the wicked.

E. (6–9) The peace of Paradise is re-established.

In the first case there is more of the very close relationship between God and His representative which we found in 1 En Sim; in the second case the pattern itself is more like that of the apocalypses.[63]

C. A more independent Messiah

There is a more independent Messianic activity in the texts in which we find the following structure:

A. Evil times.

Bg. God intervenes and sends the Messiah.

Bm. The Messiah.

C. The Messiah judges (as ruler).

D. Enemies, heathen, Belial, etc. are frustrated.

E. The righteous rejoice under the rule of the Messiah.

I select Ps Sal 17,5–51 as an example:

A. (5–22) On account of the people's sins, the heathen have been allowed to ravage and the righteous have fled and been scattered; indeed, on account of the people's iniquity, drought has come and the springs have dried up.

Bg, Bm. (23) "Take care of them, O Lord, and let their king, the Son of David, arise to rule over Israel, your servant, at the time that you have appointed".

Bm, D. (24–27) The Messiah crushes iniquitous rulers, cleanses Jerusalem of the oppressive heathens and drives out the sinners, who are punished in this way.

Bm, C, E. (28–31) The Messiah gathers a holy people, whom he rules and judges according to his wisdom.

Bm, E. (32–40) The Messiah reigns as the king of peace over a pure and splendid Jerusalem, to which peoples come in humility as pilgrims.

Cf. W. STAERK, *Die Erlösererwartung in den östlichen Religionen* (1938), 439, and SJÖBERG, *Menschensohn*, 87 ff. On the psalm as a royal psalm, see MOWINCKEL, *Psalmenstudien* II, 301 ff.; G. WIDENGREN, *Psalm 110 och det sakrala kungadömet i Israel* (1941); id., *Sakrales Königtum*, 44 ff.; JOHNSON, *Sacral Kingship*, 121 f. See also J. COPPENS, Les apports du Psaume CX (Vulg. CIX) à l'idéologie royale israélite, in *Studies in the History of Religions* 4 (1959), 333–48 (refs.).

[63] Cf. also, for example, Ez 17,22–24; Zch 6,12–15.

Bm. (41–49) The Messiah is without sin, blessed by the Lord, chosen by Him and thus a mighty and just ruler.

E. (50–51) "Blessed is he who may live in these days and may behold the salvation of Israel and the union of their tribes, which the Lord has performed." May deliverance come soon.

Thus, though this Messiah neither appears before the throne of God nor is pre-existent nor forms part of heavenly visions, he is not, of course, entirely emancipated from God. He rules with the authority of the Lord (42 ff.); it is God who saves when He sends the Messiah (23 f., 50 f.).[64]

In texts which show this variant[65] *Bm* and *E* especially are often closely related to each other, owing to the fact that, when the Messiah is described in detail, it is his activity as ruler in the time of salvation that is described, and this naturally also becomes a description of this time, which is so joyful for the redeemed people.

Finally, it may be pointed out that sometimes there is a certain caesura or fresh start in the text between God's intervention (*Bg*) in the evil situation (*A*), on the one hand, and the appearance of the Messiah (*Bm*), on the other. Thus, for example, in Test Jud 23,5–24,1 the Lord visits the wicked and re-assembles the scattered people, after which we read: "After these things shall a star arise ...".[66]

Counterparts to the pattern in the OT

There is quite a large number of OT parallels for this pattern. I shall bring forward a complex of texts which have coloured Jewish thinking to an uncommonly large extent down the centuries, viz. Ex 1–15,[67] texts which were not unimportant even to the authors we are discussing here,[68] especially on account of their function as ritual texts in the celebration of the Passover.

A. (Ch. 1) Bondage in Egypt.

Bg. (Ch. 2–3) God appears and sends Moses.

---

[64] Cf. above, 43.

[65] Besides Ps Sal 17, there is also Test Levi 17,11 – 18,14; Test Jud 23,1–25,5; Test Napht 4,1–5; Or Sib 3,265–294 (where it is doubtful who is the subject of v. 287, God or the king sent by Him; see above, 43, note 51). Also Apc Abr 27–31, where the Messianic section is to be found in 31, and, presumably, also Or Sib 3,632–761.

[66] Thus also Test Levi 18,1 f.; Test Napht 4,5; Or Sib 3,286.

[67] Cf. D. DAUBE, *The Exodus Pattern in the Bible* (1963), and further H. SAHLIN, Das Exodus-Schema als Kompositionsprinzip, in *Zur Typologie des Johannesevangeliums* (1950), 74–78; G. EDWARDS, The Exodus and Apocalyptic, in *A Stubborn Faith* (1956), 27–38; J. J. ENZ, The Book of Exodus as a Literary Type for the Gospel of John, *J. Bibl. Lit.* 76 (1957), 208–15.

[68] See, for example, 1 En 48,9 (cf. Ex 14,13, 28 ff.; 15,7, 10).

Bm. (Ch. 4–6) Moses is invested with authority.

C, D. (Ch. 7–12) Egypt is visited by scourges; judgement on "the gods of Egypt".

D, E. (Ch. 13–14) The people are saved and the Egyptians destroyed in the Red Sea.

E. (Ch. 15) The people's song of victory (in v. 17 the liberated people are planted in the sanctuary).[69]

Just as in this variant it was possible to note that the descriptions of the Messiah (*Bm*) and of the time of his rule, in which the people will be so joyful, were sometimes interwoven with each other, so we also find this state of affairs in Ps 72, in which statements on the people's salvation (v. 4, 12 ff.), on peace for the righteous (v. 7) and on the fruitfulness of the land (v. 16) are mixed with statements about the extent of the king's power (v. 8) and about his importance to the country, which is likened to that of rain (v. 6), with wishes for blessings upon him (vv. 15, 17) and with sayings on how he subjugates his enemies (vv. 9–11).[70]

Finally, we observed that in the pattern a certain caesura or fresh start was sometimes noticeable between the statements that God intervened against the powers of evil (*A, Bg*) and that He sent the Messiah (*Bm*). A similar caesura can be observed in Jr 33, in which vv. 1–13 relate that Yahweh will re-establish the now desolate Judah and Israel. Then there follows in vv. 14 f.: "Behold, the days are coming, says Yahweh, when I will fulfil the promise I made to the house of Israel and the house of Judah. (15) In those days and at that time I will cause a righteous Branch to spring forth for David."[71]

D. 4 Ez and 2 Bar

A distribution of roles between God and His Messiah which gives the impression of a conscious desire to bring order into the matter is that found in 4 Ez and 2 Bar (and also largely in the rabbinic writings[72]). We have here the following pattern:

A. Evil times, sometimes characterized as signs.

B. The Messiah appears.

C. The Messiah accuses (judges) "Antichrist" and the heathen.

D. "Antichrist", and the heathen are destroyed.

E. The joy during the limited reign of the Messiah.

I select 2 Bar 72,2–74,4 as an example:

---

[69] Other examples: Is 8,1–9,7; Jr 30–31; Ez 37,21–28.

[70] See also Is 11; Ez 34,23–31.

[71] See also Is 10–11 (11,1).

[72] For the beginning of God's kingdom, after the end of the Messianic period, cf. above, 60.

A. (72,2) After the signs have come, of which you were told before, when the nations become turbulent ...

B, (C). and the time of My Messiah is come, he shall both summon all the nations, and some of them he shall spare, and some of them he shall slay.

D. (3) These things therefore shall come upon the nations, which are to be spared by him. (4) Every nation, which knows not Israel,[73] and has not trodden down the seed of Jacob, shall indeed be spared. (5) And this because some out of every nation shall be subjected to your people. (6) But all those who have ruled over you or have known you, shall be given up to the sword.

E. (73,1) And it shall come to pass, when he has brought low everything that is in the world, and has sat down in peace for the age on the throne of his kingdom, that joy shall then be revealed, and rest shall appear.

Vv. 2–7 continue the description of this rest.

In texts with this pattern[74] the judgement motif is weak as a rule and is almost completely absent in the above example. This is connected with the fact that in 4 Ez and 2 Bar the judgement is committed to God on the verge of the coming age, which is described by one of the variants of the first main form.[75]

Counterparts to the pattern in the OT

This pattern is really so like the others—considered as a pattern—that several of the parallels which have been quoted to these others are also valid here. Mi 5,1–9 may be brought forward as an example:

A. (1, 3) Israel is oppressed.

Bm. (2) A prince from Bethlehem.

E. (4, 7) The prince watches over the flock by the authority of Yahweh and the flock is at peace.

D. (5 f., 8 f.) Assyria will be destroyed if it attacks and "the remnant"

---

[73] F. ZIMMERMANN, Textual Observations on the Apocalypse of Baruch, *J. Theol. Stud.* 40 (1939), 153, suggests that we are confronted here with a confusion of רעע and ידע, as in Si 7,20, and proposes "hurt, injure" instead of "know". (Cf. also Dn 12,4.)

[74] Other texts with this pattern: 4 Ez 7,26–29; 11,37 – 12,3; 12,32–34; 13,1–13a; 13,25–50; 2 Bar 25,2 – 30,1; 39,1 – 40,4; 70,2 – 71,1. 2 Bar 70,9 is interesting from the point of view of textual criticism. CHARLES holds that it is an interpolation (*Pseudepigrapha*, ad loc.) and perhaps he is right, but there is no support in the MSS. for this assumption. If 70,9 is deleted, we have something which very much more resembles a description of the final enemy assault (Gog and Magog) and the destruction of these enemies. It also clashes with the context in the running narrative to introduce the Messiah here, whereas this introduction takes place naturally in 72,2. On the other hand, this possible interpolation is, as such, instructive, as regards the function of the text. It was pericopes that were read and not the wider context, for in that case the present text would have seemed unnatural. Cf. above, 31, note 38, and the introduction to the present chapter.

[75] Cf. Chap. I, section 4, and above in this chapter, 55 ff., 59 f.

will be as a lion[76] among cattle among the nations. Just as, in several of the texts discussed above, the judgement motif was weak, so it is not to be found explicitly in this example.

Thus, this chapter has shown that most of these "pericopes" vary basic themes in different ways and that both these themes and the separate variants have several OT parallels. But the important thing is not the variety but the conformity, even to the extent that similar patterns of thought can be found in texts with different views on the events of the last days. Later on, in Chapter IV, we will meet some of these patterns of thought again, and consider how they function in the making of some individual texts.

---

[76] The image of the ravaging lion is used of the Messiah in 4 Ez 11,37.

CHAPTER III

Two Motifs with Varying Functions

The two previous chapters have provided us with a variegated chart of the different motifs which occur in these pericopes concerning the last things. In Chapter I they were woven into a more or less systematic account and in Chapter II they appeared in different groups of motifs, which formed varying constellations. I now propose to select two of these motifs, to determine their functions in different texts in some detail and to compare these functions in each case with the Old Testament.

The two motifs are, firstly, earthquakes and the like and, secondly, the tumult and/or the attacks made by the heathens. The functions of these motifs "vary", as they appear in different functions in different texts and are inserted at different points in the course of events in the last days. The order in which these different functions are presented is systematic rather than historical.

Here the comparison with the OT may be more detailed. In the preceding pages we have been concerned with the structure of the contents, of which we could not say more than that they had parallels in the OT. Here we get so near the actual wording that in certain cases we may conclude from them that material from definite OT texts was used in these pericopes.

1. *The Earthquake Motif*

A. 1 En 1, 3–9

In this apocalyptic text, which is one of the oldest in the selection under consideration, earthquakes are associated with God's coming to the earth, in which the universe fears the greatness of His majesty. The text accordingly describes a theophany,[1] in the same colours as several passages in the OT:

---

[1] Emphasized by N. MESSEL, *Die Einheitlichkeit der jüdischen Eschatologie* (1915), 9 ff. Cf. VOLZ, *Eschatologie*, 16, and see JÖRG JEREMIAS, *Theophanie* (1965), for the present text, 52 f. Messel counts only 1 En 1,3 ff., Ass Mos 10,3 ff. and 1 En 90,18 as theophanies (not counting 4 Ez 3,18 f., on Sinai). For parallel Greek material, see F. ADAMI, De poetis scaenicis Graecis hymnorum sacrorum imitatoribus, *Jahrbücher class. Philol.*, *Suppl.* 26 (1901), 213 ff., and K. KEYSSNER, *Gottesvorstellung und Lebensauffassung im griechischen Hymnus* (1932), 33 f.

(3) The holy great One will come forth from his dwelling,

(4) and the God of "eternity" (αἰών)[2] will tread (upon the earth)[3] on Mount Sinai

and appear in (Gr. from) His encampment

and appear in the strength of His might from the heaven (of heaven).[3]

(5) And all shall fear,

and the watchers shall quake,[4]

and great fear and trembling shall seize them unto the ends of the earth.

(6) And the high mountains shall be shaken,

and the high hills shall be made low

and shall melt like wax before the flame.

(7) And the earth shall be rent in sunder,

and all that is upon the earth shall perish,

and there shall be judgement upon all.[5]

Thus here the earthquake has its place in the description of the divine intervention (B), which passes on directly to a statement of the judgement on all men (C; 1,7). As has already been mentioned, the motif itself is here used in a way which has parallels in the OT,[6] but a closer examination also shows us a number of definite OT passages which are obviously re-echoed in this text, namely, Mi 1,3 f., together with Ex 19,11, 20, Dt 33,2 and Hb 3,6, which supplement it with details. The allusions are connected with each other by associations of motifs and key-words.[7]

The theophany referred to in these OT texts, involves in Mi 1,3 f. the divine punishment of an apostate Israel. In 1 En this theophany is taken over and placed in a wider perspective, in a pattern of thought which expects God's coming for the great last judgement on the sinners. But this pattern of thought also has OT parallels, for example, Ps 96 and 97, in which we find both God's coming, described in terms of a theophany (96,11 f., 97,3 ff.), and God's judgement of the earth (96,13; 97,8) and

---

[2] The corresponding Hebrew expression seems to be אל עולם. See E. JENNI, Das Wort ʿōlām im AT, Zschr. At. Wiss. 65 (1953), 1 ff., 33 ff., where he also discusses the possibility of rendering the word "aeon". Cf. CHARLES, Book of Enoch, ad loc.

[3] Thus the Greek text.

[4] The Greek reads "shall believe" (cf. TORREY, J. Amer. Orient. Soc. 62, 1942, 54) and adds "and they shall sing secret things in all the ends of the [earth], and all the ends of the earth shall be shaken" (cf. BURKITT, Jewish and Christian Apocalypses, 64).

[5] Eth. adds "and upon all righteous". I follow the lectio brevior, which is supported by the Greek text. Cf. BURKITT, op. cit., 63.

[6] See, for example, Jdc 5,4 f.; Ps 18,8 ff.; 68,8 f.; 77,17 ff.; 114,7.

[7] Mi 1,3 f. and Ex 19 have a subject and main word in common: God comes down (ירד — Mi 1,3, Ex 19,11) upon a mountain. The theophany on Mount Sinai is dealt with both in Ex 19 and in Dt 33,2. The latter passage is associated, by its subject and the main word Paran, with Hb 3,3. See further the analysis of the passage in Chap. IV.

the joy of the righteous (97,10 ff.; cf. 1 En 1,8).[8] Even though these psalms did not originally have this "eschatological" and universal meaning but reflected cultic events,[9] it was nevertheless natural for persons holding the views of the world and of history that these authors held to interpret them in this way.[10]

B. Or Sib 3,64 ff.

In this text it is Belial, God's great enemy, who appears instead of God in a setting in which the OT usually places God.[11] This Belial

shall raise ($\sigma\tau\acute{\eta}\sigma\epsilon\iota$)[12] the high mountains, still the sea,
shall make the great blazing sun and the bright moon
stand still, etc.

All this is deception (3,67 f.) and forms part of the evil time (A) which will precede God's great judgement (3,89 ff.).[13]

C. 1 En 102,1 f.

In this text[14] there is no longer any mention of God's "coming". The earthquake is a consequence of the fact that God "launches forth his

[8] See also Ps 50; 76; Is 30,27–33; Hb 3.

[9] See MOWINCKEL, *Psalms in Israel's Worship* I, 161 ff., and I. ENGNELL, Psaltaren, *Svenskt Bibl. Uppslagsverk* II, 618–57, esp. 645 ff; cf. H.-J. KRAUS, *Psalmen* II (2nd ed. 1961), 665 ff.

[10] A similar theophany, in which the earthquake performs the same function in the pattern of thought as in 1 En 1,3 ff., is given by Ass Mos 10,2–7, which is also built up of motifs which can be derived from quite definite OT texts. See, for example on Ass Mos 10,3: Is 13,13, 26,21, Mi 1,3, Na 1,5 f.; on 10,5: Is 13,10, Jl 2,10, 3,4; on 10,6: Ps 18,14 f., Na 1,4; on 10,7: Mi 1,7. CHARLES (ed., 1897, ad loc.) makes a conjecture on Ass Mos 10,4: he alters "(*montes humiliabuntur*) *et concutientur et convalles* (*cadent*)" to "*et colles concutientur et*". I find this conjecture unnecessary, as I am not absolutely convinced that the author really found it strange to write that mountains were shaken and valleys fell down, in spite of its having previously been stated that the mountains would be brought low. The imagery is so traditional that it would seem to be able to withstand such attacks from the logic. See Is 40,4; Hb 3,6 — Is 5,25; 64,1,3; Na 1,5 — Ez 38,20; Mi 1,4. See below, 129.

[11] See, for example, Ex 15,8; Ps 65,8; Is 38,8; Hb 3,10 f., and cf. Is 26,19. Cf. W. BOUSSET, *Der Antichrist* (1895), 115 ff., and V. MAAG, B^{e}lija'al im AT, *Theol. Zschr.* 21 (1965), 287–99.

[12] KURFESS (*ed.*, 1951, ad loc.) emends to $\sigma\epsilon\acute{\iota}\sigma\epsilon\iota$.

[13] 1 En 90,18 mentions that the earth is rent, not by God's majesty, but because God strikes it with the rod of His wrath. The result is that it swallows up the attacking enemies in a way resembling that in Nu 16,30 ff. See below, 86 f. Earthquakes are mentioned in Or Sib 3,675 ff. in a context with a similar content.

[14] For the textual problems see ZUNTZ, *J. Bibl. Lit.* 61 (1942), 197 ff.; id., The Greek Text of Enoch 102,1–3, ibid. 63 (1944), 53 f.; id., Enoch on the Last Judgement, *J. Theol. Stud.* 45 (1944), 161–70; TORREY, *J. Amer. Orient. Soc.* 62 (1942), 59 f.

word against the sinners" (or with the Greek "gives His voice against"). Phenomenologically this is only another form of theophany, such as we find in Ps 29, on how Yahweh's might is revealed in the thunder, but in this text the stress is laid not so much on the fact that creation trembles before the divine majesty as on the fact that the world and the sinners will dread the angry Judge, who will hurl fire at the sinners as He pronounces judgement.

This manner of placing the stress in the theophany is also to be found in the OT. This text is related, both in its themes and in its choice of words, to Is 30,30 f. and combines with it material from Jl 2,10 f. That is to say, it was natural for the author to apply terms and themes from a prophecy against Assyria to the sinners against whom he directs his outcries.[15]

D. Test Levi 4,1

The functions of the earthquake and some other similar natural catastrophes are more difficult to define in Test Levi 4,1:

> Now therefore, know that the Lord shall execute judgement on the sons of men.
> Because, when the rocks are being rent (ὅτι τῶν πετρῶν σχιζομένων),[16]
> and the sun quenched ...
> and the fire cowering, ...
> and Hades takes spoils through the suffering (that comes) from the Most High (ἐπὶ τῷ πάθει τοῦ ὑψίστου),[17]

---

[15] See also Ps 18,14 ff.; 46,7; 68,2 ff.; Is 13,9 ff.; Jl 4,14 ff. Cf. Test Levi 3,9: creation trembles at God's glance (cf. Ps 104,32; Si 16,19). This motif is also used in a text about the (Son of) Man in 4 Ez 13,3 f.; cf. above, 36, note 10.

We meet with another variation on this motif in 1 En 51,4, in which the mountains leap like rams in the days when the Elect One sits on the throne and the earth rejoices. Cf. Ps. 114,4, where the same expressions are used in a theophany to describe the fear of nature. (Above, 36, note 10.)

[16] I take the gen. abs. here to be temporal and the ὅτι which precedes it to be causal ("because") and introductory of the finite clause which follows the series of gen.abs. (ἄνθρωποι ... ἐπιμενοῦσιν). In order to take the gen. abs. concessively, we would have needed an introductory καίπερ (cf. Test Jos 10,5). MS. c reads καὶ ὅτι τῶν π. κτλ., and may be translated: "know that the Lord shall execute ... and that ... men will persist". The text without the καί seems to represent the lectio difficilior.

[17] In *The Greek Versions of the Testaments of the Twelve Patriarchs* (1908), ad loc., CHARLES brackets the last five words as a Christian interpolation, but in his translation in *Pseudepigrapha* (1913) he renders the phrase "through the visitations of the Most High" and thinks that a rendering by "passion" presupposes an interpolation. I accept the natural meaning "passion", "suffering", but in interpreting the genitive as a *genitivus auctoris* or *originis*, I need not assume that the Passion of Jesus is spoken of here, nor that a Patripassianist was the interpolator (CHARLES, *Greek Versions*, xlviii, and M. DE JONGE, Christian Influence in the Testaments of

men will be unbelieving and persist (ἀπιστοῦντες[18] ἐπιμενοῦσιν) in their iniquity.

On this account (διὰ τοῦτο) with punishment shall they be judged (κολάσει κριθήσονται).

As this sentence is constructed, the natural catastrophes etc. are linked with the event in the ὅτι clause, that is, with the fact that mankind will continue to commit sins. The ὅτι clause and the genitive absolute describe contemporaneous phenomena and both are included in the description of the background of evil against which God's judgement takes place (A). We do not obtain any further information on purely linguistic grounds as to the function of the earthquake in this text.

The content may give us some further hints. The Lord will judge men *because* they persist in iniquity *when* the rocks are rent and people die through the suffering that comes from God. It seems to me that there the catastrophes may characterize the final crisis and time of distress and thus be one of the signs from God which should make the sinners realize how late the time is and thus be converted.[19]

The theme of mankind persisting in sin in spite of signs from God is not unusual in the OT; we need only recall the plagues in Egypt (Ex 7–12). Another example is Ps 78, according to which Israel "still sinned and believed not",[20] although God caused rocks to be cleft in the wilderness (v. 15 f.; in order to give His people water), divided the Red Sea (v. 13) and sent death among them (v. 31).

In spite of a certain thematic similarity to the OT,[21] we must still say that the function of this motif in Test Levi 4,1 has no striking or close parallels in the OT.

E. 4 Ez and 2 Bar

With 4 Ez and 2 Bar we move on to the explicit description of earthquakes and similar catastrophes as "signs", which may be taken as indications to expect the approaching end.[22] I quote 4 Ez 9,1–4:

When you see that a certain part of the predicted signs are past, (2) then you shall understand that it is the very time when the Most High is about

---

the Twelve Patriarchs, *Nov. Test.* 4 (1960), 222 f.). On the other hand, I find it difficult to see how M. PHILONENKO's interpretation of the passage as bearing upon the Teacher of Righteousness derives any support at all from the context (*Les interpolations chrétiennes des Testaments des Douze Patriarches*, 1960, 19 ff.).

[18] MSS.*c,h,i* (=CHARLES's α), and *d* read ἀπειθοῦντες.

[19] There is a similar interpretation in MESSEL, *Einheitlichkeit*, 12, who quotes Ap 16 as a parallel, and in EPPEL, *Le piétisme juif*, 95 f.

[20] Ps 78,32 LXX: ἥμαρτον ἔτι, καὶ οὐκ ἐπίστευσαν.

[21] See also Ps 106 and Am 8,4 ff.

[22] Cf. above, 34.

to visit the world which He has made. (3) And when in the world there shall be seen quaking of places, tumult of peoples ... (4) then understand that it is of these things that the Most High has spoken ...

Here the earthquake is still associated with God's intervention, for it is one of the signs that this intervention is at hand.[23] In 2 Bar, on the other hand, it is degraded, so to speak, to the status of a sign foreboding the Messianic period, which is a different matter from God's personal and direct intervention (27,7 and 70,8).[24]

It is possible that this development from theophany to Messianic signs fits into a wider context. We shall return later to the circumstance that most of the details in these pericopes from 4 Ez and 2 Bar certainly have OT parallels but at the same time do not seem to be derived directly from distinct passages in the OT. More likely the motifs had become traditional in apocalyptic circles and been taken over in that way. But perhaps they had become worn out and in that case the authors may have wished to brighten the colours. One consequence of this may then have been that the earthquake became a "sign" preceding the coming of the Messiah, instead of accompanying a theophany. It is also perhaps typical that in these texts we also meet with omens which have no parallels in the OT.[25]

Is there any background in the OT for motifs taking on the function of "signs" presaging the end? It is not impossible that there is, but, if so, there is a lacuna between the OT and the present apocalyptic text which has to be filled with assumed speculations by the "Apocalyptists", in which they interpreted OT sayings as bearing on the last days. As I am confining my attention at present to the direct relation of the texts to the OT, the following remarks may be sufficient for the present purpose.

One point of departure in the OT may have been Jl 3,3 f.; Yahweh will give portents (מופתים) in the heavens and on the earth, the sun will be darkened, etc., before the day of Yahweh comes (לפני בוא יום יהוה, LXX πρὶν ἐλθεῖν ἡμ. κ.). The Targum, on the other hand, speaks of signs: God will give signs (אתין). Nowhere in the OT are earthquakes described as signs or wonders (אותות, מופתים), as are other catastrophes, especially the plagues of Egypt.[26] Similarly the plagues which will befall an apostate Israel, according to Dt 28, are mentioned as signs and wonders (v. 46, אות, מופת).

[23] See also 4 Ez 5,8.

[25] For 70,8, cf. Chap. II, note 74. The motif has a similar function in Apc Abr 30,6: it is included amongst the ten punishments of the heathen, which are mentioned as a reply to the question: "How long will it be?" (ch. 28). In 31,1 the "Elect One" is sent.

[25] See the next chapter, section 5.

[26] Ex 4,8 f.; Dt 6,22; 34,11; Ps 78,43; 105,27; Jr 35,20. Cf. C. A. KELLER, *Das Wort OTH* (1946), 117 ff., 136 ff.

These texts of 4 Ez and 2 Bar are not the only ones which contain "signs" presaging the end, but the term is not so common in this function as sometimes seems to be thought:[27] apart from the passages quoted from 4 Ez and 2 Bar, it is only to be found in a couple of passages in Or Sib, reckoning with the texts under consideration.[28]

Thus, as far as 4 Ez and 2 Bar are concerned, we may record that the use of the motif of the earthquake as a sign presaging the end or the Messianic period does not reveal any direct dependence on the OT but rather an apocalyptic tradition, which may certainly have adopted OT motifs but enlarged on them fairly freely.

2. *The Tumult and Assault of the Heathen*

As was indicated in Chapter I, one reason for including the heathen in reflections on the last days must have been the theocratic view of history, in which hostility to Israel was synonymous with opposition to God. National enemies, apostates among their own people and the powers of chaos, Belial and his followers—all belong to that part of the world which is rebellious against God.[29] A common motif in the Psalms is that these enemies are subjugated by God and/or His Anointed, and it is probable that originally there were cultic realities behind this motif.[30]

At the period under discussion, the motif had a long history behind it, but this was probably of little interest to the authors. On the other hand, from their special points of view they noted the mention made in the old

---

[27] Cf. for example, BILLERBECK, *Comm.* IV:2, 977 ff., where the term — and the function — are not to be found in the examples from 1 En and Jub.

[28] Or Sib 2,153; 3,796 ff. In 3,66 there is mention of Belial's signs; cf. Dt 13,2 f., 14. Sap 8,8 uses the term in a sense which is similar to that in the texts under discussion: the Wisdom "foresees signs and wonders and the events of seasons and times": σημεῖα καὶ τέρατα προγινώσκει καὶ ἐκβάσεις καιρῶν καὶ χρόνων. It is conceivable that this passage may be inserted in a chain with links such as the σημεῖα καὶ τέρατα in Egypt, the curses in Dt 28, the τέρατα of Jl 3,3 (where the Targ. reads "signs" אתין), and the "signs" in the present texts and in Mk 13, 4 par. The eschatological overtones of the Passah meal may be included. See BILLERBECK, *Comm.* I, 85; B. LOHSE, *Das Passafest der Quartadecimaner* (1953), 82; M. BLACK, *An Aramaic Approach to the Gospels and Acts* (2nd ed. 1954), 172 ff.; A. STROBEL, Die Passa-Erwartung als urchristliches Problem in Lc 17,20 f., *Zschr. Nt. Wiss.* 49 (1958), 164 ff. At any rate it is worth noting that in the Passover Haggadah Jl 3,3 is associated with Dt 26,8. (The association is, of course, via the main word מופתים, and attention is directed to the blood: Jl 3,3 — Ex 7,20.) Cf. 1 QMyst I.5.

[29] See, for example, W. EICHRODT, *Theologie des AT* I (5th ed. 1957), 309 ff.; MOWINCKEL, *Psalmenstudien* II, 50 ff.; id., *The Psalms in Israel's Worship* I, 148 ff. Cf. above, 28 ff.

[30] See above, 47, note 73.

sacred texts of the heathens "making a tumult" or attacking each other or Israel. The following discussion will show that the OT in particular played an important part in this.

We must also expect a continuous application of the "enemy" themes and problems from earlier periods until the Exile and into later Jewish times. The problem was a topical one, both in Solomon's time and that of Zedekiah and both in the Psalms and in Isaiah, Joel, Zechariah and Daniel. But, while these authors have inherited a traditional complex of problems, which becomes topical over and over again, they return to the old texts, adapt their sayings to their own situations and find new meanings in the prophecies.[31] This doubleness—traditional motif and renewed direct associations with the OT — will now be illustrated by describing in more detail how the motif of the tumult and assault of the heathen functions in these texts and how this is related to the OT.

A. 1 En 99,4

Here we meet with the motif in its simplest form. There is a brief mention that "the nations shall be stirred up, and the families of the nations shall arise on the day of destruction".[32] The exact significance of the motif is somewhat uncertain here. In the Ethiopic version it would seem as if three steps are made in describing the events of the last days. In 99,1 and 2, first of all, two woes are uttered over the sinners, each of them ending in a saying about their future fate. After this come the three steps. First, "in those days" the righteous will pray the angels to place the sins of the wicked as a testimony before God. Then, "in those days", the nations shall be stirred up etc. and finally, "in those days", the destitute will abandon their children. That is to say, the motif is included as a feature of the last evil days.

No mention is made here of the nations rising against each other or against Israel. There is a possibility that here two OT motifs have been interwoven, on the one hand, that in Ps 64,8 f. (LXX), in which the nations tremble before the power of God,[33] and, on the other, that in Jl 3,12, in which the nations are to arise and go up (יעורו ויעלו) to the valley of Jehoshaphat to be judged. However, in this case the meagre wording of the text chiefly gives the impression of reproducing a definite *topos*.

---

[31] Cf. I. L. SEELIGMANN, Voraussetzungen der Midraschexegese, *Suppl. Vet. Test.* 1 (1953), 167 ff.

[32] For the expression "day of destruction" cf. Jb 21,30; Jr 18,17; Ob 13 (יום איד); Ez 35,5 (עת אידם).

[33] Ps 64,8 f. LXX: ταραχθήσονται τὰ ἔθνη, καὶ φοβηθήσονται οἱ κατοικοῦντες τὰ πέρατα ἀπὸ τῶν σημείων σου. TM has a different reading; Pesh. = LXX.

This impression—that the passage under discussion is not particularly related to clearly definable OT passages but rather reproduces a traditional *topos* in general terms—is strengthened by the Greek version of the text. In this neither clause has a subject,[34] with the result that the sentence comes to mean that the sinners referred to in the previous sentence are afraid of the retribution to come; no "nations" or "heathens" are introduced into the picture. The choice between the two readings could be made in favour of the Greek version, since here also the principle of the *lectio brevior* may certainly be applied and also it seems easier to explain the longer reading as a supplementation rather than the Greek reading as an abbreviation. For it is possible to trace behind the Ethiopic version a desire to supplement the picture of what is to happen in the last days.

The author of the longer Ethiopian version had no lack of OT examples. He expresses himself in OT terms[35] and even in the Psalms the motif may be quite unspecified, in the sense that there is no explicit mention of any objects for the raging of the nations.[36]

B. 4 Ez 13,30 f.

In other examples from these apocalyptic texts the tumult of the nations is outlined more clearly. This is the case in 4 Ez 13,30 f.:

And there shall come astonishment of mind (*excessus mentis*) upon the dwellers on earth, (31) and they shall plan to war one against another, city against city, place against place, people against people, and kingdom against kingdom.

This is expected to take place before the revelation of the Messiah or the (Son of) Man, i.e. the motif is here included in the convulsions of mankind before the divine intervention, except that in this case the intervention is made by the Messiah and not as in the previous case by God Himself.[37]

The feature which arouses one's attention here is the clear association with two OT passages, viz. 2 Ch 15,5 f., which says of an apostate Israel

---

[34] The Greek version has: τότε συν[ταραχ]θήσονται καὶ ἀνασταθήσονται ἐν [ἡμέρ]ᾳ ἀπωλείας τῆς ἀδικίας. Cf. 1 En 1,5 and 102,3, where the inhabitants of the earth fear and tremble, but at a theophany. 99,4 is discussed by ZUNTZ in *J. Bibl. Lit.* 61 (1942), 193 ff. He assumes a reading ἀναστατωθήσονται for ἀνασταθήσονται, but the Eth. supports the text of the papyrus.

[35] See note 32 and also Ps 22,28; 46,7; 64,8 f. (LXX); 96,7; Is 64,2; Jr 6,22; 50,41; Jl 4,12.

[36] See, for example, Ps 46,7.

[37] The motif has a similar meaning and function in Or Sib 3,635 ff. and 2 Bar 48,32 (with CHARLES's conjecture; see above, 30, note 37). In the latter case it is a question of the intervention of God Himself.

that nation strove against nation and city against city, and Is 19,2, in which God says that He will throw the Egyptians into confusion, so that they fight brother against brother, friend against friend, city against city and kingdom against kingdom.[38]

The similar turn of phrase in Mk 13,8 (nation against nation, kingdom against kingdom) poses a problem to which I can see two main solutions. One would be to say that 4 Ez 13,31 and Mk 13,8 par. are each dependent on an apocalyptic tradition of describing the general motif of "the tumult of the nations in the last days" with these expressions. The other would amount to saying that 4 Ez 13,31 in its present form was influenced by Mk 13,8 par., in so far as the Christian copyist supplemented the text on the basis of the Gospels.[39] But, however we solve the problem, we still have a situation in which an adopted *topos* is expressed in terms taken directly from the OT, because the fact that it is a *topos* would seem to be beyond doubt.

The form of the motif here and its function have several OT parallels, for example, Ez 30, in which Babylon attacks Egypt on the eve of the day of Yahweh.[40]

Like so many other phenomena that are to occur during the evil time before the divine intervention, the tumult of the nations in 4 Ez and 2 Bar has also been assigned a place in the series of "signs" which are to presage the end.[41] As was evident above, this function is probably not derived directly from the OT.

C. Jub 23,23

With this passage from Jubilees we enter the group of texts in which the tumult of the heathen is aimed directly at Israel. It states that God will send a great scourge upon an apostate generation, whose wickedness is described in detail:

---

[38] The struggle among the sinners occurs in 1 En 100,1 f. without any clear connection with attacking enemies.

[39] The two alternatives can be combined: 4 Ez 13,30 f. may be formulated from an apocalyptic tradition which includes Mk 13,8 par. Cf. for example, R. BULTMANN, *Geschichte der synoptischen Tradition* (2nd ed. 1931), 129. Anyhow, in Mk 13 the combination naturally finds its place in the chain of OT associations: see below, 149.

[40] See also, for example, Is 19; Jr 50,41 ff.; Dn 11; Ob; Na 2.

[41] In 4 Ez 5,5 it is brief and "neutral" (*populi commovebuntur*, ܒܠܐܚܕ) and is framed by various omens. In 4 Ez 9,3 it is also "neutral" and is inserted after earthquakes (*populorum turbatio*, ܠܩܡܘ ܙܘܕܐ; *gentium cogitationes*, ܚܬܚܡܘ ܕܠܡܐ); on the content there, cf. Ps 2,1 f. There is the same meaning and function in 2 Bar 72,2: "signs ... when the nations become turbulent" ܠܐܡ ܚܥܘ. Cf. above, 76 f.

80

"He will wake up" (*obdormire faciet*) (Jr 6,22) against them the sinners of the Gentiles[42], "who have neither mercy nor compassion" (Jr 6,23), and "who shall respect the person of none, neither old nor young" (Dt 28,50), nor any one, for they are more wicked and strong to do evil than all the children of men.

And they shall use violence against Israel
    and transgression against Jacob,
and much blood shall be shed upon the earth,
and there shall be none "to gather and none to bury" (Ps 79,3).

These events form part of the evil time preceding the intervention of God and also serve as punishments for sins committed during the same evil time.[43]

It is hardly a coincidence that this punishment is described in terms taken from the OT descriptions of how God will send enemies against Israel as a punishment of its sins. These OT passages are here united by their common theme.[44] That is to say, we are not here faced with a record of the theme in quite general terms, concerning war and misery in the last days; the theme has a definite function and is expressed by using OT texts which emphasize this function—for him who has ears to hear what the Scriptures say and who understands this typology given in hints.[45]

The theme of enemies attacking Israel as a punishment for its apostasy is well known in the OT, and the texts alluded to above all have it.[46]

D. 1 En 90,13–19

We now come to the variant of the motif which implies that the heathen attack Israel (etc.) and are bloodily crushed by supernatural means. (This theme was of great importance to the Qumran sect.[47]) This variant has a history which is outlined in the OT and emerges in Ez 38 f. (Gog)

---

[42] The Latin fragment ends at this point.

[43] Cf. above, 56.

[44] The LXX also says in the first two cases that the enemy will come ἀπ' ἐσχάτου τῆς γῆς. On such association chains, see further below, Chap. IV.

[45] Thus the realism of the description cannot *per se* be an indication that the author was present. This is what M. Testuz assumes, because he has not noticed these OT allusions (*Les idées religieuses du Livre des Jubilés*, 1960, 167).

[46] See also, for example, Is 5,18 ff., and Jr 5. We have a similar use of this motif, more or less clearly connected with the Exile, in Test Jud 22,2 and 23,3, and in Apc Abr 27,1. See also Ps Sal 2.

[47] See, for example, J. van der Ploeg, La guerre sainte dans la "Règle de la Guerre" de Qumran, in *Mélanges ... A. Robert* (1957), 326–33, and B. Gärtner, Bakgrunden till Qumranförsamlingens krig, *Rel. o. Bibel* 19 (1960), 35–72. Cf. M. Hengel, *Die Zeloten* (1961), 279 ff.

and Zch 12,1–9.[48] The present texts are based on those of the OT but in a far from stereotyped fashion. In this case also it is true to say that, even though the basic pattern is traditional, the design is different and has renewed associations with the OT.

I first analyse 1 En 90,13–19, which forms part of a long dream allegory of history from the Creation until the reign of the Messiah. This section is obscure in so far as it seems to describe two attacks which each cause the Lord of the afflicted sheep (the people) to visit them in wrath. This led F. Martin and R. H. Charles to think that the whole thing was an account of a single attack, described in two different ways which were placed by chance one after the other.[49] The text is as follows:

(13) And I saw till the shepherds and eagles and those vultures and kites came, and they cried to the ravens that they should break the horn of that ram, and they battled and fought with it, and it battled with them and cried that its help might come.

(14) And I saw till that man came, who wrote down the names of the shepherds and carried up into the presence of the Lord of the sheep, and he helped it and showed it everything: he had come down for the help of that ram.

(15) And I saw till the Lord of the sheep came unto them in wrath, and all who saw him fled, and they all fell into shadow before his face.

(16) All the eagles and vultures and ravens and kites were gathered together, and there came with them all the sheep of the field, and they all came together, and helped each other to break that horn of the ram.

(17) And I saw till that man, who wrote the book according to the command of the Lord, till he opened that book concerning the destruction which those twelve last shepherds had wrought, and showed that they had destroyed much more than their predecessors, before the Lord of the sheep.

(18) And I saw till the Lord of the sheep came unto them and took in his hand the staff of his wrath, and smote the earth, and the earth clave asunder, and all the beasts and all the birds of the heaven fell from among those sheep, and sank down in the earth, and it covered them.

(19) And I saw till a great sword was given to the sheep, and the sheep proceeded against all the beasts of the field to slay them, and all the beasts and the birds of the heaven fled before their face.

The context is as follows. We have previously been told of bad shepherds of the flock, of how the flock is being attacked by beasts of prey

---

[48] The dating of Zch 9 ff. is intricate; see, for example, P. LAMARCHE, *Zacharie IX–XIV* (1961), 20 ff.; J. LINDBLOM, *Prophecy in Ancient Israel* (1962), 275 f.; B. OTZEN, *Studien über Deuterosacharja* (1964), 35–212 (as regards his results, see 212). On the use of earlier OT material in Ez 38 f. (cf. Ez 38,17!), see M. BURROWS, *The Literary Relations of Ezekiel* (1925), and G. GERLEMAN, Hesekielsbokens Gog, *Svensk Exeg. Årsbok* 12 (1947), 148–62. See also L. DÜRR, *Die Stellung des Propheten Ezechiel* (1923), 90 ff. For Qumran, cf. 1 QM XI.15 f. (Gog).

[49] F. MARTIN, *Le livre d'Hénoch* (1906) and CHARLES, *Book of Enoch*, ad loc. Thus also J. PEDERSEN, Zur Erklärung der eschatologischen Visionen Henochs, *Islamica* 2 (1926), 423.

and of how certain rams (the Maccabees) have arisen against the oppressive beasts of prey. Following 90,19 there is a description of God's
judgement on the fallen angels, the bad shepherds and the apostates and
of how they are to be punished (20–27). After this the time of salvation
is depicted, with a new Jerusalem, the subjection of the heathen, the
resurrection of the righteous and finally the appearance of the Messiah
(28–38). Thus the motif of the assault and destruction of the heathen is
here inserted before God's judgement (C) and is coupled with God's
personal intervention (B).

We may ask ourselves where the transition from the contemporary to
the future scene takes place, whether the attacks described in v. 13 are
part of the struggles of the Maccabees[50] or whether we are in the final
phase which the author expects will set in when Michael and also God
Himself intervene to help the people. Perhaps we may refrain from stating
the alternatives so emphatically and assume that either the transition to
the description of the final phase is made in v. 13 or that the author is
there describing a piece of history which he has experienced but which
he regards as the beginning of the struggles with the heathen in this
final phase, which will gradually lead on to their eventual destruction and
condemnation. It would seem to be clear from the association with
Dn 11,41 ff., to be dealt with below, that 90,13 is also set in this final
perspective.

Before I examine its relationship to the OT, I would remind the reader
that this text is said to render a vision. Even if we take this statement
cum grano salis—it may be a literary convention which the author has
adopted—it implies a very definite kind of narrative technique; the author paints word pictures, pictures of scenes. What he puts into his picture depends on what his imagination "sees". And what he "sees"
depends upon the concepts he has formed, in this case concepts of the
battles that are to take place at the end of time. Finally these concepts
of his are, so to speak, impregnated by the OT; the OT influences their
form and mutual combinations. We shall return to these problems in
more detail in the next chapter.

We will now see how it is possible, on the basis of the textual relationship to the OT, to explain the motifs in this text and the way in which
they are joined together and perhaps even the impression of a "doublet".

The basic picture is taken from Ez 34, in which the prophet tells how
God's sheep, Israel, are neglected by their shepherds (vv. 2 ff.) and become food for the beasts of the field (v. 8). For this reason Yahweh will

---

[50] Thus, for example, HAMMERSHAIMB, trans., ad loc. DILLMANN (*Das Buch
Henoch*, ad loc.) also gives a "political interpretation": the conflicts of Johannes
Hyrcanus with Antiochus Cyzicenus.

Himself take care of His sheep and judge the shepherds (vv. 10 ff.). But He will also judge His sheep (vv. 17 ff.) and set up David as a shepherd over them (vv. 23 f.). Thus there is in Ez 34 a basic structure which is rather like that in 1 En 90,1 ff.

The detail in the basic picture which now attracts attention is that the sheep are attacked by the beasts of the field. This is interpreted as the aggression of the heathen against God's people.[51] And as Ez 34 gives no further details of this aggression, it is associated with other OT passages, in which it seems that the author thought he had found descriptions of the same battles. In the present case, judging by the fact that Michael[52] appears, the author's thoughts went to Dn 11,41 ff., which relates that the northern king will invade the glorious land and (12,1) that at that time Israel's guardian, Michael, will arise.[53] The interpretation of this text in Daniel as referring to the great final struggle is also probably to be found in the War Scroll from Qumran,[54] in which we also find the angels taking part in the struggle.[55] A further parallel is to be found in 1 En 56, which we shall return to later and which is connected with Dn 10,20 (Gabriel and Michael battle with Persia and Greece).

We now have OT cover for the main content of 90,13 f.: God's people are attacked by heathens and an angel comes to their assistance. But a couple of details may perhaps also be explained from this quarter. Of the angel who comes to the assistance of the people, the text says: "He showed him (sc. the ram under attack) all things". This may be loosely associated with another text in Daniel, viz. chapter 10, in which an angel (Gabriel) appears to Daniel to teach him what is to happen in the days to come (v. 14). This association was then made possible by the fact that Dn 10 also mentions that Michael helps to fight against God's enemies (vv. 13, 21).

The detail that the oppressed individual calls for help starts off another series of associations; the idea that Michael appears as a helper, in accordance with Dn 12,1, presents itself. In this passage this period is described as a time of trouble (עת צרה).[56] That is to say, we may include in the associational field the idea that it is in a עת צרה that the oppressed

---

[51] There is a similar image in 6 Q14 I.6. See Dn 7 and 8 for the animal symbolism.

[52] See, for example, HAMMERSHAIMB, trans., ad loc.

[53] The motif also appears in 2 Mcc 11,6–8; cf. Is 37,36, 1 Mcc 7,41, and 2 Mcc 8,19.

[54] 1 QM I.12; XV.1. 1 QM I.11 f. mentions that "there will be a time of trouble (והיאה עת צרה) ... and in all their troubles there will be none like it (ובכול צרותמה לוא נהיתה כמוה) ... until it is completed for the eternal redemption". Cf. Dn 12,1: והיתה עת צרה אשר לא נהיתה. Cf. F. F. BRUCE, Biblical Exegesis in the Qumran Texts (1959), 63, and HENGEL, Zeloten, 252.

[55] 1 QM I.10; VII.6; XII.4, 7 ff.; XV.15; XVII.6 ff.; cf. 1 QS III.24.

[56] Cf. note 54, above.

one calls for help.[57] The expression עת צרה is not very common in the OT and in all the other cases the context speaks of help from God for the faithful in this עת צרה, help which involves the destruction of oppressors![58] It seems probable that here Is 33,2 f. played the most important part and supplied further colours to the palette of the author's imagination. Thus the oppressed individual calls for help; then not only Michael helps, in accordance with Dn 12,1, but Yahweh as well, according to Is 33,2 f.: "Be our salvation in the time of trouble" (ישועתנו בעת צרה). And the text continues: "At the thunderous noise peoples flee; at the lifting up of thyself nations are scattered" (מקול המון נדדו עמים מרוממתך נפצו גוים). Thus the association would have run to this text on account of an unstated content in the text which the thought had just been influenced by (Dn 12,1 with עת צרה). Now it supplies the continuation of our text in 1 En 90,15: God comes in wrath and those who see Him flee.[59]

Then however, the text returns to the heathen assault. This repetition could be interpreted to mean that the author was not content with the idea that the enemies will flee and fall into the shade (90,15; the meaning is uncertain).[60] He knows from other texts that the enemy will be destroyed more thoroughly, for example, from Ez 38 f. He accordingly takes up the theme again.[61]

Thus, according to 1 En 90,16, the attackers are "gathered together", as in Ez 38,7 ff. or Zch 12,2 f., and attack the horn of the ram. This forms the background to 90,17, which tells how the angel who writes the heavenly books opens the book in which the misdeeds of the bad shepherds are written. The verse is connected with two previous similar statements in the long allegory in which we now find ourselves involved,

---

[57] It is possible that 2 Mcc 11,5 f. points to an association with עת צרה in Dn 12,1 or with a similar way of thinking: it is mentioned that an angel (Michael) intervened when Lysias was pressing hard on (ἔθλιβεν) Bethsuron, and that in this situation the Jews prayed for angelic aid and recieved it. θλίβειν is a common translation of צרר.

[58] Ps 37,39; Is 33,2; Jr 14,8; 15,11; 30,7; Dn 12,1.

[59] Cf. 1 En 89,16, 20 (the same dream allegory): the Lord of the sheep comes to them and pastures them (in connection with the sending of Moses, 16); the Lord comes and the sheep smite (or, with a v.l., the Lord smites) the wolves (= the Egyptians, 20). In the present text God Himself seems to play a more prominent part.

[60] Cf. possibly Zch 12,4.

[61] It is not entirely inconceivable that the author was so influenced by Ez 38 f. that he gave us the same double account as is to be found in Ez 38,18–23 and 39,18, where Gog's downfall is twice related. See, on this point, DÜRR, Die Stellung des Propheten Ezechiel, 96 f. Another possible explanation of the "doublet" in 1 En may be the idea that the routed enemy re-groups for an attack, just as, in the War Scroll, it is expected that there will be seven conflicts between the Children of Light and the Children of Darkness. See on this point 1 QM I.14 f. Cf. how in 4 Ez 13,5 ff. the attackers gather, are frightened and then venture to fight.

namely, 89,70 f. and 89,76 f. These passages relate that the heavenly scribe writes down in his book an account of the licentiousness of the bad shepherds and that the book is read out to God, who (in the first place seals it and) places it on one side. After each of these two "refrains" a new epoch begins; in the first case the epoch of the Persian empire and in the second that extending from Alexander until the time of the Maccabees. When in 90,17 the scribe *opens* the book and lays it before God, this is an enhancement in comparison with what was said in 89,70 f. and 76 f., and the verse marks the fact that now the time of accounting is at hand. The wording of the verse is probably connected with that in Dn 7,9 f., in which the Ancient of Days sits on His throne to pass judgement and "books are opened". There too, beasts symbolize the empires which are to be judged.

Thus, on the basic picture from Ez 34, there may here be superimposed accounts of, on the one hand, how the enemy "gathers together" for the attack, in accordance with e.g. Ez 38,7 ff., and, on the other, how their misdeeds are written down in a heavenly book and brought to the remembrance of the Judge when the book is opened, in accordance with the scene of the judgement of the beasts (heathens) in Dn 7,10. As in Dn 7,11 f., the immediate consequence of the opening of the books at the time of judgement is that the beasts are destroyed—in Dn 7,11 by fire and in 90,18 by God's coming and striking the earth, so that it splits and swallows up His opponents. It seems as if the author had in his mind's eye an image of God as a shepherd with his staff (cf. Ps 23,4). This staff he then associates with the rod of Yahweh's wrath (שבט אפי) in Is 10,5 (cf. 10,24); with this rod Yahweh strikes the enemies of His flock, but the expression is that in Is 11,4 ("he shall smite the earth").[62]

The last association in the series on how God smites the earth with His staff is thus that the enemy is swallowed up by the gaping earth, like Korah and his followers in Nu 16,30 ff. To the question, why does this particular motif appear here, the answer may be that the picture of God's staff smiting the earth was simply regarded so concretely that the natural conclusion was that the earth must split as a result. The "concrete" association may, however, have been supported by the statement in Ez 38,19 ff., that Gog will be destroyed while the earth trembles and the cliffs fall. The fact that the heathen enemy in 1 En is destroyed in the same way as Korah may indicate a connection between the two passages or a more widely diffused view of the fate of the last enemy.[63]

---

[62] The association may be an assonant one: שבט פיו — אפי.

[63] The punishment is a very fitting one for the sinner who receives it, if we consider, on the one hand, that these enemies are often represented as possessed by *hubris* (for example, Is 14,13 ff.; 36 f.; Dn 7,8 ff.; 8,10 ff.) and on, the other, how

Finally there remains the statement in v. 19 on how a great sword is given to the sheep, who then proceed against the hostile beasts. Charles transfers this verse to a position after vv. 13 and 16 (which he places in parallel), but the unanimous manuscript tradition indicates that this statement must have had a meaning in its present position. It has a certain parallel in the Apocalypse of Weeks (1 En 93; 91,12–17), in which the eighth week has a sword with which to execute judgement and righteousness and in the ninth week the righteous judgement is revealed to the world.[64]

The sword which strikes the enemies of the people is in itself a common OT motif.[65] But there is a good chance that a definite passage from the OT may have contributed to the circumstance that, after the enemy has been said to sink into the earth, it is also stated that he is destroyed by the sword, however illogical this may seem. This passage is Ps 63,10 f., which says that "those who seek to destroy my life shall go down into the depths of the earth (יבאו בתחתיות הארץ), they shall give him over to the sword (יגירהו על ידי חרב)".[66] We have thus found associational links with OT passages which carry the whole of this section.

When we are confronted with a complex of OT associations like this, the following question arises. Is it really a question of association between various specific passages in the OT and not rather only a question of OT phraseology, although used to express themes which have certain associations with the OT? If the latter were the case, it would have been by pure chance that in the preceding paragraphs we were able to link motifs and OT passages with each other in the way we did. However, this is made less likely by two things: on the one hand, we shall encounter later on several cases of similar associational interweaving[67] and, on the other, there are examples of texts (from Qumran) in which the OT echoes really seem to be used phraseologically and more as a stylistic mannerism only.[68]

Nu R. explains Korah's punishment by his presumption (Nu R. 18 ad 16,32 ff.). Cf. also how similar punishments befall enemies in Ex 15,12 (Pharaoh in the Red Sea), Ps 55,16; 63,10 (enemies), and Is 14,15 (Babel). Cf. V. APTOWITZER, *Parteipolitik der Hasmonäerzeit* (1927), 167.

[64] Cf. A. C. WELCH, A Zealot Pamphlet, *Expositor Ser. 8* 25 (1923), 273–87, and J. P. THORNDIKE, The Apocalypse of Weeks and the Qumran Sect, *Rev. Qumr.* 3 (1961/62), 163–84.

[65] See, for example, Is 27,1; 31,8; 34,5 f.; 66,16; Jr 47,6; Ez 38,21; Mi 5,6. Cf. 1 QM XI.11 f.; XV.3; XVI.1; CD VIII.1; IX.7 f. (Zch 13,7 quoted), 10, 13.

[66] Ez 38,21 may have aided the association.

[67] The examples presented in Chap. IV are by no means isolated ones. Cf. below, 112, note 48.

[68] Cf. below, 138 f.

My conclusion is accordingly that, in its way of describing the assault and annihilation of the heathen on the eve of the last judgement, 1 En 90,13 ff. reveals an influence from the OT which is expressed both in its composition and choice of imagery and in its content and minor details.

E. 1 En 56,5–8

This example too contains a description of the heathen assault, which is miraculously overcome. The description is in 1 En Sim, at the very end of the second parable. This portion of text shows us another way of inserting this struggle in the series of final events, and the associations with the OT which we also find here refer to other texts than those in the preceding cases.

From 55,3 onwards the text relates the judgement and punishments of the fallen angels, who are thrown into the valley of punishment to be tormented there. Their punishment is carried out by avenging angels. Then follows the portion of text under discussion and is later followed in 57,1 by a description of how Israel returns from the Dispersion. Thus here the motif has been inserted after a judgement (*C*) and before the time of salvation (*E*). In order to demonstrate how the elements of the text are related to the OT, I first quote the passage in full:

(56,5) And in those days "the angels shall return"[1] (Dn 10,20)
and hurl themselves to the east upon the Parthians and Medes[2]
in order to "stir up the kings" so that the "spirit" (Jr 51,11) of commotion
    comes upon them,
and they shall rouse them from their thrones,
so that they "break forth as lions"[3] from their lairs,
and "as hungry wolves" (Ez 22,27) in their flock,
(6) and they shall go up and tread under foot the land of his elect ones,
and the land of his elect ones shall be before them as a threshing-floor
    and a highway.[4]
(7) But the city of my righteous shall be a hindrance to their horses,
and they shall begin a "fight among themselves" (Is 19,2),
and "their right (hand) shall be strong against themselves" (Zch 14,13),
and a man shall not know his brother,
nor a son his father or his mother,
till "the number of the corpses" (Na 3,3) is (full) through their slaughter,
and their punishment is not to be in vain.
(8) In those days "Sheol shall open its jaws" (Is 5,14),
and they shall go down therein,
and their "destruction shall be at an end" (Ps 9,7);
"Sheol shall devour" (Nu 16,30) the sinners in the presence of the elect.

---

[1] A variant "assemble".

[2] Cf. מדי ופרס in Dn 5,28 and 6,9.

[3] The expression is found in Jr 4,7; 49,19; 50,44.

[4] The last clause is regarded as an interpolation by CHARLES. I do not think that his reason—that it makes the stanza too long—is a tenable one.

This time it is either Zch 12,2–4 which provides the basic outline, to which details from other sources are added, or a general idea of how in the last days the enemy will appear and be destroyed which forms a framework for this mosaic, in which anyhow the particular portions inspired by Zch 12,2 ff. take up a great deal of space.

(2) Lo, I am about to make Jerusalem a cup of reeling to all the peoples round about; it will be against Judah also in the siege against Jerusalem. (3) On that day I will make Jerusalem a heavy stone for all the peoples; all who lift it shall grievously hurt themselves. And all the nations of the earth will come together against it. (4) On that day, says Yahweh, I will strike every horse with panic, and its rider with madness. But upon the house of Judah I will open my eyes, when I strike every horse of the peoples with blindness.

One detail which gives rise to the inclusion of several OT motifs in this text is that it speaks of "kings" instead of "heathens" or "nations". This is hardly a coincidence, since in 1 En Sim "the kings", "the mighty" or "those who possess the earth" are common concepts in contrast to "the elect", "the righteous", etc., in the same way as the concept of "the sinners".[5] However, there would seem to be somewhat different associations connected with "kings" in this particular text as compared with 1 En 38,5 or 46,4: here they are the leaders of the attacking heathen enemies and in 38,5 and 46,4 they are synonymous with "sinners".

What is to be described is, then, how these kings attack Jerusalem to their own undoing. The context has referred to the angels who betake themselves to the valley of punishment. The text starts from this detail and it is therefore these angels who hurl themselves to the east. We then have the following chain of events. The angels "return" from the valley, according to Dn 10,20, in which Gabriel "returns" from the revelation to Daniel to fight against Persia. However, the פרס in Daniel has been interpreted as referring to the Parthians,[6] who were of greater topical interest at the period when the text originated and were therefore inserted in it. But in Esther and Daniel the "Medes and Persians" are a permanent combination,[7] which is probably the reason why "the Medes" are joined with the Parthians in 1 En 56,5.[8] Now it seems natural for the author, in thinking of these heathen enemies, to let their kings personify them. Thus it comes about that "Medes" is the key-word leading over to Jr 51,11,

---

[5] See 1 En 38,5; 46,4 f.; 48,8; 53,5; 54,2; 55,4; 62,3, 9; 63,1. Cf. LADD, *Biblioth. Sacra* 110 (1953), 42 f.

[6] A similar shift of meaning from "Persians" to "Parthians" is to be met with, for example, in b BQ. 117a; cf. b MQ. 18a.

[7] Persians and Medes: Est 1,2, 14, 18 f.; Medes and Persians: Dn 5,28; 6,9, 13, 16; 8,20.

[8] Cf. Ac 2,9.

where we find the phrase "(Yahweh) will stir up (הֵעִיר) the spirit of the kings of the Medes".[9] Our text is linked up with this phrase and gives a paraphrase of the expression "spirit" included in Jr 51,11. The saying on how these kings are stirred up is now expanded with similar motifs in the second half of 56,5. First, with the statement that they are roused from their thrones, a turn of phrase which occurs several times in 1 En Sim[10] and which is probably related to the phrase in Ps 2,2 about the kings who rebel against Yahweh and His Anointed.[11] To this is added the motif which is used of bad Jerusalemite kings in Zph 3,3 (princes are compared with lions and wolves) and in Ez 22,27 (wolves). But the particular expression "break forth as lions" has its closest parallels in Jeremiah, where it is used in 50,44 of enemies approaching Babylon.[12] Thus the theme of hostile princes or bad rulers would seem to have acted as a kind of associative link.

In 56,6 is described the deployment of these hostile rulers, a deployment which is briefly related in Zch 12,3 in the statement that all the peoples will be gathered together against Jerusalem. In the present text the enemy are said to tread under foot the holy land, which to them becomes a threshing-floor and a highway. As far as I can see, this is not linked up with any clearly definable passages in the OT, but the motifs recur in Isaiah and Jeremiah in texts which deal with military aggression against Babylon and Judah.[13]

At 56,7 we reach the point at which the destruction of the enemy is to be described. The statement that the city will be a hindrance to the enemy's horses is probably based on Zch 12,3 f., where those who lift the

---

[9] This phrase is common in the OT: see 1 Ch 5,26; 2 Ch 21,16; Ezr 1,1, 5; Jr 51,11; Hg 1,14. Yahweh is the subject in every case. That here the work has been split off and assigned to angels may be regarded as an expression of a Jewish tendency to emphasize God's transcendence out of reverence for His majesty. See CHARLES, *Book of Enoch*, ad loc., and BOUSSET & GRESSMANN, *Religion*, 321, 329. For a substantial modification, see H. BIETENHARD, *Die himmlische Welt im Urchristentum und Spätjudentum* (1951), 103 f.

[10] See 1 En 46,4; 62,3. And cf. above, this Chap., note 41.

[11] The expression is also to be found in Is 14,9. Ps 2 is interpreted as referring to Gog and Magog in b Ber. 7b, b Ab.Zar. 3b, Tanch. חֻ 24 (Buber), Pesiq.d.RK. 9 (79 a), Midr. Ps ad 2,1 and 118,9. Cf. DALMAN, *Worte Jesu* I, 219 ff. See also 4 QFlor. I.18 f.

[12] Otherwise also Jr 4,7 and 49,19.

[13] See, for example, Is 5,5 and Jr 12,10 (the country is trodden down); Jr 51,33 (Babel like a threshing floor, cf. Is 21,10). A curious coincidence is that in Zch 12,3 the LXX reads: "Jerusalem shall be a stone that is trodden upon by all peoples. All who tread her down shall scoffing scoff" (λίθον καταπατούμενον πᾶσιν τοῖς ἔθνεσιν· πᾶς ὁ καταπατῶν αὐτὴν ἐμπαίζων ἐμπαίζεται). This presumes the reading of רמס instead of עמס and perhaps forms of שׂחק instead of שׂיש.

stone (Jerusalem) will be cut in pieces and the horses will be smitten with panic and blindness and the riders with madness.[14] This makes an easy transition to the description given in Zch 14,13 of the tumult in a similar situation among the enemy gathered against Jerusalem.[15] This is expressed in the form of a bloody internal conflict.[16] But the theme again attracts turns of phrase and motifs from other passages in the OT via associations of key-words and themes. Thus, the reference in the text to the enemy's internal conflicts is worded in terms of Is 19,2 (there is civil strife, a man does not know his brother) and Mi 7,6 (divisions in the family).

After the confusion on the eve of destruction has been described, there remains the description of the destruction itself, which is briefly mentioned in Zch 12,9: God will seek to destroy all the nations that come against Jerusalem. This is now depicted in colours taken from other texts in which enemies are destroyed, viz. Na 3,3 (the destruction of Nineveh)[17] for the multitudes of corpses, Nu 16,30 ff. (the destruction of Korah)[18] for Sheol swallowing up the enemies, and Ps 9,7 (enemies are conquered by the power of God) for the detail that the enemy will be destroyed. Thus, once again it is Korah's fate that befalls the attackers.[19]

Thus, in 1 En 56,5–8 we have found a complex of associations with the OT resembling that which we found in 1 En 90,13 ff. but here containing for the most part different details and associations with different OT texts.

F. Or Sib 3,663–697

Because of the epic style and hexameter line adopted, this text cannot approach as near the wording of the OT as the others, but the use of OT material is still clear enough.

The text is preceded by an oracle to the effect that the Messiah will be sent down to earth and will set up his kingdom (652 ff.) (B). This is followed by a description of the time of salvation (702 ff.) (E). Between these passages, then, we find the description of an unsuccessful attack

---

[14] See also Hg 2,23 and Zch 10,5.

[15] In the different passages TM has different expressions for this "confusion". On the other hand, the LXX uses ἔκστασις in both passages.

[16] The theme recurs several times in similar contexts: Jdc 7,22; 2 Ch 20,23; Ez 38,21; Hg 2,23.

[17] See also Ps 110,6; Is 37,36; Ez 39,4 ff.

[18] But the wording is partly derived from Is 5,14. On this phenomenon, by which—to put it simply—one text is reproduced with words from others, see below, Chap. IV. Is 5,14 is given a similar interpretation in 4 QpIs^b II.5–8: the mockers who reject the law.

[19] See above, 86.

on the part of the heathen. This picture of the order of events in the last days is the same as in Ez 37 ff., where 37,24 ff. mentions the Messiah ("my servant David") and his reign, 38 and 39 Gog's attack on the holy land and his destruction, and 40 ff. the new Temple and the new Jerusalem.[20]

This agreement between Ez 37 ff. and Or Sib 3,652 ff. seems to be more than a coincidence, judging from the portion of text we are now to examine. This turns out to be built upon the foundation laid by Ez 38 f. I shall now give an exposition of Or Sib 3,663 ff. point by point and show the OT background for each point.

663 f.: The kings of the nations will attack the holy land to their own undoing. Ez 38,7 ff.; Gog collects troops and invades the holy land.[21] 665 f.: They will attempt to plunder the Temple. Ez 38,12 f.: Gog will pillage and carry off silver and gold.[22] 667 f.: Each of the kings will set up his throne round the city. Jr 1,15: Each of the tribes from the north will set up its throne round Jersusalem (extensive verbal agreement). This association accordingly involves a step away from the Ezekiel text, presumably via a thematic association from Ez 38,15, in which Gog comes from the north, to Jr 1,15, in which Yahweh calls upon the tribes in the northern kingdoms and they come.[23]

669 f.: God will speak to each of the vain peoples. There is no absolutely clear association with Ez 38 f. here, but the following explanation is perhaps a reasonable one. A picture has now been painted of the hostile kings on their thrones round Jerusalem, and in Ez 38 we have reached v. 18, which says that the wrath of Yahweh will arise, and v. 19, in which Yahweh speaks in anger, although not expressly to Gog. As in other cases,[24] Ps 2 may also have made a contribution here, but this time from the LXX version (v. 2: The kings of the earth approached (παρέστησαν) ... and gathered together (συνήχθησαν ἐπὶ τὸ αὐτό) and v. 5: God will speak to them in wrath and terrify them in His rage). The expressions in Ez 38,18 f. and Ps 2,5 are so alike in the LXX as to constitute favourable conditions for a key-word association, which may moreover be assumed to be supported by a thematic association.[25]

---

[20] The outline is also to be found in Ap 20,4–22,21.

[21] See also Jr 1,15; 25,9; Zch 12,2 f.; 14,2.

[22] See also 2 Rg 25,13 ff., and Jr 52,4 ff.

[23] The "north" motif is common in these contexts: see Is 14,31; Jr 1,14; 6,22; Ez 26,7; Dn 11,40; Jl 2,20, and cf. Is 14,13. See J. Ph. HYATT, The Peril from the North in Jeremiah, *J. Bibl. Lit.* 59 (1940), 499–513; A. LAUHA, *Zaphon: Der Norden und die Nordvölker im AT* (1943), esp. 72 ff., and A. S. KAPELRUD, *Joel Studies* (1948), 93–108.

[24] See above, note 11.

[25] The LXX has the same expression in both cases: Ez 38,18: ἀναβήσεται ὁ

In 670b–672 we are back at Ez 38. Or Sib: Their judgement (κρίσις) will come from God and they will perish. Ez 38,22 (LXX): I will judge (κρινῶ) him with death and blood.[26] In 673–681 the destruction is described in close association with Ez 38,19 ff. 673 f.: Swords of fire and lightning flashes from heaven. Ez 38: v. 19, God speaks in the fire of His wrath, and v. 22, fire will rain down.[27] 675: Earthquake. Ez 38,19: Earthquake. 676–679: Fishes, beasts, birds, men and every sea shall shudder before the face of God. Ez 38.20: Before the face of the Lord shall tremble fishes, birds, beasts and men. 680 f.: The mountains are rent, and the abyss (κυάνεον ἔρεβος) appears. Ez 38,20 (LXX): The mountains are rent, and the ravines (or abysses: φάραγγες) fall.

In 682–684 the author again digresses and relates how the ravines and mountains are full of dead, there flows blood on the rocks, and the torrents fill the plain with blood. The wording is for the most part to be found in Ez 35,8 (LXX). The link with this passage must have taken place via key-words (φάραγγες etc.[28]) and been supported by the motif of slaughter which is to be found in the otherwise unused v. 21 in Ez 38, according to which a man's sword will be directed against his brother.

In 685 we are "home" again: all the walls (τείχεα ... ἄπαντα) of the enemies shall fall. Ez 38,20: Every wall (πᾶν τεῖχος) shall fall. 686–688 give an explication: because they did not know the law nor the judgement of God, but in their folly raised their lances against the holy (ἐφ' ἱερόν).[29]

θυμός μου; v. 19: ἐν πυρὶ τῆς ὀργῆς μου ἐλάλησα ..., and Ps 2,5: λαλήσει ... ἐν ὀργῇ αὐτοῦ, καὶ ἐν τῷ θυμῷ αὐτοῦ ταράξει αὐτούς. I do not find M. BUTTENWIESER's argument very convincing, when he holds that the TM of Ps 2 was modelled on Ez 38 f. (The Psalms, 1938, 792 f.).

[26] See also Jl 4,12 and Zch 12,9.

[27] Perhaps the expression in 674 is a parallel association with Nu 16,35: it speaks of flames of fire in their midst (εἰς μέσον ἀνδρῶν).

[28] Either an association from the ὄρη βουνοί and ἔρεβος mentioned in Or Sib 3,680 f. or from Ez 38,20 (which lies behind it) with φάραγγες and ὄρη, or most likely from both, in combination with Ez 35,8 (LXX), where Edom is to be stricken: "I will fill your hills (βουνούς) and your ravines (φάραγγας) with your slain, and on all your plains (πεδίοις) those slain with the sword in you shall fall". In 3,682 mention is made of φάραγγες ἐν οὔρεσιν and of πεδίον. In Judith 2,8 the φάραγγες are filled with slain and each χείμαρρους and ποταμός shall be filled with corpses.

[29] The natural translation of ἱερόν is "the holy", i.e. the Temple. As far as I can see, the lingustic usage in Or Sib 3 does not give any reason for abandoning this translation. See H. G. LIDDELL, R. SCOTT and H. S. JONES, Lexicon (1925–40), and R. STEPHANUS, Theasurus (1841), sub voce. And cf. the translations: H. C. O. LANCHESTER, in Pseudepigrapha, "the Holy One"; H. N. BATE, in the SPCK Translations of Early Documents (1918), "the holy place", and KURFESS (ed.), "Tempel". If—contrary to expectation—it is God they are raising their lances against, there are points of contact in Ez 38 f.; see 38,16, 22; 39,7.

689–693 again relate to Ez 38, in which we have now rea hed vv. 22 f. 689–690: God will judge all men with war and sword and fire and drenching rain (ὑετῷ τε κατακλύζοντι). Ez 38,22: God will judge with death and blood and drenching rain (ὑετῷ κατακλύζοντι). 691–693: There shall be brimstone from heaven, stones and hail; the four-footed shall die, and then shall they know God. Ez 38: v. 22, (God judges) with hailstones and causes it to rain fire and brimstone, and v. 23, God will become known to many nations.

694–697 form an epilogue, which is not related to Ez 38 f. It speaks of a general outcry in the land, a theme which was perhaps inspired by Zch 12,10 ff.,[30] of the great rivers of blood after the battle (cf. Is 34,7) and of the beasts which will gorge themselves on the battlefield.[31]

Here it is evident that the author of this section of Or Sib was not only generally and indefinitely inspired by the ideas in Ez 38 f. but also deliberately made use of the OT text in the LXX version. He translated it into an epic style and only added here and there supplementary details, which he derived from OT texts with closely related motifs. He did not make any real re-interpretation of Ez 38 f. On the other hand, his use of Ps 2 may go back to a textual exegesis in the synagogue, a source which may also be traced in other texts similar in content to that just analysed.[32]

While in the preceding examples of this motif the associations went from text to text more freely and (especially in the case of 1 En 90) may have had a definite text as a basic outline for a more freely painted picture, the author of the present example follows a single text more closely and reproduces it to a greater extent. The associational technique is the same when it appears, but he returns to the text he is reporting after his digressions.

G. 2 Bar 48,37

The theme is probably also represented in 2 Bar 48,37:

And many shall be stirred up (Syr. ܘܢܬܬܙܝܥܘܢ[33]) in anger to injure many
and they shall rouse up armies in order to shed blood,
and in the end they shall perish together with them.

The context of this passage is a description of the evil time before the coming of the Judge (48,39) and thus belongs to the stage which was called A above. Like its context, it is related to OT motifs[34] but not to clearly distinguishable passages in the OT. One has the impression that

---

[30] See also Ex 12,30, Ez 32,16, and Am 5,16.

[31] See Jr 7,33; Ez 29,5; 32,4; 39,4, 17 ff.

[32] See above, note 11.

[33] Cf. 2 Bar 48,32 (conjecture!), and 4 Ez 5,5 (Syr.).

[34] Cf. Ps 3,2; Is 59,7; Jr 50,41; Ez 26,3; 38,4 ff.; 39,4.

here the theme is a traditional *topos*, only enveloped in a mysterious veil, owing to the use of the indefinite "many", a mannerism which the author may have learned from Dn 11 f.[35] The place in the pattern of thought occupied by these enemy attacks also has a parallel in these two chapters in Daniel, where 11,41 ff. corresponds to the present theme and is set in a time of distress, like the text in 2 Bar.[36] But the correspondence is not so close as to enable us to draw the positive conclusion that Dn 11,41 ff. played an active part in the composition of the present text.

H. 4 Ez 13,5–11 and 13,34–38

There is a variation on the theme of the assault of the hostile peoples and their miraculous defeat in 4 Ez 13,5–11 and 13,34–38, where it is the (Son of) Man who is attacked by and destroys the enemy.[37] The former text describes the whole thing as part of a vision, while the latter forms part of the interpretation of the vision.

In both these texts we shall see, on the one hand, how the motifs seem to have been polished by traditional use and, on the other, how the material taken over was supplemented by new material from the OT.

We then take first the part of the vision (4 Ez 13,5–11). In vv. 2–4 the prophet has seen the (Son of) Man arise from the sea and all things trembled in his presence (this is expressed in terms similar to those in Ps 68,2 f.).[38]

(5) And after this I saw, and lo! there were gathered together a multitude of men innumerable, from the four winds of heaven to fight with the Man who came up out of the sea. (6) And I saw that he cut out for himself a great mountain and flew upon it. (7) But I sought to see the region or place whence the mountain had been cut out, but could not. (8) And after this I saw, and lo! all who were gathered together to fight with him were in great fear, but yet they dared to fight. (9) And when he saw the violence of their multitude that came, he did not lift up his hand, neither did he hold spear nor any of all the weapons of war; (10) but I saw how he sent out of his mouth only as it were waves of fire, and out of his lips a breath of flame, and he was shooting forth glowing coals of storm. (11) And these were all

---

[35] See Dn 11,10 f., 13 f., 18, 26, 33 f., 39 ff., 44; 12,2 ff., 10.

[36] Dn 12,1 עת צרה. Cf. the beginning of the section in 2 Bar, of which this passage is a part: "that time shall arise which brings affliction" (v. 30, ردحا ,رلم; Dn 12,1 Pesh.: رلمخمو; ردحا).

[37] It is likely that Test Jos 19,8–12 also represents this variant: Joseph sees a virgin, from whom is born a lamb, which is then attacked by all beasts and overcomes them. As regards the symbolism, cf. 1 En 90,12 ff. (above, 84). However, as the text has probably been so heavily edited by Christian writers that its present state would seem to make it impossible to get at the orginal version, I shall not analyse it in any detail here. See further DE JONGE, *Nov. Test* 4 (1960), 215 ff.

[38] Cf. above, 36.

mingled together—the waves of fire, and the breath of flame, and the mass of the storm;[39] and they fell upon the violence of the multitude that was prepared to fight, and burned them all up, so that nothing was visible of that multitude of men without number save only dust of ashes and smell of smoke.

After this the text goes on to describe in vv. 12 f. how this Messianic figure gathers God's dispersed people together and brings the heathen under his dominion. Thus here the motif is assigned to the beginning of the Messianic era.

If we compare the relation of this text to the OT with that of the previous example, we shall see a clear difference. OT motifs are certainly used but, if I may say so, more casually and more superficially. To be sure, the image of the (Son of) Man was inspired by Dn 7,13 and Is 11,4,[40] but this combination is not a new one. It was used long before, in 1 En Sim.[41] It is worth noting how, when this text is associated with Is 11,4 (4 Ez 13,10), it expands the statement that the scion smites the earth with the rod of his mouth and slays the wicked with the breath of his lips so that the enemy is reduced to reeking ashes by rivers of fire and flames. While in the earlier texts the authors were content with, so to speak, building with stones from the OT, it seems as if the author of the present text built with stones which had become traditional and were not taken directly from the OT. Moreover he gave some of these building stones which were originally taken from the OT some extra adornment to make them more impressive.[42]

There is one point on which this text may be original and would in that case provide us with an indication that, even when the writers followed the beaten track, they still returned to the OT and fetched new material from its stores. I am referring to the passage in which the (Son of) Man is said to cut out a mountain and fly on it, whilst the prophet cannot see from whence it was cut (4 Ez 13,6 f.).[43]

[39] F. ZIMMERMANN, Underlying Documents of IV Ezra, *Jew. Quart. Rev.* 51 (1960/61), 123, suggests that "storm" (*tempestas*) is a mistranslation of the Heb. זִקִּין ("sparks") as if it were the Aram. זִיקָא.

[40] 4 QpIs[a] also interprets (IV.1 ff.) Is 11,4 as referring to the vanquishing of enemies in the last days. Magog is expressly mentioned in IV.4. Box (*Ezra-Apocalypse*, 283) denies a dependence of 4 Ez 13,3 on Dn 7,13. The argument that the Latin has *homo* and not *filius hominis* is weakened by the fact that the Syr. has ابر ومهﻣﺎ ودحزبعا, with which we may compare Dn 7,13 Pesh. اﺑﺮ حﻧﺎﻟﻌﺒ ﻠﻞ. Cf. DALMAN, *Worte Jesu*, 200 f., and H. GRESSMANN, *Der Messias* (1929), 379 ff.

[41] 1 En 49,1 ff.

[42] Cf. above, 76.

[43] 4 Ez 13,6: *Et vidi, et ecce sibimetipso sculpsit montem magnum et volavit super eum. (7) Ego autem quaesivi videre regionem vel locum unde sculptus esset mons, et non potui.*

It is highly probable that here we have a kind of new usage of a part of the dream vision in Dn 2,31–35 (on the colossus with the feet of clay).[44] There (vv. 34 f.) a stone is cut out without hands, which breaks the image and becomes a great mountain, filling the whole earth. In the same chapter of Daniel the dream is interpreted, in that the different parts of the statue are said to stand for four different world empires (vv. 38–43) and the stone for the kingdom which God will establish and which will break all other kingdoms and stand for ever (vv. 44 f).

It is probably this interpretation of the dream vision in Dn 2,31–35 which is the reason for its being mentioned at all in connection with the (Son of) Man. He is described just before this verse in this text, in wording adopted from Dn 7,13. But Dn 7,2–14 also contains a dream vision, in which the four world empires appear and are destroyed, after which the Son of Man receives everlasting dominion. The intention is clearly to relate the Son of Man in Dn 7,13, conceived as an individual, to the empire which God will establish according to Dn 2,44,[45] by having the (Son of) Man fly on the stone.

When the dream vision in 4 Ez 13,2 ff. is interpreted later on in this chapter, however, the detail of the flying stone is given a somewhat different interpretation from that in Dn 2. We now pass on to the second text in 4 Ez.

This text (4 Ez 13,27 f.) reports the detail that fire will stream forth from the mouth of the (Son of) Man and that unarmed he will destroy the attacking host. The text says that this will now be interpreted. Then vv. 29–31 first give the description of the turbulence of the people, to which I referred above,[46] a feature which it is difficult to find any justification for in the vision itself. After these "signs" the (Son of) Man (here called *filius meus*) is revealed. When the peoples hear his voice, they are said to leave their dwelling-places and their own wars and to gather together to fight against him (32–34).

Then the detail of the stone which becomes a mountain is interpreted. "(36) But he will stand on the top of Mount Sion. (36) But Sion will come and be revealed to all, prepared and erected, as you saw the mountain cut without hands." V. 37 mentions that the (Son of) Man will reprove (*arguet*) and punish the nations for their ungodliness.[47]

---

[44] Thus also KEULERS, *Eschatologische Lehre des 4 Ez*, 132. For other "midrashic" details in 4 Ez, see ZIMMERMANN, *Jew. Quart. Rev.* 51 (1960/61), 126 ff.

[45] On the two Dn texts, see also M. NOTH, "Die Heiligen des Höchsten", in *Gesammelte Studien* (1957), 274–90, esp. 283 f. The stone has a Messianic interpretation in Tanch. תולדות 20 and תרומה 6 (A. SCHLATTER, *Das AT in der johanneischen Apokalypse*, 1912, 33), and Nu R. 13,14.

[46] See above, 79 f.

[47] The exact meaning is somewhat uncertain. The fire, flames and storm could

Thus the author supplements his traditional motif of the assault and destruction of the heathen with a new interpretation of an OT text, an interpretation which has its origin in the text's own interpretation in the OT—that the stone–mountain is God's eternal kingdom. This is expressed more precisely here, so that the mountain becomes the heavenly Sion, made without hands, from which the Messiah (the (Son of) Man) will judge the hostile nations and to which he will re-assemble the people of God (13,39 ff.).[48]

I. 2 Bar 70,7–71,1

We meet with the motif of the heathen attack on Israel in a sort of hybrid form in 2 Bar 70,7 – 71,1. There a vision is interpreted as meaning that in the last days great evil and misery will prevail among mankind. This also includes the circumstance that (70,7) God will "reveal those peoples whom He has prepared before, and they shall come and make war with the leaders that shall then be left". The text goes on to say that mankind will be destroyed in earthquakes, fire and famine (8). Those of the victors and vanquished who survive will fall into the hands of the Messiah (9). "(10) For all the earth will devour its inhabitants. (71,1) And the holy land shall have mercy on its own, and it shall protect its inhabitants at that time."

Here we recognize wellnigh every detailed motif from our previous examples but they are combined in a single mixture. If we follow Charles and delete 70,9 on how the remnant of the victors and the vanquished

be interpreted as accusations and punishments from the (Son of) Man and this is how Box interprets them (op. cit., ad loc.). But the Latin actually allows the peoples' *impietates* to be compared to *tempestates*. On the other hand, the flames are interpreted as *cruciamenta quibus incipient cruciari*. The Syriac version says that the (Son of) Man will destroy his enemies by the law, which is compared to the fire. The Lat. (except MSS. M, N; on the MSS., see B. VIOLET, *Die Esra-Apokalypse* I, 1910, XVIII f.) reads "*improperabit coram eis mala cogitamenta ... et cruciamenta ...; et perdet eos sine labore et legem, quae igni adsimilata est*". This Latin variant must be a Christian offshoot of the Syriac version just cited, which is hardly original (cf. VIOLET, op. cit. II, 1924, ad loc.).

[48] I feel dubious about Box's distinction between, on the one hand, the earthly Sion in 13,35, and, on the other, the heavenly Sion in 13,36. On the contrary, I find here a further manifestation of the idea of a new Temple, made without hands (ἀχειροποίητος), associated in the NT with Jesus and His consciousness of Himself as the Messiah (Mk 14,58; Jn 2,19; cf. Ac 7,48; 17,24). See E. G. SELWYN, *Comm. 1 Pt* (2nd ed. 1947/1955), 286 ff.; A COLE, *The New Temple* (1950); M. SIMON, Retour du Christ et reconstruction du Temple, in *Mélanges ... M. Goguel* (1950), 246 ff., esp. 251 f.; D. FLUSSER, Two Notes on the Midrash on 2 Sam.vii: I. The Temple "Not Made with Hands" in the Qumran Doctrine, *Isr. Expl. J.* 9 (1959), 99–104; B. GÄRTNER, *The Temple and the Community in Qumran and the NT* (1965).

will fall into the hands of the Messiah[49]—the sentence is certainly incompatible with its context—we have a text which is in somewhat better agreement with itself and with the texts with similar contents which we have just discussed.

But, however we regard 70,9, it is clear that what is described is set in the evil times which will precede the Messianic empire. The relationship with the OT seems to be an indirect one: the motifs belong to the OT but their wording is such that it is difficult to find connections with definite OT texts. Bearing in mind that we have met with the motifs in other pericopes and that here we have to do with one of the very latest of the texts, it is reasonable to conclude that here the theme has become traditionally apocalyptic. In this example the motifs are not directly derived from the OT, at least not in such a way as to enable us to perceive it as clearly as in the previous examples.

J. Ps Sal 17,23–27

The last stop on our rather long journey through these pericopes is Ps Sal 17,23–27, in which the motif of the heathen enemies functions in a manner which we have not so far discussed. We find ourselves at the beginning of that part of the psalm which describes the Messiah and his reign:

(23) Behold, O Lord, and raise up to them their king, the son of David,
at the time in which you see, O God,
that he may reign over Israel, your servant.
(24) Gird him with strength, that he may shatter unrighteous rulers.
(25) Purge[50] Jerusalem from the nations that trample it down[51] to destruction.
(26) Wisely, righteously,[52] he may thrust out sinners from the inheritance;
"he may destroy" the pride of the sinners "as a potter's vessel,
with a rod of iron he may break in pieces" (Ps 2,9) all their substance (ὑπόστασις);
(27) "he may destroy the godless" nations "with the word of his mouth" (Is 11,4),

---

[49] Cf. above, Chap. II, note 74.

[50] The Greek has the imperative; on the other hand, the Syr. subordinates the clause to the imperative in v. 24. The fact that v. 33 reads καθαριεῖ with the Messiah as subject is a confirmation of the Syr. reading and thus of an amendment to an infinitive. However, it must be emphasized that it is a slight confirmation, for, if in v. 25 God is asked to purify, this does not clash with the statement in v. 33 that God's Messiah will perform this purification. See also KUHN, *Die älteste Textgestalt der Psalmen Salomos*, 69.

[51] Cod. Voss. misc. 15 reads ἀπατούντων instead of καταπατούντων. See W. BAARS, A New Fragment of the Greek Version of the Psalms of Solomon, *Vet. Test.* 11 (1961), 441–44.

[52] The Syr. lacks equivalents for both these expressions.

so that the nations flee before him at his rebuke,
and he may reprove the sinners for the thoughts of their heart.

The actual heathen attack or, to put it more exactly, occupation has already been mentioned in vv. 5 ff. It has the effect of a punishment and is part of the evil time of preparation preceding the Messianic kingdom (*A*). We now turn our attention to that part of the motif in which the land is "purged" of these oppressors during the reign of the Messiah (that is, during *E*).

This view of how the heathen are to be vanquished has a definite relation to the OT, just as much as the majority of the variants we have previously discussed. It has a particular relation to several of the "royal" psalms, in which God gives the king victory over the nations and his reign is distinguished by the nations' making their submission to him.[53]

The relevance of these particular psalms in the OT as comparative material for the theme in general becomes clear when we consider in somewhat more detail how the OT is used in these few verses.

The Messiah is here depicted, first of all, with features from Jr 30,9[54] (the promise of a David *redivivus*). To this is connected the fact that he is girded with strength, so that he is able to crush princes, a metaphor probably inspired by Ps 18,39 f. (33), a psalm of David (cf. 2 Sm 22).[55] The harsh rule of the Messiah over sinners and heathens in v. 26 is described with a quotation from Ps 2,9[56] and his power as judge from Is 11,4.

It is clear that the Messiah is the central figure here and the result is that the heathens and their activities are only accessory characters. This is also shown by the fact that they have, so to say, no OT passages that apply primarily to them, as is the case with the Messiah.

When v. 24 mentions that Jerusalem will be "purged" of the heathen who "trample her down", we have here a terminology that is common in intertestamental times. It has certain possible origins in the OT, among which may be mentioned the following: Ps 79,1 (heathens have defiled (טמאו) the Temple) and Dn 8,13 f. (the Temple is trodden under foot and shall be cleansed). In the books of the Maccabees this expression often recurs: the heathens trample things under foot and they must be cleaned (this, of course, applies primarily to the Temple).[57]

In so far as the description of the enemy here is independent of the

---

[53] For example, Ps 2; 18; 21; 68; 110.

[54] J. VITEAU (*Les Psaumes de Salomon*, 1911, ad loc.) refers instead to Ez 37,21–25 and does not even mention Jr 30,9.

[55] See also Nu 24,17 and Ps 110,5.

[56] Cf. SEELIGMANN, *Suppl. Vet. Test.* 1 (1953), 173 f., and MAAG, in *Das Böse*, 72 ff.

[57] See, for example, 1 Mcc 1,37 f.; 3,45, 51; 4,36 ff.; 2 Mcc 2,18; 5,15 f.; 8,2; 10,3 ff. See also Ps Sal 2,1 ff., 20.

Messianic passages in the OT, it seems to be traditional, in the sense that it seems to illustrate a prevalent fashion of describing the occupation without including any distinct OT passages and placing them in the mouth of the ancient author.

If we now look back upon this chapter, we may see that it has shown us that both these motifs—the earthquake and the enmity of the nations —appear in the most widely varying combinations with other motifs, in very different places in the events of the last days and with functions that vary considerably. In most cases we found OT parallels for the combination, the order and the function.

However, we have now got so close to these texts that we are justified in assuming a direct influence from the OT, as regards the two motifs and the combinations and functions they have in these texts. As regards most of the texts, we have been able to show how leavened they are in this respect by OT material,[58] and have also been able to analyse in detail how this OT material for both the motifs was interwoven in accordance with certain lines of association.

Finally we have been able to note, as regards these motifs, a certain tendency in 4 Ez and 2 Bar, the latest of our texts, for motifs originally derived from the OT to become traditional. The expressions for these motifs lose their association with specific OT passages. At the same time there is a tendency to "embellish": new and fanciful elements, which are not taken from the Scriptures, are mixed with these traditional motifs. But still we cannot speak of any emancipation from the OT. On the contrary, we find examples of how the traditions were supplemented by new associations with OT texts.

---

[58] Cf. H. ELMGREN, *Philon av Alexandria* (1939), 100 ff. R. BULTMANN (Weissagung und Erfüllung, *Zschr. Theol. Ki.* 47, 1950, 360 ff.) maintains that the method of using the whole OT as a prophetic book is due to a Hellenistic and Stoic tradition. But so early a work as the Deuteronomic historical books gives instances of this way of regarding even "non-prophetic" parts of the OT as prophetic, and it is scarcely possible to refer this work to any Hellenistic and Stoic tradition. Thus I cannot see any reason why this distinction of Bultmann's should hold good as regards the present texts. See CARLSON, *David*, 263 ff.

CHAPTER IV

An Inquiry into the Composition of Some Apocalyptic Texts

1. *Introduction*

We have now established the existence of various patterns of thought in the texts under discussion and seen (in Chap. III) the different ways in which a couple of distinct motifs functioned in these patterns. The parallels to these patterns in the OT and the closeness to the OT of the functions of the motifs investigated in Chap. III should not in themselves surprise us, if we bear in mind the important part which the OT played in post-Exilic Judaism, as the quintessence of God's revelation to the chosen people.[1]

In this chapter I shall examine a few texts in even more detail and attempt to get at their content structure by closer analysis, i.e. I now want to carry out on whole pericopes an investigation similar to that which I devoted to the individual motifs of the earthquake and the tumult of the people in the previous chapter.

However, I wish for the moment to limit the field of view and to try to elicit the part played by OT allusions and phrases in the composition of certain texts. Actually, in the majority of texts this does not signify a restriction but rather a more precise definition of the task, since the OT ferment is so conspicuous. On the other hand, it means only an imperfect beginning to a wider research task, viz. the investigation of the part played by the OT in Jewish apocalyptic and in the pseudo-epigraphical writings. Here only a couple of flowers can be culled from this abundant flora and examined in due form.

There are some complicating factors in an inquiry like this. When we attempt in this way to get an insight into the creative process behind these texts, as it is reflected in the way in which the author uses the OT, there immediately crops up the awkward question "Which author?" The fact that we otherwise know nothing about him is a negligible difficulty, but is it even possible to speak of "an author" in the singular?[2]

[1] See, for example, F. WEBER, *Jüdische Theologie* (2nd ed. 1897), 14 ff.; SCHÜRER, *Geschichte* II, 545 ff.; BILLERBECK, *Comm.* III, 126 ff.; G. F. MOORE, *Judaism* I (1927), 235 ff.; J. BONSIRVEN, *Le judaïsme palestinien* I (1934), 247 ff.; H. A. WOLFSON *Philo* I (2nd ed. 1948), 19 ff., 87 ff.; R. H. PFEIFFER, *History of NT Times* (1949), 46 ff.; H. BRAUN, *Spätjüdisch-häretischer und frühchristlicher Radikalismus* I–II (1957), passim. See further note 7, below.

[2] The problem is indicated by ENGNELL, *Biblioth. Orient.* 8 (1951), 188, and by K. KOCH, *Was ist Formgeschichte?* (1964), 94 f.

And if we now assume that a certain writing was the work of *one* author, what was there to prevent later editors from substantially altering the original version?

Accordingly we have here a complication deriving from the history of the writing's transmission and are compelled to reduce our question to a simple inquiry into the detailed structure of the existing text, as regards its use of the OT.[3] Thus the creative process which we are trying to analyse may in itself be distributed over several persons and periods.

There is a further complication in the fact that, of all the texts used here, only Or Sib is available in the original language, while all the rest have been preserved only in translation. For example, large parts of 1 En have only been preserved in an Ethiopic translation of a Greek translation of the original text in Hebrew or Aramaic.[4] Obviously in this process of translation and re-translation associations with the OT, expressed by a characteristic turn of phrase, may disappear, while a translator or a copyist may very well have added others.

This complication may have contributed to produce a state of affairs in which the present texts seem to have largely been neglected during the intense effort which has been devoted, particularly in the last two decades, to investigating and elucidating the part played by the OT in both other Jewish texts of the period and in early Christian thought.[5]

---

[3] I.e., the same restriction on the questions as we observed earlier. Cf. above, 53.

[4] See, for example, CHARLES, *Book of Enoch*, lvii ff., and HAMMERSHAIMB, trans., 74 ff. (But cf. E. ULLENDORFF, An Aramaic "Vorlage" of the Ethiopic Text of Enoch?, in *Atti del Convegno Internazionale di Studi Etiopici 1958*, 1960, 259–68; he answers the question in the affirmative.) There would seem to be a similar state of affairs in Ass Mos, where the way leads from a Hebrew original through a Greek translation to the Latin MS. we now possess. See CHARLES, *Ass Mos* (1897), xxxviii ff.; D. H. WALLACE, The Semitic Origin of the Assumption of Moses, *Theol. Zschr.* 11 (1955), 321–28; B. NOACK, trans. (1963), 320.

[5] The Chicago dissertation by L. R. HAMMILL, *Biblical Interpretation in the Apocrypha and Pseudepigrapha* (1951), was not available to me, but it must be an exception. Cf., on the other hand, the abundance of works, of which the following is only a selection: N. G. COHEN, Josephus and Scriptures, *Jew. Quart. Rev.* 54 (1963/64), 311–32; S. G. SOWERS, *The Hermeneutics of Philo and Hebrews* (1965). (On the use of the OT by Philo and Josephus, see also the literature in L. FELDMAN, *Scholarship on Philo and Josephus 1937–62* [1963], 12 ff. and 47.) E. HOSKYNS, N. DAVEY, *The Riddle of the NT* (rev. ed. 1936); C. K. BARRETT, The OT in the Fourth Gospel, *J. Theol. Stud.* 48 (1947), 155–69; T. W. MANSON, The OT in the Teaching of Jesus, *Bull. J. Ryl. Libr.* 34 (1951/52), 312–32; C. H. DODD, *According to the Scriptures* (1952); J. DUPONT, L'utilisation apologétique de l'AT dans les discours des Actes, *Ephem. Theol. Lovan.* 29 (1953), 289–327; B. GÄRTNER, The Habakkuk Commentary (DSH) and the Gospel of Matthew, *Stud. Theol.* 8 (1954), 1–24; K. STENDAHL, *The School of St. Matthew* (1954); E. E. ELLIS, *Paul's Use of the OT* (1957); A. SUHL, *Die Funktion der alttestamentlichen Zitate und Anspielungen im Markusevangelium* (1965).

In the case of the Qumran texts the situation is a different one. Between the available text and the Hebrew Bible concordance there is in most cases only the problem of which Bible text (more or less resembling the TM) was used by the author. Annotated editions of the text give frequent references to Biblical passages,[6] and special investigations of the part played by the OT in these texts appeared only a few years after the texts had been published.[7]

I begin by putting a question as to the relationship between the external form of the texts and their internal structure. Here the principal problem is the visions and the question is, "Has the fact that a text takes the form of a description of a vision any significance, when we attempt to discover how this text was composed?" In conjunction with this question, it will be necessary to discuss the relationship between an author's ideas and his work. In other words, we must touch upon such matters as "inspiration", analysis of associations and so on, with particular reference to the texts under discussion. This will be followed by a discussion of the use of the OT in certain texts and an attempt to plot their structure by isolating the OT associations and motifs and their possible mutual connections.

Firstly, as regards their external form, these texts are linked especially with the Prophetic Books in the OT. Thus one of the most common literary forms in them is the oracle, in the shape of a prophecy,[8] a "parable" (משל),[9] or an oracle of judgement ("woe unto you ... for ...").[10]

---

[6] See, for example, *Die Texte aus Qumran*, ed. E. LOHSE (1964), *The Thanksgiving Hymns*, ed. M. MANSOOR (1961), and *La Règle de la Guerre*, ed. J. CARMIGNAC (1958).

[7] B. J. ROBERTS, The Dead Sea Scrolls and the OT Scriptures, *Bull. J. Ryl. Libr.* 36 (1953/54), 75–96; GÄRTNER, op. cit.; STENDAHL, op. cit., 183 ff.; P. WERNBERG-MØLLER, Some Reflections on the Biblical Material in the Manual of Discipline, *Stud. Theol.* 9 (1955), 40–66; J. CARMIGNAC, Les citations de l'AT dans "la Guerre des Fils de Lumière contre les Fils de Ténèbre", *Rev. Bibl.* 63 (1956), 234–60, 375–90; id., Les citations de l'AT et spécialement des Poèmes du Serviteur, dans les Hymnes de Qumrân, *Rev. Qumr.* 2 (1959/60), 357–94; J. A. FITZMYER, The Use of Explicit OT Quotations in Qumran Literature and in the NT, *NT Stud.* 7 (1960/61), 297–333. Further W. H. BROWNLEE, Biblical Interpretation among the Sectaries of the Dead Sea Scrolls, *Bibl. Archaeol.* 14 (1951), 54–76; K. ELLIGER, *Studien zum Habakuk-Kommentar vom Toten Meer* (1953), 118–64; BRUCE, *Biblical Exegesis*; O. BETZ, *Offenbarung und Schriftforschung in der Qumransekte* (1960).

[8] For example, the Apocalypse of Weeks (1 En 93,1–10; 91,12–17). On the question of the relation of these forms to the pseudonomity etc., see, for example, RUSSELL, *Method and Message*, 118 ff., 127 ff.

[9] 1 En Sim (37–71).

[10] For example, 1 En 84 ff.

It may be inserted in the framework of a farewell speech like Jacob's in Gn 49 or Moses' benediction in Dt 33.[11]

A very common form is that in which the oracle is communicated within the framework of a dialogue between the prophet who puts the questions and a divine person who answers them (an angel or God Himself).[12] This method of providing a setting for the oracle was also inspired by the OT.

Here we also encounter a form of representation which must be considered in a little more detail, viz. the visions. Thus the whole of 1 En Sim is cast in this mould, and we meet with it in both 4 Ez and 2 Bar, in a form which was in all probability deliberately associated with Daniel and Ezekiel. The prophet is carried away by ecstasy, sees the vision (for example, some wild beasts, a man or dark and light streams of water), reflects upon it and then has it interpreted.

The question now is whether these visionary narratives are only literary stereotypes or whether they go back to extraordinary experiences.[13] Of course, it is difficult to give a definite answer. What is related in the framework narrative in 4 Ez is in itself preparation which might have formed a good starting-point for hallucinations and the like: we read of long fasting and concentrated prayer (5,20; 6,31, 35) and of preparations by means of a special diet (9,23 ff.). Indeed, certain details may be interpreted as indicating the use of a special drink, which gives "inspiration" (14,38 ff.). Other texts provide similar examples.[14] It is a recognized fact that an author who uses well-established, conventional, literary forms for rendering visions may nevertheless cast his own visionary experiences in precisely these forms which he has taken over.[15]

We may now go a step further. If the convention of the external form does not in itself indicate whether we are to assume visionary experiences of these authors or not, what about the content of these visionary narratives? For this also displays the use of conventional material in a conventional style. "Conventional" may mean both traditional themes

---

[11] 1 En 91,1–11, 18–19; 92,1–5; Test XII Patr. See EPPEL, *Piétisme juif*, 1 ff., and J. MUNCK, Discours d'adieu dans le NT et dans la littérature biblique, in *Mélanges ... M. Goguel* (1950), 155–70, esp. 157 ff.

[12] Thus, for example, in 4 Ez, Apc Abr, 2 Bar.

[13] There is a more detailed discussion of this question in RUSSELL, op. cit., 158 ff. Cf. WIDENGREN, *Literary and Psychological Aspects*, 116 ff., and LINDBLOM, *Prophecy in Ancient Israel*, 105–202.

[14] Apc Abr 9,7; 2 Bar 5,7; 9,2 etc.

[15] For example, W. BOUSSET, *Die Offenbarung Johannis* (1906), 13; PORTER, *Messages*, 26, 40 f.; T. ANDRÆ, *Mystikens psykologi* (1926), 215–405, passim; KAUFMANN, Apokalyptik, *Enc. Jud.* II, 1145 f.; C. SCHNEIDER, *Die Erlebnisechtheit der Apokalypse des Johannes* (1930); Å. V. STRÖM, *Der Hirt des Hermas, Allegorie oder Wirklichkeit* (1936), 7 ff.

(*topoi*) in Jewish expectation concerning the last days and, above all, associations with the OT, in which it is sometimes possible, as we saw in the previous chapter, to isolate series of associations from passage to passage, within the framework of a pattern of thought of the type presented in Chap. II. Under these circumstances, is it also possible to assume that visions, hearing of voices, etc. may have underlain some of these texts? The answer to this question must be that a convention of this kind does not exclude a basis of extraordinary experiences either.[16]

Here I cannot refrain from quoting A. Farrer, who worked on the same question in relation to Revelations: "The difficulty would vanish, if we could suppose that the angel made the poem and St. John suffered the ecstasy; that he passively received a verbal comment on the visions, as well as the visions themselves. The angel (in effect) dictated the book, St. John wrote it down. But if so, what a very late first-century, Asia-Minor, Greco-Semitic, apostolico-rabbinical angel!"[17]

Thus, whatever experiences a prophet may have, when he writes down what he wishes to communicate of what he has experienced, he expresses himself in words which are coloured by the tradition of which he is a representative. This means that, as regards what has been seen and written down, we cannot draw any clear distinction between texts whose authors reproduce visions and texts whose "ordinary" author describes visually what he wishes to say. In the milieu we are now studying, both types of author employ the same devices, as regards form, language and style.

It should then be true to say of these authors—whether visionaries or not—that their imaginations, which (possibly under the influence of "visionary" experiences) produce what they formulate in words, are working with ideas which have been previously learned.[18] To quote a programmatic sentence by H. Ebbinghaus: "Die Phantasieleistungen sind nichts anderes als Gedächtnisfunktionen".[19]

We may wonder whether the question about the background of experience in these texts has turned out to be superfluous. If both the visionary and the "ordinary" author only reproduce previously learned material in what they write, although in fresh combinations, what advantage is there in including visions, hearing of voices, etc. in investigating the making of these texts?

---

[16] See the preceding note.

[17] A. FARRER, *The Revelation of St. John the Divine* (1964), 23 f.

[18] I use the word "learn" in a wider sense, i.e. not only referring to an active and conscious study. See, for example, J. DEESE, The Psychology of Learning (2nd ed. 1958), 1 ff., and passim.

[19] H. EBBINGHAUS, *Grundzüge der Psychologie* II (4th ed. 1919), 247.

I think that here we have to take into consideration the difficult factor of "inspiration". To express it more exactly: we shall keep in view that we have to reckon with different degrees of consciousness in the creative imagination.[20] We disregard hysterical phenomena, such as automatic writing and the like.[21] It is a fact that has been vouched for in various ways that authors can work with different degrees of conscious selection and rejection of expedients for expressing what they have "seen", "conceived", etc.

Let us take an example of how an author may describe himself as being in the hands of something stronger than himself, viz. Friedrich Nietzsche, who describes the origin of *Also Sprach Zarathustra* as follows:

> Provided one has the slightest remnant of superstition left, one can hardly reject completely the idea that one is the mere incarnation, or mouthpiece, or medium of some almighty power. The notion of revelation describes the condition quite simply; by which I mean that something profoundly convulsive and disturbing suddenly becomes visible and audible with indescribable definiteness and exactness. One hears—one does not seek; one takes —one does not ask who gives; a thought flashes out like lightning, inevitably without hesitation—I have never had any choice about it.[22]

On the other hand, Stephen Spender, in describing how he works, quotes two extremes as regards inspiratory concentration: Mozart, who composed his music rapidly in his own mind before he wrote it down; and Beethoven, who worked in note-books and then wrote and re-wrote his rough drafts over and over again. Spender seems principally to classify himself as a Beethovenian type.[23] He describes how he works out a poem from an original idea over a long period.[24]

We have to reckon that such introspective descriptions of the creative process may be rationalizations and may have been unconsciously touched up, in order to present a conscious or unconscious picture of how an artist should work.[25] But nevertheless we have so much evidence from artists who have tried to describe the creative process behind their work that we are justified in speaking of different degrees of conscious selection

---

[20] See on this point and on the following exposition, for example, H. Høffding, *Psykologi i Omrids* (6th ed. 1911), 233 f.; Andræ, op. cit., ibid. and 581–619.; H. Delacroix, L'invention et le génie (in G. Dumas, *Nouveau traité de psychologie* VI, 1939, 447–544), 512 ff.; B. Ghiselin, Introduction to *The Creative Process* (1952), 5 ff.

[21] See, for example, J. Jastrow, Automatic Writing, *Dict. of Philosophy and Psychology* I (1928), 94 f.

[22] Cit. from the anthology of Ghiselin (op. cit.), 209 f.

[23] S. Spender, The Making of a Poem, in Ghiselin, op. cit., 115 f.

[24] Spender, op. cit., 116 ff.

[25] Cf. Ghiselin, op. cit., 17 f.

and testing in the creative process;[26] of the fact that the material which is learned in different ways and which the "imagination" works on is combined and re-organized with different degrees of involvement of the conscious, intellectual part of the mind; and of the fact that the "inspiration" may be both Paul Valéry's *ligne donnée*,[27] the original idea which is then purposely worked on, and the Mozartian "hearing of the *tout ensemble*", in which the composer takes his music "out of the bag of his memory" and quickly commits it to the paper.[28]

Considerations like these seem to be of relevance to anyone who tries to isolate associational threads in texts like those we are considering here. It would seem that an author who writes under the influence of a vision or a similar experience does not expose his associations so much to the sifting action of his scrutinizing consciousness during the creative process. Even though the visionary's opus may be derived from less controlled associations, we can scarcely use the impression that his series of associations is more "intuitive" than consciously thought out as a criterion of the genuineness of his experience. On the whole, we have to realize that this field has been too little investigated for us to venture to set down any definite theses in this connection. But at least these considerations may open our eyes to the fact that the associational fabrics in these texts may have highly complicated patterns and that we should not be surprised if the threads in the fabrics run in the most peculiar coils. A man's associations do not always follow straight lines.

The aspect of the composition of these texts which will be dealt with here is then their use of the OT. However, there is actually no such use, in the sense that OT passages are *explicitly* quoted, discussed or referred to. On the other hand, as has already been mentioned, these texts are leavened by the OT in another way, in that the learned intellectual content on which the authors' imaginations work comes to a very large extent from the OT. In the previous chapter it was shown that "OT" must mean, at least to some extent, "a more than private interpretation of the OT". Thus, for example, the interpretation of Ps 2 as referring to

---

[26] See also R. THOMSON, *Tänkandets psykologi* (1963), 176 ff. A certain amount of pioneer work in attempting to elucidate the creative process was carried out in the 1930s by C. PATRICK. See her dissertation entitled *Creative Thought in Poets* (1935), and also her Creative Thought in Artists, *J. Psychol.* 4 (1937), 35–73, and lately *What is Creative Thinking?* (1955). Similar problems have lately been dealt with in *Contemporary Approaches to Creative Thinking* (ed. H. E. GRUBER, G. TERRELL, M. WERTHEIMER, 1962).

[27] Cf. the section by P. VALÉRY in GHISELIN, op. cit.: The Course in Poetics: First Lesson (92–105).

[28] A (possibly unauthentic) letter of Mozart, cited in GHISELIN, op. cit., 34 f.

Gog (and his equivalents) in Or Sib 3,669 f. would seem to go back to a more general Jewish exegetical tradition.[29] As regards this contact between apocalyptic and general Jewish Biblical exegesis, A. Schlatter has written a pioneering work on Revelations, in which he has demonstrated how the author makes use of the OT in a fashion which, it would seem, can to a very large extent be traced back to the textual exegesis given by the rabbis in the Jewish synagogue.[30]

We get a certain idea of how the creative mind of the author worked with the material it had learned when we are able to determine certain "stations" for the processes of association, determine which OT passages are echoed in the text and then consider how it came about that the author recalled these particular passages and why his "intuition" or his exploring mind sought out just this or that passage in the OT.

Here, of course, we are treading the time-honoured paths of psychology. Even Aristotle mentioned associations and the ways in which they arose, on account of similarity, proximity, etc.[31] The psychology known as associationism went so far as to conceive of the whole spiritual life as consisting of elements associated with each other in accordance with the "laws of association".[32] Various correctives have been applied to this view during the present century, especially by Gestalt psychologists such as W. Köhler.[33]

As regards the texts under discussion, this means that we have to expect not only different degrees of consciousness behind different combinations of this Biblical material but also that the authors will to a certain extent have "guided" associations and that even the most unconscious links between the OT passages will be under the moulding and guiding—though very cautious—control exercised by the whole (the "Gestalt"), i.e. one of the patterns of thought of which we found some formulations in Chap. II.

That this mode of expression fostered by the OT is not specific of Jewish apocalyptic in particular is shown by the Revelation of St. John in the NT, which is charged with OT material, to a large extent dependent

---

[29] See above, 90, note 11.

[30] SCHLATTER, Das AT in der johanneischen Apokalypse. The summary of his results is on 104 ff.

[31] Aristotle, De mem. 2. See further, for example, EBBINGHAUS, Grundzüge I, 677 ff.

[32] Representatives of this persuasion were James and John Stuart Mill (father and son), A. Bain, T. Ribot, T. Ziehen, G. E. Müller.

[33] W. KÖHLER, Psychologische Probleme (1933). Criticisms from different points of departure were made by H. BERGSON, for example, in Matière et mémoire (15th ed. 1919).

on the Jewish tradition.[34] But this technique is not reserved exclusively to strictly apocalyptic writers, as is shown by the hymns in Lk 1 f.[35] and by the psalms of the Qumran sect,[36] as well as by the later Odes of Solomon.[37] On the other hand, it is possible that an investigation of the details in their use of the OT would give a picture different from that we find in the present texts. Several detailed investigations are still necessary on this point, but at any rate it is clear that a technique of authorship that makes an intensive use of the OT for content, ideas and phraseology is not a special feature of the present texts.

Nor is this attachment to the OT a feature which distinguishes, say, post-Biblical Jewish literature from the earlier, more independent OT books. It would certainly seem that the character of Judaism as a religion based on a revelation in holy scripture appeared much more clearly in the post-Exilic period, especially during the struggles for spiritual independence. But we find even in Biblical texts, and not only in the latest of these texts, this habit of copying conventional thoughts, words and phrases from earlier authoritative literature. For example, Dn 12,2–4 makes use of passages from Isaiah and Amos.[38] We know that Micah is somewhat related to the Isaiah tradition.[39] Portions of Jeremiah are said to make use of earlier and more authentic texts,[40]

---

[34] See SCHLATTER, op. cit., and further BOUSSET, *Die Offenbarung Johannis*, 13; E. LOHMEYER, *Comm.* (2nd ed. 1953), 195 f.; FARRER, *Comm.*, 30 ff.; J. CAMBIER, Les images de l'AT dans l'Apocalypse de Saint Jean, *Nouv. Rev. Théol.* 87 (1955), 113–22; L. CERFAUX and J. CAMBIER, *Comm.* (1955), 207 ff.; E. LOHSE, Die alttestamentliche Sprache des Sehers Johannes, *Zschr. Nt. Wiss.* 52 (1961), 122–26; A. VANHOYE, L'utilisation du livre d'Ézéchiel dans l'Apocalypse, *Bibl.* 43 (1962), 436–76. For further references, see A. FEUILLET, *L'Apocalypse* (1963), 65 ff.

[35] Cf. DALMAN, *Worte Jesu*, 31 f.; P. GAECHTER, *Maria im Erdenleben* (1953), 28; M. D. GOULDER and M. L. SANDERSON, St. Luke's Genesis, *J. Theol. Stud.* 8 (1957), 12–30. For further refs., see also R. LAURENTIN, Traces d'allusions étymologiques en Luc 1–2, *Bibl.* 37 (1956), 435–56; 38 (1957), 1–23.

[36] See, for example, CARMIGNAC, *Rev. Qumr.* 2 (1959/60), 357–94.

[37] R. HARRIS and A. MINGANA, *The Odes and Psalms of Solomon* II (1920), 110 ff. But cf. J. CARMIGNAC, Un Qumrânien converti au christianisme: l'auteur des Odes de Solomon, in *Qumran-Probleme* (1963), 75–108.

[38] See A. FEUILLET, Le Fils de l'homme de Daniel et la tradition biblique, *Rev. Bibl.* 60 (1953), 183 ff., 336 f.; H. L. GINSBERG, The Oldest Interpretation of the Suffering Servant, *Vet. Test.* 3 (1953), 400–04; RUSSELL, *Method and Message*, 188 f. And cf. H. JUNKER, *Untersuchungen über literarische und exegetische Probleme des Buches Daniel* (1932), 35 f.

[39] See EISSFELDT, *Einleitung*, 552, and the references given there.

[40] W. L. HOLLADAY, Prototype and Copies: a New Approach to the Poetry–Prose Problem in the Book of Jeremiah, *J. Bibl. Lit.* 79 (1960), 351–67. If the idea of traditionist circles is brought into the problem, the alternative of authentic or unauthentic immediately becomes more intricate: see I. ENGNELL, Profeter, *Svenskt Bibl. Uppslagsverk* II, 593 f., and id., Traditionshistorisk metod, ibid., 1256 ff.

and the men behind the Deuteronomic work[41] habitually use early traditions, including the Psalms and the Prophetic Books.[42]

Thus, even though the actual attachment to early Biblical texts is not in itself anything new, it would nevertheless seem that, at the time when the present texts originated, most of the OT had in practice become canonical, in the sense that men scrutinized it and believed that they could find the truth in it—not only a divine revelation but *the* divine revelation.[43]

This authoritative function of the OT was the point of departure from which the Scriptures were interpreted and applied in Judaism. The reason why I mention this is that the way in which these texts use the OT seems to be akin to that in the *midrashim*, partly owing to the fact that the *midrashim*, with their *Sitz im Leben* in the rabbinical schools and the synagogues, probably contributed in various ways to the material worked on by the creative imagination of the authors and partly owing to the actual technique.

We know what part was played in the OT by *jeux de mots* of various kinds. The authors not only play with sounds, which may sometimes make the expressions more drastic (cf. the *mashal* literature[44]), but also make this play with sounds produce consequences as regards content. This applies especially to the Prophetic Books, which swarm with verbal fireworks, for example, Jr 1,11 f., in which the prophet sees a rod of an almond tree (שָׁקֵד), which means that Yahweh is watching over (שֹׁקֵד) His word to perform it.[45] Here we may also recall, in passing, all the popular etymologies of various proper names, for example, Gn 30,20, in which Zebulun is explained partly by "gift" (זבד) and partly by "dwell" (זבל).

This fact—that sound similarities have consequences as regards content in the OT—is one of the starting-points for the *midrash* exegesis.[46] In this exegesis, associations on account of the similarity in form of identi-

---

[41] Cf. above, 26, note 13.

[42] H. H. ROWLEY, The Prophet Jeremiah and the Book of Deuteronomy, in *Studies in OT Prophecy*, presented to Th. H. Robinson (1950), 157–74; WIDENGREN, *Sakrales Königtum*, 59 ff. (2 Sm 7); CARLSON, *David*, passim. Cf. M. GASTER, *Samaritan Eschatology* (1932), 77 ff., and also B. W. ANDERSON, Exodus Typology in Second Isaiah, in *Israel's Prophetic Heritage* (1962), 177–95, and G. W. BUCHANAN, Midrashim prétannaites, *Rev. Bibl.* 72 (1965), 227–39.

[43] SEELIGMANN, *Suppl. Vet. Test.* 1 (1953), 176 ff., and J. W. DOEVE, *Jewish Hermeneutics in the Synoptic Gospels and Acts* (1953), 52 ff. And see above, note 1.

[44] See, on this point and on the following exposition, G. BOSTRÖM, *Paronomasi i den äldre hebreiska maschallitteraturen* (1928), 1 ff.

[45] Cf. WIDENGREN, *Literary and Psychological Aspects*, 124 f.

[46] SEELIGMANN, op. cit., 157 ff.

cal or similar words in different texts is of great importance.[47] Both the "etymologizing" interpretation and the interpretation from the fact that an expression is *bis legomenon* are both psychologically and interpretatively related to the way in which these authors sometimes work, a way of which we had partial proof in the previous chapter.

I shall now analyse some of these texts as regards their use of the OT and try to elucidate the associational paths.[48] I shall present the text phrase by phrase with the Biblical passages I have found relevant set out in five columns alongside the phrases, after which I shall analyse the passage. In the first column of Biblical passages I quote passages of which I am certain that they and no others influenced the text *and* that in this connection the wording of the text was considerably influenced by the passage (it becomes almost a quotation). This "quoting" part of the text is printed in italics.

In column 2 I include passages which I am still certain have influenced the text (these passages and no others), without the text being so "quoting" as in the first case. Column 3 includes passages in which the motif of the text is definitely to be found. Column 4 includes passages in which motifs which resemble those in the texts are to be found. Column 5, finally, includes passages in which examples of the phraseology used in the text are to be found. This column 5 is even more selective than columns 3 and 4. It is obvious that sometimes one may be doubtful as to which column a Biblical passage should be inserted in, but I nevertheless considered it to be of value that the material should be classified somehow.[49]

2. 1 En 1,3–9

The oracle is preceded in vv. 1–3*a* by some lines which partly serve as an introduction to the whole of 1 En or to the first "book"[50] and partly as an introduction to the text under discussion. This introduction begins with a preliminary exordium in 1,2*a* ("he took up his parable

[47] W. BACHER, *Die älteste Terminologie der jüdischen Schriftauslegung* (1899), 14 f.; G. AICHER, *Das AT in der Mischna* (1906), 118 ff.; J. Z. LAUTERBACH, Talmud Hermeneutics, *Jew. Enc.* XII (1906), 32 f.; S. LIEBERMAN, *Hellenism in Jewish Palestine* (1950), 49 ff.; SEELIGMANN, op. cit., 159 ff.; E. STARFELT, *Studier i rabbinsk och nytestamentlig skrifttolkning* (1959), 50 f., 93 ff. Cf. M. KADUSHIN, *The Rabbinic Mind* (1952), 61 ff., and DOEVE, op. cit., 65 ff.

[48] I hope to have a later opportunity of publishing a more comprehensive collection of analyses of this kind.

[49] I deliberately refrain from making several of the various detailed observations which could be made, for example, as regards the variant readings and the relations to the readings of the OT versions.

[50] See CHARLES, *Book of Enoch*, 2, and HAMMERSHAIMB, trans., 69.

and said"), but then further information about Enoch and the secrets he learned of is inserted as a parenthesis. This information is certainly determined, as regards its content, by what is to be discussed later on but is also influenced by the Balaam sayings in Nu 23 f., with which this exordium in 1,2a is also linked.[51] After 1,9 comes 2,1, the content of

---

[51] Although this introduction is not one of the "pericopes" I am dealing with here, I give the following analysis of it.

1,1 *The word of blessing* of Enoch, *how he blessed*	Dt 33,1
the elect righteous who will be	Is 45,4 65,9, 15,22
in the day of tribulation	Jr 16,19 Ob 14 Na 1,7 Hb 3,16 Zph 1,15
to remove all the enemies;	Na 1,2 (LXX)
and the righteous will be saved.	Ps 18,28 Is 10,20 Ez 14,14 Dn 12,1

The Greek version used above has, in my opinion, preserved the original reading in second line from the end. We then get a play upon words which gives the significance of the "day of tribulation" (יום צרה): on that day the "enemies" (צרים) will be removed. CHARLES (*Book of Enoch*, ad loc.) thinks instead that the Greek is corrupt. For the expression "elect righteous", cf. 1 QH II.13. (It has a Mandaean parallell pointed out by G. WIDENGREN in a review article in *J. Royal As. Soc.* 1961, 125.)

1,2 And *he took up his parable* *and said*	Nu 23,7 24,3		
—Enoch, a righteous man, *whose* *eyes were opened by God*—*he* *saw the vision of the Holy One* in the heavens,	Nu 24,4		
which the angels showed me; and from them I heard every- thing, and from them I under- stood as I saw,		Dn 8,15 ff. 10,12 ff.	Nu 22,31
but not for this generation, but *for a remote one, which is for* *to come.*	Ps 78,4 ff.		

The associations here probably proceed from the fact that the following text is characterized as a parable (παραβολή, משל). Thus it has been natural to employ

which differs from that of 1,3–9, which can thus be treated as a separate unit.

The pattern of thought encountered here says nothing about an evil time which will be the background and preparation for the divine intervention (B). This intervention is made by God Himself and is accompanied by judgement (C), punishment for sinners (D) and general joy for the faithful (E). The stress is placed mainly on the theophany (B) and on the description of the future joy of the faithful (E). We shall now see how this general pattern of thought is combined with the more specific associations in the making of this oracle.

		Zch 2,13 (17)	
1,3b. The Holy great one *will* *come forth from His dwelling*,	Is 26,21 Mi 1,3		
4. and the God of the eternity[52] *will tread (upon the earth)*[53]	Am 4,13 Mi 1,3		
on Mount Sinai,		Ex 19,11, 20	
		Dt 33,2 Dn 7,10	
and appear with (Gr. from) His hosts (encampment)[53]			Ne 9,6
and appear in the strength of His might from the heaven (of heavens).[53]	Hb 3,3 f.		Ps 148,4

The sayings in 1,3b and 4 are based on Mi 1,3, which describes a theophany which introduces punishment for Judah and Israel: "Behold, Yahweh is coming forth out of his place, and will come down (ירד) and tread upon the high places of the earth." It may surprise the reader to find that it is on Sinai that this theophany preceding the universal judgement is to take place. The association leading to this specification of the location has presumably been made via identity of key-words and similarity of motif. In Ex 19 a theophany like that in Mi 1 is described and God "comes down" (Ex 19,11 ירד) on a mountain.

The continuation in 1,4 is linked with Dt 33,2: "Yahweh came from

the wording from Nu 24,3: "he took up his parable and said". But the context of Nu 24,3 gives the stimulus for a closer description of Enoch and his message from what is said of Balaam in v. 4. This is supplemented by material from narratives of Daniel's visions. The validity of these messages for the age in which the author lived is expressed in terms of Ps 78,4 ff. This is an example of association on account of context (we shall meet with more of these below): the main idea of משל is to be found in v. 2 of Ps 78: "I will open my mouth in a parable" (במשל). Otherwise Balaam, both amongst the Jews and in the early Church, was the type of the wicked and idolatrous man; see K. G. Kuhn, Βαλαάμ, *Theol. Wörterb.* I (1933), 521–23, and P. Janzon, Nikolaiterna i NT och i fornkyrkan, *Svensk Exeg. Årsbok* 21 (1956), 82–108.

[52] See above, 72, note 2.

[53] This is the Greek reading. For the Greek variant in 1,5, see above, 72, note 4.

Sinai ... he shone forth from Mount Paran, he came from the ten thousands of holy ones''. The step in this direction was taken via the common motif: God appears on Sinai. The same motif also attracted the writer in Hb 3,3, which also concerns a theophany, this time from Mount Paran, which served as a key-word from Dt 33,2, where the same mountain is mentioned.

5. And all shall fear,		Ex 19,16	Is 29,23
		20,18	Mi 7,17
		Hb 3,6	
and the watchers shall quake,[54]			
and fear and great trembling shall seize them unto the ends of the earth.		Ps 67,8	Ex 15,10
6. And the high mountains shall be shaken,		Ex 19,18	
		Jdc 5,5	
		Is 64,1,3	
		Na 1,5	
and the high *hills shall be made low,*	Is 40,4		
	Hb 3,6		
and *shall melt like wax before the flame.*	Ps 97,5	Ps 68,3	
	Mi 1,4		
	Is 64,2 (LXX)		
7. And *the earth shall be rent in sunder,*	Hb 3,9	Is 24,19	
		Hb 3,6	
and all that is upon the earth shall perish,		Gn 7,21 ff.	
and there shall be a judgement upon all.[55]		Ps 7,9 96,13 Is 66,16	
		98,9	
		Jr 25,31	
		Dn 7,10	
		Jl 4,2	

Here it is largely the same texts which provide the raw material, viz. Ex 19, Mi 1 and Hb 3.[56] We presumably have here a collection of Biblical

[54] I take the similarity with the LXX reading of Thr 4,14 to be a coincidence: ἐσαλεύθησαν ἐγρήγοροι αὐτῆς (TM נעו עורים). These allusions and the use of OT texts which are almost quotations are in the majority of cases not picked out atomistically from a context which does not deal with a related subject or a subject interpreted as being related, in comparison with the present apocalyptic text. See below, 126. The watchers mentioned in Thr 4,14 in all probability do not have anything to do with the watchers of 1 En, who are angels. See, for example, 10,9, 15; 12,22 ff.; 13,10. See BIETENHARD, *Die himmlische Welt*, 210.

[55] The Eth. adds "and upon all righteous", which in HAMMERSHAIMB's opinion (trans., ad loc.) is a dittography.

[56] Possibly the step from 1,6*b* to 1,6*c* was taken via a play upon words: 1,6*b* in linked with Hb 3,6: "the high hills are made low" (שֵׁחוּ from שחח). The LXX here reads שָׂחוּ (from שיח): ἐτάκησαν, "they melted". 1,6*c* says precisely that the mountains will melt, though alluding to OT passages which use a different word than שיח (which moreover is not to be found at all in TM).

motifs and texts which are in part made topical by 1,3–4 and which ramify out from the idea that God will come in a theophany to judge. The fear mentioned in 1,5 is the constantly recurring reaction on the part of man and the rest of the creation in the presence of the divine revelation.

8. But with the righteous He will make peace,	Nu 6,26	Ps 85,9	Is 9,6 f. Hg 2,10
and will protect the elect,	Nu 6,24		
and mercy shall be upon them,	Nu 6,25	Ps 67,2 Is 49,13 Am 5,15	Tob 13,9 Sap 3,9 4,15
and they shall all belong to God,		Ex 19,5 Jr 30,22 31,1 32,38 Ez 11,20 Ho 1,9 f.	Ps 100,3
and they shall be prosperous,		Ps 1,3 Jr 32,39	Is 48,5
and they shall be blessed,[57]	Nu 6,24	Ps 24,5 67,2	
and (the) light (of God)[58] shall appear unto them,	Nu 6,25	Ps 67,2 80,4, 97,11 Is 9,2 60,1 f.	Is 62,1 f.
(and He will make peace with them).[59]	Nu 6,26		

This description of the future felicity of the elect is introduced here in virtue of the pattern of thought, in which the fate of the wicked is in contrast with the considerably pleasanter lot of the godly.

On closer inspection it turns out that this pasage has so much affinity with the Aaronite blessing that it is possible to assume that we have here a paraphrase of Nu 6,24–26. In that case Nu 6,24–26 was interpreted as dealing with the blessing of God's faithful people in the time of consummation.[60] What makes this assumption somewhat uncertain is the fact that, although a large number of key-words in the text certainly have equivalents in Nu 6, 24–26, they are arranged in a different order.[61]

Some not entirely dissimilar paraphrases are to be found in the Manual of Discipline and Formulary of Blessings of the Qumran sect.[62] The

[57] The Gr. adds "and he shall aid all and shall help us".
[58] The bracketed words not in the Gr.
[59] Not in the Eth.
[60] Cf. RIESENFELD, Jésus transfiguré, 211; see also VOLZ, Eschatologie, 384.
[61] It is noteworthy that the longer Greek reading in the last line actually extends the text so that the whole of Nu 6,26 is continuously paraphrased.
[62] 1 QS II.2 ff. And cf. the blessings in 1 QSb and their relations to the OT (TH. H. GASTER, The Scriptures of the Dead Sea Sect, 1957, 113 ff.). For Nu 6,24–26, see

116

Manual follows the OT text more closely than 1 En 1; in the Formulary the text is somewhat freer. The great difference is that in the Qumran documents the paraphrase also is explicitly a blessing.

9. And behold! *He comes with ten thousands of His holy ones*	Dt 33,2	Dn 7,10		
to execute judgement upon all,		Dn 7,10	Ps 96,13 Jr 25,31 Dn 7,26 Ml 3,5	Dt 10,18
and He will destroy the ungodly,		Is 66,15 f. Jr 25,31	Ps 1,5	
and *He will convict all flesh* of all that the sinners and the ungodly have done and committed against Him.[63]	Is 66,16 f. Jr 25,31			

Here we are back in the theophany again. At the end of 1,7 the approaching judgement was briefly indicated. Here it is a subject of greater interest (owing to the pattern of thought?).[64] The connection with the preceding theophany is established in words from Dt 33,2, a passage which was discussed previously. With it is now associated Dn 7,10, which has a motif in common with Dt 33,2, viz. the great court of heaven. To this we must add the circumstance that both in Dt 33,2 and in the context of Dn 7,10 it is said that God "comes" (אתה).

The judgement connected with this theophany is mentioned in terms which resemble in part those in Is 66,15 f. and Jr 25,31. One possible explanation of this associational interweaving is that Is 66,15 f. takes up from Dt 33,2 the motif that God "comes" (יבוא), supplies the motif that Yahweh will execute judgement on all flesh" (נשפט . . . את כל בשר) and then leads on to Jr 25,31, where the same phrase is to be found.[65] Jr 25,31 is then made to help in wording the description of the destruction of the ungodly, which is also indicated in Is 66,16 f. ("those slain by

esp. 1 QSb II.22–III.21. Cf. also M. GERTNER, Midrashim in the NT, *J. Sem. Stud.* 7 (1962), 273 ff. (Lk 1,76–79 a midrash on Nu 6,24–26).

[63] The Gr. reads for the last few lines: "and He will convict all flesh of all the works of ungodliness which they have ungodly committed, and of the hard words which they have spoken, and of all that ungodly sinners have spoken against Him". The last two clauses are reminiscent of Dn 7,25: the last horn's insolent speech against God, for which it is condemned. If there is a positive relation between the present variant and this Dn passage, this reading is in the same field of association as the first lines of 1,9, where the judgement scene is modelled on Dn 7,10 ff. The present 1 En passage is quoted in a similar form in Jd 14 f.

[64] In theophany texts it is common for a judgement to be mentioned, for example, in Ps 96,13; Mi 1,2 ff.; Ml 3,5.

[65] Only these two passages.

Yahweh shall be many; they shall come to an end altogether"; Jr 25,31: "the wicked he will put to the sword").

One question suggests itself: have those who translated this text shown that they had noted these associations with the OT by linking them with "their" translation of the Bible? I am not in a position to give any opinion about the Ethiopic text,[66] but we also have a Greek version of the present text and there it seems as if the translator missed most of the echoes from the OT. The only ones which are like any Greek version of the Bible (the LXX) are a couple of very striking passages, viz. the turn of phrase from Nu 24,4 in 1 En 1,2 and the phrase about the melting wax in 1,6.

Thus, we have been able to note in 1 En 1,3–9 that the numerous echoes from the OT are probably not unconnected with each other and that the connection is established partly via motif and key-word associations and partly on the basis of the underlying pattern of thought.

3. 1 En 46,1–8

Here we find ourselves among the parables. The context is as follows. The present section is demarcated from the preceding one, in which the second parable begins in 45,1, primarily by the content: 45,1–6 forms a separate whole in which the subject and speaker is God. V. 46,1 introduces a section in which, on the other hand, the speaker is the visionary himself. After 46,8 there seems to be a formal fresh start in the threefold "in those days" which introduces the description of the judgement in 47–48.[67]

The content of the oracle is as follows. The visionary sees the Head of Days and the Son of Man (1) and has his vision commented on by an angel, who gives a more detailed description of the Son of Man (2–3). The Son of Man accuses and punishes sinners and mighty ones (4–6), whose wickedness is described (7–8).

46,1. And *there I saw One who*   Dn 7,9
    had a head of days
and *His head was white like wool,*   Dn 7,9
and *with Him* was another *being,*   Dn 7,13
    whose countenance had the ap-
    pearance of a man,
and his face was full of gracious-   Jdc 13,6   Dn 10,6
    ness like one of the holy   1 Sm 29,9
    angels.   Zch 12,8

---

[66] Cf. above, 18.
[67] See above, 63.

2. And I asked one of the angels who went with me and showed me all the hidden things
  Dn 7,16 Is 6,6
    8,13 Zch 2,2

concerning that Son of Man who he was, and whence he was (and) why he went with with the Head of Days.
  Dn 7,16

Thus the author here relates what he "saw"—if he saw anything—in terms clearly borrowed from Daniel's vision of God and the Son of Man.[68] In so far as the secrets are explained by the visionary questioning an angel (46,2), the narrative technique is also linked with the same passage in Daniel.

A comparison of the face of the Son of Man with that of an angel is linked with his presentation in 46,1 in terms derived from Dn 7,13. This comparison may have been inspired by the fact that immediately afterwards (46,2) an angel plays a part in the narrative. However, it may also be worth noting that this comparison is often used in the OT of David.[69] This is shown especially in Zch 12,8; in the time of salvation the house of David will be as a god, as Yahweh's angel. Thus this late text seems consciously to adopt the David epithet from the earlier texts. There seems to me to be good reason for assuming that the present text also does not use this comparison by chance.

If the above assumption is correct, this comparison would mean that the Davidic Messiah was identified with the Son of Man. In that case it was also this underlying identification which made the association possible, supported by the presence of the Daniel angel on the scene further on in the text.

3. And he answered and said unto me:
  Dn 7,16   Gn 23,5
                     41,16

this is the Son of Man who has righteousness,
  Jr 23,5 f. Is 9,6 f. Is 53,11
    33,15 f.   11,3 ff.
         Zch 9,9

with whom dwells righteousness,
         Is 32,16 Is 1,21

and who reveals all treasures of that which is hidden,
  Is 45,3

because the Lord of Spirits has chosen him,
  Is 42,1 1 Sm 16,10 Is 45,3 f.
   43,10   ff.
   49,7

---

 [68] M. BLACK (The Eschatology of the Similitudes of Enoch, *J. Theol. Stud.* 3,1952, 3) calls 1 En 46 "a midrash on Dan. 7,13".

 [69] 1 Sm 29,9; 2 Sm 14,17, 20; 19,28. J. COPPENS (Le Fils d'homme daniélique..., *Ephem. Theol. Lovan.* 37, 1961, 15 f.) thinks, as many other scholars too (see the refs. ibid.), that the expression places the Son of Man among the angels.

and whose lot has the preemi-nence before the Lord of Spirits in uprightness for ever.	Ps 2,8 f. 16,5 f.

The angel's answer combines in a revealing way OT motifs which were evidently all associated with each other in their application to the Son of Man, because they were seen to be applied to the same divine ruler.

The Son of Man is described here as "he who has righteousness" Cf. Jr 23,5 f.: Yahweh shall "raise to David a righteous (צדיק) branch, who shall execute judgement and justice (צדקה) in the land ..., and his name is 'Yahweh our righteousness' (צדקנו)'" and Jr 33,15: the branch of righteousness (צדקה) grown up to David shall execute judgement and justice (צדקה) in the land.[70]

It is possible that the expression "righteousness dwells with" (the Son of Man) goes back to Is 32,16, which says of the coming time of salvation that then "the judgement (משפט) shall dwell (שכן) in the wilderness and the righteousness (צדקה) shall dwell (תשב) in the fruitful field". Even though this association may only be assessed as possible, the association with the Jeremiah passages on the Righteous Branch is a probable one.

The next "station" for the associations between the attributes of the Son of Man is Is 45,3. The Son of Man "reveals all treasures of that which is hidden". In Is 45,3 the Lord says to Cyrus, His anointed "I will give you the treasures of darkness and the hoards in secret places" (אוצרות חשך ומטמני מסתרים). The association seems undeniable.

When later the Son of Man is said to be chosen by God, he is again given the epithet from Deutero-Isaiah, in which the Servant is very often said to be chosen by God.[71]

In the relatively broad description of the divine ruler which we have hitherto encountered in this pericope, the author has accordingly applied to the Daniel Son of Man epithets which in the OT are applied to David, the Davidic Messiah, the Righteous Branch and the Servant of Yahweh. From this we may reasonably suppose that he started from a Biblical interpretation which identified these figures with each other.[72]

---

[70] Cf. Midr. Ps 21 (J. Bowman, The Background of the Term 'Son of Man', *Exp. Times* 59, 1947/48, 287).

[71] The fact that the attribute "Elect" naturally ranges itself amongst other attributes of the Son of Man, derived from different passages in the OT, occasions a certain hesitation in relation to the attempts to prove that there are different sources in 1 En Sim, in which texts concerning the Elect One would be distinguished from those concerning the Son of Man. Cf. above, 39, note 28.

[72] Nevertheless I feel dubious about the correctness of a conclusion from this that amounts to saying that this Son of Man was a suffering Messiah. In the intertesta-

	Is 14,9	Ps 2,2	Is 49,7	Is 52,15
4. And this Son of Man whom you have seen, shall *raise up the kings and the mighty* from their seats, and the strong *from their thrones,*				
and shall loosen the reins of the strong		Ps 2,3	Is 52,2	Ps 116,16
and *break the teeth of the sinners.*	Ps 3,8		Ps 58,7	

It is difficult to distinguish the path from the foregoing description to the echoes from Is 14,9.[73] However, one quite conceivable process of association is as follows. One of the texts which mentions how the Servant was chosen by God is Is 49,7. However, the same verse also says that kings shall arise (קָמוּ) in the presence of the Servant.[74] This arouses associations with the rebellious kings in Ps 2 and also with the kings in Sheol in Is 14,9, who are raised up (הֵקִים) from their thrones. It is this latter passage that is responsible for the wording, and this allusion to a section on enemies who are punished in Sheol is not alone. This particular theme occurs later on in 46,6 and there the contact with Is 14 is re-established.

However, it is the fact that these kingly enemies rise up that leads on to the saying about loosening the reins, which was probably inspired by Ps 2,3. In that case it was the context of Ps 2,3 which was the point of attachment for the associations (Ps 2,2: "the kings of the earth stand up" (יִתְיַצְּבוּ, Targ. קָיְמִין), followed by v. 3: "let us burst their bonds and cast their cords from us"). The context indicates that this reply should be thought of as coming from the rebellious kings.[75] But, as there is no

mental period the interpretation of *ebed* in Deutero-Isaiah is not uniform and the same witness does not give all the *ebed* passages the same meaning. This is the case with the LXX, and later also with the Targ. Jon. Thus it seems hazardous to me to ascribe *e silentio* to the Son of Man features from other *ebed* texts than those which actually resound in the texts. The idea of a suffering Son of Man is asserted by JOACH. JEREMIAS (Erlöser und Erlösung im Spätjudentum und Urchristentum, *Deutsche Theol.* 2, 1929, 106–19; cf. also id., Zum Problem der Deutung von Jes. 53 im palästinischen Spätjudentum, in *Mélanges ... M. Goguel*, 1950, 113–19, and id., παῖς θεοῦ, *Theol. Wörterb.* V, 1954, 686 f.). Thus also W. MANSON, *Jesus the Messiah* (1943), 173 f.; W. D. DAVIES, *Paul and Rabbinic Judaism* (2nd ed. 1955), 279 f.; ENGNELL, *Biblioth. Orient.* 8 (1951), 187–92. On the other hand, see E. SJÖBERG, Känna 1 Henok och 4 Esra tanken på den lidande Människosonen?, *Svensk Exeg. Årsbok* 5 (1940), 163–83; id., *Der verborgene Menschensohn,* 255 ff. For other refs., see SJÖBERG, *Der verborgene,* ibid., and recently also M. RESE, Überprüfung einiger Thesen von Joachim Jeremias zum Thema des Gottesknechtes im Judentum, *Zschr. Theol. Ki.* 60 (1963), 28 ff.

[73] This allusion seems to make unnecessary the suggestion by TORREY, *J. Amer. Orient. Soc.* 62 (1942), 55 f., of reading "cast down" from an Aram. *yaṭṭēl.*

[74] Cf. above, 90, note 11.

[75] Thus also, for example, Midr. Ps ad Ps 2,3 and Ex R. 50,1 (ad 37,1).

explicit indication in the text that it is these kings who utter this reply, another interpretation was possible. In a period of oppression for the chosen people, when they were waiting for deliverance and the deliverer, it was evidently reasonable to apply the sentence to the shackles the strangers had imposed upon them, shackles which the coming deliverer was expected to break. Thus this little allusion allows us to imagine a combination of the triumphant Anointed One in Ps 2 with the heavenly Son of Man in Dn 7.

It is then perhaps via a motif association that 1 En continues by saying that the Son of Man will break the teeth of the sinners. The passage is an echo of Ps 3,8, in which Yahweh arises and delivers the afflicted man from his enemies. The common motif would then be the divine chastisement of the enemies.[76]

5. And he shall *put down the kings from their thrones and kingdoms,*	Dn 5,20		Is 26,5	Jb 12,18 Is 47,1 Dn 7,26	
because they do not extol and praise Him		Dn 4,27, 34		Dn 7,25	
nor with thankfulness *acknowledge* whence *the kingdom was bestowed* upon them.	Dn 4,22, 29 5,21				
6. And he shall put down the countenance of the strong			Jb 40,11 f. Ps 18,28 Is 2,11 13,11 Ez 21,26	Ps 36,13 Is 52,15 Jr 46,15 Dn 5,21	
and shall fill them with shame,			Jb 8,22 40,13 (LXX) Ps 83,17 Hb 2,16	Ps 35,26 132,18 Ez 7,18	
and *darkness* shall be their dwelling	Jb 17,13				
and *worms* shall be *their bed*	Is 14,11	Jb 17,14		Jb 21,26	
and they shall have no hope of rising from their beds,		Jb 17,15	Ps 41,9	Jb 15,22 Is 38,18 Am 5,2	
because they do not extol the name of the Lord of Spirits.		Dn 4,27	Is 38,18	Dn 7,25	Ps 34,4

After the description in 46,4 of how the kings and mighty ones will be browbeaten by the Son of Man, this theme is carried further in 46,5 with the aid of material from Dn 4 f., which deals with how Nebuchadnezzar

---

[76] The association may have been aided by the fact that the context of several of the previously "quoted" passages speaks of deliverance: this is the case in Is 43,11 f.; 49,8; Jr 23,6; 33,16, as well as in Ps 3,8 f.

was driven from his throne for a time on account of his arrogance. The step to this passage may have been taken via key-words (kings, kingdoms and thrones) and also via the common theme (mighty enemies who have exalted themselves are punished). In both the texts it is moreover the king of Babylon who is spoken of.

The continuation in 46,6 a involves a further development of the same theme of the chastisement of the haughty. The motif is a general one in the OT and if we bear in mind, on the one hand, the slightly vague wordings and, on the other, the manifold translations the text has undergone, we shall realize that it is hazardous to decide whether any particular OT passages have contributed to the present text.[77]

The next few lines are more precise. Here the future fate of these high and mighty ones is described by associations with Jb 17,13 ff. and Is 14,11. It seems likely that the process of association was as follows. These rulers are seized by *hubris* and are put down; they descend into Sheol, just as in Is 14 Babylon is overwhelmed by the same fate.[78] Is 14 was topical above in the discussion of 1 En 46,4 and may have remained in the author's mind. Is 14,11 says of Babylon that "worm is spread (יֻצַּע רִמָּה) under you, and worms (תּוֹלֵעָה) cover you". This is reflected in 46,6 ("worms shall be their bed"). However, רמה and יצע, as key-words, lead on to Jb 17,13 ff. and these verses moreover colour the lines in 46,6.

---

[77] One conceivable process of association would be as follows. In Dn 4,34 and 5,19, 22, i.e. in close connection with the passage just quoted, it is stated that the King of Babylon did not "humble" his heart, and that he could "humble", "put down", whom he would. The verb which is used in all the passages is שפל (Aram.). This context may have suggested the theme of how God "humbles, puts down", (שפל) the arrogant. Among the OT passages that have this theme is Jb 40,11 ff. in which it is said (v. 11): "look on every one that is proud, and abase him" (הַשְׁפִּילֵהוּ) and continues (v. 13): "Hide them all in the dust together; bind their faces in the secret place" (פְּנֵיהֶם חֲבֹשׁ בַּטָּמוּן). The LXX reading is "Fill their faces with shame" (ἀτιμίας ἔμπλησον). Cf. G. RICHTER, *Textstudien zum Buche Hiob* (1927), ad loc. This LXX reading corresponds well with the reading of the present text. If it was this passage from Job that lay behind the present text, it must consequently have emanated from a reading which we now only know from the LXX. But after what has happened lately in textual criticism, this need not shock us. (See F. M. CROSS, *The Ancient Library of Qumrân*, 1958, 124 ff.; P. W. SKEHAN, Qumran and the Present State of OT Text Studies; the Masoretic Text, *J. Bibl. Lit.* 78, 1959, 21–25; H. M. ORLINSKY, Qumran and the Present State of OT Text Studies: the LXX Text, ibid., 26–33, and cf. P. E. KAHLE, *The Cairo Geniza*, 2nd ed. 1959, 218 ff.) The theme "hide them in the dust" (Jb 40,13) then merges naturally into the Sheol and sepulchre themes in the continuation.

[78] In Is 14,11 the saved people say to Babel: "Your pomp (גְּאוֹנְךָ) is brought down to Sheol". Ideas such as גאה and גאון are common in the texts listed above as parallels to 1 En 46,6 a. Thus there are several possibilities of finding associative links.

The association between Is 14,11 and Jb 17,13 ff. is connected with the following details in 17,13 ff. V. 14 says: "I say to the worm (רמה): my mother and my sister" and v. 13 mentions "my bed (יצועי) in darkness". That is to say, it was key-words in the context of what was more clearly quoted (in 46,6) that were the point of attachment for the associations.

The following material from Jb 17,13 ff. now provides material for 46,6: v. 13, "Sheol is my *house* (ביתי), I have my bed in *darkness*" and v. 15, "Where is now my hope, my hope, who shall see it?" (cf. 1 En 46,6: "they shall have no hope of rising from their beds").

The following is the order of the actual passages from the OT: Jb 17,13, Is 14,11, Jb 17,14, Jb 17,15. It would then be reasonable to regard Is 14,11 as a temporary deviation from an association series according to Jb 17,13 ff. However, I took another course above, one which I find preferable for the following reasons. The context makes use of Is 14 (v. 9 in 46,4 and v. 13 in 46,7 a). For this reason it is probable that Is 14 was the starting-point. Between the theme of the passage in 1 En and Is 14 there is a connection of motifs which should facilitate the explanation of how the author used Is 14 to give substance to the account in 1 En 46. On the other hand, Jb 17,13 ff. deals with Job's bitter reflections in relation to his future. Finally, we should not be too quick to assume that such association series as we are now trying to analyse will reveal simple straightforward lines of thought.

These motifs from Jb 17,13 ff. have accordingly now been applied to the arrogant rulers. The associations now revert to a previous point of attachment, viz. Dn 4,27 and 34, in which Neduchadnezzar exalts himself in *hubris* (v. 27) and after his punishment expresses his changed state of mind as follows (v. 34): "now ... I praise and extol and honour the king of heaven ... those who walk in pride he can abase (השפלה[79]; cf. "put down" in 46,5 a and 6 a).

7. And these are they who judge the stars of heaven,	Is 14,13			Dn 8,10
and raise their hands against the Most High,	Jb 15,25			
and tread upon the earth and dwell upon it,	Dn 7,19, 23			
and *all their deeds manifest unrighteousness,*	Ez 21,29			
and their power rests upon their riches,	Ps 49,7 52,9	Prv 11,28		
and their faith is in the gods which they have made with their hands,		Dt 4,28 Is 2,8	Ps 115,4 ff.	

---

[79] Cf. note 77 above.

and they deny the name of the Lord of Spirits,	Jr 5,12 Ps 74,10		
8. and they persecute the houses of His congregation	Ex 14,8 f. Ps 69,27 109,16 119,86	Dn 7,25	Ps 74,8
and the faithful who hang upon the name of the Lord of Spirits.		Ps 33,21 52,11	

Thus in v. 7 *a* Is 14 once more, so to speak, comes to the surface. In v. 13 the king of Babylon said: "I will ascend into heaven, I will exalt my throne above the stars of God".

The motif of *hubris* which re-echoes in Is 14,13 connects with each other the text passages which probably contributed to the continuation in 46,7. In Jb 15,24 f. it is said of the wicked man that "distress and anguish terrify him, ... because he had stretched forth (נטה) his hand against God and bids defiance (יתגבר) to Shaddai". The context of Dn 7,19 and 24 mentions how the fourth beast "spoke great things" (v. 20), and how the last king "shall speak words against the Most High" (v. 25). The beast "stamped the residue with his feet" (v. 19) and it is said that the kingdom which it represents will "devour the whole earth, and trample it down, and break it into pieces" (v. 23). Thus, finally, this motif of *hubris* being punished is also to be found in the context of Ez 21,29, which contributed some wording to 46,7: in Ez 21,31 the Lord says to the wicked prince "abase (השפיל) that which is high (הגבה)".

Finally, Ps 52,9 has also been drawn in here, presumably on account of its context. It says of him who boasts of mischief: "See the man who did not make God his refuge (מעוזו), but trusted in the abundance of his riches, and strengthened himself in his wickedness" (יעזו בהותו). This pride also expresses itself in all kinds of evil speaking (vv. 4–6; cf. Dn 7,20, 25, quoted above).[80]

The remainder of 1 En 46,7 f. certainly contains OT motifs, but I have found it impossible to fix upon any precise OT passages which were used and from which it may be possible to trace how they were combined.

This analysis of 1 En 46 has revealed a somewhat different structure than that of 1 En 1,3–9 (analysed above), in that here the pattern of thought about the events of the last days does not seem to guide the creative process to the same extent. On the other hand, we may expect that nevertheless a certain conception moulded and formed a framework for the interweaving of the motifs. The section shows a clear structure: the Son of Man appears (46,1), he is presented in greater detail (2–3),

---

[80] It is this context that leads me to assume that it is Ps 52,9 and not Ps 49,7 that resounds here.

his relation to the arrogant rulers is made clear (4–5), the punishment he is to give them is stated (5–6) and their wickedness is described in detail (7–8).

One peculiar phenomenon is the contextual associations, i.e the fact that links are made from one text to another via the context of either or both. This shows that the OT texts were not regarded here in so atomistic a fashion as it is often assumed was the case in contemporary Judaism.[81] A typical wording from a text draws with it its context,[82] so that this context may form a spring-board or goal for a new association. In this connection I may also point out that practically 100 % of the OT passages to which allusion is made "fit", i.e. they have not been lifted out of their contexts and have not had their meanings radically altered.

The two texts which we have analysed so far are both from the preChristian period.[83] However, we may also glance at a couple of portions of text from a somewhat later period.

4. *Ass Mos 10,1–10*

Ass Mos can be dated with considerable certainty in a period which approximately coincides with Jesus' public ministry or immediately prior to it.[1]

The context is as follows. In ch. 8 "the king of the kings of the earth" appears. There is a period of distress, persecution and torture. In ch. 9 the mysterious Taxo is introduced;[2] he exhorts his sons not to

---

[81] See, for example, MOORE, *Judaism* I, 248; F. MAASS, Von den Ursprüngen der rabbinischen Schriftauslegung, *Zschr. Theol. Ki.* 52 (1955), 148; E. E. ELLIS, Jesus, the Sadducees, and Qumran, *NT Stud.* 10 (1963/64), 275; RUSSELL, *Method and Message*, 179 f. But cf., for example, KADUSHIN, *The Rabbinic Mind*, 98 ff.

[82] Cf. DODD, *According to the Scriptures*, passim, BRUCE, *Biblical Exegesis in the Qumran Texts*, 68 f., and S. L. EDGAR, Respect for Context in Quotations from the OT, *NT Stud.* 9 (1962/63), 55–62. For a downright criticism of Edgar's views, see R. T. MEAD, A Dissenting Opinion about Respect for Context in OT Quotations, *NT Stud.* 10 (1963/64), 279–89.

[83] As regards 1 En Sim, opinions are divided, as is well known, but as regards the other parts of 1 En, discussion would seem to be superfluous. See above, 19 f.

[1] CHARLES in *Pseudepigrapha*, 411, and C. CLEMEN in KAUTZSCH, *Apokryphen* II, 313 f.

[2] See, for example, C. C. TORREY, "Taxo" in the Assumption of Moses, *J. Bibl. Lit.* 62 (1943), 1–7; id., "Taxo" Once More, ibid. 64 (1945), 395–97; H. H. ROWLEY, The Figure of "Taxo" in *The Assumption of Moses*, ibid., 141–43. It would seem that the problem has been solved from the Qumran texts, where מחוקק is supposed to be the equivalent of τάξων. See S. MOWINCKEL, The Hebrew Equivalent of Taxo in Ass. Mos. ix, *Suppl. Vet. Test* 1 (1953), 88–96; M. DELCOR, Contribution à l'étude de la législation des Sectaires de Damas et de Qumrân IV: Le Meḥoqeq du document de Damas et Taxo dans l'"Assomption de Moïse" IX, *Rev. Bibl.* 62 (1955), 60–66, and cf. ROWLEY (*Relevance*, 149 ff.), who is doubtful.

apostatize and with them dies for his faith. Ch. 10 begins by describing God's intervention. Together with the rest of ch. 10, this context corresponds to the pattern of thought isolated above, viz. *A* (evil times), which may include Satanic empires which will persecute the faithful in the period preceding *B* (the divine intervention). This intervention will involve judgement and punishment for the enemies of God's people (*C, D*; 10,7 and 10) and will lead to the exaltation and joy of the godly (*E*; 10,8–9).[3]

Ass Mos reaches its culmination in 10,10 and the conclusion begins with 10,11. We are again set in the narrative framework of the book, in which Moses instructs Joshua on the eve of his departure from this life: the content here is that Joshua must preserve the book along with what Moses has just said (10,11 ff.).

Within the framework of this pattern of thought there is a definite theme—God's theophany for vengeance—around which the detailed motifs in ch. 10 are clustered. We shall see that here it is not possible to find very many association paths, in the sense that, within a certain ruling pattern, we may distinguish how one detail provides another in complete chains. Here the individual details are rather grouped around certain main motifs, i.e. instead of the image of a chain, we could select that of a key-ring with keys hanging from it.

10,1. Et tunc *parebit regnum*	Is 40,9		Ps 102,17	
illius	(Targ.)		Is 60,2	
in omni creatura illius,		Is 40,5		
et tunc diabolus[4] finem habebit,				Dn 7,26
et tristitia cum eo adducetur.		Is 35,10		
		51,11		
2. Tunc implebuntur manus		Dn 12,1		
nuntii qui est in summo constitutus,				
qui protinus vindicavit ab inimicos eorum			Dt 32,43	Is 35,4
			Is 1,24	
			Na 1,2	

One gets the impression that what inspired the author here was a targumic interpretation of a Biblical text. At any rate it is Targ. Is which, although it is a late work, explains how material from Is 40 and Is 35 was combined here. In Targ. Is, Is 40 and Is 35 are combined, because

---

[3] Cf. above, 55 ff.

[4] The MS. reads *zabulus*. Professor G. WIDENGREN has informed me that in the next edition of *Sakrales Königtum* he intends to amend his suggestion as regards *zabulus* (88 f.), and to adopt the usual reading *diabolus*; *z-* instead of *di-* is a not uncommon phenomenon in Vulgar Latin (see E. DIEHL, *Inscriptiones latinae Christianae veteres* I, 1961, 237, § 1223 (*zaconus — diaconus*)).

the interpretative paraphrase makes them both expressly deal with the deliverance of God's people and their restoration to Sion. The result is that the two chapters also have key-words which connect them together, besides their common theme. Thus, in Is 40,2, the Targ. reads: "She (sc. Jerusalem) is about to be filled with the people of her exiles" (מעם גלותהא), in 35,6: "the exiles of Israel (גלותא דישראל) gathered", and in 35,10: "the redeemed of the Lord shall be gathered together from among the exiles (מביני גלותהון) and shall enter into Sion". In 40,3 furthermore the Targ. speaks not of "Yahweh's way" but of a way (אורחא) before the people and of treading down paths (כבישו ... כבשין) for it. This increases the affinity with Is 35, where in v. 8 the Targ. speaks of a trodden and straight way (כיבש אורח ותיקון), in which the redeemed walk.

It would seem to be obvious that the first two lines and the last line in 10,1 received their motifs from these two texts. Line 1 reproduces a paraphrase of Is 40,9 like that in the Targ. In Is 40,5 we read that "the glory of Yahweh shall be revealed" and that "all flesh shall see it together" (line 2 in the above analysis: *in omni creatura illius*). The last line is linked with Is 35,10: "sorrow and sighing shall flee away" (Targ.: "shall cease").

It is even possible that the line *"tunc diabolus finem habebit"* may be anchored in Is 35,9. The Biblical text says of the above-mentioned way: "No lion shall be there, nor any ravenous beast shall go up thereon". The Targ. interprets this as follows: "no king that does evil shall be there, and no ruler that oppresses shall march thereon". A similar paraphrase may conceivably have given us the line on the devil's end.[5]

That "God's kingdom shall be revealed" implies vengeance. In 10,2 it is (probably[6]) Michael who has this task delegated to him. Here two OT motifs are brought together: on the one hand, the vengeance which in the OT God Himself is to wreak and, on the other, Michael's appearance, in accordance with Dn 12,1, in the transition from the period of the last great Satanic empire (Dn 11,21 ff.; Ass Mos 8) to the time of salvation (Dn 12,1 ff.). This divine vengeance is mentioned in Is 35, on which we have just been dwelling: v. 4 says "God comes with vengeance" (נקם יבוא).

---

[5] The Targ. may conceivably have started from the comparison of bad rulers with ravening lions and other beasts (see, for example, Jr 50,17, Ez 22,27, and Zph 3,3). If the present text goes back to a comparison between the Devil and a lion, it has a parallel in 1 Pt 5,8, where reference is made to the OT and the Devil is compared to a ravening lion. However, this comparison is quite unique in the Bible. Cf. W. MICHAELIS, λέων, *Theol. Wörterb.* IV (1942), 256–59.

[6] See, for example, the edition by R. H. CHARLES (1897) and C. CLEMEN's trans. in KAUTZSCH, *Apokryphen* II (1900), ad loc. But cf. T. W. MANSON, Miscellanea Apocalyptica, *J. Theol. Stud.* 46 (1945), 43 f. (*nuntius* = Eliah).

3. [Exur]get enim caelestis a sede regni sui		Nu 10,35 Ps 12,6 68,1; 76,10 Is 2,19 14,22 28,21	1 Rg 9,5
et *exiet de habitatione* sancta *sua*	Is 26,21 Mi 1,3	Zch 2,13 (17)	Dt 26,15 Is 63,15
cum indignatione et ira[7]		Is 13,13 Na 1,5 f.	
propter filios suos,			
4. et tremebit terra, usque ad fines suos[8] concutietur,		Is 13,13 Ps 59,14 Na 1,5 f. Jl 2,10 Hb 3,6	
et alti montes humiliabuntur		Is 2,12 ff. Mi 1,4 40,4 Hb 3,6	
et concutientur		Is 5,25 64,1, 3 Na 1,5 Hb 3,6	
et convalles cadent.[9]		Ez 38,20 Mi 1,4	

It is obvious that the description of this theophany is built up of OT material. It is principally Mi 1,3 f., Na 1,4 ff. and Is 13,13 which seem to have supplied this material. Motifs have been taken sometimes from one text and sometimes from another, in most cases without our being able to say which. It is more the author's own conception which structures the passage than the associations with OT texts, even though this conception is expressed with the aid of associated OT motifs.

5. Sol non dabit lumen et in tenebris convertent se cornua lunae		Is 13,10 Jl 2,10 3,4; 4,15 Zch 14,6	Ez 32,7
et confringentur			
et tota *convertit se in sanguine*	Jl 3,4		
et orbis stellarum conturbabitur[10]		Is 13,10 Jl 2,10 4,15	Sap 13,2
6. et mare usque ad abyssum decedet[11]		Na 1,4 Ps 114,3 Ps 107,26 Is 19,5	

---

[7] The MS. has the acc. after this *cum*.

[8] The MS. reads *suas*.

[9] I cannot accept CHARLES's conjecture: see above, 73, note 10.

[10] MS. *conturuauitur*.

[11] MS. *-it*.

et[12] fontes aquarum deficient		Ps 18,16 f. Ho 13,15	Ps 42,2
		Is 19,5	Jl 1,20
		Ez 30,12	
		Jl 1,20	
et flumina expavescent,	Na 1,4	Ps 114,3	

After the earth's trepidation at this time has been described in 10,4 with details from a batch of theophany texts, there comes in 10,5 the turn of the heavenly phenomena, a picture in which the colours are mainly taken from Jl, though Is 13, v. 13 of which was echoed in 10,3, may have contributed something here from v. 10.

In 10,6 attention is called to the waters, which retire at God's revelation of Himself. Perhaps this motif was taken primarily from Na 1,4: "He rebukes the sea and makes it dry and dries up all the rivers". The theophany in Na 1 was also mentioned in connection with 10,2–4. But here again it is true to say that the author's line of thought seems to move along a quiet path, which directs attention to the effect of the revenging theophany first on the earth, then on the heavens and finally on the waters. The OT is adduced rather than forms the narrative itself.

7. quia exurgit summus deus		Nu 10,35	Dt 33,27
aeternus		Ps 76,10	Dn 6,26
		Is 2,19, 21	Su 35
		14,22	(LXX)
et palam veniet ut vindicet		Ps 59,6	
gentes		96,13	
		Is 3,13	
		26,21	
et *perdet omnia idola* eorum. Mi 1,7		Ez 30,13 Is 2,20	

The description of the results of the theophany in 10,4–6 was introduced in 2 and 3 with a mention of Michael's vengeance and of God rising and leaving His habitation in wrath. This has a pendant here on the other side of the theophany. The motifs are all perfectly of the OT type but are nevertheless so general that it is not possible to trace the exact texts.

8. Tunc *felix eris tu Istrahel*	Dt 33,29		
et ascendes supra cervices	Dt 33,29		
	(Targ.)		
et alas aquilae	Is 40,31		
	(Targ.)		
et inplebuntur,	Is 40,2?		
9. *et altabit te* deus	Ps 37,34		
et faciet te haerere[13]		Ps 37,34?	Is 14,13 1 Rg 8,39
			Dn 12,2

---

[12] MS. *ad.*

[13] MS. *he-.*

130

caelo stellarum
loco habitationis earum,[14]
10. et conspicies[15] a summo et   Ps 37,34   Ps 91,8
    videbis[16] inimicos tuos in ter-   92,12
    ra[17] et cognosces et gaudebis   118,7
    et ages[18] gratias et confitebe-   Is 66,14,24
    ris creatori tuo.

In 10,8*a* we have what is probably a deliberate echo of Dt 33,29, which concludes Moses' blessing on the plains of Moab and is followed by the narrative of his death, i.e. it has largely the same place as in the present text. The author has read a variant which is repeatedly vouched for outside TM.[19]

The next line also (on *alas aquilae*) probably goes back to a targum. At any rate Targ. Jon. on Is 40,31 may be translated "they shall mount on the wings of eagles".[20] The interpretation in Targ. Is of the end of Is 40 is in good accord with Ass Mos 10: it mentions that the ungodly shall stumble, that they who have waited for the salvation of the Lord shall be gathered from among their exiles.

As regards the composition of this section, we have here a kind of circular composition. We have already noted that 2–3 and 7 are parallel to one another. Now there arises in 8 an association with the same text (Is 40) with the same themes as we noted in 10,1. Indeed, the effect is a kind of chiasmus.[21] This effect is strengthened if Cheyne's conjecture in the next line is correct as regards content (*et inplebuntur dies luctus tui*,[22] which should be connected with Is 40,2: "her warfare is accomplished"). Further phenomena which fit well into a chiasmus like this are those in 10,1 (*tristitia adducetur*) and 10,10 (*gaudebis*) and the association with Dn 12,1 f.,[23] which is probable at the beginning and admissible at the end.

---

[14] MS. *eorum*.

[15] MS. *conspiges*.

[16] MS. *vides*.

[17] MS. *terram*.

[18] MS. *agis*.

[19] LXX, Targ. Jon., Targ. Onk., Pesh., Vulg. See Charles, ed. Ass Mos, 42.

[20] Charles, ed., ad loc. The text reads דסליק על גדפי נשרין. J. F. Stenning (ed. Targ. Is., 1949) translates instead as: (feathers) "that come up on the wings of eagles".

[21] On such composition patterns in the OT, see N. W. Lund, *Chiasmus in the NT* (1942), 3–136, and Carlson, *David*, passim. See also B. Thiering, The Poetic Forms of the Hodayot, *J. Sem. Stud.* 8 (1963), 189–209.

[22] In *Pseudepigrapha*, ad loc., Charles disregards his earlier acceptance (ed. of Ass Mos, ad loc.) of this conjecture and suggests others. J. Bonsirven (*La Bible apocryphe*, 1953, ad loc.), however, has accepted it.

[23] These observations argue against the assumptions that 10,1–2 are a later insertion, as Charles suggests in *Pseudepigrapha*, ad loc.

Finally, it seems probable to me that, in its description of the future joy of the elect, 10,9 f. takes its starting-point from Ps 37,34:[24] "He shall exalt you to inherit the land; when the wicked are cut off, you shall see it" (וירוממך לרשת ארץ בהכרת רשעים תראה). There may be some doubt about 9b (*haerere*; MS. *herere*): has the translator, whose proficiency in Latin is not exactly impressive, rendered κληρονομεῖν by this word? The whole psalm has a content which should have facilitated the taking over of material for the present section: God will cause misfortune to befall the wicked, but the righteous shall inherit the land.[25]

If we now look back at the portion of Ass Mos analysed, we see a very coherent text which makes use of OT material in what appears to be a well-considered composition. This material is taken from texts whose contents were evidently interpreted as dealing with the same subject as Ass Mos 10. In other words, we find here also a faithfulness to the context similar to that which we noted above.[26] This picture can be supplemented by saying that the text gives indications that the author has made use of a text recited in public worship in an interpretative translation or of a textual exegesis which was represented also in a later targum. As regards the texture of this OT material, I would like to revert to the image I mentioned at the beginning, the image of the key-ring, to which are attached units which are little related to each other. The pattern of thought and the composition guide the OT associations and these associations have in common only what unites them to Ass Mos, viz. the common theme.

5. *4 Ez 6,13–28*

With 4 Ez we advance a generation further forward in time compared with Ass Mos, to a period after the fall of Jerusalem.[27] The context is as follows. The second vision begins in 5,20. Within its framework the question, who will bring about the final visitation, is asked in 5,56 and this question is answered. In 6,7 the question, where is the boundary between the present and the future age, is asked and the answer is the puzzling saying about Esau's heel, which Jacob held on to.[28] From 6,11 onwards

---

[24] It is possible that Is 40,21 and Ps 37,34 are connected by a main word, but, if so, the main word is not a particularly marked one, for the phrase is common. Is 40,31 has קוי יהוה and Ps 37,34 קוה אל יהוה.

[25] The psalm is given a similar interpretation in 4 QpPs 37, though the interpretation has not been preserved as far as v. 34.

[26] See above, 126.

[27] See EISSFELDT, *Einleitung*, 849.

[28] See A. STROBEL, *Untersuchungen zum eschatologischen Verzögerungsproblem* (1961), 37 ff.

the theme is the last signs of the end. After the present pericope the author reverts in 6,29 to the framework narrative which concludes this vision.

In this section stress is placed on the signs of the end, as is also indicated by the introductory petition for knowledge of the signs (6,11 f.), but an equally large amount of space is occupied by the description of the joy in the time of salvation. These two themes (*A* and *E*, to use the notation given in Chap. I) predominate in 6,20–24 and 25–28 respectively. But other parts of a pattern of thought are also perceptible: the signs precede God's intervention (*B*; 6,18), when He will call the wicked to account (*C, D*; 6,19).

13. Et respondit et dixit ad me: *Surge super pedes tuos*		Ez 2,1	Dn 10,11	Dn 8,18		
et audies vocem plenissimam sonus.			Dn 10,6	Ez 1,24		
14. Et erit, si commotione commovebitur *locus in quo stas super eum* 15. in eo quoloquitur,		Ex 3,5	Is 6,4			
tu non expaveas,	Dn 10,12					
quoniam *de fine* verbum,	Dn 8,17,19					
et fundamenta terrae intelleget,[29] 16. quoniam de ipsis sermo;						
tremescit et commovebitur,					2 Sm 22,8 Ps 82,5 Is 13,13 24,18	
scit enim, quoniam finem eorum oportet commutari.			Ps 102,27			
17. Et factum est, cum audissem						
et surrexi super pedes meos			Ez 2,2; 3,24 Dn 10,11			
et audivi, et ecce vox loquens,			Ez 2,2 Dn 10,9	Ez 3,24		
et sonus eius *sicut sonus aquarum multarum.*		Ez 1,24 43,2				Is 17,13 Jr 51,16

This section forms an introduction to what is to come, in which divine secrets will be revealed to the prophet. The way in which this introduction is linked with the OT reveals, to my mind, a desire on the part of the author to give his own message the same character as is inherent in the revelations which, according to the OT, were received by the men of God of earlier times, especially Daniel and Ezekiel and presumably also Moses and Isaiah.[30] Thus 6,13–15 and 17 contain material from the descriptions

---

[29] So with the Syr. (ܡܣܬܟܠ); Lat. *intellegetur*. See VIOLET's ed., ad loc.

[30] The pseudonomity is part of the same psychological picture. See, for example, RUSSELL, *Method and Message*, 130 ff.

of Daniel's visions in Dn 8 and 10 and of Ezekiel's in Ez 1 ff. In addition, there are fragments of the story of Moses and the burning bush (Ex 3) and probably also from Isaiah's vision in Is 6.

6,16 seems to expand the motif of the trepidation of the place, partly by extending this trepidation to apply to the foundations of the world and partly by giving an explanation of why they tremble—they are afraid at the prospect of their destruction. We noted above[31] that the earthquake in 4 Ez 5,8 had no direct connection with a theophany and was "tamed" into a sign of the end. Here the connection with the theophany remains to a certain extent, in so far as the earth shakes when God speaks, but the explanation which is given breaks up the connection considerably. It is not because God speaks that creation trembles but because it knows that soon it must come to an end.

18. et dicit: ecce dies venient				Jr 7,32; 9,25
et erit, quando appropinquare		Is 40,10		
incipio		Ml 3,5		
ut *visitem habitantes in* terram,	Is 26,21	Is 13,11	Ps 89,33	
			Is 24,21	
			26,14	
19. et quando inquirere in-		Is 13,11		Gn 9,5
cipiam ab eis qui iniuste no-		26,21		Dt 23,21
cuerunt iniustitia sua,				
et quando *suppleta fuerit humi-*	Is 40,2			
litas Sion,				
20. et cum supersignabitur			Jb 9,7	
saeculum,				
quod incipit pertransire,			Gn 6,17	
			Ps 102,27	
			Dn 7,26	
haec signa faciam:				

This little section, which relates in one breath what it is that the signs portend, is dominated by the author's ideas about the last days. The few clear associations with the OT are taken from texts which describe how God "comes" and further motifs in 18 and 19*a* have parallels in such texts, without there being on that account any clear connection with one text or the other.

20*b*. *Libri aperiuntur*	Dn 7,10		
ante faciem firmamenti		Ez 1,22 ff.	
et *omnes videbunt simul*	Is 40,5	Ez 20,48	Ps 97,6
21. et anniculi infantes loquen-		39,21	Is 52,10
tur vocibus suis,			
et praegnantes immaturos pa-			
rient infantes trium et quat-			

---

[31] See above, 76.

22. et subito apparebunt semi- nata loca non seminata			Jr 2,2	
et plena prumptuaria subito in- venientur vacua;		Jr 17,13 Ho 13,15 Jl 1,17		
23. et tuba canet cum sono,	Am 3,6 Jl 2,1	Is 18,3 27,13		
quam cum omnes audierint subito expavescent.	Am 3,6 Jl 2,1	Ex 19,16		
24. Et erit in illo tempore debel- labunt amici amicos ut ini- mici	Is 19,2	Zch 14,13	2 Ch 20,23 Is 3,5 Jr 9,4 f. Zch 8,10	
et expavescet terra cum his qui inhabitant eam;		Jr 51,29 Ps 33,8	Ps 76,9	Ps 24,1
et venae fontium stabunt, ut non decurrant			Ps 74,15 Jr 51,36 Ho 13,15	
in horis tribus.			Dn 12,7	

In 20*b* we are referred to Daniel again, as well as to Ezekiel's vision
in Ez 1 f. The three OT passages underlying 20*b* may be associated with
each other as follows. Both Dn 7,9 ff. and Ez 1,22 ff. reproduce a vision of
the Supreme Being upon the Throne. In the Daniel vision it is related
that judgement is passed and "books are opened", and in Ez 1,22 ff. it
is in the "firmament" that Yahweh's glory (כבוד) appears. But in Is
40,5 it is just Yahweh's glory (כבוד) that is revealed "and all flesh shall
see it together".

As regards the "signs" presented in 6,21, we have only to note that
they do not seem to go back to the OT.[32] 22*b* has certain OT parallels,
23 is connected with Jl 2,1 (Am 3,6) which deal with the day of Yahweh,
and the motif of the internal struggle in 24*a* has a similar context in Is
19 and Zch 14.

25. Et erit omnis qui derelic- tus fuerit ex omnibus istis, quibus praedixi tibi, ipse sal- vabitur		Is 4,2 f. 10,22 37,22 Ez 14,22 Jl 3,5	Ps 91,15 Is 11,11,16
t videbit salutare meum t finem saeculi mei.	Ps 91,16	Ps 50,23 Ez 7,2 ff. Dn 8,19 12,13	

---

[32] A. Kaminka, Beiträge zur Erklärung der Ezra-Apokalypse, *Monatsschr. f.
Gesch. u. Wiss. d. Jud.* 77 (1933), 347, thinks that they are interpolated. Cf. L.
Gry, Essai sur la plus ancienne teneur et la fortune du Catalogue des Signes de la
Fin, *Rev. Sci. Phil. Théol.* 29 (1940), 264 ff.

26. Et videbunt, qui accepti sunt homines qui mortem non gustaverunt a nativitate sua			Gn 5,24 2 Rg 2,11 Si 48,9 49,14	
et mutabitur cor inhabitantium et convertetur in sensum alium	Ml 4,6	Ez 11,19 36,26	1 Rg 18,37 1 Ch 29,18	Ex 14,17 1 Rg 18,37 Ps 105,25
27. Delebitur enim malum,			Is 11,9 Ps 7,10 37,9	
et extinguetur dolus,			Jb 18,5 Zph 3,13	
28. florebit autem fides,	Ps 85,12		Ps 72,7 92,13	
et vincetur corruptela, et ostendebitur veritas, quae sine fructu fuit tantis temporibus.			Is 38,19	

Here again one has the impression that the author's belief as regards what is to happen some day results in his having a secure hold on the narrative. Here and there, there peeps forth a hint of a closer association with the OT, but it would seem to be obvious that here we are at a considerably greater distance from the OT than was the case in the texts analysed previously.

Many—indeed the majority—of the motifs are certainly from the OT but, considered against the background of the preceding texts, this passage from 4 Ez gives the impression of representing an apocalyptic *tradition*, in which the motifs originally taken from the OT have now lost any distinct associations with it. We saw above in Chap. III (the interpretation of the stone which struck the colossus with feet of clay[33]) that the author nevertheless draws water out of the well of the OT and have found instances of it in the analysis of the introduction to the present section, for which Daniel and Ezekiel supplied basic material. (Perhaps it was more than a coincidence that it was in both cases Daniel in particular which was the subject of interest.)

Another feature which shows the reverence of the author of 4 Ez for the OT is the zeal for the Law which is evidenced here, more clearly than in the majority of these texts.[34] Nevertheless the impression which was

---

[33] Cf. above, 97. And see D. SIMONSEN, Ein Midrasch im IV. Buch Esra, in *Festschrift I. Lewy* (1911), 270–78 (on 4 Ez 7,132–139).

[34] 4 Ez 3,19 ff.; 7,72, 81, 94; 8,29; 9,31 ff.; 13,54. And see, for example, MUNDLE, *Zschr. At. Wiss.* 47 (1929), 227 ff. This is not to say that the authors and redactors of other apocalyptic texts under discussion had a negative attitude to the Torah: see W. D. DAVIES, *Torah in the Messianic Age and/or the Age to Come* (1952), 39 ff.

received above in Chap. III is confirmed—the impression of an apocalyptic tradition which has established itself and which is sometimes overlaid with layers of new material derived from the OT.

Concluding Remarks

What follows now is not a summary, gathering together for the reader the results of the preceding discussions and drawing certain conclusions. On the contrary, I want to widen the field of vision a little and indicate some consequential problems into which the analyses debouch and for the assessment of which they are relevant.

First of all, however, I would remind the reader of the limitations placed on the inquiries made in the previous chapters. The selection of pericopes which provides the material for Chaps. I and II is a relatively ample one. But Chaps. III and IV are concerned with a very limited selection: two motifs isolated—though they occur quite commonly—and four pericopes analysed. Even if I had devoted more space to presenting more analyses in Chap. IV[35] and thus produced more examples of texts structured by and with the aid of OT material, a "gap" would arise, as regards demonstrating the influence of the OT on the literature under discussion. The clear allusions and the distinct motif associations are certainly undeniable proofs that the authors used the OT, and used it thoroughly, but, as regards the patterns of thought, we cannot in most cases go further than seeing parallels to them in the OT. In isolated cases (as in 1 En 90,13 ff. and Or Sib 3,663 ff.),[36] a distinct dependence of the composition on the OT is demonstrable, but in the majority of cases this is not so. I only find it probable that the observable associations with details in the OT indicate that the parallels to the patterns of thought in the OT may also mean that the authors were dependent on the OT in these respects too. This is nevertheless a point at which it would seem to be realistic to expect a broad background to these texts, including a large number of factors (religious, psychological, cultural and others), several of which would seem to be impossible to establish objectively. As I pointed out in the introduction, however, I have restricted myself to trying to determine the association with the OT and the part played by the OT in these texts as they exist at present. The fact that I deliberately neglected to examine my material genetically and comparatively is ex-

---

Cf., for example, G. H. Dix, The Enochic Pentateuch, *J. Theol. Stud.* 27 (1926), 29–42, and G. Hölscher, Problèmes de la littérature apocalyptique juive, *Rev. Hist. Phil. Rel.* 9 (1929), 101 f.

[35] Cf. above, 112, note 48.
[36] See above, 81 ff. and 91 ff.

plained by the necessity for concentration and is not a denial that it can and should be examined in this way.

I mentioned at the beginning of Chap. IV that the Qumran texts were rapidly investigated, as regards at any rate a number of problems concerning their relation to the OT.[37] We may now ask ourselves whether the ways in which the authors of the texts under discussion here made use of the OT have any counterpart in the writings left behind by the Qumran sect. In order to get at least a preliminary answer to this question, I have extracted a few passages which disclose, even at a rapid glance, an abundance of echoes of the OT. Hence they would scarcely seem to be typical of the Qumran texts in this respect. I have examined these passages in the same way as I did the texts in Chap. IV. They are the War Scroll (1 QM) XI. 8–15, and XII. 7–16, and the Thanksgiving Psalms (1 QH) III.7–36.

It appears that a number of phenomena from the apocalyptic texts are recognizable. Thus, there are contextual associations between OT allusions or quotations,[38] and likewise it happens that such associations are linked with one another by key-word associations.[39] We also find examples of the phenomenon that probably *one* OT text, so to speak, carries a portion of text, but the actual expressions are taken from other OT texts.[40]

However, differences are also noticeable. Firstly, of course, there is the fact that in these Qumran texts we find ourselves on what is textually much safer ground. As regards the use of the OT, there seems to be a substantial difference in relation to some of the passages investigated in Chap. IV, in that the OT material is, so to speak, more passive. (In other words, the situation is reminiscent of that in Ass Mos 10.[41]) It is the author who decides: the text is logically built up and the thought

---

[37] See above, 104, and note 7, ibid.

[38] 1 QM XII.11: "Place 'your hand on the necks of your enemies' (Gn 49,8) and your foot on the heaps of the slain; 'smite the nations that oppress you' (Nu 24,8)". In the context of both Gn 49,8 (v.9) and Nu 24,8 (v.9) we read: "he couched as a lion, and as a lioness; who dares rouse him up?". The Hebrew is largely identical in the two passages. They are both eschatologically "loaded" in the Qumran texts: cf. 1 QSb V.27–29; 1 QM XI.6 f.; 4 QTest. 9–13; CD VII. 19 f.

[39] 1 QM XII.14 f.: "'All that have afflicted you shall bow down to you' (Is 60,14) and ['they shall lick] the dust (15) [of your feet'] (Is 49,23)". In both these texts the enemy is abased at the feet of the victor (רגלך), and in both "he falls down" (Is 60,14 השתחוו, Is 49,23 ישתחוו).

[40] Is 60,5–14 "carries" 1 QM XII.12*b*–14, but does not come up to the surface, so to speak, until XII.14. Cf. CARMIGNAC, *La Règle de la Guerre*, ad loc., E. NIELSEN (in E. NIELSEN and B. OTZEN, *Dødehavsteksterne*, 2nd ed. 1959), ad loc., and Y. YADIN, *The Scroll of War* (1962), ad loc.

[41] See above, 132.

moves methodically from one main motif to another. When these main motifs are to be put into writing, the OT text is adduced, often only in the form of phrases and terms, while the author himself is more actively and consciously responsible for the images and the lines of thought. The result is that these OT phrases and indeed whole sentences are adopted to serve the author's purpose and in their original context they may refer to quite different matters than those the author uses them for. This accordingly points in another direction than the contextual associations and the rule in the texts analysed above, that quotations and allusions do not radically alter their meanings when they are transferred to the apocalypse. In the Qumran texts, on the other hand, the author does not seem always to have borrowed from the OT with any sense of fidelity to the context of the passages borrowed. (Moreover the *pesher* exegesis of the Qumran sect also shows an atomistic manner of regarding and using the Scriptures.) Thus the War Scroll describes God's army in XII.9 by a term from Ez 38,9,16, which in its original context describes Gog, and in XII.11 it says of the army of the children of light (or of God?) "take your booty", an expression which in the OT is only used of the enemies of God's people.[42]

This gives us reason to recur briefly to the reflections above as to the different degrees of consciousness in authors in their choice of means of expression. In analysing some pericopes in Chaps. III and IV, I surmised that the OT material the author had learned was "active", i.e. the author's own conscious selection of associational material was not particularly noticeable, but he followed, so to speak, consciously or unconsciously, the associations between the OT materials stored in his mind. In the Qumran texts it seems as if we are at the other end of the scale. Their authors' way of working leads J. Carmignac to write: "It is understandable that the author should be satisfied with his work when he concluded this hymn with its fine poetic flight ...: in less than ten lines he succeeded in cramming in about thirty quotations".[43]

This fact—that the apocalyptic texts reveal so profound a dependence on the OT, not only in language and style but also as regards internal structure and details in the description—gives us reason to touch upon the question of the origin of the apocalyptic and eschatological ideas, especially the idea of the Son of Man. To restrict the argument to the latter, it has often been assumed, ever since W. Bousset,[44] that Iranian ideas of the primordial man were more or less transferred to Jewish literature. A

---

[42] Is 10,6; Ez 29,19; 38,12 f.

[43] CARMIGNAC, op. cit., 185.

[44] W. BOUSSET, *Hauptprobleme der Gnosis* (1907), 209 ff., 219 ff.; id., *Religion* (2nd ed. 1906), 301 ff., 404 ff. See the surveys of research in STAERK, *Die Erlösererwartung*, 422 ff., and in MOWINCKEL, *He That Cometh*, 422.

modern protagonist of a similar idea was S. Mowinckel.[45] On the other hand, it has been asserted that domestic Jewish ideas concerning the sacral kingship (I. Engnell[46]) or other OT concepts are sufficient as a basis of explanation.[47]

It would seem to be clear that 1 En contains much that it is natural to assume external inspiration for, for example, many of the celestial and astronomical speculations.[48] *Per analogiam* we should therefore expect a similar state of affairs also as regards the themes which are "spun" around the Son of Man. But there are a couple of "buts". One is the fact that the OT supplies both the warp and the weft in the fabric of the Son of Man texts examined.[49] Practically all the *anthropos* features that may be enumerated for the Son of Man in 1 En Sim can be traced back, in the form they have there, to the OT in the way we traced them above, and it is obvious that at least two texts are also based directly on Dn 7,10 ff. The other "but" is that, if an original *anthropos* myth lies behind these texts, it has, figuratively speaking, been broken into fragments as a myth. In that case several of these fragments may certainly be found in these texts but with Jewish OT overpainting.

Nevertheless it seems to me that these two "buts" are not sufficient to deny the possibility of external influence. However much Dn 7 and other OT passages may have inspired 1 En Sim, whence comes the idea of the heavenly Son of Man in Dn 7 and the markedly individual interpretation of this passage? Even Daniel tells of Jewish contact with all kinds of Chaldaean wisdom and it is probable that the cultural conditions were such that the Jews knew of and were influenced by Iranian religion.[50]

Combining the phenomenological and cultural data with the above analysis, I am led to assume that Jewish contact with Iranian ideas gave rise to the idea of the Son of Man, but that this idea took on its own form, coloured by the saturated Jewish and OT tradition.[51]

---

[45] S. MOWINCKEL, Opphavet til den senjødiske forestilling om Menneskesønnen, *Norsk Teol. Tidsskrift* 45 (1944), 189–244, and id., *He That Cometh*, 420 ff.

[46] ENGNELL, *Biblioth. Orient.* 8 (1951), 190 ff., and id., Människosonen, *Svenskt Bibl. Uppslagsverk* II, 229–32.

[47] For example, GLASSON, *Second Advent*, 14 ff., and COPPENS, *Ephem. Theol. Lovan.* 37 (1961), 17 ff.

[48] See, for example, P. GRELOT, La géographie mythique d'Hénoch et ses sources orientales, *Rev. Bibl.* 65 (1958), 33–69, and id., La légende d'Hénoch dans les apocryphes et dans la Bible, *Rech. Sci. Rel.* 46 (1958), 5–26, 181–210.

[49] They are not isolated: I have analysed most of the Son of Man texts in 1 En Sim and the picture is the same in all of them.

[50] BOUSSET, *Religion* (2nd ed.), 548; WIDENGREN, *Suppl. Vet. Test.* 4 (1957), 197–241, and id., *Iranisch-semitische Kulturbegegnung in parthischer Zeit* (1960).

[51] MOWINCKEL's views (*He That Cometh*, 425 ff.) do not seem to differ so much from this, when he has put forward all his modifications.

This leads us on to a further question, a question of great and fundamental importance but which can only be indicated here. The motifs worked over in the preceding pages, above all in the last two chapters, may largely be described as mythical elements.[52] It is interesting to note that these mosaics are made up of fragments of myths and that, because they are fragments, they may have varying functions. We had some examples of this in Chap. III above.[53] On the other hand they may—because they are mythical fragments (both mythical and fragments!) —be put together in order to describe a figure or an event, in such a way that they seem to contradict one another. This sometimes led the textual editors of later times to amend the texts so that they agreed with the coherent myth which the editor wished to find! One example is the twofold attacks in 1 En 90,13 ff. discussed above[54] and another is the way in which the Son of Man is endowed with both Davidic Messianic attributes and with that of Wisdom in being pre-existent.[55] This means that these mythical fragments may have begun to be transformed into parts of a symbolic language.

This is not the place for an investigation of the extent to which this transformation from myth in fragments to symbolic language took place in the works of these authors or of how far they were conscious that the myth fragments expressed something beyond or other than the straightforward words. But it is probably clear that, for example, the statements about God's "coming" to earth in 1 En 89 f.[56] was understood as symbolic language. The authors were certainly as alien to anthropomorphism as this. What is more, these statements were given an image function, by being placed within the framework of a vision.

It would seem to be beyond all doubt that there was a transformation of the myth in fragments to symbols, at any rate here and there. In other words, they were used in speaking with human and worldly concepts of what was apprehended as divine and transcendent. A conceptual material was then used which was regarded as having been sanctified by the transcendent God, viz. material taken from the Holy Scriptures.

---

[52] On the notion, see, for example, WIDENGREN, *Religionens värld*, 132 ff.; J. SLØK, Mythos und Mythologie I, *Rel. in Gesch. u. Geg.* IV (1960), 1263–68 (refs.), and J. HAEKEL, Mythos und Mythologie II, ibid., 1268–74 (refs.).

[53] Cf. I. HERMANN, *Begegnung mit der Bibel* (1962), 29 ff.

[54] See above, 81 ff.

[55] 1 En 46,1 ff.; 48,3. Nothing is said about his co-operation in the Creation. Cf. SJÖBERG, *Menschensohn*, 88 ff., and MOWINCKEL, *He That Cometh*, 371 f., 430.

[56] 1 En 89,16, 20; 90,15, 18. See also 1 En 1,4.

PART TWO

Traditio-Historical Analyses of the
Eschatological Discourse

The Eschatological Discourse in the Gospels of Mark and Matthew in Relation to the OT, Especially Daniel

1. *Introduction*

A glance at the eschatological discourse in Nestle's edition of the NT shows that the editors have printed in bold type a number of echoes from and allusions to Daniel. In this chapter we shall see that these four or five references are not coincidences but, on the contrary, reveal an association with Daniel which in other respects upholds and inspires the main part of this "discourse". After a short introduction to the actual texts in Daniel, I will examine the eschatological discourse in the Matthew–Mark version in the same way as I analyzed several Jewish texts in Chap. IV above and the knowledge which we gained as to how OT associations may be interwoven in the most complicated patterns may here be of advantage.

In the introduction to his version Mark makes Peter, James, John and Andrew ask (13,4): "Tell us, when will this be, and what will be the sign when these things are all to be accomplished?" (μέλλη ταῦτα συντελεῖσθαι πάντα). This seems to be a conscious allusion to Daniel 12,7 on the part of the evangelist. In this passage Daniel asked (v. 6) how long it would be till the end,[1] and the angel answered "that, when the shattering of the power of the holy people comes to an end, all these things would be accomplished" (LXX συντελεσθήσεται ταῦτα πάντα).

A man who posed Daniel's question at the beginning of the Christian era could go to the Book of Daniel and there also find sayings as to what "all these things" were. The questions raised in later times about Daniel's isagogic problems would not, of course, have worried him, neither those on the consistency of the book nor those on how the different military enterprises, the horns and the beasts are to be related to history.[2] Instead he would in all probability have taken seriously the statements in the book that parts of its content refer to the end of time[3] and the

---

[1] The passage is a doubtful one; see A. BENTZEN (2nd ed. 1952) and O. PLÖGER (1965), *Comm.* ad loc.

[2] See on this point O. EISSFELDT, *Einleitung* (3rd ed. 1964), 693 ff., and the references given there.

[3] Dn 8,17, 19; 9,26 f.; 11,27, 35, 40; 12,4, 9, 13.

fact that dreams and visions end with sayings that the kingdom of God will be set up and/or the power of evil will be cut off for ever.[4] Above all, the following sections from Daniel would presumably have come into the foreground, viz. 2,27–45 (Nebuchadnezzar's dream of the great image, and its interpretation), 7,2–27 (the vision of the four beasts, of the Ancient of Days and the Son of Man, and its interpretation), 9,22–27 (Gabriel interprets Jeremiah's prophecy of the seventy years' captivity), and ch. 11–12 (the *angelus interpres* speaks of the kingdoms of the north and the south, of attacks on the people of God and of their afflictions and the final deliverance).

A man who meditated on these texts would find that they overlap to a great extent; they are all concerned with similar matters and on these points may complement each other.[5] A glance at the Daniel texts just quoted shows that they are connected together by a no means paltry number of similarities. Thus the four kingdoms appear in ch. 2, 7, 8 and 11; a last king appears and acts blasphemously and speaks "great words" against God (ch. 7, 8 and 11);[6] he intrudes upon the cult worship (ch. 7, 8, 9 and 11)[7] and scourges and persecutes the chosen people (ch. 7, 8, 9 and 11);[8] he will be destroyed (ch. 2, 7, 8, 9 and 11); that will be the end of time (ch. 8, 9, 11 f.); God's kingdom will be set up (ch. 2 and 7, cf. 12). In addition there are a number of details which connect these texts.[9] It would therefore be almost unnatural if these pericopes, which from the beginning were so closely associated with each other, were not also readily kept together in the exposition.[10]

Before I enter upon a detailed examination of the relationship between the eschatological discourse and the Daniel pericopes, I will briefly establish the existence of certain resemblances in the picture as a whole given in both the texts. A brief synthesis of the accounts of the events of the last

---

[4] Dn 2,45; 7,14, 18, 27: the kingdom of God; Dn 2,45; 7,11, 26; 8,25; 9,26 f.; 11,45: the evil is cut off.

[5] Cf., for example, B. RIGAUX, *L'Antéchrist* (1932), 151–68, and PLÖGER, op. cit., 54 ff., 118 f., 130 f., 143, 172 ff.

[6] Cf. Dn 3,5 ff.; 4,22 ff.; 5,18 ff.; 6,7 f.

[7] Cf. Dn 5,2 ff.

[8] Cf. Dn 3,12 ff.; 6,16 ff.

[9] For example, דקק Dn 2,40, 44; 7,7, 19, 23; רמס–רפס Dn 7,19; 8,10; הצליח Dn 8,12, 25; 11,36; והדקת (· · ·) די לא בידין Dn 2,34, 45 — באפס יד ישבר Dn 8,25; השחית Dn 8,24 f.; 9,26; שמם Dn 8,13, 27; 9,26 f.; 11,31; 12,11; מרמה Dn 8,25; 11,23; גדל Dn 8,4, 8–11, 25; 11,36 f.; נחרצה Dn 9,26 f.; 11,36; a time, two times, and half a time, Dn 7,25; 12,7.

[10] This manner of regarding the texts is the background of the rabbinic rule בנין אב, which is mostly used for halakic exegesis but is also applicable to the haggadah. See W. BACHER, *Die älteste Terminologie der jüdischen Schriftauslegung* (1899), 9 ff., and H. STRACK, *Introduction to the Talmud and Midrash* (1959), 93 f.

days given in these Daniel texts would be roughly as follows. After the four empires which have succeeded each other, in part during wars, a warlike ruler will appear, who will also attack Palestine, blaspheme against God, persecute the faithful ("those who are wise"), seduce some of God's people into apostasy and desecrate the Temple by "the abomination of desolation". Finally he will be destroyed when God's kingdom is set up (the Son of Man) and those who have held out will be saved for the eternal kingdom. The order of these events varies. The texts are written in a prophetic style, mostly within the framework of the description of a vision with the interpretations added. A parenetic element is perhaps to be found, but it does not occupy a prominent position in these particular pericopes.[11]

If we compare this with the eschatological discourse in the Mark and Matthew version, we find certain similarities of content. There we read of war, catastrophes, persecutions, apostasy (Mt), the abomination of desolation, false Messiahs and false prophets and lastly the arrival of the Son of Man and his ingathering of the elect. The parenetic feature is prominent and the prophecies often do duty as reasons for parenetic sayings, for example, Mt 24,6 "be not alarmed, *for* this must take place". There are no obscure references to time, such as "a time, two times, and half a time", and the figure of the warlike and blasphemous king does not appear.

I shall now pass on to analyse the use of the OT and especially of the Book of Daniel in the eschatological discourse according to Mark and Matthew. In doing so, I leave aside some sections, which will instead be examined later in this chapter (sections 3–4).

2. *A Preliminary Survey*

A. Mk 13,5*b*–8/Mt 24,4*b*–8

Take heed that no one leads you astray.	Jr 29,8	
/5[12] (For + *Mt*) many will come in my name saying,	Jr 29,9	Dt 18,17 ff.
		Jr 14,14
		23,21,25
"I am (the Christ + *Mt*)"	Ex 3,14	Is 14,13 f.
	Dt 32,39	Jr 48,26,42
	Is 41,4	Dn 7,8,25
	47,8,10	8,10 f.
And they will lead many astray.	Jr 23,13,32	Dn 8,24 f.
	Ez 13,10	11,32

---

[11] Cf. Dn 12,3, 12; on the other hand Dn 3 (and 6).

[12] The italic figures in the translation refer to St. Matthew's Gospel.

			Dn 12,4[13] Mi 3,5	
7/6 And when you (*Mt*: and you will) hear of wars and rumours of wars,		Dn 7,21 9,26 11,4–27	Jr 51,46 Dn 8,24	Jr 4,19 Dn 2,39 f.
do not be (*Mt*: see that you are not) alarmed;			Jr 51,46	
(for + *Mt*) *this must take place,*	Dn 2,28 f., 45; 8,19			
but the end is not yet.		Dn 11,27	Dn 9,26 11,35	
8/7 For *nation will rise against nation*	2 Ch 15,6	Dn 11,25 ff.		Jr 6,22 51,27 f.
and *kingdom against kingdom,*	Is 19,2	Dn 11,25 ff.		Jr 51,27 f.
(and + *Mt*) there will be earthquakes in various places,		Dn 2,40 LXX?	Is 24,18 f. 29,6 Jr 51,29 Ez 38,19 Dn 2,40 LXX Hg 2,22	
there will be famines;[14]			Dt 28,48 32,24 Jr 14,12 15,2	
8 (all + *Mt*) this is but the beginning of the sufferings (ὠδῖνες).			Is 13,8 21,3 Jr 22,23 25,29	

I leave the first two verses on one side for the time being and begin with Mk 13,7/Mt 24,6 on wars and rumours of wars. Now war is the theme which determines the whole of the first part of Dn 11, in which the north and the south are involved in incessant controversies. We also find it in Dn 11,21 ff., where the "contemptible person" exercises his dominion and in vv. 25 ff. struggles against the king of the south. Dn 9,26 states of the rule of the same prince: "to the end there shall be war" (עד קץ מלחמה). In Dn 7,21 it is also said of the last horn that it made war with the saints.

We encounter the same warlike ruler in Dn 8,23 ff. and there his activity is included in what the angel says to Daniel in 8,19: "I will make known to you what shall be (אשר יהיה, LXX ἃ ἔσται) at the latter end of the indignation" (cf. the δεῖ γενέσθαι in Mk 13,7). Here, however, we may also insert Dn 2,29–45, in which four kingdoms arise and the last one breaks and crushes. This forms part of the dream which in 2,28 f.

---

[13] For the reading, see below, note 83.

[14] *Mt*: there will be famines and earthquakes in various places.

148

and 45 is said to reveal "what shall be" (מה די להוא, LXX ἅ/ὅσα δεῖ γεν-έσθαι, 45: τὰ ἐσόμενα).

It is incontrovertible that the phrase "this must take place" in this text is related to Daniel; it is possible that the war theme may have been inspired by Daniel but without further evidence it is no more than possible.

The position in Daniel is that the war theme, which is only hinted at or briefly mentioned in ch. 2, 7, 8 and 9, is further developed in ch. 11. If, however, we assume that Daniel inspired the war motif in this text, this assumption is immediately reinforced by the following points. The text goes on to say: "but the end is not yet" (οὔπω (ἐστὶν + Mt) τὸ τέλος). We saw that in Dn 9,26 it was said that "to the end there shall be war". In Dn 7,21 the war against the saints passes over into the judgement (v. 22). There should therefore be reason for the expositor of Daniel to try to relate this war to the end of time. This is possible by making use of the verses in ch. 11 which deal with the contemptible person's war against the king of the south (v. 25 ff.): the description of this military undertaking closes (v. 27) with the words: "the end is yet to be at the time appointed" (כי עוד קץ למועד).[15] The words οὔπω τὸ τέλος in Mark must be said to be very closely related to this sentence.

In Mk 13,8/Mt 24,7 this statement about the coming wars is confirmed by further OT passages to which the association moved via the common themes, viz. 2 Ch 15,6 (nation against nation) and Is 19,2 (kingdom against kingdom). The two passages are connected by a common catch-word, which is not to be seen in the Gospel text, namely, the phrase "city against city" (עיר בעיר), which only occurs in these two passages in the OT. The theme which carried the association is perhaps not only that the kingdoms and nations will attack one another but also that in Dn 11 it is Egypt (the south) which is involved in struggle just as in Is 19. The context of 2 Ch refers to great disturbances and distress (v. 5 f.) and also contains the exhortation: "Take courage; do not let your hands be weak, for your work shall be rewarded" (v. 7), that is to say, themes that harmonize well with the text under consideration (v. 8/8 f., 13/13, 19/21).

The verses which follow (v. 8 b/7 b) speak of famine and earthquakes. If we seek for a background for this in the OT, we should probably regard the motifs as loosely associated with this passage from several OT descriptions of times of tribulation and war, possibly with "eschatological" overtones: the enemy approaches, the ground trembles in his presence, famine, pestilences (Lk!) and death are rife and confusion and

---

[15] LXX: ἔτι γὰρ συντέλεια εἰς καιρόν.

fear spread around.[16] These motifs would seem to have formed part of this context, not because the OT texts used gave occasion for it but because these OT motifs had come to occupy a relatively permanent position in the expectations of the distress that would prevail in the last days.

The last line, on the beginning of the sufferings (travail), gives the impression of being a commentary with no direct relationship with the OT.[17]

B. Mk 13,9–13/Mt 24,8–14

In these verses Mark and Matthew go their separate ways. We shall return to the details later and will now only touch on two verses which contain themes and material which are common to both Mark and Matthew.

> (9) They will deliver you up to councils (*9* They will deliver you up to tribulation) ... (13/*13*) But he who endures to the end will be saved.

In the pericopes from Daniel persecutions are also mentioned.[18] This is the case in Dn 7,25, in 8,24 f. and in 11,30 ff., where the description is more extensive. The wording in v. 9/9 παραδώσουσιν may have been influenced by Dn 7,25, which says that the saints "shall be given" into the hand of the last blasphemous king (יתיהבון בידה, LXX παραδοθήσεται πάντα (!) εἰς τὰς χεῖρας αὐτοῦ) for a time, two times, and half a time.

For v. 13 we turn to Dn 11. When the persecutions are described there, v. 32 says: "The people who know their God shall be strong" (יחזקו, LXX κατισχύσουσι). This steadfastness under persecution and apostasy is in good agreement with the Synoptic ὁ ὑπομείνας.[19] That the perseverance will last "to the end" (εἰς τέλος) may link up with the same Daniel text, in which v. 35 says that the wise ones will be chastened "until the time of the end" (עד עת קץ).[20] But also in Dn 7,25 the afflictions under the

---

[16] See, for example, Dt 28,20 ff.; Is 13,4 ff.; Jr 4,19 ff.; 6,22 ff.; 49,20 ff.; 50,41 ff.; Ez 7,5 ff.; Jl 2,1 ff. Though it is scarcely worth basing even hypotheses on, we may note that the image of the woman giving birth (the ὠδῖνες!) is often associated with these tribulations (see, for example, Jr 4,31; 6,24; 49,22; 50,43).

[17] This is so, even though an imaginative Midrashist might conceivably find both "the beginning" and "the travail" in Dn 11,26 חילו, חללים or Dn 9,21 בתחלה.

[18] Cf. PH. CARRINGTON, *Comm. Mk* (1960), 277.

[19] Cf. also Dn 12,12 f., which is stressed by T. F. GLASSON, Mark xiii. and the Greek OT, *Exp. Times* 69 (1957/58), 215.

[20] This is an argument against the idea that τέλος has different meaning here from in v. 7 and means "finally, completely", etc., as is maintained by V. TAYLOR (1952) and C. E. B. CRANFIELD (1959), *Comm. Mk*, ad loc.

blasphemous king are fixed as to duration, and afterwards the end will ensue with the judgement (v. 26).

The fact that those who persevere will finally be saved may either be regarded as a simple supplement to the saying on steadfastness or also related to Daniel. There the last days are referred to in 12,1 as "a time of trouble" from which the chosen will be "delivered". (ימלט).

If we now look back for a moment and ask ourselves what we have so far learned about the relations between the eschatological discourse and Daniel, the answer seems to be that so far a Daniel connection has only been shown to be possible, but that it may be judged to be probable if further and less ambiguous connections with Daniel can be demonstrated.

C. Mk 13,14–20/Mt 24,15–22

14/15 When you see the *abomination of desolation* (spoken of by the prophet Daniel + *Mt*)	Dn 11,31 12,11		Dn 9,27	Ps 74,4	
(*Mk*: set up where it ought not to be)		Dn 11,31			
(*Mt*: standing in the holy place)		Dn 9,27?[21]			Is 60,13
—let the reader understand—				Dn 9,23,25	
16 then let those who are in Judaea *flee to the mountains;*	Gn 19,17	Dn 12,1?	Ez 7,16 1 Mcc 2,28	Jr 50,8 51,6,45 Zch 2,10 f. 14,5	
15/17 let him who is on the housetop not go down (nor enter + *Mk*) to take what is in (*Mk*: anything from) his house;				Ex 12,4 ff. Is 46,2 Jr 10,17 Ez 7,11 ff.	
16/18 and let him who is *in the field not turn* back to take his mantle.	Gn 19,17			Am 2,16	
17/19 And alas for those who are with child and for those who give suck in those days!				2 Rg 15,16 (Is 54,1) Thr 4,4 Ho 14,1 Am 1,13	
18/20 Pray that it may not happen (*Mt*: that your flight may not be) in winter (or in a Sabbath + *Mt*).				Ex 16,29	
19/21 For in those days there will be *such tribulation as has*	Dn 12,1		Dt 31,17,21 2 Ch 15,6	Jr 6,24	

---

[21] Cf. below, note 57.

not been from the beginning of the creation which God created *until now*, and never will be.[22]	Jr 30,7 Hb 3,16 Zph 1,5 ff.	
20/22 And if the Lord had not shortened the days (*Mt*: pass.) no human being would be saved; but for the sake of the elect (whom he chose + *Mk*) he shortened the (*Mt*: those) days (*Mt*: pass.).	Dn 12,1(?)	Dn 9,24 Is 65,9,15

We encounter "the abomination of desolation"[23] in Daniel in passages dealing with persecutions and oppression, which strengthens the possibility of the association of this theme with Daniel discussed above. In the eschatological discourse the concept of the abomination of desolation no longer stands for the Zeus altar set up by Antiochus IV in the Temple at Jerusalem but has other associations, though it is difficult to say exactly which. Bearing the context in mind, both in the Gospels and in Daniel (which was interpreted eschatologically), it seems probable that the symbol in question refers to some form of blasphemy which will characterize the last days.[24] In addition, at least in the text as it now stands, it seems that the devastation of Jerusalem and Judaea was associated with it.[25]

The faithful are now exhorted to flee from this "abomination of desolation". It seems undeniable that this flight is mentioned with allusions to the story of Lot's flight from the overthrow (הפכה) of Sodom, as related in Gn 19. Is it now possible to find out how this association arose? In order to try to find an answer to this question, we will first see how the destruction of Sodom is mentioned in two passages in the OT. Dt 29 refers to Egypt's idolatrous abominations (v. 16 שקוצים): if the people do such things, the wrath of God will strike the whole land (vv. 19–22) in a way resembling that in which Sodom and Gomorrah were overthrown (v. 22 מהפכת ס׳ ועמ׳).

In Thr 4,6 we read: "The iniquity (עון) of the daughter of my people has been greater than the sin (חטאת) of Sodom, which was overthrown

---

[22] Mt has a somewhat different reading.

[23] A new impulse to the interpretation of the expression in Dn was given by E. NESTLE in Der Greuel der Verwüstung, *Zschr. At. Wiss.* 4 (1884), 248, in which he demonstrated the background of בעל שמים.

[24] A. LOISY (1912), E. KLOSTERMANN (4th ed. 1950), E. LOHMEYER (rev. ed. 1953), J. SCHMID (4th ed. 1958), *Comm. Mk*, ad loc., and A. H. M'NEILE, *Comm. Mt* (1915), ad loc. Cf. CARRINGTON, op. cit., 279 f. See also Theodor of Heraclea, *Fragm. 122* (ed. J. REUSS, 1957).

[25] TAYLOR and CRANFIELD, *Comm. Mk*, ad loc.

152

(ההפוכה) in a moment, no hand being laid on it" (ולא חלו בה ידים).26 In these and other examples Sodom is the prototype of grave sin and blasphemy and its punishment is an illustration of how God's wrathful judgement is a merciless destroyer.27

Then we return to the Daniel pericopes. The abomination of desolation is, then, referred to in Dn 9,27, 11,31 and 12,11, in all these passages in connection with the narrative of how the Tamid sacrifice is taken away, a sacrilege which, according to 9,27, will be punished: "Until the decreed end is poured out on the desolator" (עד כלה ונחרצה תתך על שמם).28

The fact that the Tamid sacrifice is taken away, according to Dn 8,11, is interpreted in the same chapter (v. 25) as meaning that the last evil king "shall rise up against the Prince of princes", which continues: "but, without hand (באפס יד), he shall be broken". We would seem to be justified in combining this with Thr 4,6, quoted above, in which Sodom was destroyed "no hand being laid on it", for it seems as if this expression is restricted to the Daniel passages and to Thr 4,6. We may also introduce into the picture the fact that, according to Dn 7,11, the blasphemous beast will be destroyed and given over to be burned with fire.29

If we now combine these details, it seems as if the bridge between the Daniel texts on the abomination of desolation and Gn 19 was the idea that an ungodly or blasphemous place or thing will be destroyed by God's wrathful judgement. This could also answer the question above as to why the text speaks of flight; it is a matter of escaping from God's punishment, the judgement that will befall an ungodly thing.30

If this is the case, it is striking that this judgement is not explicitly mentioned in the text, while it is mentioned in Lk 21,21 f.: "Let those who are in Judaea flee to the mountains ... for these are days of vengeance". 2 Ths 2,8 mentions the destruction of the lawless one, and Lk 17,26 ff. compares the day of the Son of Man with the events around the time of the Flood and with the story of Lot and the overthrow of Sodom in fire and brimstone. That is to say, we find in other passages of the NT a sort of typology which compares the end with the destruction of

---

26 The translation of חול is extremely uncertain: see, for example, W. GESENIUS and F. BUHL, *Lexicon* (16th ed. 1915), sub voce. LXX: οὐκ ἐπόνεσαν ἐν αὐτῇ χεῖρας.

27 See also Is 13,19; Jr 49,18; 50,40; Am 4,11; Zph 2,9. Cf. Lk 17,29; 2 Pt 2,6; Ap 11,8. See also the material in P. BILLERBECK, *Kommentar zum NT aus Talmud und Midrasch* I (1922), 571 ff., III (1926), 785 f.

28 The first words in the Hebrew phrase (כ׳ וג׳) are to be found, apart from Dn 9,26 f., only in Is 10,23 and 28,22, in which God's wrath falls upon "all the earth" (or "all the land").

29 The same destruction awaits the last empire, according to Dn 2,34, 45.

30 Similarly G. HARDER, Das eschatologische Geschichtsbild der sog. kleinen Apokalypse Markus 13, *Theol. Viat.* 4 (1952), 83 ff.

Sodom. In the present text Lot's flight has been lifted from the same comparative text.

V. 19/21 sheds further light on the problem. It does not give the reason for the flight from the place where the abomination of desolation will appear, but the circumstances under which it will take place, in that it speaks of the time of a great trouble (θλῖψις).

The passage quotes Dn 12,1: "At that time shall arise Michael, the great prince who has charge of your people. And there shall be a time of trouble (עת צרה), such as never has been since there was a nation till that time; but at that time your people shall be delivered (ימלט), every one whose name shall be found written in the book".[31]

Thus the situation in the Gospel text is as follows. When the abomination of desolation appears, the faithful must take to headlong flight. This is described with side glances at Lot's flight from Sodom. The faithful are exhorted to pray that the flight may not be in winter, *for* "at that time" (τότε Mt) or "those days" (αἱ ἡμέραι ἐκεῖναι Mk) shall be a trouble. It seems to me highly probable that here we have a fundamental answer to the question above about the flight. Underlying this text is a collocation of passages in Daniel on the abomination of desolation with the description of the time of trouble in Dn 12,1. This text mentions that the faithful shall be delivered—or shall flee—during the trouble, and this is then transposed to become a flight from the abomination, a flight which we find to be patterned in Lot's flight from Sodom. What is more, we may record that the same verb is used of the flight in Dn 12,1 and in Gn 19, namely, nif. of מלט.[32]

At this point we will, for the time being, leave this section, which has proved to a great extent to be based on material from the Daniel pericopes grouped together above. It has attracted other biblical material to itself via thematic associations which presuppose a definite interpretation of the texts used. The connection we found with Daniel (apart from the direct "quotations") must be regarded as strengthening further the possibility of such a connection in the sections previously discussed. We will return later to the verse on the shortening of the time, as well as to some further details.

D. Mk 13,21–23/Mt 24,23–25

(And + *Mk*) then if any one
says to you, "Look, here is the
Christ!" or "(Look + *Mk*), there
he is!",

---

[31] For the use of Dn 12,1 in Jewish texts, see above, 84 f.

[32] Gn 19,17, 19, 20, 22. Moreover we can note the appearing of angels in both texts.

do not believe it.		Dt 13,4,9	Jr 23,16	
22/24 (For + *Mt*) false Christs	Dt 13,2		Jr 2,18	Dt 18,20
and false *prophets will* arise			5,31	Is 9,15
and show (great + *Mt*) *signs*			23,15	
and wonders,				
(so as + *Mt*) to lead astray, if		Dt 13,6 f.		
possible, (even + *Mt*) the elect.		Dn 8,24?		
23/25 (But take heed; *Mk*) (Lo,				
Mt) I have told you (all				
things + *Mk*) beforehand.				

After this point Mt introduces three logia, the first designed as a parallel to v. 23 and typically enough beginning with οὖν, while the second and third are associated with the context by theme. However, the logion in v. 23 ("here–there") is associated in Lk 17,23 f. directly with that in 24,27 (the lightning).

If we now consider Dn 11 f., we find that so far the following have been used or at least have had equivalents in our text: 11,21–30 war, 30–35 persecutions, endurance to the end, the abomination of desolation, 12,1 trouble, flight (deliverance). Ch. 11,36–45 occurs in the middle of this section, where vv. 37 f. say that the evil king "shall give no heed to the gods of his fathers" (v. 37: על אלהי אבתיו לא יבין), that "he shall honour a god which his fathers did not know" (v. 38: לאלוה אשר לא ידעהו אבתיו יכבד).

The Jew who knew his Bible and who read these lines in Daniel at the period in which the discourse came into existence could hardly avoid associating them with the emphatic warnings against idolatry in Dt 13, where v. 7 says "Let us go and serve other gods, which neither you nor your fathers have known" (אלהים אחרים אשר לא ידעת אתה ואבותיך). A check with a concordance shows that the mode of expression which unites the two passages only occurs in them and in Dt 28,64.

The conclusion of this combination between Dn 11,37 and Dt 13 must be that behind our text's allusions to Dt 13 in the description of the misleading signs of the false prophets lies an exposition of Dn 11, which found via a key-word association that the activity of the false prophets was predicted therein. Emphasis is laid on the statement that these men of lies will lead the faithful astray with their signs, a feature which must also have been taken from Dt 13: v. 7 "entice" (סות hif.), vv. 6,11,14 "draw away" (נדח hif.).[33] It may be worth while noting finally that in Dt 13 these seducers are called "sons of Belial" (v. 14 בני בליעל), i.e. the passage is open to later associations with the great antagonist of God.

---

[33] LXX: v. 7 παρακαλέω; v. 6 πλανάω; vv. 11, 14 ἀφίστημι (aorist I act.).

E. Mk 13,24–27/Mt 24,29–31

(*Mk*: But in those days, after that tribulation (θλῖψις)) (*Mt*: Immediately after the tribulation of those days) *the sun will be darkened,*	Jl 2,10 4,15		Is 13,10 Ez 32,7 Jl 3,3	
and *the moon will not give its light,*	Is 13,10		Ez 32,7 Jl 2,10 4,15	
25 and *the stars will fall from heaven,*	Is 34,4			Is 13,10 Ez 32,7 Jl 2,10 4,15
and *the powers in* (*Mt*: *of*) *the heavens* will be shaken;	Is 34,4			
(*30* then will appear the sign of the Son of Man in heaven, + *Mt*)		Is 11,10 f.		Is 18,3 66,19
and then (*all the tribes of the earth will mourn,* and + *Mt*)	Zch 12,12,14		Ez 32,9 f.	Is 13,7 f.
26 *they will see the Son* of Man *coming in* (*Mt*: *on the*) *clouds* (*of heaven* + *Mt*)	Dn 7,13			Is 19,1
with (*great* + *Mk*) power and (*great* + *Mt*) glory,		Dn 7,14		
27/*31* and (*then* + *Mk*) he will send out the (*Mt*: his) angels			Zch 14,5	Dn 7,10
(*with a loud trumpet* call, + *Mt*)		Is 27,13		
and (they will + *Mt*) *gather his elect from the four winds,* (*Mk*: *from the ends of the earth to the ends of heaven.*) (*Mt*: *from one one end of heaven to the other.*)	Dt 30,3 f. Zch 2,10 LXX		Ps 106,47 Is 43,5 ff. 56,8 Jr 29,14 31,8 ff. 32,37 Ez 28,25 34,12 f. 37,21	Is 27,12 49,5 Jr 30,10 Zch 2,10 ff. (6 ff.)

In the centre of this section there is again a quotation from Daniel, that concerning the Son of Man's appearance with the clouds. The last main point in the group of pericopes from Daniel, that referring to the setting up of God's kingdom, has hereby been taken up. Ch. 8, 9 and 11 only mention the negative side, that the evil king will be annihilated. Ch. 12 refers to the joy of the elect and in ch. 2 and 7 the whole thing results in a positive saying on the kingdom of God, in ch. 7 symbolized by the Son of Man.

Certain re-interpretations have taken place in the eschatological discourse. It is no novelty that the Son of Man is an individual, either in the Gospels or in their environment. But it would seem to be an original re-interpretation that the Son of Man is here not, as in Daniel, brought to God's throne.[34] And a relevation of God (the Ancient of Days) is not mentioned, nor is His judgement (Dn 7,9 ff.). Instead the Son of Man has taken over God's function of coming to gather together the scattered people of God (even though the angels, sent by the Son of Man, gather them together); and a judgement is explicitly mentioned only in the extended form of the discourse, in Mt 25,31 ff.

It is in keeping with the fact that here the Son of Man appears in place of God that the celestial phenomena which accompany this appearance[35] are associated in the OT with theophanies on the Day of Yahweh.[36] The texts used in vv. 24 f./29 are bound together by a common theme and by key-words. Thus in Jl 2,10 and 4,15 we read of the coming Day of Yahweh: "The sun and the moon are darkened (שמש וירח קדרו), and the stars withdraw their shining". And Is 13,10 has the same theme: "The stars of the heavens and their constellations will not give their light; the sun will be dark at its rising, and the moon will not shed its light" (חשך השמש בצאתו וירח לא יגיה אורו). Is 34 has the same theme and motifs: v.4, "All the host of heaven shall rot away (נמקו כל צבא השמים),[37] and the skies roll up like a scroll. All their host shall fall" (כל צבאם יבול).[38]

Here, as also in v. 7/8 above, we encounter the phenomenon we found exemplified in Chap. IV in Jewish texts, namely, that the basis consists of *one* text from the OT, while the description is expanded with (or alternatively is made up of) other textual quotations and textual allu-

---

[34] Similarly B. WEISS (1910), J. KNABENBAUER (3rd ed. 1922), P. GAECHTER (1964), *Comm. Mt.*, ad loc.; SCHMID, *Comm. Mk*, ad loc.; R. B. Y. SCOTT, 'Behold, He Cometh with Clouds', *NT Stud.* 5 (1958/59), 131. Cf. CARRINGTON, *Comm. Mk*, 284.

[35] There is a certain possibility of finding a contrast association with the previous verses: it may be possible to interpret these celestial phenomena as "wonders" in accordance with Jl 3,3 f.: "I will give wonders (מופתים) in the heavens and on the earth ... The sun shall be turned to darkness, and the moon to blood ..." These wonders would then be contrasted with the signs and wonders of the false prophets (Dt 13,2 אות או מופת). Moreover the Targ. Jon. in Jl 3,3 reads "signs" (אתין). Cf. Or Sib 3,64 ff., in which Belial (Dt 13,14!) makes misleading signs appear in the heavens. See above, 73.

[36] Cf. above, 35 f., 71 ff.

[37] 1 QIs[a] begins with והעמקים יתבקעו ו instead. Cf. Mi 1,4. The words were associated with this passage in Is on account of ונמסו (ה)הרים, which is common to Is 34,3 and Mi 1,6. The LXX lacks the first clause of the verse in TM.

[38] GLASSON, *Exp. Times* 69 (1957/58), 213 ff., seems to overstress the agreement with the LXX reading of Is 34,4 (τακήσονται πᾶσαι αἱ δυνάμεις τῶν οὐρανῶν ... καὶ πάντα τὰ ἄστρα πεσεῖται). Cf. T. W. MANSON, The OT in the Teaching of Jesus, *Bull. J. Ryl. Libr.* 34 (1951/52), 316.

sions, to which associations are made from a common theme and/or via key-words.

The quotation from Dn 7,13 is expanded with the adverbial phrase "with great power and glory" (so Mark). This may well have been inspired by Dn 7,14: "And to him (viz. the Son of Man) was given dominion and glory and kingdom" (שלטן ויקר ומלכו).[39]

Finally, with the description of how God's kingdom will set in with the Parousia the author associates the traditional theme of the gathering together of the scattered people of God. While the OT usually says that it is God Himself who "gathers", here it is the angels who carry out this task and it is reasonable to assume that they entered the picture the more easily in that the heavenly court is also presented in the Daniel text which provides the main point of this section, namely, 7,10: "A thousand thousands served him (viz. the Ancient of Days) and ten thousand times ten thousand stood before him".

The OT passages which have contributed most to the wording of this "gathering" seem, as far as Matthew is concerned, to be Zch 2,10 (6) and Dt 30,4, both principally in the LXX variant and, as far as Mark is concerned, these two, together with Is 43,6. All these passages are united by their having themes and key-words in common. Zch 2,10 (6) reads: "I shall gather you from the four winds of the heavens" (ἐκ τῶν τεσσάρων ἀνέμων τοῦ οὐρανοῦ συνάξω ὑμᾶς).[40] And in Dt 30,4 we find: "If your dispersion is from one end of the heaven to the other end of heaven, from there the Lord your God will gather you" (ἐὰν ᾖ ἡ διασπορά σου ἀπ᾽ἄκρου τοῦ οὐρανοῦ ἕως ἄκρου τοῦ οὐρανοῦ, ἐκεῖθεν συνάξει σε κύριος ὁ θεός σου).[41] Is 43,6 finally also refers to the great gathering: "Yahweh will call His children from all quarters and will say to the south: 'Bring my sons from afar, and my daughters from the end of the earth' " (מקצה הארץ, LXX ἀπ᾽ἄκρων (codd. SC sing.) τῆς γῆς).

The manner in which we have been able to derive the last-mentioned parts of the eschatological discourse directly or indirectly from Daniel must be considered to have further reinforced the probability that the parts of the discourse first discussed are also based on these texts in Daniel about the last days. Taken altogether, the conclusions arrived at so far give us reason to assume that the main part of the eschatological discourse is based on a coherent exposition of or meditation on these texts in Daniel, which even in Daniel are in part said to be "for the time

---

[39] LXX: ἐξουσία (88-Syh + καὶ τιμὴ βασιλική). CARRINGTON (Comm. Mk, ad loc.) suggests Ps 8,5.

[40] Cf. TM "I have spread you abroad as the four ..." (כארבע ... פרשתי).

[41] Cf. TM "If your outcasts are in the uttermost parts of heaven, from there ..." (בקצה השמים).

of the end". Such an assumption must be considered now to have acquired a certain justification and if it is true, we should be able to get more details in the discourse elucidated in the same way as some parts have already been elucidated. And conversely, if we can fix further details in the discourse in these Daniel texts, this will strengthen the probability of the assumption.

3. *A Second Survey*

A. Mk 13,5*b*–8/Mt 24,4*b*–8

We accordingly now turn back to the beginning of the eschatological discourse and discuss some details that were passed over at the first survey.

As far as Mk 13,4 is concerned, we have already considered the formulation of the introductory framework in conjunction with Dn 12,7.[42] It seems clear from our previous experience of Daniel associations that this must be more than a coincidence. We will have occasion later on to decide on our attitude to the place of this framework in the history of the tradition of this pericope.[43]

We then direct our attention to the first verses of the discourse (Mk 13,5*b* f./Mt 24,4*b* f.), which read: "Take heed that no one leads you astray. (For + *Mt*) many will come in my name, saying 'I am (the Christ + *Mt*)', and they will lead many astray".

The core of these words is that people will come and say wrongly: "I am—ἐγώ εἰμι". (In company with most commentators, I take the ὁ χριστός in Matthew as secondary.)[44]

Several exegetes have assumed that this ἐγώ εἰμι here is a paraphrase, which means that he who says these words of himself is calling himself by the name of God.[45] The probability of this interpretation is strength-

---

[42] See above, in this chapter, section 1.

[43] See below, 219 ff. and 240 f.

[44] See, for example, M'NEILE, W. C. ALLEN (3rd ed. 1912), and J. SCHMID (3rd ed. 1956), *Comm. Mt*, ad loc.; G. R. BEASLEY-MURRAY, *Mark 13* (1957), ad loc.; W. MANSON, The ΕΓΩ ΕΙΜΙ of the Messianic Presence in the NT, *J. Theol. Stud.* 48 (1947), 140; HARDER, *Theol. Viat.* 4 (1952), 75; E. STAUFFER, *Jesus, Gestalt und Geschichte* (1957), 130.

[45] MANSON, *J. Theol. Stud.* 48 (1947), 137–45; C. E. B. CRANFIELD, St. Mark 13, *Scot. J. Theol.* 6 (1953), 288; D. DAUBE, The 'I Am' of the Messianic Presence, in *The NT and Rabbinic Judaism* (1956), 325–29; H. ZIMMERMANN, Das absolute "Ich bin" in der Redeweise Jesu, *Trierer Theol. Zschr.* 69 (1960), 13 ff. Cf. LOHMEYER, *Comm. Mk*, and also J. A. BENGEL, *Gnomon NT* (1742/1862), ad loc. On this paraphrase of the *shem hammephorash*, see, apart from the works already quoted, C. H. DODD, *The Interpretation of the Fourth Gospel* (1953), 93 ff.; C. K. BARRETT, *Comm. Jn* (2nd ed. 1956), 282 f.; STAUFFER, op. cit., 130 ff.; H. ZIMMERMANN, Das

ened by the background in Daniel which we shall now try and demonstrate for this text.

'Εγώ εἰμι is thus a LXX form of the OT revelation formula אני הוא.[46] However, it is also used in Is 45,18 to paraphrase (ואין עוד) אני יהוה; LXX ἐγώ εἰμι (καὶ οὐκ ἔστιν ἔτι). The Hebrew formula has a variant אני ואפסי עוד in Is 47,8, 10 and Zph 2,15 and in all these cases אני is translated by ἐγώ εἰμι, i.e. the pronoun has been understood as a paraphrase of the name of God. Several later exegetes think that the translators of the LXX, by using this paraphrase, have hit on the truth.[47] In Is 47, however, it is Babylon which "in its heart" (בלבבה) blasphemously calls itself by the name of God,[48] and before we return to Daniel, we shall recall that Babylon in Jewish and Christian apocalyptic was a pseudonym for Rome or the great Satanic heathen enemy at the end of time.[49]

And now to Daniel. In Dn 7,8, 11 and 20 we meet with the horn that speaks great things (ממלל רברבן), and in v. 25, as an interpretation of this, with the king who "shall speak words against the Most High" (מלין לצד עליא ימלל). The same phenomenon is to be met with in ch. 8. There a horn grows great (תגדל) in v. 10 "even to the host of heaven", and v. 11 says that "it magnified itself, even up to the Prince of the host" (עד שר הצבא הגדיל). V. 25 interprets this as "in his heart he shall magnify himself (ובלבבו יגדיל), he shall even rise up (יעמד) against the Prince of princes". Finally we encounter the motif also in Dn 11,36; "the king ... shall exalt himself (יתרומם) and magnify himself (יתגדל) above every God, and shall speak astonishing things (נפלאות) against the God of gods".

As a background to Daniel here, I will quote a text which probably provided the themes of Dn 8, namely, Is 14,13 f.[50] This says of Babylon who must go down into Sheol: "You said in your heart (בלבבך, cf. Dn 8,25), 'I will ascend (אעלה) to heaven; above the stars of God I will set

absolute 'Εγώ εἰμι als die neutestamentliche Offenbarungsformel, *Bibl. Zschr.* 4 (1960), 54–69, 226–76; A. HAIDUK, "Ego eimi" bei Jesus und seine Messianität, *Communio Viat.* 6 (1963), 55–60.

[46] See Dt 32,39; Is 41,4; 43,10; 52,6.

[47] See, for example, P. VOLZ (II, 1932), and E. J. KISSANE (II, 1943), *Comm. Is*, ad loc.

[48] In Zph 2,15 it is Nineveh.

[49] 4 Ez 3,1 f., 28; 2 Bar 11,1 f.; Or Sib 5,143, 158 f. Cf. BILLERBECK, *Comm.* III, 816. In the NT 1 Pt 5,13; Ap 14,8; 17,5 f.; 18,2 ff. See P.VOLZ, *Die Eschatologie der jüdischen Gemeinde* (2nd ed. 1934), 280. For Nineveh (Zph 2,15), see Gn R. 16 (BILLERBECK, op. cit., 812).

[50] See J. A. MONTGOMERY (1927), E. W. HEATON (1956), A. JEFFERY (1956), and N. M. PORTEOUS (1962), *Comm. Dn*, ad loc. Cf. 1 En 46,7 (above, 125), 2 Mcc 9,10; Ap 12,4; b Ḥag. 13a.

my throne on high (cf. Dn 8,10 f.) ... I will make myself like 'Aelyon'"
(אדמה לעליון).[51]

It would have been reasonable for a Jew who knew his OT and who meditated on these Daniel texts at the beginning of the Christian era to associate the great words and self-exaltation[52] of the horn (king) with the rising of Babylon above the stars and its making itself like 'Aelyon and Babylon's use of the paraphrase of God's name in Is 47,8, 10 respectively.

Thus the origin of the nucleus of the wording in Mk 13,6 seems to be explained. The saying that people will come saying ἐγώ εἰμι was originally an interpretation of the great words and arrogance of the horn (king) in Dn 7 f. and 11.

If we now connect with Dn 8,25, however, we also get an explanation of what follows in the eschatological discourse. We read in Daniel: "By his cunning he shall make deceit prosper (הצליח מרמה) under his hand, and in his heart he shall magnify himself. Without warning he shall destroy many (בשלוה ישחית רבים);[53] and he shall even rise up against the Prince of princes." We recognize the second and fourth sentences from the previous discussion. The first and third, on the other hand, give the impression of underlying the sentence in the eschatological discourse about those who say, "I am": "they will lead many astray" (πολλοὺς πλανήσουσιν). Hif. of שחת may also mean "destroy in a moral or religious respect",[54] and מרמה is translated in Prv 14,8 (LXX) by πλάνη.

Further on in Mk 13/Mt 24 the text speaks of leading astray, viz. in v. 22/24 and in Mt also in v. 11. We may then ask ourselves whether the section on leading astray to apostasy at the beginning of the discourse was extracted by the author who edited the text from a position connected with the "abomination of desolation". However, it may be questioned if such a hypothesis is not based on a premise that the content of the discourse is to describe a curve, in which blasphemous and misleading elements such as these belong to a later stage logically and temporally.

If, on the other hand, we compare the arrangement of the eschatological discourse with the Daniel pericopes, we find precisely the same thing in Dn 7,20 f.: the prophet asks about "the horn which had eyes and a mouth that *spoke great things*, and which seemed greater than its fellows. As I looked, this horn *made war* with the saints ..."

There is a further detail in this context. Daniel speaks of *one* horn and *one* king, the eschatological discourse of "many" coming and saying "I am". That is to say, the expositor of Daniel or perhaps one of his

---

[51] Cf. also note 55 below.

[52] For הגדיל in the sense of "to exalt oneself (in *hubris*)", see also Jr 48,26, 42.

[53] LXX: ἀφανιεῖ πολλούς; Theod. διαφθερεῖ π.

[54] For example, Gn 6,12; Dt 4,16; Is 1,4; Zph 3,7.

successors regarded this king as a personification of several individuals, which was not too remote, as associations with Babylon, a kingdom, were in his mind.[55]

The continuation in Mark and Matthew—wars, rumours of wars, famines and earthquakes, including the statement in v. 7/6 "the end is not yet"—was discussed above and, since we have now related its context to Daniel, it would seem that the close connection of this section with Daniel has been proved, as near as may be.

B. Mk 13,14–23/Mt 24,15–25

I will discuss the complicated passages Mk 13,9–13 and Mk 24,9–4 separately below. A large part of Mk 13,14–20/Mt 24,15–22 could be explained above as consisting partly of direct associations with Dn 11,31 (9,27) (the abomination of desolation) and 12,1 (time of trouble, delivery), and partly of exhortations to headlong flight, in terms of Gn 19 (of Lot and Sodom).

Matthew writes in v. 15 that the abomination of desolation stands "in the holy place" (ἐν τόπῳ ἁγίῳ). It is probably pure coincidence that these particular words are to be found in Is 60,13;[56] on the other hand, there is possibly a connection with Dn 9,27.[57] There the LXX (and Theod.) read: ἐπὶ τὸ ἱερὸν βδέλυγμα τῶν ἐρ., which would be the equivalent of the Hebrew על הקדש instead of the על כנף in TM. In any case it is probable that Daniel supplied this adverbial phrase, for the context of both 9,27 and 11,31 makes it clear that the abomination is in the Temple.[58]

The sayings on the flight and its circumstances in vv. 14–18/16–20 may have been spun out with the help of separate logia. Thus vv. 15 f./19 have a separate parallel in Lk 17,31; v. 17/18 has a separate variant in Lk 23,29. I will return to these questions later.[59]

[55] This is further facilitated by the fact that behind Dn 8,10 we may also see Ps 75,5 f.: "I say to the boastful (plu.), 'Do not boast', and to the wicked (plu.), 'Do not lift up your horn; do not lift up your horn on high, or speak with insolent neck' ". (BENTZEN, Comm. Dn, ad loc.) Cf. 1 Jn 2,18, 22, 26; 4,1, 3; 2 Jn 7, and see below, 235 ff.

[56] Cf., for example, also Ex 3,5; Jo 5,15.

[57] For example, E. KLOSTERMANN (2nd ed. 1927) and SCHMID, Comm. Mt, ad loc. Cf. RIGAUX, L'Antéchrist, 241, on כנף—ΠΤΕΡΟΝ—ΙΕΡΟΝ. A. RESCH (Der Paulinismus und die Logia Jesu, 1904, 392) compares with Dn 11,31 וחללו המקדש.

[58] If we accept the thesis that to the interpreter the Dn pericopes could constitute a group of texts in which the units illustrated each other, the difficulty of deciding whether it is Dn 9,27 or 11,31 or even 12,11 which is quoted disappears. Cf. D. DAUBE, The Abomination of Desolation, in The NT and Rabbinic Judaism (1956), 418–37, and B. RIGAUX, Βδέλυγμα τῆς ἐρημώσεως Mc 13,14; Mt 24,15, Bibl. 40 (1959), 675–683.

[59] See below 226. In its comments on Gn 19,16, Gn R. makes Lot complain that he had to abandon great riches in Sodom. See also 1 Mcc 2,28.

There is also some possibility that Matthew's longer and probably secondary[60] reading in v. 20 on the flight on the Sabbath may also be related to the text on Lot's flight. Gn 19,12 says: "Bring them (viz. the sons-in-law etc.) out of the place" (הוצא מן המקום), and Lot's words to his sons-in-law in v. 14 are almost similar: "Get out of this place" (צאו מן המקום הזה). The expression מקום + יצא מן used of men is rare in the OT; it is to be found only in Ex 16,29, Ru 1,7 and Jr 22,11. Of these, Ex 16,29 contains a Torah commandment on the Sabbath.[61] It says, à propos of collecting manna on the Sabbath: "Let no man go out of his place on the seventh day" (אל יצא איש ממקמו). That is to say, in his further meditations on the flight described in the words of Gn 19, the author of Matthew would have observed the similarity of the expression in Gn 19,12, 14 and Ex 16,29 and was led to word the text in this way out of respect for the commandment in Ex 16,29. This would then be the formal aspect of the association: it must also have had an aspect as regarded the content—that the Sabbath was a problem for the author and his milieu.

We will now pass on to the saying about the shortening of the days, v. 20/22. Several OT texts have been suggested as a possible background, but none of the suggestions seem convincing.[62] Bearing in mind that so far we have already found so many associations with Daniel, I would like to propose the following solution.

In the Greek phrase the actual main word κολοβοῦν is really somewhat peculiar. It has a concrete meaning, "to mutilate", "to cut short", "to curtail", and is used, for instance, of tree trunks or dogs' tails.[63]

---

[60] ALLEN, M'NEILE, and TH. H. ROBINSON (1928), Comm. Mt, ad loc. Cf. KLOSTERMANN, Comm. Mk, 135. On the other hand, see B. WEISS, Comm. Mk, Lk (1901), A. LOISY, Les évangiles synoptiques II (1908), and M.-J. LAGRANGE, Comm. Mt (3rd ed. 1927), ad loc.

[61] It was also from this passage that the scribes determined how far it was permissible to travel on the Sabbath. See Mek. Ex 16,29; p Erub. IV.21,6; T. Erub. IV.11 (BILLERBECK, Comm. II, 1924, 590 ff.). Cf. W. O. E. OESTERLEY, Le Sabbat (1935), 62 f., 77 f. Note furthermore the vocabulary in 1 Mcc 2,34, in which the pious Jews refuse to fight on the Sabbath: οὐκ ἐξελευσόμεθα; see further M. D. HERR, The Problem of War on the Sabbath (Hebrew), Tarbiz 30 (1960/61), 243 f. (Eng. summary, vii).

[62] B. W. BACON, The Gospel of Mark (1925), 128 (Is 28,22); M.-J. LAGRANGE, Comm. Mk (4th ed. 1929), ad loc. (Dn 9,24 Theod.); W. BOUSSET, Antichrist (1895), 143 (Dn 12,7); F. BUSCH, Zum Verständnis der synoptischen Eschatologie: Markus 13 neu untersucht (1938), 96 (Dn 9,24; Is 54,7 f.; Hg 2,6). Cf. BEASLEY-MURRAY, Mark 13, ad loc.

[63] H. STEPHANUS, Thesaurus IV (1841), F. PASSOW II (rev. ed. 1847), W. PAPE I (2nd rev. ed. 1888), J. H. MOULTON and G. MILLIGAN IV (1920), F. PREISIGKE I (1925), H. G. LIDDELL and R. SCOTT (rev. ed. 1925–40), W. F. ARNDT, F. W. GINGRICH (1957), sub voce.

When the large lexica give a figurative meaning, "to shorten" (of time), the only example quoted is the present passage.[64] A survey of several concordances gives the same negative result. We should then at least be able to conclude that this figurative use is, if not unique, then somewhat original, and this originality must attract some attention.

The text which is quoted immediately before this problematic verse is Dn 12,1 on the great trouble at this time. The quotation closes with the words מהיות גוי עד העת ההיא ("since there was a nation till that time"). If now we take the words גוי עד, make ד and ע change places and read the two words as one word, we get the word גוידע. To drop a י and to create a new combination such as this would have been a trifle to a Jewish scribe at the beginning of the Christian era.[65] We then have a sentence which reads גודע העת ההיא, which means: "one who cuts short that time"! If we so wish we may conjure up a subject and an article from מהיות and get: (ו)יה) הגודע ה' ה' ה' "Yahweh is he who shortens that time".

This solution fits well with the continuation of both the eschatological discourse and Dn 12,1. Dn 12,1 goes on immediately to say that the people shall be delivered (ימלט), "every one whose name shall be found written in the book". The words in the Gospels (20/22), that, if the Lord did not shorten that time, "no flesh should be saved (οὐκ ἂν ἐσώθη πᾶσα σάρξ), but for the sake of the elect ... he shortened the days" (Mk), are in good agreement with this. The step from being "written in the book" to being "elect" is not a long one.[66]

Then follows the section Mk 13,21–23/Mt 24,23–25 about the false Christs and false prophets. We found above that this was based on Dn 11,36 ff., in that the statements on the evil king's contempt for the gods of his fathers carried over to Dt 13, which refers to false prophets, sons of Belial, who perform signs and wonders. There we also found a point of attachment for the sentence that the purpose of these prophets' work is said to be to lead astray—(ἀπο-)πλανᾶν—the elect.

---

[64] However, one example is 3 Bar 9 with ἡμέρας as object (the text is in *Apocrypha anecdota* II, ed. M. R. JAMES, 1897, 91). The LXX uses the word only in 2 Rg 4,12, and there in a concrete sense (obj. χεῖρας). On the other hand, it is used in figurative sense (of πνεῦμα and ψυχή) in Symm. Jb 21,4 and Aq. Jdc 16,16; Jb 21,4 and Zch 11,8 (G. DELLING, κολοβόω, *Theol. Wörterb.* III, 1938, 823).

[65] See, for example, K. STENDAHL, *The School of St. Matthew* (1954), 185 ff.; W. H. BROWNLEE, *The Text of Habakkuk in the Ancient Commentary from Qumran* (1959), 118 ff. (ואשם — וישם) in 1 QpH IV.9, והרעל — והערל in XI.9); A. ROSENZWEIG, Die Al-tikri-Deutungen, in *Festschrift I. Lewy* (1911), 204–53, esp. 226 ff. See also J. W. DOEVE, *Jewish Hermeneutics in the Synoptic Gospels and Acts* (1953), e.g. 88 f.

[66] This election may possibly be mentioned as early as Dn 11,35. Here TM says that some of those who are wise shall fall, to refine and to cleanse among them: ובּרר וללבן. The versions of the LXX and Theod. both use a form of ἐκλέγεσθαι.

C. Mk 13,24–27/Mt 24,29–31

Finally we return to the section on the Parousia (Mk 13,24–27/Mt 24,29–31). We found above that the description was composed of OT material which was linked together via motifs and key-words which described the coming of the Son of Man in terms of Yahweh's theophany on the Day of Yahweh for the "gathering" of his people. Matthew's text also contains some further OT allusions. Between v. 29 on phenomena among the sun, moon and stars and the quotation from Dn 7,13 (the Son of Man on the clouds of heaven) in v. 30 c, we find the following words: "Then will appear the sign of the Son of Man in heaven, and then all the tribes of the earth will mourn".

It has been suggested that the sentence on the sign of the Son of Man was inspired by Is 11,10–12:[67] "The root of Jesse shall stand as an ensign to the peoples" (נס עמים), the Lord will recover the remnant of His people from the different nations (v. 11), and (v. 12) "will raise an ensign for the nations (נס לגוים), and will assemble the outcasts of Israel (אסף נדחי י׳), and gather (יקבץ) the dispersed of Judah from the four corners of the earth" (מארבע כנפוכ הארץ).[68]

This context of the motif in Is 11 seems to me to argue that the suggestion is correct. For it is clear that key-word and thematic associations connect Is 11,10 ff. with Mt 24,31 and constituted part of the bridge by which the motif of the sign found its way into the text. The key-words may be the Hebrew ones in the OT passages which underlie v. 31 (קבץ, ארבע), or the Greek ones in either the LXX version of these passages or the Gospel text (συνάγειν, τέσσαρες).

If we pose the question why this allusion comes so early and not in connection with the actual point of association (the "gathering"), the answer is as follows. Matthew identified "the root" in Is 11 with the Son of Man.[69] When the text says that "the root shall stand as an ensign to the peoples", this was found to correspond with the revelation of the Son of Man on the clouds of heaven. Thus the sign is seen ἐν οὐρανῷ, and this is co-ordinated with the other celestial phenomena in v. 29.

According to Isaiah, the root stood as an ensign "to the peoples" (v. 10 עמים, v. 12 גוים). It is therefore not a long step from Is 11,10 ff. to the next quotation in Mt 24,30, that from Zch 12,12, 14 on the mourning of all tribes of the earth. The quotation is mainly taken from v. 12: "the land shall mourn, each family by itself" (ספדה הארץ משפחות משפחות)

---

[67] M'NEILE, *Comm. Mt.* ad loc., and cf. T. F. GLASSON, The Ensign of the Son of Man (Matt. xxiv. 30), *J. Theol. Stud.* 15 (1964), 299–300.

[68] In v. 10 the LXX reads: ὁ ἀνιστάμενος ἄρχειν ἐθνῶν, and in v. 12: ἀρεῖ σημεῖον εἰς τὰ ἔθνη, καὶ συνάξει ... ἐκ τῶν τεσσάρων πτερύγων τῆς γῆς.

[69] Cf. 1 En 46,3 (above, 120).

and is coloured by v. 10: "They (viz. the inhabitants of Jerusalem) shall mourn" (ספדו), and by v. 14: (they shall mourn) "all the families that are left" (כל המשפחות הנשארות).[70]

We may now ask ourselves how this quotation from Zch 12,10 ff. came to be associated with this text; did Is 11,10 ff. or the following quotation from Dn 7,13 play any part? The fact that Dn 7,13 and the same form of a quotation from Zch 12,10 ff. are combined in Ap 1,7[71] may indicate that it is between these two passages that we should primarily look for a connection. One possible explanation is that an interpretation of Zch 12,10 ff. on the Parousia of the Son of Man was partly favoured by ideas like these in 1 En Sim, where the revelation of the Son of Man results in "sinners", "mighty ones" and kings being put to shame, for example, 1 En 48,8: "In these days downcast in countenance shall the kings of the earth have become".[72] Dn 7,14 may also have served as a starting-point for the motif: "All peoples, nations, and languages shall serve him" (viz. the Son of Man) (כל עממיא אמיא ולשניא לה יפלחון).[73]

As long as we know no more about the early history of the Gospel material, we must also allow for the possibility that the combination of Zch 12,10 ff. and Dn 7,13 may be found in its original form in Mt 24,30: in this case Is 11,10 ff.—the peoples round the root as an ensign—may have played a part in the origin of the combination.

Finally we also find in Mt 24,31, after the saying on the Parousia of the Son of Man, a saying that the angels of the Son of Man will be sent out to gather in the elect "with a loud trumpet call" (μετὰ σάλπιγγος μεγάλης). The expression is taken from Is 27,13 and it seems highly probable that the context of the passage formed a bridge for the associations. Is 27,12 f. says: "In that day ... you will be gathered one by one ... And in that day a great trumpet will be blown (יתקע בשופר גדול) and those who were lost in the land of Assyria and those who were driven out to the land of Egypt will come ..."[74] Thus here, as in the case of the ensign in Is 11, the great gathering is the motif, in the context of the words

---

[70] LXX: v. 10: κόψονται; v. 12 κόψεται ἡ γῆ κατὰ φυλὰς φυλάς; v. 14 πᾶσαι αἱ φυλαὶ αἱ ὑπολελειμμέναι.

[71] See on this point STENDAHL, School, 212 ff.; A. J. B. HIGGINS, The Sign of the Son of Man (Matt. xxiv. 30), NT Stud. 9 (1962/63), 380—82; B. LINDARS, Books of Testimonies, Exp. Times 75 (1963/64), 174. Cf. M'NEILE, Comm. Mt, ad loc.

[72] See also 1 En 38,1 ff.; 45,6; 46,4 ff.; 62,1 ff. This is so, provided that this κόψονται is not instead a sign of conversion. Thus A. FEUILLET, Le discours de Jésus sur la ruine du Temple, Rev. Bibl. 56 (1949), 78 f. On the other hand, see, for example, TH.ZAHN (2nd ed. 1905) and SCHMID, Comm. Mt, ad loc.

[73] LXX: πάντα τὰ ἔθνη τῆς γῆς κατὰ γένη καὶ πᾶσα δόξα λατρεύουσα αὐτῷ.

[74] LXX: συναγάγετε ... σαλπιοῦσιν τῇ σάλπιγγι τῇ μεγάλῃ, καὶ ἥξουσιν οἱ ἀπολόμενοι ...

quoted, that carries the association. Nevertheless it is probable that the additions in Matthew (v. 30 f.) do not only depend on key-word and thematic associations; in the last case a desire to supplement the Parousia picture with traditional motifs may also have played a part.[75]

Finally we may note that the motif which characterizes the eschatological discourse after the parable of the fig tree and the logia associated with it (Mk 13,28–32/Mt 24,32–36), is the imperative "watch" (γρηγορεῖτε, ἀγρυπνεῖτε). This motif may perhaps have been supported by the closing words of Dn 12,12: "Blessed is he who waits" (המחכה).[76]

This second survey seems to me to have confirmed the assumption that the parts of the eschatological discourse so far discussed have as their foundation an exposition or meditation based on texts in Daniel about the last things, especially 7,8–27; 8,9–26; 9,24–27; 11,21–12,13 and to some extent 2,31–45.

4. *Mk 13,9–13 and Mt 24,9–14*

Since the texts in Mark and Matthew are not parallel at this point, we will discuss the versions separately. (The real parallel text in Matthew to Mk 13,9–13 is in Mt 10,17–22 in connection with the charge to the twelve disciples.) We discovered above that the main concept (παραδοθῆ-ναι) may find support in Dn 7,25 and that the final verse of the section may be based on Dn 11: v. 32 ("stand firm") and v. 35 (refining until the time of the end). We found the persecution as a motif in Dn 7,24 f. and 8,24 f., and in more detail in 11,30 ff.

A. Mk 13,9–13

If we first consider the Mark text, it proves to consist of three small sections, all introduced by a form of παραδιδόναι. The first includes v. 9 f. and is concerned with being handed over to different authorities for the sake of Jesus. To this is added (v. 10) a logion about the preaching of the Gospel to all the world. The second section (v. 11) promises the support of the Holy Spirit when the persecuted are to defend themselves before law courts, and the third finally (v. 12) speaks of divisions in the family. The fact that in another context (Lk 12,11 f.) Luke transmits an equivalent to the second section means that we should take into account that at least this section may have been an isolated logion which was incorporated later.

---

[75] Cf. Ps Sal 11,1; 4 Ez 6,23; Apc Abr 31,1; *Shemone esre* 10 (KLOSTERMANN and SCHMID, *Comm. Mt*, ad loc.).

[76] LXX: ὁ ἐμμένων; Theod. ὁ ὑπομένων.

9 But take heed of yourselves; for they will deliver you up to councils;		Dn 7,25		
and you will be beaten in synagogues;				
and you will stand before governors and kings for my sake			Ps 119,46 Dn 6,13 ff.	
for a testimony against them.[77]			Ps 119,46	Dt 31,26
10 And the gospel must first be preached to all nations.				
11 And when they bring you to trial and deliver you up,		Dn 7,25		
do not be anxious beforehand what you are to say; but say whatever is given you in that hour, for it is not you who speak, but the Holy Spirit.		Ex 4,11 ff.	Jr 1,7 ff.	
12 And brother *will deliver up brother* to death,	Mi 7,2 Targ.		Is 9,19 ff. 19,2 Ez 38,21 Am 1,11 Mi 7,2, 5 Hg 2,23 Zch 7,10 14,13	
and the father his child, and *children will rise against parents*	Mi 7,6		Ez 22,7	
and have them put to death; 13 and you will be hated by all for my name's sake.	Mi 7,6	Ps 106,41	Ps 25,19 69,5 105,25	Is 66,5
But he who endures		Dn 11,32 12,12 Mi 7,7		
to the end		Dn 11,35		
will be saved		Dn 12,1	Mi 7,7	

The associations with Daniel which we indicated above do not seem to have increased in number here. The echoes of the OT are otherwise quite weak, apart from those in v. 12 on divisions in the family.

Vv. 12–13*a* are carried by this motif. It may be of interest to note that the previous connection with the OT which we found in Mark's version (v. 8) was with Is 19,2, which also has this particular motif:[78]

---

[77] For this translation, see L. HARTMAN, A Linguistic Examination of Luke 21,13, in *Testimonium linguae* (1963), 57 ff.

[78] Vv. 8 and 12 are regarded as belonging together also by E. WENDLING, *Die Entstehung des Marcus-Evangeliums* (1908), 156.

"They will fight, every man against his brother, and every man against his neighbour" (איש באחיו ואיש ברעהו). It is but a short step from this to Mi 7,2: "They all lie in wait for blood, and each hunts his brother with a net" (איש את אחיהו יצודו). However, it seems to be a targumic interpretation like that in Targ. Jon. that sounds throughout this text, for Targ. Jon. reads: "A man delivers up his brother to destruction" (גבר ית אחוהי מסרין לגמירא). And Mi 7,5 f. says: "Put no trust in a neighbour (רע), have no confidence in a friend, ... for the son treats the father with contempt (מנבל), the daughter rises up (קמה) against her mother, the daughter-in-law against her mother-in-law; a man's enemies are the men of his own house" (איבי איש אנשי ביתו). This last verse also corresponds to 13a on the hatred of all men, and the author has trodden the same paths as the LXX and Targ. in his interpretation. The LXX reads "a man's enemies are *all* the men in his house", and Targ. Jon. literally: "those who *hate* a man (סנאוהי דגברא) are the men ...".

Finally, however, this Micah text provides us with a bridge over to the continuation in 13b. Mi 7,7 says: "But as for me, I will look (אצפה) to Yahweh, I will wait (אוחילה, LXX ὑπομενῶ) for the God of my salvation".

B. Mt 24,9–14

Then they will deliver you up to tribulation		Dn 7,25		
nd put you to death;	Dn 11,33			
nd you will be hated by all nations for my name's sake.		Ps 106,41	Ps 25,19 69,5 105,25	Is 66,5
0 And then *many will fall away*	Dn 11,41[79] LXX	Dn 11,33,35		
nd betray one another			Dn 7,25	
nd hate one another.			Is 66,5	
And many false prophets will arise	Dn 11,32,34			
nd *lead many astray*.	Dn 12,4[80]	Dn 11,32,34		
2 And because *wickedness is multiplied*,	Dn 12,4[80]			
ost men's love will grow cold.			(Ct 8,7)	
3 But he who endures		Dn 11,32 12,12 Mi 7,7		
the end		Dn 11,35		
ll be saved		Dn 12,1	Mi 7,7	

---

[79] MSS. 88–Syh. The reading may be influenced by Mt (J. ZIEGLER, ed., ad loc.).
[80] For the reading, see below, 171.

14 And this gospel of the king-	Dn 11,33	Dn 12,3
dom will be preached		
throughout the whole world,		
for a testimony to all nations;	Dn 11,35?	
and then the end will come.	Dn 11,35	
	12,4	

Compared with the Mark text just discussed, this section of Matthew yields far more associations with the OT, especially Daniel and with the verses in Daniel which deal with persecutions, especially 11,32–35:

He shall seduce with flattery (יחניף בחלקות) those who violate the covenant: but the people who know their God shall stand firm and take action. (33) And those among the people who are wise shall make many understand and they shall fall (נכשלו) by sword and flame, by captivity and plunder, for some days. (34) When they fall (בהכשלם), they shall receive a little help. And many shall join themselves to them with flattery (בחלקלקות); (35) and some of those who are wise shall fall (מן המשכילים יכשלו) to refine among them and to cleanse and to make them white, until the time of the end, for it is yet for the time appointed (כי עוד למועד).

The closeness of Matthew's "put to death" to the phrase "fall by sword" in Dn 11,33 is clear but is of no significance unless the context can also be associated with the same passage in Daniel. However, this is the case: v. 10a, "many will fall away" (σκανδαλισθήσονται), corresponds satisfactorily with Dn 11,35, many of the wise "shall fall" (יכשלו). The LXX even translates יכשלו in 11,41 by σκανδαλίζεσθαι.[81]

V. 11 then refers to false prophets. This may have a possible origin in 11,32 and 34. V. 32 "he shall seduce with flattery" etc. reads in the LXX and Theod. "those who violate the covenant shall seduce with flattery" (i.e. יחניפו instead of יחניף). Both in vv. 32 and 34 we may therefore find apostates who practise "flattery"—חלקות and חלקלקות. Now the fairly unusual noun חלק is used of the deceit of the false prophets in Is 30,10 and Ez 12,24. The expositor who wished to interpret the apostates' appearance in Dn 11,32 and 34 accordingly had not far to go to find false prophets concealed in the Daniel sayings on those who have betrayed the covenant and on those who joined themselves to the wise "with flattery", a "flattery" which then also included their misleading activities (πλανῆσαι).[82]

When, however, the prophecy of the many being led astray is to be put into words, Dn 12,4 is adduced. Dn 11,35 and 12,4 are linked with

---

[81] MSS. 88–Syh.; in 11,35 the LXX reads διανοηθήσονται (from a Hebrew ישכילו). Cf. note 79.

[82] Cf. Is 13,10 דברו לנו חלקות חזו מהתלות, LXX ἡμῖν λαλεῖτε καὶ ἀναγγέλλετε ἡμῖν ἑτέραν πλάνησιν.

each other by similar themes: 11,35; "some of the wise shall fall ... to cleanse them ... until the end", and 12,4 may be read: "until the time of the end many shall go astray, and evil shall increase." This translation presupposes a different text than TM, which reads "many shall run to and fro (ישטטו), and knowledge (הדעת) shall increase". The LXX, however, has a variant which supports the assumed text and therefore presupposes ישטטו (go astray) and הרעה (evil).[83] Thus, it appears that the continuation in Matthew (v. 12a) on the increasing wickedness also has support in Daniel!

If accordingly the persecutions and apostasy were described on the basis of Dn 11,32–35, it would be natural after this point, with the support of 11,35, to speak of endurance "to the end" (11,35: "to refine, ... until the time of the end"). We previously connected the endurance with v. 32 ("be strong") and in so far as the final deliverance is to be linked with Dn 12,1 (ימלט), the author here takes the first step towards the theme worked out in vv. 15 ff.

Between the verses on the persecution and the next section, however, comes Mt 24,14 on the preaching of the gospel throughout the whole world. It has a parallel in Mk 13,10: "and the gospel must first be preached to all nations". There the verse is inserted between the words on being brought before various courts and the promise of the help of the Holy Spirit in making a defence. It is a little strange to see that we may in fact find support in Daniel for this missionary logion, even in this particular section in Dn 11 which describes the persecutions. Verse 11,33 says: "Those among the people who are wise shall make many understand" (משכילי עם יבינו לרבים). In Dn 12,3 they are called "those who turn many to righteousness" (מצדיקי הרבים). To interpret "the many" as "the whole world" was not difficult for the Biblical expositor of the time.[84]

Matthew closes v. 14 with the words "and then the end will come". Bearing in mind that the persecutions, apostasy, errors and mission of the preceding verses are contained in Dn 11,32–35, it is fairly probable that this sentence is connected with the end of Dn 11,35: "until the time of the end, for it is yet for the time appointed" (עד עת קץ כי עוד למועד).[85] What is described in vv. 32–35 will last until the end: conversely, one

---

[83] LXX: ἕως ἂν ἀπομανῶσιν οἱ πολλοὶ καὶ πλησθῇ ἡ γῆ ἀδικίας. Note הדעת — הרעה — ארעא (earth)! (Cf. MONTGOMERY, Comm. Dn, ad loc.)

[84] See JOACH. JEREMIAS, πολλοί κτλ., Theol. Wörterb. VI (1959), 536 ff.

[85] There is even a slight possibility that an imaginative Midrashist might find an εἰς μαρτύριον in the למועד in this verse. We have a למועד which was translated by εἰς μαρτύριον in 1 Sm 9,24. Cf. HARTMAN, Testimonium linguae, 64 ff.

might argue that, when all this has happened, then, after this ($\tau\acute{o}\tau\varepsilon$),[86] the end will come.

We have now analysed the main part of the eschatological discourse in its relation to the OT and the results of the analysis seem to me to have confirmed step by step what we supposed at an earlier stage in this chapter, namely, that an exposition or meditation on Daniel texts about the last days underlies the discourse. At the same time the results open up the most intricate problems concerning the tradition of the discourse. However, we may already draw one conclusion of relevance for the work on the discourse in the following two chapters, namely, that, if we disregard the problematical passage Mk 13,9–11, the discourse in Mark's version is a considerably more coherent unit than has generally been assumed. The above results seem to me to indicate clearly that the view of the discourse as a conglomeration of small fragments cannot be maintained.[87]

5. *Survey of the Relation to Daniel*

I will now give a summary and somewhat schematic survey of the links in the eschatological discourse, according to the results achieved so far. In the left-hand column I give in brief the eschatological discourse in its Marcan form but insert in parentheses some elements peculiar to Matthew. I shall leave out Mk, vv. 9–11,[88] and as regards Mt, vv. 9–14, the account in section 4 above will have to suffice for the time being. The right-hand column gives the OT passages which provide support for the discourse: in some cases the OT reference is italicized in order to make clear a possible link. The middle column gives a brief description of how the link was established, for example, by thematic association or keywords.

5 Be not led astray.		
6 Many will say, "I am";	The horn magnifies itself—the blasphemy of Babylon in Is 14,13; 47,8.	Dn 7,8, 11, 20; *8,10 f.*, *25*; 11,36
they will lead many astray.		8,25

[86] See ARNDT and GINGRICH, *Lexicon*, sub voce, and W. G. KÜMMEL, *Promise and Fulfilment* (1957), 97. Cf. A. H. M'NEILE, Τότε in St Matthew, *J. Theol. Stud.* 12 (1910/11), 127 f.

[87] Cf. P. VIELHAUER, Apokalyptik des Urchristentums, Einleitung (in E. HENNECKE and W. SCHNEEMELCHER, *Apokryphen* ... II, 3rd ed. 1964), 434 f.: "Diese 'Rede' ist, wie die kritische Analyse gezeigt hat, eine Komposition aus grösseren und kleineren Einzelstücken verschiedener Herkunft und oft divergierender Tendenz". It may be questioned if an analysis does not prove to show something quite different!

[88] Cf. below, 213 ff.

7 Wars and rumours of wars.	The blasphemy–war sequence in Dn 7,20 f.	7,21; 9,26; *8,23 ff.;* 11,25 ff. 2,28 f., 45; *8,19*
Be not alarmed; this must take place; the end is not yet.	"War" in 11,25 ff.–"end" in 11,27	11,27
8 Nation against nation, kingdom against kingdom;	Associated themes ("war"). 2 Ch 15,6 and Is 19,2 are joined by key-words in their contexts; associated themes.	2 Ch 15,6 Is 19,2
earthquakes, famines.	More loosely associated with the theme or war.	
The beginnings of the travail. (9–11)		
12 Delivering up: a brother delivers up his brother	Connection with Is 19,2, just quoted; key-words in the context; associated themes.	Dn 7,25 Is 19,2 Mi 7,2 ff.
Children–parents.	Further on in Mi 7; the same theme.	Mi 7,6
13 Hated by all. He who endures	Mi 7,7 may facilitate the return to Daniel.	Mi 7,6 Mi 7,7 Dn 11,32
to the end will be saved. 14 The abomination of desolation;		Dn 11,35 Dn 12,1 11,31; 12,11; 9,27
flee to the mountains.	Sodom as a type of the abomination; an implicit point of association: the destruction.	Gn 19,17
15 Nothing from the house; 16 he who is in the field must not turn back.	Separate logion? (Cf. Lk 17,31).	Gn 19,17
17 Alas for those with child and those who give suck.	Separate logion? (Cf. Lk 23,29.)	
18 May it not happen in winter (or on a Sabbath).	Key-word association from Gn 19 ("go out from the place").	Ex 16,29
19 Tribulation.	Cf. "flee"—"be delivered" in the same text (Dn 12,1).	Dn 12,1
20 The days are shortened.	Re-vocalization of Dn 12,1 just quoted in the text.	12,1
21 "Here is the Christ". 22 False prophets showing signs and wonders	Association from "god whom his fathers did not know" in 11,38 to the same phrase in Dt 13,7.	Dn 11,37 f. Dt 13,2
to lead astray. 24 The sun is darkened;	Still in Dt 13. The Day of Yahweh.	Dt 13,7 Jl 2,10

the moon does not shine;	The Day of Yahweh; key-word and thematic association.	Is 13,10
25 the stars fall, the powers are shaken.	The Day of Yahweh; key-word and thematic association.	Is 34,4
(The sign of the Son of Man;	Key-word and thematic association ("gather", "four").	Is 11,10 ff.
the tribes mourn.)	Cf. Ap 1,7.	Zch 12,12, 14
26 The Son of Man in clouds		Dn 7,13
with great power and glory.		Dn 7,14
(A great trumpet-call.)	Association via the context (the "gathering").	Is 27,13
27 The angels gather the elect together.	The traditional motif of the gathering together is connected with the Danielic consummation (the eternal Kingdom). The passages are joined by common themes and key-words.	Dt 30,3 f. Zch 2,10 (Is 43,6)

6. The "Midrash" in Relation to the Parenetic Function of the Discourse

If we wanted to call this "exposition" on the basis of Daniel a midrash,[89] the designation would not be completely inappropriate. For want of a better, I shall in what follows use this designation, but within quotation marks. But many things must have happened to this "midrash" before the eschatological discourse took on the form it has now. To continue with the rabbinic terminology, the original "midrash" is well on the way to becoming a "mishna". This is a development which may be seen in some rabbinic traditions, where a (halakic) midrash has lost its distinct connections with the text interpreted, and the traces of the exegetical work have to a great extent been effaced, so that what remains is the (halakic) result of the exegesis, a mishna.[90]

This opens up the following problems. Ever since T. Colani an increasing number of scholars have for a century assumed that the eschatological discourse consists of or has as its main ingredient a slightly Christianized

---

[89] F. GILS (*Jésus prophète*, 1957, 128) uses the expression "apocalyptic Dn midrash" of Mt 24,9–13, 15–25 par., but has only recorded the present conspicuous OT quotations. Cf. also J. BOWMAN, *The Gospel of Mark. The New Christian Jewish Passover Haggadah* (1965), 239–53.

[90] See J. Z. LAUTERBACH, Midrash and Mishna, in *Rabbinic Essays* (1951), 163–256; R. BLOCH, Écriture et tradition dans le Judaïsme, *Cah. Sion.* 8 (1954), 19 ff.; B. GERHARDSSON, *Memory and Manuscript* (1961), 83 f. And cf. id., *The Good Samaritan — the Good Shepherd?* (1958), for a possible similar development, so that the presence of an underlying OT text is no longer so clear.

miniature apocalypse taken over from Judaism.[91] Could we not then assume that this miniature apocalypse was our "midrash", which was later reformed, especially by the addition of the parenetic sentences? If we do not wish to venture so far into the sphere of guesswork, we may still put the following question: now that we have succeeded in producing what may be, if not altogether a distinct, yet a distinguishable groundwork for the eschatological discourse, do the parenetic sayings belong to this groundwork?

First of all, we must repeat a couple of old observations, namely, that it is uncommon in the Jewish apocalypses for the eschatology to be so closely bound up with parenesis as it is here; indeed, even the detail of the constant form of address in the second person plural is rare.[92]

Our "midrash" is thus interwoven with admonitions, but it is also followed by them. This applies to all three versions. But while the interwoven parenesis is common to them all, they differ in what follows Mk 13,32 par., even though the motif is similar ("watch"). If we assume that Mark's was the first Gospel to be written down and that the writer of the Matthew and Luke Gospels knew of and used Mark's, the conclusion must be that the parenesis in the discourse was present at the latest when Mark's Gospel was written down and that the closing parenesis was more loosely attached to the "midrash", as the closest parallels to the end of Mark's Gospel (13,33–37) are scattered in Matthew and Luke.[93] The closing verses of Luke are peculiar to his Gospel,[94] and Matthew expands his text with Parousia parables up to and including ch. 25. If we say that Luke did not adopt Mark's closing verses because he had "used" the material before (in 19,12 f.; 12,38, 40)[95] and that Matthew was unwilling to close his discourse as early as Mark and collected more material on the subject in his usual fashion,[96] the conclusion is still precisely that the closing admonitions do not seem to have been so closely bound up with the discourse in the tradition.

---

[91] T. COLANI, *Jésus Christ et les croyances messianiques de son temps* (2nd ed. 1864). The history of the research on this subject is described in G. R. BEASLEY-MURRAY, *Jesus and the Future* (1954).

[92] J. WELLHAUSEN, *Comm. Mk* (1909), 100; LOHMEYER, *Comm. Mk*, ad loc.; G. R. BEASLEY-MURRAY, The Rise and Fall of the Little Apocalypse Theory, *Exp. Times* 64 (1952/53), 348 f.; SCHMID, *Comm. Mk*, 237.

[93] Cf. R. BULTMANN, *Die Geschichte der synoptischen Tradition* (2nd ed. 1931), 124 f., 187 f.

[94] BULTMANN, op. cit., 126, calls it "eine ganz späte hellenistische Bildung". Cf. the Semitic substratum for "snare" — "travail" (1 Ths 5,3) pointed out in the next chapter (see 192, below).

[95] J. M. CREED (1930), and cf. J. SCHMID (3rd ed. 1955), *Comm. Lk*, ad loc.

[96] For example, KLOSTERMANN and P. BONNARD (1963), *Comm. Mt*, ad loc., SCHMID, *Comm. Mt*, 333 f.

Then if we compare the content of the admonitions within the "midrash" with that of the concluding admonitions, we see that the great theme of the latter is "to watch", for the day will come "suddenly", while the interwoven parenesis warns the disciples against "Antichrist" occurrences and against being led astray during the "travail". Altogether this indicates that, in judging the parenetic parts of the discourse, we must not equate the parenesis within the "midrash" with the concluding one. In order to come to some conclusion as to whether the Daniel "midrash" and the interwoven parenesis belonged together from the beginning, wholly or in part, we will now return to the OT texts used and see what basis there may be there for the admonitory sentences.

The first admonition we meet with in the discourse is that in 13,5b: "Take heed that no one leads you astray" (πλανήσῃ), which is combined with the sentence on the many who say "I am" and who "will lead many astray" (πλανήσουσιν). The prophecy on the leading astray of the many is based, as I found above to be probable, on Dn 8,25: "he shall destroy many". The admonition therefore arose through a simple transition from indicative to imperative, from the prophecy of a danger to a warning of it.

The next warning is that in 13,7, in connection with the prophecy on war: "When you hear of wars and rumours of wars, do not be alarmed" (μὴ θροεῖσθε). The reason for the admonition is given in connection with Dn 8,19: "it must take place"; the wars are further explained by the combined quotation from Is 19,2 and 2 Ch 15,6. Anxiety in connection with war is a common theme in the OT,[97] but it is possible that Is 19 and 2 Ch 15 may have made a special contribution here. Is 19,1 and 3 refer to the confusion of the Egyptians and in 2 Ch 15,7 we meet with an admonition which is reminiscent of the one under discussion: "But you, be strong (חזקו, LXX ἰσχύσατε)! Do not let your hands be weak" (אל ירפו, LXX μὴ ἐκλυέσθωσαν).

The admonition in 13,9a ("take heed to yourselves") involves not least a change of perspective in the account. While in the preceding verses attention was concentrated on the world-wide convulsions, in v. 9 it is concentrated on the very obvious personal troubles of the persons addressed.[98] In 13,11 the help of the Holy Spirit in making defences before the courts of law is promised: "do not be anxious beforehand what you are to say". This admonition forms part of the problematic vv. 9–11, which we found above to break out of the context, in that they are not so closely associated with the OT.

---

[97] See, for example, Is 13,6 ff.; 17,14; Jr 4,19 ff.; 6,24 ff.; Jl 2,1 ff.; Na 2,11.
[98] See, for example, BEASLEY-MURRAY, *Mark 13*, and W. GRUNDMANN, *Comm. Mk* (2nd ed. 1959), ad loc. Cf. LOHMEYER, *Comm. Mk*, ad loc.

Then we come to 13,14, the commandment to flee to the mountains. Here the admonition, as we saw above, is directly included in the "midrash". It is taken from Gn 19,17, like the prohibition on turning back in v. 16. The prohibition against going down from the roof and entering the house is parallel with the latter and seems to lack any association with the OT. 13,18 ("pray that it may not happen in winter") has no obvious OT background either.

When, on the other hand, we come to 13,21, the admonition not to believe (μὴ πιστεύετε) those who say "Look, here is the Christ!" etc. is clearly connected with Dt 13, used in the passage. Dt 13,4 says: "You shall not listen (לא תשמע) to the words of that prophet ...", and v. 9 on the enticing member of the family: "You shall not yield (לא תאבה) to him or listen (לא תשמע) to him".

Thus we have seen that in two passages (13,14 ff. and 13,21) the parenesis associated with the "midrash" is so closely bound up with the text expounded that it is most natural to assume that there "midrash" and parenesis are one.[99] We may well consider that this is the case also in v. 5 b (where the indicative "lead astray" gave rise to a warning against being led astray) and in v. 7 (anxiety at the prospect of war) the connection is possible. In any case, the conclusion is that our "midrash" had at least some of its parenetic elements connected with it from the beginning.

It now remains to bring forward some further details which were not, so to speak, directly taken from the texts used. They are briefly as follows. (a) 13,6: *many* say "I am"; (b) they do so "in my name" (ἐπὶ τῷ ὀνόματί μου); (c) 13,8c: "this is the beginning of the travail" (ἀρχὴ ὠδίνων ταῦτα); (d) 13 b: the hate "for my name's sake" (διὰ τὸ ὄνομά μου); (e) 15 a: he who is on the housetop ...; (f) 17 f.: alas for those with child ..., may it not be in winter; (g) 21: "Look, here is the Christ"; (h) 14: "those who are in *Judaea*". Of these, (e) may be a formation in parallel with the context and (c) an explanatory comment. (f) seems to be, so to speak, theologically innocent and here it may be a matter of an early expansion or of incorporated logia. (b), (d) and (g), like (a) and (h), may have something to do with the early history of the eschatological discourse and with its different usage and interpretation in the early Church. We accordingly have reason to return to the subject in Chap. VII, on the history of the tradition of the text.

---

[99] Cf. J. THEODOR, Midrash Haggadah, *Jew. Enc.* VII (1904), 550 ff.

CHAPTER VI

The Eschatological Discourse and the Letters to the Thessalonians

1. *Introduction*

The subjects discussed in the first and second Letters to the Thessalonians are very like those in Mk 13 and here and there the similarities of expression are striking.[1] These similarities have been explained in a great variety of ways.[2] Thus scholars have assumed that Paul was directly dependent on an early form of Mk 13 or Mt 24;[3] some of them have thought that Q may have been involved in this relation.[4] It has also been suggested that the similarities are due to both Thessalonians and Mk 13 being based on Jewish material in the form of a written apocalypse.[5] Other arguments seem to proceed on the basis of the assumption that the similarities are connected with the common theme of the Parousia and what is to precede it.[6] These possible solutions have a by no means inconsiderable number of variants, which are related partly to the individual scholar's view of the origin and development of the eschatological discourse and partly to the view of the authenticity of 2 Ths. Thus we have a whole range of views, from one according to which both the Letters to the Thessalonians are genuine and, as regards large portions of the eschatological material, are based on a form of the discourse written down at an early date—the discourse mainly going back to Jesus Himself—and supple-

---

[1] See the table in B. RIGAUX, *Comm. Ths* (1956), 98 ff. Also J. B. ORCHARD, Thessalonians and the Synoptic Gospels, *Bibl.* 19 (1938), 19 ff., and J. P. BROWN, Synoptic Parallels in the Epistles and Form-History, *NT Stud.* 10 (1963/64), 45.

[2] See for the following paragraph BEASLEY-MURRAY, *Jesus and the Future*, esp. 232 ff., and RIGAUX, *Comm.*, 95 ff.

[3] See B. H. STREETER, *The Four Gospels* (1924), 493; ORCHARD, op. cit.; C. C. TORREY, *Documents of the Primitive Church* (1941), 36 ff.; E. COTHENET, La IIe Épître aux Thessaloniciens et l'Apocalypse synoptique, *Rech. Sci. Rel.* 42 (1954), 5–39. Cf. D. BUZY, Saint Paul et Saint Matthieu, *Rech. Sci. Rel.* 28 (1938), 473–78, and BEASLEY-MURRAY, op. cit., 234.

[4] BEASLEY-MURRAY, loc. cit.

[5] G. HÖLSCHER, Der Ursprung der Apokalypse Mrk 13, *Theol. Blätter* 12 (1933), 199 f., and C. H. DODD, *The Apostolic Preaching* (1936), 37 ff.

[6] Cf. e.g. B. RIGAUX, *Saint Paul et ses lettres* (1962), 181 f.

mented by Q,[7] to a view in which 2 Ths is deutero-Pauline, neither 1 nor 2 Ths has any positive relation to the "discourse" or parts of it and this discourse contains little, if any, of the teaching of Jesus, consisting instead of apocalyptic material borrowed from Jewish sources.[8]

Here I refrain from discussing in detail the question of the authenticity of 2 Ths[9] and assume, with many scholars from different camps, that the Letter is authentic.[10] The two main problems are the strange literary similarities between 1 and 2 Ths and the fact that the eschatology of the two letters may seem inconsistent. The latter problem is now generally held to be hardly a serious one and the further investigations in this chapter will confirm this view. Recently computers have also provided material for the discussion,[11] but it seems that in this connection computer methods have not been sufficiently elaborated as yet.[12]

The previous chapter indicated that an exposition of Daniel is the basis of the eschatological discourse. If this exposition existed before the discourse was written down in Mark's Gospel,[13] a comparison with 1 and 2 Ths may tell us something of the earlier history of this discourse and also something of 1 and 2 Ths. In this comparison I shall not primarily direct attention to the verbal correspondences[14] but to the function of the expressions in the exposition.

Paul, the former disciple of Gamaliel,[15] made use of and taught traditions (παραδόσεις) in his work as a missionary.[16] That which is

---

[7] BEASLEY-MURRAY, loc. cit.

[8] P. VIELHAUER, Apokalyptik des Urchristentums (in HENNECKE, Apokryphen II, 3rd ed. 1964), 429 ff.

[9] See the exhaustive discussion of this subject in RIGAUX, Comm., 121–52. Also W. G. KÜMMEL, Das literarische und geschichtliche Problem des ersten Thessalonicherbriefes, Suppl. Nov. Test. 6 (1962), 213 ff., where K.-G. ECKART's article Der zweite echte Brief des Apostels Paulus an die Thessalonicher, Zschr. Theol. Ki. 58 (1961), 30–44, is critically examined.

[10] E. VON DOBSCHÜTZ, A. VON HARNACK, M. DIBELIUS, J. WEISS, A. OEPKE, M. GOGUEL, B. RIGAUX, W. G. KÜMMEL, H. VON CAMPENHAUSEN.

[11] A. Q. MORTON and J. McLEMAN, Christianity and the Computer (1964), 33: 1 and 2 Ths are indistinguishable, as they show the same linguistic picture.

[12] See, for example, T. M. KNOX, The Computer and the NT, Svensk Exeg. Årsbok 28–29 (1963–64), 111–16; G. B. CAIRD, Do Computers Count?, Exp. Times 76 (1964/65), 176; H. K. McARTHUR, Computer Criticism, ibid., 367–70.

[13] I assume that St. Mark's was the first Gospel to be written down.

[14] Thus in particular ORCHARD, Bibl. 19 (1938), 19 ff. In a still unpublished manuscript H. BURKHARDT interprets many of these word-correspondences as simanim for Gospel tradition, following up GERHARDSSON in Memory and Manuscript.

[15] Ac 22,3. And see below, 187, note 50.

[16] See on this and the following points GERHARDSSON, op. cit., 288 ff.

"transmitted" is to a great extent what the Apostle himself "received" (παραλαμβάνειν; for example, 1 Co 15,23). If we take him at his word —and why should we not do so?[17]—he passed on these traditions in his work in the churches, and in his letters he only reminds his readers of them and repeats parts of them.[18] It seems to me to be an inescapable fact that among these παραδόσεις there were several sayings of Jesus and that Paul regarded these sayings as being of special importance.[19]

Among the παραδόσεις which Paul passed on was the teaching that Christ would return to judge and to save. This also forms part of the *kerygma* which he shares with other missionaries of the early Church.[20] It sometimes happens, however, that scholars who hold this view at the same time deny that these teachers of the Church gave any detailed teaching on this Parousia, viz. on "apocalyptic".[21] This is because they presuppose that Mk 13 has no essential element in common with the teaching of Jesus and that 2 Ths is deutero-Pauline. The idea which they form of Jesus and of the content of the apostolic teaching with the aid of other texts leads them to this conclusion. Perhaps an analysis of a couple of portions of 1 and 2 Ths against the background of the results achieved in the previous chapter may shed light on these problems as well.

---

[17] Cf. R. BULTMANN, Die Bedeutung des geschichtlichen Jesus für die Theologie des Paulus, *Theol. Blätter* 8 (1929), 137–51, and H.-J. SCHOEPS, *Paulus* (1959), 48 ff.

[18] See 1 Co 11,2, 23 ff.; 15,1 ff.; Gl 1,9; Phil 4,9; Col 2,6. And cf. O. MOE, *Paulus und die evangelische Geschichte* (1912), 34 f.

[19] This is denied by W. HEITMÜLLER, Zum Problem Paulus und Jesus, *Zschr. Nt. Wiss.* 13 (1912), 320–37; BULTMANN, in his article in *Theol. Blätter* (see note 17) and in *Das Verhältnis der urchristlichen Christusbotschaft zum historischen Jesus* (1960), 9; W. SCHMITHALS, Paulus und der historische Jesus, *Zschr. Nt. Wiss.* 53 (1962), 145–60. Cf. M. DIBELIUS, *Die Formgeschichte des Evangeliums* (3rd ed. 1959), 239 ff. The collection of material in RESCH's book *Der Paulinismus und die Logia Jesu*, seems to have fallen undeservedly into oblivion in his native country. See also C. H. DODD's works History and the Gospel (1938), 63 ff., Matthew and Paul, in *NT Studies* (1953), 53–66, and The Primitive Catechism and the Sayings of Jesus, in *NT Essays ... in mem. T. W. Manson* (1959), 106–18; W. D. DAVIES, *Paul and Rabbinic Judaism* (1955), 136 ff. For current discussions, see W. G. KÜMMEL, Jesus und Paulus, *NT Stud.* 10 (1963/64), 163–81.

[20] See, for example, DODD, *The Apostolic Preaching*, 7 ff.; VIELHAUER, in HENNECKE, *Apokryphen* II, 429; H. VON CAMPENHAUSEN, Die Begründung kirchlicher Entscheidungen beim Apostel Paulus, in *Aus der Frühzeit des Christentums* (1963), 35 f.

[21] DODD, op. cit., 37 ff.; VIELHAUER, op. cit., 430.

2. 1 Ths 4,13–18

In the first part of the Letter (1,2–3,13) Paul spoke with joy and thankfulness of the spiritual status of the Thessalonian church and recalled his work among the people he was addressing. The second, parenetic part of the Letter begins at 4,1 with exhortations, consolation and eschatological teaching (4,1–5,24). This is the main purpose of the Letter.[22] Thus 4,1 begins with exhortations to the Christian way of life, especially in sexual matters (vv. 3–8). Vv. 9–11 consist of exhortations to brotherly love and in v. 11 the readers are admonished to "live quietly, to mind your own affairs, and to work with your hands, as we charged you ...".

With 4,13 the Apostle enters upon a new theme, the fate at the Parousia of the Christians who have already died. The subject of the Parousia has been glanced at earlier in the Letter: in 2,19 f. the Thessalonians are to be Paul's glory and joy in the presence of Jesus Christ at His Parousia and in 3,12 he prays that the Lord may make them abound in love, so that He may establish (στηρίξαι) their hearts unblamable in holiness before God at the Parousia of Christ with all His holy ones. That is to say, Paul is writing his Letter with the same early prospect of the Parousia as that which gave rise to the anxiety of the Thessalonians, leading to Paul's statement in vv. 13 ff. in answer to the Thessalonians' question, viz. whether the surviving Christians will be privileged before the dead at the Parousia. It is difficult to determine exactly what it really was that worried the Thessalonians. We may leave this question on one side[23] and content ourselves with the knowledge that they *were* worried and that Paul wished to comfort them by increasing their knowledge.

Let us first consider his line of thought. The Thessalonians are not to grieve; they have a hope (v. 13b). The reason for this hope is given in v. 14: *for* (γάρ) faith in the death and resurrection of Jesus also implies (εἰ πιστεύομεν ... οὕτως καί) faith that God will bring forth (ἄξει) those who have fallen asleep in Christ,[24] together with Him (σὺν αὐτῷ). This is a thesis which must be explained in more detail, and this

---

[22] Rigaux, *Comm.*, 54 f.

[23] See instead the commentaries, particularly Rigaux, ad loc., and also F. Guntermann, *Die Eschatologie des hl. Paulus* (1932), 36 ff., and J. Dupont, Σὺν Χριστῷ. *L'Union avec le Christ suivant saint Paul* (1952), 40 f.

[24] The interpreters are doubtful as regards to which word διὰ τοῦ Ἰησοῦ is to be attached, as well as the exact meaning of the expression. See Rigaux, *Comm.*, ad loc. I give here the translation by M. Dibelius (3rd ed. 1937) and A. Oepke (6th ed. 1953), *Comm. Ths*, ad loc.

explanation is given in v. 15: *for* (γάρ), Paul declares by the (a) word of the Lord (ἐν λόγῳ κυρίου), the survivors will not precede (οὐ μὴ φθάσωμεν) the dead at the Parousia. At the same time as the explanation of v. 14 continues in vv. 16 f., vv. 16 f. also form a more detailed explanation of v. 15 (ὅτι). It consists of an account of the Parousia, according to which the Lord will descend from heaven and those who have died in Christ will arise first. Then they, together with the survivors, will be caught up (ἁρπαγησόμεθα) in the clouds to meet the Lord. After that they will always be with the Lord. With this the argument ends and in v. 18 the Apostle concludes (ὥστε): "comfort one another with these words".

One of the many problems posed by this text is the word of the Lord quoted. To what does it refer in the text?[25] To v. 15*b* and, if so, how much further? Furthermore, what does the expression mean? Is the Apostle basing his words on an agraphon[26] or on a personal "revelation"[27] or is he alluding to some saying of Jesus which is preserved in the Gospels? Mk 9,1, Mt 22,32 or parts of Mk 13 par. have been suggested for the latter.[28]

First, we must remember that λόγος does not necessarily mean "logion". Like its Hebrew equivalent (דבר), it may be used both of a complex of doctrine and of parts of such a complex.[29] That is to say, the λόγος κυρίου which is mentioned may, as far as the terminology is concerned, be, for example, a "discourse" or parts of one, and the expression may thus also be translated "a teaching", "an instruction of the Lord" or something of that kind.

The problem on which Paul has now to give an opinion concerns a point of doctrine which is not directly bound up with directives for conduct, church order, etc. We might call it a non-halakic decision.[30]

---

[25] Cf., for example, K. WEGENAST, *Das Verständnis der Tradition bei Paulus und in den Deuteropaulinen* (1962), 109.

[26] G. WOHLENBERG (2nd ed. 1909), DIBELIUS, J. E. FRAME (1912), *Comm. Ths*, ad loc. JOACH. JEREMIAS, *Unbekannte Jesusworte* (3rd ed. 1963), 77 ff. Cf. BULTMANN, *Theol. Blätter* 8 (1929), 139, and id., *Geschichte*, 136.

[27] G. MILLIGAN (1908), E. VON DOBSCHÜTZ (1909), and O. LINTON (1964), *Comm. Ths*, ad loc.; J. G. DAVIES, The Genesis of Belief in an Imminent Parousia, *J. Theol. Stud.* 14 (1963), 105 ff. Cf. BULTMANN, loc. cit. Against this view argues, for example, VON CAMPENHAUSEN, op. cit., 37.

[28] See the commentaries; RESCH, *Paulinismus*, 38; D. M. STANLEY, Pauline Allusions to the Sayings of Jesus, *Cath. Bibl. Quart.* 23 (1961), 28.

[29] See BACHER, *Die älteste Terminologie*, 17 ff.; M. JASTROW, *Dictionary* (1926), sub voce; GERHARDSSON, *Memory*, 295 f.

[30] For the epithet "non-halakic", see, for example, A. MARMORSTEIN, Agada, *Enc. Jud.* I (1928), 951 f.

182

For comparison, I will now produce two other passages in which the situation is similar, namely, 1 Co 11,17 ff. and 1 Co 15,1 ff.[31]

In 1 Co 11,17 ff. Paul is to censure the wrongful behaviour of the Corinthians at "the Lord's Supper" (τὸ κυριακὸν δεῖπνον). In vv. 17–22 he describes the unsatisfactory state of affairs at Corinth: there are divisions (σχίσματα) in the church and this is manifested in the fact that at the meetings each person eats what he has brought with him. As a result some are hungry and others are drunk. Paul's opinion is that: "it is not the Lord's supper that you eat" (v. 20). He does not approve their conduct (οὐκ ἐπαινῶ, v. 22).[32] From v. 23 onwards Paul begins his own argument, in order to put things right. He has received from the Lord (ἐγὼ γὰρ παρέλαβον ἀπὸ τοῦ κυρίου) a tradition which he also passed on (παρέδωκα) to the Corinthians.[33] Then this tradition is quoted, i.e. the words of institution of the Eucharist, the nucleus of which are Jesus' words about the bread as "my body" and the wine as "my blood" (vv. 23b–25). To this Paul adds in v. 26 his explanation of ἀνάμνησις: when you eat and drink "you proclaim (καταγγέλλετε) the Lord's death until He comes".[34]

In v. 27 Paul begins his application and conclusion (ὥστε); he who unworthily eats this bread and drinks this cup of the Lord is guilty of profaning the body and blood of the Lord. Instead, a man is to examine (δοκιμάζειν) himself and discern the body,[35] judging himself in order that he may not be judged (vv. 28–32). At v. 33 Paul has reached a concrete conclusion (ὥστε): the Corinthians are to wait for each other at the meetings, and those who are hungry should eat at home.

The structure is accordingly as follows: the problem (vv. 17–22), reference to and quotation of a Jesus tradition (vv. 23–25), (an explanation of part of this tradition (v. 26)), the Apostle's conclusions from and exhortations on the basis of the tradition quoted (vv. 27–32),

---

[31] See GERHARDSSON, op. cit., 320 ff. For halakic decisions, see ibid., 311 ff. Also L. CERFAUX, La tradition selon saint Paul, in Recueil L. Cerfaux II (1954), 253 ff.

[32] On the value of this expression, see A. FRIDRICHSEN, Non laudo. Note sur I. Cor. 11,17–22, Horae Soederbl. 1 (1944), 28–32.

[33] For a more detailed analysis of the tradition terminology here, see GERHARDS-SON, loc. cit. For the hypothesis of the Hellenistic community as mediators of the tradition, see the recent criticism in E. LARSSON, Paulus och den hellenistiska församlingsteologin, Svensk Exeg. Årsbok 28–29 (1963–64), 81–110.

[34] See, for example, H. LIETZMANN, Comm. Co (4th ed. by W. G. KÜMMEL, 1949), ad loc. For καταγγέλλειν in the sense of cultic recitation, see G. B. GRAY, Sacrifice in the OT (1925), 395, and H. ODEBERG, Comm. Co (1953), ad loc. Cf. also H. SCHLIER, Die Verkündigung im Gottesdienst, in Die Zeit der Kirche (3rd ed. 1962), 246 ff.

[35] For this difficult sentence, see the commentaries, ad loc.

and a practical conclusion from the entire preceding argument, and a direct answer to the problem posed (vv. 33 f.).

In the second example, the much-discussed passage from 1 Co 15,1 ff.,[36] Paul is to refute those in Corinth who deny the resurrection of the dead (v. 12). But this is inserted in connection with the more comprehensive purpose of giving teaching on the Resurrection. Here Paul begins by recalling the tradition (παρελάβετε, v. 1; παρέδωκα, v. 3) which he himself received as such (παρέλαβον, v. 3). This tradition, this λόγος (v. 2), consists of a series of clauses which summarize some essential events related to Jesus' death and resurrection (vv. 3–7).[37] As in the previous example, the end of the tradition is followed by an explanation by the Apostle (vv. 8–11), who in these verses describes how he himself became involved in these events. With v. 11, however, attention is again drawn to the *logos* quoted: "whether then (it was) I or they, so we preach (κηρύσσομεν) ...".

The problem which is to be dealt with first then emerges in v. 12— the denial by some Corinthians of the resurrection of the body. At the same time the wording shows what element in the *logos* quoted provides the starting-point for Paul's argument—its content that Christ arose from the dead: εἰ δὲ Χριστὸς κηρύσσεται ὅτι ... ἐγήγερται, πῶς λέγουσιν ... This κηρύσσεται takes up the κηρύσσομεν of v. 11. In vv. 13–19 Paul develops an argument which forms the chain "the Apostles' *kerygma* is true, Christ has been raised, the dead are raised". None of the links can be denied without the others also being denied. V. 20 closes this part of the argument, and this part also forms a basis for the continuation: "But now in fact (νυνὶ δέ)[38] Christ has been raised from the dead, the first fruits of those who have fallen asleep".

Thus the structure here is as follows: reference to and quotation of a tradition on the resurrection of Jesus (vv. 1–7), (comments on a part of this tradition (vv. 8–11)), the problem (v. 12), argument on the basis of the tradition (vv. 13–19), a positive conclusion which involves a refutation of the denial which formed the problem (v. 20).[39]

---

[36] See on the following exposition GERHARDSSON, op. cit., 296 ff., 322 f.

[37] On the length of the quotation, see GERHARDSSON, op. cit., 299 f., and references there, together with E. BAMMEL, Herkunft und Funktion der Traditionselemente in 1. Kor. 15,1–11, *Theol. Zschr.* 11 (1955), 401–19; H.-W. BARTSCH, Die Argumentation des Paulus in I Cor 15,3–11, *Zschr. Nt. Wiss.* 55 (1964), 263 f., in which some of the German literature on the passage is quoted; J. ROLOFF, *Apostolat–Verkündigung–Kirche* (1965), 45 ff.

[38] For this nuance in νυνὶ δέ, see E. SCHWYZER, *Griechische Grammatik* II (1950), 571.

[39] For examinations of the exposition in 1 Co 15 as a whole, see H. RIESENFELD, Das Bildwort vom Weizenkorn bei Paulus, in *Studien z. NT in hon. E. Klostermann* (1961), 43–55, and M. E. DAHL, *The Resurrection of the Body* (1962).

The main difference in relation to 1 Co 11 is that the problem is not presented at the beginning. This is in good agreement with the circumstance that the confutation of those who deny the resurrection forms part of a more comprehensive instruction.

In both these cases, as in 1 Ths 4,13 ff., the basis of the Apostle's argumentation is a tradition which is assumed to have an indisputable authority. Otherwise, if we compare the structure of 1 Ths 4,13 ff. with that in the two examples, we find here also how the Apostle gathers together at the end (v. 18) the whole of the preceding argument in a sentence which is related to the problem he is faced with: "comfort one another"[40] in relation to v. 13, "you may not grieve". While in 1 Co 11 it was easy and in 1 Co 15 only slightly difficult to determine the beginning and end of the tradition quoted, the situation in 1 Ths 4 is somewhat different. We get the impression that Paul is interweaving with a tradition his own interpretation and application of it: "... the Lord shall descend, and the dead in Christ will rise first; then *we* who are alive ...".[41]

We will now take a closer look at 1 Ths 4,13 ff. and, in doing so, compare the text with the eschatological discourse. Against the background of the previous chapter I put forward the following hypothetical statements. The eschatological discourse has proved to be based on a "midrash" on Daniel. *If* Paul knew of this discourse, there is a strong possibility that he was also acquainted with its "midrashic" basis. It would be highly probable that he would use the material when he was to give his opinion on these eschatological questions.

(13) Οὐ θέλομεν δὲ ὑμᾶς ἀγνοεῖν, ἀδελφοί, περὶ τῶν κοιμωμένων, ἵνα μὴ λυπῆσθε καθὼς καὶ οἱ λοιποὶ οἱ μὴ ἔχοντες ἐλπίδα. (14) εἰ γὰρ πιστεύομεν ὅτι Ἰησοῦς ἀπέθανεν καὶ ἀνέστη, οὕτως καὶ ὁ θεὸς[42] τοὺς κοιμηθέντας διὰ τοῦ Ἰησοῦ ἄξει σὺν αὐτῷ.

Thus, when Paul is to console the depressed Thessalonians, he begins in v. 14 with a wider saying which takes the form of a somewhat forced protasis–apodosis construction. The εἰ clause there perhaps

---

[40] The phrase also shows similarities with contemporary letters of condolence; see A. DEISSMANN, *Licht vom Osten* (4th ed. 1923), 143 ff. (DUPONT, *L'Union avec le Christ*, 41).

[41] On the change in Paul's expectation of living to see the Parousia, see W. GRUNDMANN, Überlieferung und Eigenaussage im eschatologischen Denken des Apostels Paulus, *NT Stud.* 8 (1961/62), 17 ff., and J. A. SINT, Parusie-Erwartung und Parusie-Verzögerung im paulinischen Briefcorpus, *Zschr. Kath. Theol.* 86 (1964), 54 ff. Cf. C. K. BARRETT, NT Eschatology, *Scot. J. Theol.* 6 (1953), 143 f.

[42] MSS.B *1739* pc syr^harcl attach καί to τοὺς κοιμηθέντας instead of to the whole sentence: οὕτως ὁ θεὸς καὶ τ.κ, This seems to be a secondary reading, depending on a desire to adjust the content.

contains a quotation of some confessional formula.[43] This is the basis of the assurance in the apodosis that God will also bring (ἄξει) those who have fallen asleep "through Jesus" with Him (σὺν αὐτῷ). The basic thought resembles that in 1 Co 15,12 ff., where Christ is said to be "the first fruits" (vv. 20 and 23): even as Christ certainly died but also arose from the dead, so also the harvest (the first fruits of which have been taken)—the Christians who are in communion with Him—will also arise. But the thought in 1 Ths only resembles that in 1 Co, which was written later: the text in Thessalonians does not carry on any argument on the basis of any ἀπαρχή ideology.

What then is the ground for Paul's assertion, based on the statement on the death and resurrection of Jesus, that God will bring those who have fallen asleep through Jesus with Him? It seems to me that the somewhat mysterious expression ἄξει σὺν αὐτῷ, rightly understood, may show us a solution. The attempts here to paraphrase σύν by "in communion with" are not altogether convincing and we should beware of giving the preposition the meaning of "into communion with".[44] The simple straightforward translation means that God "brings" Christ and that He "brings" those who have fallen asleep "with Him". In my opinion it is quite clear that Dn 7,13 underlies these formulations—the text which otherwise provides the basic quotation from the OT for the description of the Parousia in the eschatological discourse. Dn 7,13 says:

I saw in the night visions,
and behold, with the clouds of heaven
there came one like a son of man,
and he came (מטה; LXX παρῆν; Theod. ἔφθασε) to the Ancient of Days,
and *they brought him* (הקרבוהי; LXX οἱ παρεστηκότες προσήγαγον αὐτόν;[45]
   Theod.[A] προσήγαγον αὐτόν; Theod.[B] προσήχθη αὐτῷ; Theod.[MSS.] προσηνέχθη
   αὐτῷ) before him.

Thus, according to Paul, it is the risen Jesus who is the Son of Man who is brought forward in Dn 7,13 and Paul means that the dead Christians will then be brought forward together with Him.

We may then ask ourselves how it comes about that Paul can introduce a multitude along with this Son of Man in Dn 7,13. However, this is fairly plausible, since the second part of Dn 7 interprets the

---

[43] For example, K. STAAB, *Comm. Ths* (3rd ed. 1959), ad loc. Cf. RIGAUX, *Comm.*, ad loc., and E. STAUFFER, *NT Theology* (1955), 338 f.

[44] Thus when Ac 13,23 and He 2,10 are quoted as parallels (RIGAUX, *Comm.*, ad loc.).

[45] This text is selected by J. ZIEGLER (ed. 1954), and is supported by Syh[mg] (*vid.*), Just. and others. 88-Syh[txt] read ὡς πάλαιος ... and παρῆσαν αὐτῷ (= the text of RAHLFS's ed.).

vision of the Son of Man so far as to state that the saints of the Most
High will have kingdom and dominion (v. 27). There is also a possibility that Paul knew of a Daniel reading which is now to be found in
certain MSS. of the LXX[46] and in which we find: "There came one
like a son of man, and one like an Ancient of Days was there (παρῆν)
and those standing by (οἱ παρεστηκότες) were with Him (or: came to
Him)" (παρῆσαν αὐτῷ). These παρεστηκότες are the thousands which in
Dn 7,10 παρειστήκεισαν before the Ancient of Days. Paul may have
found this multitude in a reading such as this. Be that as it may, it is
elsewhere clear that Paul thought of the Parousia of Christ as being
combined with a collective Parousia. Thus he speaks in 1 Ths 3,13
(already quoted) on "the Parousia of our Lord Jesus with all His holy
ones" (μετὰ πάντων τῶν ἁγίων αὐτοῦ),[47] where these holy ones are
angels, saints or both.[48] The critical point for Paul's argumentation
here, however, is the participation of the Christians who have fallen
asleep in this collective Parousia.

(15) Τοῦτο γὰρ ὑμῖν λέγομεν ἐν λόγῳ κυρίου, ὅτι ἡμεῖς οἱ ζῶντες οἱ
περιλειπόμενοι εἰς τὴν παρουσίαν[49] τοῦ κυρίου οὐ μὴ φθάσωμεν τοὺς κοιμηθέντας.

Thus, in v. 14 Paul gave an assurance without stating any further
grounds for it that those who had fallen asleep would be "brought
forward" together with Christ. Here in v. 15 he gives his first explanation of the grounds on which he gave this assurance (γάρ).

When Paul sat at the feet of Gamaliel,[50] the process of discussion
must have got into his blood; a problem was posed, statements of

[46] See the previous note.

[47] This is a quotation from Zch 14,5. See also 2 Ths 1,10, and cf. 1 Co 6,2, Jd
14 and 4 Ez 7,28.

[48] See RIGAUX, Comm., ad loc.

[49] Perhaps there is also an association with Dn 7,13 in παρουσία. The Son of
Man came (אתה, LXX παρῆν) to the Ancient. Cf. P. L. SCHOONHEIM, Een sema-
siologisch Onderzoek van Parousia (1953), 167 ff., 276 f. Moreover it is not altogether
clear how εἰς τὴν κτλ. is to be combined with the sentence; see, for example, A.
WIMMER, Trostworte des Apostels Paulus an Hinterbliebene in Thessalonich,
Bibl. 36 (1955), 273–86.

[50] Ac 22,3; cf. Phil 3,5. The arguments put forward for thinking that Paul was
not a pupil of Gamaliel and had never been in Jerusalem are not very convincing.
If Gl 1,22 is to be used to support this idea, it must be assumed that "the Churches
of Christ in Judaea" were personally acquainted with the pupils of the rabbinic
collegia! Cf. HEITMÜLLER, Zschr. Nt. Wiss. 13 (1912), 327; BULTMANN, Theol.
Blätter 8 (1929), 137; E. HAENCHEN, Comm. Ac (1959), ad 22,3. On the other hand,
see G. BORNKAMM, Paulus, in Rel. in Gesch. u. Geg. V (3rd ed. 1961), 167 f. And to
claim that the Apostle did not use the Scriptures as a rabbi, on the grounds that
he was too free and used the LXX, seems to oversimplify the matter. Cf. HAEN-
CHEN, loc. cit., and, on the other hand, GERHARDSSON, Memory, 280–323.

opinion were made and supported by references to the Scriptures or
to traditions handed down from earlier teachers (Rabbi N. said in the
name of Rabbi N. etc.).⁵¹ Though Paul's past may have influenced
his mode of argument in some passages,⁵² it is nevertheless in a wholly
different milieu that he is now, in his capacity as an Apostle of God
and of Christ, deciding his attitude to a problem. Thus perhaps λέγομεν
in v. 15a may be comparable with the countless אמר in the rabbinical
writings.⁵³ But Paul here is not relying on the saying of a rabbi nor
on the Scriptures, but on a *logos* from the divine Lord who sent him.
It is doubtful whether λέγομεν ἐν λόγῳ κυρίου means that he intends
to repeat a received tradition, as in 1 Co 11 and 1 Co 15. On the other
hand, the wording could be interpreted in this way, that Paul "says"
with reference to a *logos*⁵⁴ (for example, a "midrash"!) from the Lord
which he interprets and supplements for his own purpose. This seems
to me at least to be what in fact has happened here (I disregard for
the time being the question of authenticity⁵⁵). The "explanation" in
v. 15 would then be a Pauline dictum (v. 15b) and he says that he is
basing his dictum on a *logos* from the Lord.

(16) ὅτι αὐτὸς ὁ κύριος ἐν κελεύσματι, ἐν φωνῇ ἀρχαγγέλου καὶ ἐν σάλπιγγι θεοῦ, καταβήσεται ἀπ᾽ οὐρανοῦ, καὶ οἱ νεκροὶ ἐν Χριστῷ ἀναστήσονται
πρῶτον, (17) ἔπειτα ἡμεῖς οἱ ζῶντες οἱ περιλειπόμενοι ἅμα σὺν αὐτοῖς
ἁρπαγησόμεθα ἐν νεφέλαις εἰς ἀπάντησιν τοῦ κυρίου εἰς ἀέρα. καὶ οὕτως
πάντοτε σὺν κυρίῳ ἐσόμεθα.

Here Paul gives the support (ὅτι) for the dictum which he gave in
v. 15 and which was based on the *logos*. His wording shows striking
similarities to the eschatological discourse. Each of the details quoted
in the description of the Parousia can certainly be parallelled in con-

---

⁵¹ This is, of course, extremely brief. The terminology is more abundant; no
distinction has been made between halakic and haggadic discussions, nor between
the problems of explaining obscure Scripture passages and the problems concerning
the rabbinic tradition. See I. JELSKI-COLDIN, *Die innere Einrichtung des grossen
Synedrions zu Jerusalem* [1893], 82 ff.; BACHER, *Terminologie*; S. B. HOENIG, *The
Great Sanhedrin* (1953), 106 f.; GERHARDSSON, op. cit., 245 ff.

⁵² See GERHARDSSON, op. cit., e.g. 311 ff.

⁵³ For example, b Ber. 3b: "R. Zerika says (that) R. Ammi said (that) R. Joshua
ben Levi said: 'A verse in the Scripture says'"; (or "R.Z. says in the name of R.A.,
(who says) in the name of …'") אמר רבי ז' אמר ר' א' אמר ר' י' ב' ל' כתוב אחד אומר

⁵⁴ The expression is to be found in 1 Rg 20,35: "one of the sons of the prophets
said (אמר) to his fellow by the word of Yahweh (בדבר יהוה) …"; LXX (21,35):
εἶπεν … ἐν λόγῳ κυρίου. Cf. 1 Ch 21,19. This mode of expression can scarcely be
cited in support of the revelation theory (cf. note 27 above); it supports my interpretation just as much. Cf. DAVIES, *J. Theol. Stud.* 14 (1963), 106. The interpretation "with reference to" etc. is also given by BURKHARDT, op. cit. (see note 14 above).

⁵⁵ See below, 245 ff.

temporary Jewish literature, both "the descent", the angel(s) and the trumpet blasts, and they have to a large extent an OT background.[56] The individual details would, then, hardly constitute by themselves a reason for assuming that Paul is using a tradition closely related to Mt 24 par.,[57] but the combination of these details seems to do so. Thus, in Mt 24,30 b f. we find the Son of Man coming in the clouds of heaven. He will send out His angels with great trumpet blasts, and they will gather together His elect. The nucleus of this passage in the eschatological discourse is the quotation from Dn 7,13 which we found underlying ἄξει in 1 Ths 4,14.

In Chap. V we noted that in the group of pericopes from Daniel the coming of God's kingdom is referred to in several places and in different ways. In Dn 2,44 f. it is symbolized by the stone which crushed the great image, in 7,13 f. the Son of Man appears, in 7,27 kingdom and dominion are given to the people of the saints, in 8,25 b the evil king shall be broken by no human hand, and in 12,1 f. the elect will be delivered. The "midrash" which we traced in the previous chapter combined these texts with each other and the expositor formed a composite picture of them.

It seems to me that Paul proceeded as follows. He knew about the "midrash" structure of his *logos* and how it was based on Daniel. Faced with a question on the time of consummation, he finds the answer to be in the application of not only Dn 7 but also Dn 12,2 f., which refers to the resurrection: "Many of those who sleep in the dust of the earth shall awake, some to everlasting life, and some to shame and everlasting contempt". The statement that a multitude may be present at the Parousia may be based on Dn 7,27; the statement that the saints will have the dominion would then mean that they will also be present at the Parousia. I also mentioned the LXX variant which introduced a multitude in Dn 7,13, but the statement that precisely "those who have fallen asleep" will be included in this multitude is probably taken from Dn 12,2 f. The probability that Paul here used Dn 12,2 f. is strengthened by the similar terminology of both texts; death is spoken of as a sleep from which one awakes.[58]

We note also in the continuation of Paul's exposition that it is Daniel

---

[56] See the commentaries, ad loc., and DUPONT, *L'Union*, 97 ff.

[57] The trumpet blasts at the Parousia are only mentioned in Mt, not in Mk and Lk. Cf. 1 Co 15,52.

[58] 1 Ths 4 κοιμᾶσθαι, Dn 12 ישן, LXX, Theod. καθεύδειν; 1 Ths 4 ἀναστήσεσθαι, Dn 12 קיץ, LXX ἀναστήσεσθαι, Theod. ἐξεγερθήσεσθαι; 1 Ths 4 πάντοτε, Dn 12 עולם, LXX, Theod. αἰώνιος. In all probability Dn 12,3 underlies Mk 13,43, and is perhaps reflected in Col 3,4. See DUPONT, op. cit., 80 ff.

that colours his account via some form of the eschatological discourse. Thus the detail that the Christians will be caught up to meet the Lord "in the clouds" (v. 17) evidently goes back to Dn 7,13, which forms the cornerstone in Mk 13,26 par.

Two details give the impression of having been influenced by an image of the Parousia which is also expressed in some sayings of Jesus in the Gospels. This is the case with the expression ἀρπαγησόμεθα, which may have as its background ideas related to a saying such as that in Mt 24,40 f.: "two men will be in the field: one is taken (παραλαμβάνεται) and one is left ...".[59] The wording εἰς ἀπάντησιν τοῦ κυρίου may also be directly or rather indirectly related to expressions such as εἰς ὑπάντησιν τοῦ νυμφίου in Mt 25,1 and ἐξέρχεσθε εἰς ἀπάντησιν in 25,6.[60]

If we summarize the results achieved so far in the comparison between 1 Ths 4,13 ff. and Mk 13 par., it must be admitted that we have been able to display a series of possibilities that Paul used a form of the eschatological discourse. However, these possibilities seem to combine to indicate that the working hypothesis we drew up above is true. It explains several obscure points in 1 Ths 4: ἄξει, the nature of the *logos* used and how it was used here and the general picture of the Parousia.

3. 1 Ths 5,1 ff.

(1) Περὶ δὲ τῶν χρόνων καὶ τῶν καιρῶν, ἀδελφοί, οὐ χρείαν ἔχετε ὑμῖν γράφεσθαι. (2) αὐτοὶ γὰρ ἀκριβῶς οἴδατε ὅτι ἡμέρα κυρίου ὡς κλέπτης ἐν νυκτὶ οὕτως ἔρχεται.

With this περὶ δέ Paul begins a new section which is closely related in theme to the preceding one. We may compare it with 1 Co 7,1, where περὶ δὲ ὧν ἐγράψατε introduces a new section on the ethics of marriage. 1 Co 7,25 ff. belongs to the same group of themes, and begins with περὶ δὲ τῶν παρθένων.[1] In 1 Ths 4 Paul has discussed the

---

[59] In the same direction goes A. FEUILLET, Le sens du mot Parousie dans l'Evangile de Matthieu, in *Background ... in hon. C. H. Dodd* (1956), 265.

[60] E. PETERSON's idea of a Hellenistic background (Die Einholung des Kyrios, *Zschr. System. Theol.* 7,1929/30, 682–702) is critically examined by DUPONT (op. cit., 64 ff.), who emphasizes the apocalyptic background and the OT ideas behind it. N. JOHANSSON (*Det urkristna nattvardsfirandet*, 1944, 115) assumes, in conjunction with H. B. SWETE (*The Parables of the Kingdom*, 1921, 125), that it was a misinterpretation of the parable of the ten virgins that worried the Thessalonians, and also compares the κέλευσμα in this text with κραυγή in Mt 25,6. This can scarcely become more than a hypothesis.

[1] For περί in a similar use as introducing a heading, see, for example, 1 Co 8,1, 4; 12,1. C. E. FAW (On the Writing of First Thessalonians, *J. Bibl. Lit.* 71, 1952,

Parousia and in 5,1 ff. he takes up a fresh point in connection with it: since the time of the Parousia is uncertain, we must watch and be prepared. How close the two sections were in the mind of the writer is indicated by the fact that the conclusion of this section is related to the Thessalonians' anxiety (dealt with in the previous section) on behalf of those who have fallen asleep before the Parousia and to Paul's reassurance (1 Ths 4,13 ff.). Thus, in conclusion, the Apostle writes "... so that whether we wake or sleep, we might live with Him. Therefore encourage one another and build one another up, just as you are doing" (5,10 f.).

When Paul begins this parenesis on watchfulness, he does it by linking it up with something which may form a basis for what follows. That is to say, he uses a method of argumentation which resembles that used in the pericopes from 1 Co 11, 15 and 1 Ths 4 which we have just discussed. In 1 Ths 4 this basis was a λόγος κυρίου; here are quoted some passages which are introduced by ἀκριβῶς οἴδατε (vv. 2–3). In them the day of the Lord is compared to a thief; the verses tell how destruction will strike the heedless suddenly, as travail comes upon a woman with child. At v. 4 Paul moves from this reported speech into direct speech: ὑμεῖς δέ, ἀδελφοί, and begins a parenesis which is related to the concepts of day/night and light/darkness and in which the contrast of watching and sleeping occupies a prominent place.

The expression "you know well" (ἀκριβῶς οἴδατε) and similar expressions are fairly common in Paul's writings. He uses them to introduce generally recognized facts,[2] passages from the Scriptures[3] or basic Christian truths which he obviously presumed were known to his readers.[4] Here we have the latter case[5] and it is fairly common for scholars to assume that Paul is here referring to a saying of Jesus.[6] The point of interest, as far as the present purpose is concerned, is

220 ff.) finds that in Paul's writings the formula is "confined to the answering of specific questions on problems brought up in letters from the churches to which he is writing". Before we take this expression as proving such a detailed statement as to the present text, it ought to be shown that its frequency in Epictetus (*Diatr.*) or Philo (*De spec. leg.*) or *Didache* (7,1; 9,1; 11,3, for example) does not undermine the argument.

[2] For example, Rm 6,16; 1 Co 5,16; 9,24.

[3] For example, Rm 11,2; 1 Co 9,13.

[4] For example, 1 Co 3,16; 6,3, 9, 15 f., 19.

[5] For J. R. HARRIS, the many οἴδατε in 1 Ths indicated that a letter to Paul from the church had shown what they "knew" (A Study in Letter-Writing, *Expositor Ser. 5* 8,1898, 168 ff.). For T. W. MANSON this was a reason for assuming that 2 Ths was earlier than 1 Ths (The Letters to the Thessalonians, in *Studies in the Gospels* ..., 1962, 274).

[6] See, for example, FRAME, RIGAUX, and STAAB, *Comm. Ths.* ad loc.

that these sayings of Jesus are to be found at the end of the eschatological discourse.

The first sentence, about the thief coming in the night, thus has a close parallel in Mt 24,43/Lk 12,39: "If the householder had known in what part of the night (φυλακή, Lk ὥρα) the thief was coming, he would have watched".[7] It is convenient to arrange the continuation as follows:

1 Ths 5,3	Lk 21,34-36
When they say, "Peace and security",	But take heed to yourselves, lest your hearts be weighed down with dissipation (κραιπάλη καὶ μέθη), and cares of this life,
then sudden destruction will come upon them (αἰφνίδιος αὐτοῖς ἐπίσταται ὄλεθρος),	and that day come upon you suddenly (ἐπιστῇ ἐφ' ὑμᾶς αἰφνίδιος ἡ ἡμέρα ἐκείνη)
as travail (ὥσπερ ἡ ὠδίν) comes upon a woman with child;	(35) like a snare (ὡς παγίς); for it will come upon all who dwell upon the face of the whole earth. (36) But watch (ἀγρυπνεῖτε) at all times,
and there will be no escape (οὐ μὴ ἐκφύγωσιν).	praying that you may have strength to escape (κατισχύσητε ἐκφυγεῖν) all things that will take place, and to stand (σταθῆναι) before the Son of Man.

In 1 Ths 5,6 f. we meet with turns of phrase that are related to further details in the verses quoted from Luke, viz. the exhortations to watch (γρηγορεῖν), to be sober and not drunk (μεθύσκειν). The closeness of the parallel texts may be thought to be less than it is in fact, as regards the comparison with the travail (ἡ ὠδίν) and with the snare (ἡ παγίς). It is an ambiguity in the Hebrew roots חבל, which underlies this passage: if we vocalize them as חֵבֶל, they mean "travail", but if we vocalize them as חֶבֶל, they mean "snare".[8]

The similarities between the two texts are so great that it seems necessary to assume that 1 Ths uses the same tradition as Lk 21,34 ff.

---

[7] The actual introduction περὶ δὲ τῶν χρόνων καὶ τῶν καιρῶν reminds us of Mk 13,32 (/Mt 24,36) περὶ δὲ τῆς ἡμέρας ἐκείνης ἢ τῆς ὥρας οὐδεὶς οἶδεν. However, similar expressions were so common at the period that the similarity has scarcely any appreciable value as an argument; cf. Dn 2,21; 4,23; 7,12; Ne 10,34; 13,31; Sap 8,8 (RIGAUX, Comm., ad loc.).

[8] See J. T. MARSHALL, Did St. Paul Use a Semitic Gospel?, Expositor Ser. 4 2 (1890), 75; RESCH, Paulinismus, 341. There is the same possibility in an Aramaic text: חֶבְלָא travail, חַבְלָא (חֶבְלָא) rope, snare. This ambiguity was also used in Ps 18,6 LXX (cf. Ac 2,24) and Ps 18,5 Targ. Jon. (similarly 2 Sm 22,5 Targ. Jon.) (E. LÖVESTAM, Son and Saviour, 1961, 41). Cf. 1 QH III.7 ff.

In addition to the mere parallelism, there is the fact that αἰφνίδιος occurs only in these two passages in the NT and that ἐφίστημι only occurs in 2 Tm 4,2, 6 among the letters attributed to Paul in the NT, and elsewhere only in Luke's Gospel and the Acts of the Apostles.[9] We may also note the similarity of basic mood between 1 Ths 5,3a (peace and security) and Mt 24,37 ff. (before the Flood)/Lk 17,26 ff. (before the Flood; Sodom and Lot).

Paul's parenesis after the quoted words of Jesus uses the watch/sleep motif in relation to "day/night/thief" in the preceding verses. But the turns of phrase and the combinations of motifs are such that several authors have assumed that general early Christian catechetic and/or parenetic traditions underlie this passage.[10]

We recall that 1 Ths 4,13 ff. and 5,1 ff. are closely related. In the previous section we found it probable that Paul knew of and used an account of the last days like that in Mk 13 par. and also knew of its character as a "midrash" on Daniel. The part of this "midrash" he used was the final section, that dealing with the Parousia. The pericope we have just discussed uses the same metaphor of the thief which is to be found at the end of the eschatological discourse in Mt 24 and a series of logia which appears at the close of Luke's version of this discourse.

This indicates that Paul knew of and used in 1 Ths 4,13–5,11 not the "midrash" alone but the "midrash" and the additional logia on the last days (which are not a biblical exposition).[11]

4. Further Details in 1 Ths and Preliminary Conclusions

If the preceding arguments are correct, they will shed some light on certain details in the Letter. I shall now discuss them briefly.

1 Ths 3,1 ff.: Paul was anxious about the Thessalonians and sent Timothy to establish them in their faith (3) τὸ μηδένα σαίνεσθαι ἐν ταῖς

---

[9] See further B. RIGAUX, Vocabulaire chrétien antérieur à la première épître aux Thessaloniciens, in Sacra Pagina II (1959), 385.

[10] See PH. CARRINGTON, The Primitive Christian Catechism (1940), 51, and E. G. SELWYN, Comm. 1 Pt (1947), 369 ff., 386 ff. Cf. E. LÖVESTAM, Spiritual Wakefulness in the NT (1963), 45 ff., 95 ff.

[11] In principle we may, of course, also consider that Paul first made this collocation in 1 Ths and that later the church tradition took it up, so that Matthew and Luke are ultimately dependent on Paul here. Against this we have the fact that Paul expresses himself in such a way as to indicate that he is associating himself with existing tradition in these pericopes and that he is then also taking over certain complexes of motifs which are to be found in other parts of the NT. See LÖVESTAM, loc. cit.

θλίψεσιν ταύταις. αὐτοὶ γὰρ οἴδατε ὅτι εἰς τοῦτο κείμεθα. (4) καὶ γὰρ ὅτε πρὸς ὑμᾶς ἦμεν, προελέγομεν ὑμῖν ὅτι μέλλομεν θλίβεσθαι, καθὼς καὶ ἐγένετο καὶ οἴδατε.

Paul writes on the eve of the Parousia (1 Ths 2,19 f.). With this in prospect, he has taught the Christians of Thessalonica about the θλίψεις of the last days, and he reminds them of this teaching with an οἴδατε resembling that in 1 Ths 5,2. Θλῖψις is referred to in the eschatological discourse (Mk 13,19 par., Mt 24,9).[12] It is highly probable that it was a form of this discourse which formed the basis of the teaching on θλῖψις.

1 Ths 2,19; 3,13; 4,15 and 5,23 use the term παρουσία: it may be more than a coincidence that this term is used in the Gospels only in Mt 24.[13]

In summarizing the argument so far, I find that the parallels between 1 Ths and Mk 13 par. which we have just examined seem to act like a combination lock. It is the combinations of a relatively large number of details in the two texts which seem almost to compel us to assume the existence of a connection between them, but, taken by themselves, these details have little significance. On the other hand, we can hardly draw the conclusion that this relation subsists in Paul's quotation of the wording of an early written text of the Gospel—for example, a Proto–Mark—which the Synoptic Evangelists also used later on. However, if a *logos* about the last days, which was based on a "midrash", was known to Paul, then we have here material whose nucleus may be relatively solid. Its outlines, however, are soft as to make conceivable this combination of restriction and freedom in relation to the tradition, which we have met with in 1 Ths. The echoes of the logia in Lk 21,34 ff., however, allow us also to surmise that in this case this "midrash" had linked with it, as early as a few years before 50 A.D., logia on watching in expectation of the sudden occurrence of the Parousia. For Paul must have come into contact with it at that time, if he was able to impart the knowledge of its content to the church at Thessalonica during his missionary work there.[14]

---

[12] Cf. RIGAUX, op. cit., 384. See also J. C. FENTON, Paul and Mark, in *Studies in mem ... R. H. Lightfoot* (1955), 109 f., and J. MUNCK, I Thess.i. 9–10 and the Missionary Preaching of Paul, *NT Stud.* 9 (1962/63), 96 ff.

[13] There are also some curious points in common of 1 Ths 2,14 ff. and Mt 23,29 ff. Cf. ORCHARD, *Bibl.* 19 (1938), 20 ff., and RIGAUX, *Comm.*, 103.

[14] Paul must have reached Thessalonica about 50 A.D. See RIGAUX, *Comm.*, 7 ff., and A. WIKENHAUSER, *Einleitung in das NT* (2nd ed. 1956), 257 f.

5. 2 Ths 2,1-17

In 2 Ths 1 the thanksgiving[15] for the Christian virtues of the Thessalonians in their endurance of the persecutions merges into a survey of the Parousia, together with the judgement and especially the glorification of the faithful. Against this background ch. 2 begins with a new section, which contains exhortations to calmness in this eschatological perspective (vv. 1-3a), followed by teaching which justifies the exhortations (vv. 3b-12). In conclusion, vv. 13-17 re-open the prospect of the final salvation and hope, and of the divine election, call and comfort to the church of Thessalonica.

I shall first give an account of the structure of the text as regards its content.

(1) Ἐρωτῶμεν δὲ ὑμᾶς, ἀδελφοί, ὑπὲρ τῆς παρουσίας τοῦ κυρίου ἡμῶν Ἰησοῦ Χριστοῦ καὶ ἡμῶν ἐπισυναγωγῆς ἐπ᾽ αὐτόν, (2) εἰς τὸ μὴ ταχέως σαλευθῆναι ὑμᾶς ἀπὸ τοῦ νοὸς μηδὲ θροεῖσθαι, μήτε διὰ πνεύματος μήτε διὰ λόγου μήτε δι᾽ ἐπιστολῆς ὡς δι᾽ ἡμῶν, ὡς ὅτι ἐνέστηκεν ἡ ἡμέρα τοῦ κυρίου. (3) μή τις ὑμᾶς ἐξαπατήσῃ κατὰ μηδένα τρόπον. ὅτι ἐὰν μὴ ἔλθῃ ἡ ἀποστασία πρῶτον καὶ ἀποκαλυφθῇ ὁ ἄνθρωπος τῆς ἀνομίας,[16] ὁ υἱὸς τῆς ἀπωλείας, (4) ὁ ἀντικείμενος καὶ ὑπεραιρόμενος ἐπὶ πάντα λεγόμενον θεὸν ἢ σέβασμα, ὥστε αὐτὸν εἰς τὸν ναὸν τοῦ θεοῦ καθίσαι, ἀποδεικνύντα ἑαυτὸν ὅτι ἐστὶν θεός. (5) οὐ μνημονεύετε ὅτι ἔτι ὢν πρὸς ὑμᾶς ταῦτα ἔλεγον ὑμῖν;

In v. 1 the two technical expressions παρουσία and ἐπισυναγωγή indicate the subject which is to be dealt with, for ὑπέρ here is synonymous with περί.[17] Vv. 2-3a give exhortations connected with this subject ("be not shaken or excited; let no man deceive you"). Then v. 3b gives the doctrinal justification of these exhortations (ὅτι): first the apostasy must come and the man of lawlessness be revealed. His epithets are piled up in v. 4 in such a way that the passage becomes an anacoluthon. What the Apostle has just said—the teaching and/or the preceding exhortations—is referred to in v. 5: it is what Paul has spoken of on his visit, i.e. his words summarize earlier teaching given to the church in a fashion like that in 1 Ths 5,2 (οἴδατε) or 1 Co 11,23 (παρέδωκα ὑμῖν).

(6) καὶ νῦν τὸ κατέχον οἴδατε, εἰς τὸ ἀποκαλυφθῆναι αὐτὸν ἐν τῷ αὐτοῦ καιρῷ. (7) τὸ γὰρ μυστήριον ἤδη ἐνεργεῖται τῆς ἀνομίας. μόνον ὁ κατέχων ἄρτι ἕως ἐκ μέσου γένηται.

---

[15] See on this point P. Schubert, *Form and Function of the Pauline Thanksgivings* (1939), and E. Mócsy, De gratiarum actione in epistolis Paulinis, *Verb. Dom.* 21 (1941), 193-201, 225-32.

[16] A 𝔐 D G *pm* lat syr Ir read ἁμαρτίας. For the textual criticism, see Rigaux, *Comm.*, ad loc.

[17] See Arndt and Gingrich, *Lexicon*, sub voce.

With v. 6 the problems begin to accumulate. Here indeed we have a *crux interpretum* which has been a crux ever since the earliest exegesis—the much-discussed verses on ὁ κατέχων—τὸ κατέχον[18] and τὸ μυστήριον τῆς ἀνομίας.[19] This is something which those addressed know about "now". This "now" is in most cases stated as being in opposition to the earlier point of time (ἔτι ὤν).[20] Even though this is by no means self-evident, v. 6 is at any rate characterized by these present particles νῦν, ἤδη, ἄρτι.

(8) καὶ τότε ἀποκαλυφθήσεται ὁ ἄνομος, ὃν ὁ κύριος Ἰησοῦς[21] ἀνελεῖ τῷ πνεύματι τοῦ στόματος αὐτοῦ καὶ καταργήσει τῇ ἐπιφανείᾳ τῆς παρουσίας αὐτοῦ, (9) οὗ ἐστιν ἡ παρουσία κατ' ἐνέργειαν τοῦ σατανᾶ ἐν πάσῃ δυνάμει καὶ σημείοις καὶ τέρασιν ψεύδους (10) καὶ ἐν πάσῃ ἀπάτῃ ἀδικίας τοῖς ἀπολλυμένοις, ἀνθ' ὧν τὴν ἀγάπην τῆς ἀληθείας οὐκ ἐδέξαντο εἰς τὸ σωθῆναι αὐτούς. (11) καὶ διὰ τοῦτο πέμπει αὐτοῖς ὁ θεὸς ἐνέργειαν πλάνης εἰς τὸ πιστεῦσαι αὐτοὺς τῷ ψεύδει, (12) ἵνα κριθῶσιν πάντες οἱ μὴ πιστεύσαντες τῇ ἀληθείᾳ ἀλλὰ εὐδοκήσαντες τῇ ἀδικίᾳ. (13) Ἡμεῖς δὲ ὀφείλομεν εὐχαριστεῖν τῷ θεῷ πάντοτε περὶ ὑμῶν, ἀδελφοὶ ἠγαπημένοι ὑπὸ κυρίου, ὅτι εἵλατο ὑμᾶς ὁ θεὸς ἀπαρχὴν[22] εἰς σωτηρίαν ἐν ἁγιασμῷ πνεύματος καὶ πίστει ἀληθείας, (14) εἰς ὃ καὶ ἐκάλησεν ὑμᾶς[23] διὰ τοῦ εὐαγγελίου ἡμῶν, εἰς περιποίησιν δόξης τοῦ κυρίου ἡμῶν Ἰησοῦ Χριστοῦ. (15) Ἄρα οὖν, ἀδελφοί, στήκετε, καὶ κρατεῖτε τὰς παραδόσεις ἃς ἐδιδάχθητε εἴτε διὰ λόγου εἴτε δι'ἐπιστολῆς ἡμῶν.

At v. 8 the subject of the future prospect (τότε) is taken up again and the description dwells still further on the man of lawlessness, who here is called ὁ ἄνομος. He will be revealed (ἀποκαλυφθήσεται), i.e. the description is related to ἀποκαλυφθῇ in v. 3. Vv. 8*b* and 9 describe the lawless one in two relative clauses: at His Parousia Jesus

---

[18] Apart from the commentaries, see the following recent publications: A. STROBEL, *Untersuchungen zum eschatologischen Verzögerungsproblem* (1961), 98 ff.; F. F. BRUCE, Christianity under Claudius, *Bull. J. Ryl. Libr.* 44 (1961/62), 309–26; O. BETZ, Der Katechon, *NT Stud.* 9 (1962/63), 276–91; L. SIRARD, La parousie de l'Antéchrist, 2 Thess. 2,3–9, *Analecta Bibl.* 18 (1963), 89–100; D. W. B. ROBINSON, II Thess. 2,6: "That which restrains" or "That which holds sway?", *Stud. Evangelica* 2 (1964), 635–38.

[19] See the preceding note, and cf. 1 QH V.36; 1 QMyst I.2; 1 QM XIV.9. (Cf. K. G. KUHN, Die in Palästina gefundenen hebräischen Texte und das NT, *Zschr. Theol. Ki.* 47, 1950, 205).

[20] See the commentaries. Cf. G. Vos, *The Pauline Eschatology* (1953), 130.

[21] Β Ψ ℵ *pm* omit the word.

[22] Thus Β Α G *33 al f* vg syr^harcl; ἀπ' ἀρχῆς ℵ Ψ ℵ D *pm* it syr^pesh. See RIGAUX (*Comm.*, ad loc.), who choses the second reading.

[23] Β Α D* *pc* it read ἡμᾶς. Note the itacism. See B. M. METZGER, *The Text of the NT* (1964), 191 f.

will destroy him (v. 8); the activity (ἡ ἐνέργεια)[24] of the lawless one at his parousia is Satan's activity, including lying signs and wonders (v. 9) and all kinds of wicked deception (ἀπάτη ἀδικίας) (v. 10a). This deception is located in those who perish (10a), and the text dwells on them and their fate, as far as v. 12. The continuation (vv. 13 f.) is in contrast with this:[25] those addressed are called "beloved by the Lord", "elect", "first-fruits to salvation" and the like. This bright prospect gives rise to a closing and summarizing admonition in v. 15: "so then (ἄρα οὖν)[26] stand firm and hold to the traditions (παραδόσεις) which you were taught by us, either by word (cf. v. 5 ἔλεγον) or by letter". Then vv. 16 f. close the section with a prayer for divine help for those addressed.

A comparison between this pericope and the eschatological discourse reveals several similarities. The wording in v. 1 of the subject to be dealt with is notable; that we meet with παρουσία here and in Matthew's introduction to the eschatological discourse is perhaps not so strange as the fact that the expression ἐπισυναγωγή is used here. This is the only time it is used in the corpus Paulinum: in Mk 13,27/Mt 24,31, on the other hand, the angels gather in (ἐπισυνάξουσιν) the elect at the Parousia.

The admonition in v. 2 tells the Thessalonians not to be quickly shaken (σαλευθῆναι) or excited (θροεῖσθαι), because some people make out that the day of the Lord has come (ἐνέστηκεν).[27] We should compare this with the beginning of the eschatological discourse (Mk 13,5 ff.): "Take heed that no one leads you astray (μή τις ὑμᾶς πλανήσῃ). Many will come in my name, saying 'I am', and they will lead many astray (πλανήσουσιν). And when you hear of wars and rumours of wars, do not be alarmed" (μὴ θροεῖσθε). The fact that the verb θροεῖσθαι only occurs in these two passages in the NT (and the root only in one place in the LXX—Ct 5,4) and occurs in similar contexts has led several commentators to assume a direct connection between them.[28]

V. 3 repeats the warnings (μή τις ὑμᾶς ἐξαπατήσῃ), and in the verses

---

[24] It is difficult to assess the relationship to ἐνεργεῖται in v. 7.

[25] This close connection with the preceding verses makes me unwilling to join the commentaries in drawing a marked borderline between vv. 12 and 13. When these two verses are kept together, v. 15 has a natural place in the account. Cf. RIGAUX's idea that v. 15 breaks the train of thought, and, on the other hand, FRAME, Comm., and C. MASSON, Comm. Ths (1957), ad loc.

[26] In the NT the expression is only found in the corpus Paulinum: Rm 5,18; 7,3, 25; Gl 6,10; Eph 2,19; 1 Ths 5,6.

[27] See F. TILLMANN, Die Wiederkunft Christi (1909), 10, and RIGAUX, Comm., ad loc (and cf. id., Antéchrist, 251).

[28] WOHLENBERG, MILLIGAN, VON DOBSCHÜTZ, RIGAUX, Comm., ad. loc.

of the discourse just quoted we encounter an analogous exhortation (μή τις ὑμᾶς πλανήσῃ). If we now add to this the possibility that what men may be misled into thinking in 2 Ths is that the day of the Lord has come, the similarity becomes quite great between this and the statement in Matthew that the danger is that people will appear and say that they are the Christ and in Luke that the time is at hand (ὁ καιρὸς ἤγγικεν). Indeed, if we read Mark (and Luke) with no expository prepossessions, we also find this meaning there: many will say falsely that they are Jesus, i.e. Jesus returned to earth. In that case the differences between the Synoptic Gospels and 2 Ths is only that, in the first case, men are deceived into believing people who say that they are Jesus who has returned to earth and, in the second case, men are deceived into believing people who say that He has returned.

However, the analysis in Chap. V showed that this passage in the Synoptic apocalypse was underlain by a "midrash" on the Daniel sayings on the horn (king) who magnifies himself and speaks great things; ἐγώ εἰμι has the significance of a formula of divine revelation. One of the Daniel passages concerned was 11,36 and this passage is quoted in 2 Ths 2,3 about the blasphemous man of lawlessness! This poses questions as to the nature of the relation between the two texts, to which we shall return later.

Before the day of the Lord the apostasy[29] will come and the man of lawlessness be revealed. Judging by what follows, where the apostasy does not play any independent part but the qualities and the activities of the lawless one take up all the space, it is not advisable to distinguish the apostasy and the revelation of the lawless one sharply from each other.[30]

This man of lawlessness is now described with the help of some OT allusions:[31] first, to Dn 11,36 on the king who exalts himself above every god (יתרומם ויתגדל על כל אל, LXX παροργισθήσεται καὶ ὑψωθήσεται

---

[29] It is tempting to translate ἀποστασία by "rebellion" (RSV) in comparison with the wars and rumours of war and the fact that nation will raise against nation in Mk 13,7 f. par. However, the LXX usage, the definite article, the close connection with ἀνομία and the associations with idolatry seem to indicate that "apostasy" is preferable. See RIGAUX, Comm., ad loc., and below on Dt 13. Cf. TILLMANN, op. cit., 130 ff., and GUNTERMANN, Die Eschatologie des hl. Paulus, 91 ff.

[30] Cf. RIGAUX, Comm., ad loc. The man of lawlessness "is revealed" (ἀποκαλυφθῇ). This is to some extent parallel with the fact that the apostasy "comes" (ἔρχη), and this, taken together with the usage of ἀποκάλυψις about Jesus' Parousia in 2 Ths 1,7 indicates that the proposal to give it the meaning of "to reveal a criminal" or "to punish" cannot be effected, either here or in vv. 6 and 8 (thus SIRARD, Analecta Bibl. 18, 1963, 90 f.).

[31] These ideas are placed in a larger phenomenological context by V. MAAG in Der Antichrist als Symbol des Bösen (in das Böse, 1961), 68 ff.

ἐπὶ πάντα θεόν). However, this is combined with features from Is 14,13 f. on the blasphemous Babylon: "You said in your heart: 'I will ascend (אעלה) to heaven, above the stars of God I will set my throne on high (ארים); I will sit (אשב) on the mount of assembly in the far north'". Likewise details from Ez 28,2 ff. on the ungodly king of Tyre: "Your heart is proud (גבה) and you have said: 'I am a god, I sit in the seat of the gods (מושב אלהים ישבתי) in the heart of the seas'" (see also vv. 6 and 9).[32]

In vv. 8 ff. this man of lawlessness is again mentioned: according to v. 8, Jesus will destroy him at the Parousia, which is described with reference to Is 11,4, according to which the shoot from the stump of Jesse will destroy his enemies.[33] According to vv. 9 f., the "parousia" of the lawless one is "after the activity of Satan, with all power and with lying signs and wonders and with all wicked deception". God sends the activity of deception (ἐνέργεια πλάνης, v. 11). These wordings lead one's mind to Dt 13, where prophets[34] appear with signs and wonders (vv. 2 f.: מופת, אות, LXX σημεῖον, τέρας), the whole thing taking place to mislead people into idolatry (v. 6 סרה, LXX πλανῆσαι); these children of Belial wish to seduce people into apostasy (vv. 11,14 נדח hif., LXX ἀποστῆσαι) from Yahweh. These quotations also shed light on some further details in 2 Ths 2. On the one hand, the apostasy (ἡ ἀποστασία) is connected with Dt 13,11, 14 (ἀποστῆσαι), and, on the other, we are here in a position to establish, in a concrete text with some modification, Bousset's old surmise that behind the expression ὁ ἄνθρωπος τῆς ἀνομίας lay the word בליעל.[35] We may trace this back to Dt 13,14 אנשים בני בליעל, LXX ἄνδρες παράνομοι.[36]

In the preceding chapter we found most of these OT associations with the same functions in the eschatological discourse. Thus Dn 11,36 was one of the Daniel texts referring to the arrogance of the last evil king,[37] which, together with Is 14, underlay Mk 13,6 par. on ἐγώ εἰμι.

---

[32] Cf. Ex R. 8,2; b Ḥul. 89a; Mek. Ex 15,11 (49a); Tanch. וארא § 7 ff. (11b) (BILLERBECK, *Comm.* II, 462 ff.; III, 44, 378). It is especially the echoes from the OT that impair M. BRUNEC's thesis that the man of lawlessness means the contemporary unbelieving Jews (De "Homine peccati" in 2 Thess. 2,1–12, *Verb. Dom.* 35, 1957, 3–33).

[33] Cf. Ps Sal 17,27; Ap 19,15, 20; and see above, 99 ff.

[34] The Targ. Jon. writes נבי שקרא.

[35] BOUSSET, *Antichrist*, 99 ff.; also id., *Die Religion des Judentums* (3rd ed. by H. GRESSMANN, 1926), 255. Cf. SIRARD, op. cit., 94, who combines ἀποστασία and Belial departing from 1 Rg 20 (TM 21), 13 LXX and a number of Aquila passages. (The expression is found only in LXX^A.)

[36] Targ. Jon.: arrogant men (גברין זדינין); Targ. Onk.: men of wickedness (ג׳ בני רשעא).

[37] Moreover Dn 7,8, 11, 20, 25; 8,10, 24 f.

That is to say, this OT background to Mk 13,6 and the subsequent interpretation of ἐγώ εἰμι form a perfect parallel, as regards content, with 2 Ths 2,4, which, however, expresses the same factual content by an association also with Ez 28,2 ff. The meaning of this passage has, however, been distorted in a remarkable fashion; instead of saying that the lawless one sits in the seat of gods (מושב אלהים, LXX κατοικία θεοῦ) in the seas, the author says that he sits in the Temple of God (εἰς τὸν ναὸν τοῦ θεοῦ).[38] It is highly probable that this feature was ultimately taken from Daniel's sayings on the abomination of desolation. Taken by itself, it could be the context in Daniel[39] which caused the writer to locate the blasphemous phenomenon to the Temple. However, it is remarkable that both Mt 24,15 (ἐν τόπῳ ἁγίῳ) and 2 Ths 2,4 (εἰς τὸν ναόν) resemble the variant reading of Dn 9,27 (ἐπὶ τὸ ἱερὸν βδέλυγμα τῶν ἐρημώσεων)[40] represented in the LXX and Theod. Mt 24,15 and 2 Ths 2,4 may have both been separately derived from Daniel or one of these texts may have been the mediator for the other.[41]

If we now continue on the other side of the verses on the "now" situation and κατέχων, the text says, with reference to Is 11,4, that the Lord will slay the lawless one with the breath of His mouth. On this point we may note, on the one hand, how the evil king in Daniel is destroyed in different ways in connection with the execution of divine justice[42] and, on the other, how we found above that the motif which probably formed the link with the description of the flight from the abomination in terms of Gn 19 (on Lot and Sodom) was the divine wrath which strikes an ungodly and blasphemous phenomenon.[43] Here also the text that inspired 2 Ths may have been Daniel or an (older) form of the eschatological discourse.

We compared above the details of the lying signs made by the lawless man and his deceit with Dt 13. But Mk 13,22 par. is related to the same passage in the way which we indicated in the previous chapter.[44] We may accordingly compare Mk 13,22 ἐγερθήσονται δὲ

---

[38] מושב א׳ hap.leg. Otherwise מושב is used (and in the LXX κατοικία) of Sion in Ps 132,13: in all other cases in the OT it refers to human dwellingplaces and seats.

[39] Possibly in the light of passages such as 1 Mcc 1,54, 59; 6,7; 2 Mcc 6,2.

[40] Cf. above, 162, note 57.

[41] If we introduce a possible (but improvable) intermediate link, the various theoretical possibilities are increased. J. B. ORCHARD assumes that Paul here used Mt 24, took the reference to Dn in 24,15 ad notam and thus dragged Daniel material into 2 Ths 2 (St. Paul and the Book of Daniel, Bibl. 20, 1939, 172–79). R. SCHNACKEN-BURG (Die Johannesbriefe, 1953, 128 f.) connects 2 Ths 2,4 with Mk 13,14.

[42] Dn 7,10 f., 26; 8,25; 9,26 f.; 11,45.

[43] See above, 152 ff.

[44] See above, 155.

ψευδόχριστοι καὶ ψευδοπροφῆται καὶ ποιήσουσιν σημεῖα καὶ τέρατα πρὸς τὸ ἀποπλανᾶν, with 2 Ths 2,9 f. ἐν πάσῃ δυνάμει καὶ σημείοις καὶ τέρασιν ψεύδους καὶ ἐν πάσῃ ἀπάτῃ ἀδικίας. Here we may ask whether 2 Ths does not have Mk 13 par. between it and the OT.

However, we have been able to establish the following facts. The introductory admonitions in 2 Ths 2,2 use a terminology which in all probability derives from a form of the eschatological discourse. The description of the man of lawlessness uses the same texts from Daniel and Dt 13 with the same interpretation and in the same consecutive order as in the eschatological discourse and with a choice of words that is in places quite parallel. Altogether this state of affairs cannot, it seems to me, yield any other conclusion than that behind 2 Ths 2,1 ff. there is a form of the eschatological discourse and that the author of the Letter was aware, as in the case in 1 Ths, of the OT texts which underlay the discourse.[45]

This form of the eschatological discourse is presented in 2 Ths 2,5, not explicitly as a tradition (παράδοσις), but with a reference to Paul's earlier teaching: "do you not remember?" (οὐ μνημονεύετε). Here we come quite close to the οἴδατε which we discussed in connection with 1 Ths 5,1 ff.[46] The expression may here serve in a fashion resembling that in 1 Co 4,17, where Paul says he will send Timothy to Corinth to remind (ὃς ... ἀναμνήσει) the Corinthians "of my ways (ὁδοί) in Christ, as I teach (διδάσκω) them everywhere in every church". Here Paul's apostolic teaching is a binding norm which the messenger is to re-instate in its full force in the church, by "reminding" the members of it.[47] In 2 Ths 2,15, however, the concept of παράδοσις is also explicitly introduced. In this verse a period is set to the preceding text in a fashion which results in what "has been told" to those addressed and what they should "remember", according to 2,5, also being plausibly introduced into these παραδόσεις: "So then (ἄρα οὖν), brethren, stand firm and hold to the traditions (κρατεῖτε τὰς παραδόσεις) which you were taught (ἐδιδάχθητε) by us, either by word (cf. 2,5!) or by letter".[48]

[45] Cf. L. O. BRISTOL (Mark's Little Apocalypse: A Hypothesis, *Exp. Times* 51, 1939/40, 302 f.), who thinks that the author of Mk 13,14 is influenced by Paul in 2 Ths.

Perhaps the much-discussed *katechon* may also have fresh light shed on it by these links with the OT and the eschatological discourse. I have as yet no new suggestion to make, but (in spite of the Qumran parallels) I am surprised that the sense "restraining" is so readily accepted by the majority of scholars. Perhaps the fourth beast and חזק in Dn 11,21, 32 played some part?

[46] See above, in this chapter, section 3.

[47] See on this point GERHARDSSON, *Memory*, 293, 304 f. Cf. 2 Tm 2,8; 2 Pt 3,2; Jd 17.

[48] See further RIGAUX, *Comm.*, ad loc., and VON CAMPENHAUSEN, *Begründung*,

The eschatological tradition, which in 1 Ths 4 f. was called λόγος κυρίου (4,15) and which those addressed were presumed to ἀκριβῶς εἰδέναι (5,2), at least in certain parts, is the same tradition as those addressed in 2 Ths were presumed to remember and to be holding to, except that different parts of it are used in the two Letters.[49]

Now that we have established this connection between 2 Ths 2 and a form of the eschatological discourse, we must also note the following point. 2 Ths 2 describes as a single phenomenon what the eschatological discourse divides into three, viz. those who come and say "I am" (Mk 13,6 par.), the abomination of desolation (13,14 ff. par.) and the false Christs and prophets who make misleading signs and wonders (Mk 13,22 par.).[50]

However, there is some evidence which indicates that the Matthaean version (Mt 24,3 ff.) holds together certain sections of the discourse in a way which is reminiscent of 2 Ths 2.[51] If we begin at the end, v. 29 clearly shows that the appearance of the false prophets (vv. 23 f.) is included in the θλῖψις which is mentioned in v. 21 (v. 29: "Immediately after the θλῖψις of those days ..."). But the θλῖψις of v. 21 is the state of affairs during which people are to flee from the abomination of desolation (vv. 15 ff.). In Mark's Gospel too the abomination and the false prophets are kept together in the same way. In Matthew's Gospel, however, the section on the abomination is introduced almost as if it gave another aspect to what had gone before or as a re-association with a certain theme after a short break (v. 14?).[52] For Matthew begins with ὅταν οὖν ἴδητε, i.e. perhaps the deceit of the false prophets

---

39. Cf. WEGENAST, *Verständnis der Tradition*, 116 ff. For a conceivable connection with early Christian parenetic tradition here, see CARRINGTON, *Catechism*, Chap. IV, and SELWYN, *Comm. 1 Pt*, 382 ff., 439 ff.

[49] So it also turns out that the various apologetic artifices used for and against the interpretation of 2 Ths 2,15 as a basis for the old theory of the two sources of revelation, Scripture and Tradition, do not do the text justice. Cf. A. STEINMANN, *Comm. Ths* (1918), ad loc., and WEGENAST, loc. cit. On the other hand, see STAAB, and RIGAUX, *Comm.*, ad loc.

[50] Cf. Origen (*Hom. in Jer.* IV.3), who refers to the words of the Lord in the Gospel and says that "he who is to come" (ὁ ἐλευσόμενος; note the singular!) will make signs and do wonders (L. E. WRIGHT, *Alterations of the Words of Jesus*, 1952, 141).

[51] Cf. the *Comm. Mt*, ad loc., by M'NEILE, KLOSTERMANN, A. SCHLATTER (*Der Evangelist Matthäus*, 1929), J. SCHNIEWIND (5th ed. 1950), SCHMID, F. V. FILSON (1960), BONNARD, and GAECHTER.

[52] B. WEISS, and M'NEILE, *Comm.Mt*, ad loc., connect οὖν with τέλος. Similarly ZAHN, *Comm.Mt*, ad loc. KNABENBAUER, *Comm. Mt*, ad loc., connects οὖν with the disciples' question at the beginning of the discourse.

and the wickedness mentioned in Mt 24,11 ff. are joined by this οὖν with the abomination.[53]

One consequence of these observations is that we may reduce somewhat the difference between the eschatological discourse and 2 Ths. Another result is that we can establish a probable meaning for the τότε which occur in these possibly combined parts of Matthew. In that case they would not mean "then" (= "thereafter")[54] but "then" (= "at that time"), although with a less demonstrative function as regards the determination of time, almost approaching a function such as that in *waw consecutivum*.[55]

Twice in this comparison Matthew's version of the eschatological discourse has yielded the closest parallel to 2 Ths 2, viz. the term παρουσία and "the holy place" (24,14). We may add that in 1 Ths it was Matthew's Gospel that was the sole basis for certain parallels: the trumpet (24,31), the ἀπάντησις (25,1, 6), the thief in the night (24,43; Luke had it in another context), and the μεθύσκειν (24,49).[56] This agrees with other observations that Paul seems to use a Gospel tradition that is related to Matthew.[57]

Above[58] I hinted at a problem on which I must now give an opinion, viz. the relation between Mk 13,5-7/Mt 24,4-6 and 2 Ths 2,2 f. First the circumstances of the case. In 2 Ths 2 those addressed are not to θροεῖσθαι by the rumours that the day of the Lord has come. They must allow no one to lead them astray, for the man of lawlessness must first be revealed. In Mk/Mt no one must be allowed to lead the disciples astray, for many will say "I am (the Christ)". When they hear of wars, they must not θροεῖσθαι, for this must take place; but the end is not yet. Θροεῖσθαι, which occurs in the NT only here, binds the two passages closely together and μή τις ὑμᾶς ἐξαπατήσῃ (2 Ths 2,3) and μή τις ὑμᾶς πλανήσῃ (Mk 13,5 par.) are at least closely parallel.

---

[53] We may compare this with the function of οὖν in 24,26, in which v. 26 provides supplementary logia, involving just a variant or another aspect of the subject of v. 23. It is also possible to go back to θλῖψις in v. 9 and thus have a single block of text from v. 9 to v. 29, characterized by θλῖψις, apostasy, "Antichrist" and false prophets.

[54] This sense is strongly emphasized by KÜMMEL, *Promise*, 97. However, v. 14 is perhaps an exception.

[55] M'NEILE, *J. Theol. Stud.* 12 (1910/11), 172 f.

[56] To parallel ἀνομία in Mt 24,12 and ἄνθρωπος τῆς ἀνομίας or μυστήριον τ. ἀν. in 2 Ths 2,3 and 7 respectively seems to me to be looking too much at isolated words, while disregarding their meaning in the context. Cf. ORCHARD, *Bibl.* 19 (1938), 34 f. There is the same collocation in BURKHARDT, op. cit. (see note 14 in section 1 of this chapter).

[57] Cf. BUZY, *Rech. Sci. Rel.* 28 (1938), 473 ff., and DODD, *Matthew and Paul.*
[58] See above, 198.

Θροεῖσθαι has a fairly similar sense in both passages: "Be not alarmed, for the end is not yet" and "for before the day of the Lord the man of lawlessness must be revealed" respectively. But the detailed circumstances in which they are not to be alarmed are different; in 2 Ths it is false gossip that the Parousia has already taken place and in Mk/Mt it is wars and rumours of war. However, in a way the really difficult problem as regards the relation between these so similar expressions is concentrated in the exhortation "let no one lead you astray". For the error in 2 Ths is the belief that the Parousia has already occurred, while in fact first the man of lawlessness must come, he who will proclaim himself to be God. In Mk 13, on the other hand, the error is the seduction practised by those who say "I am". In other words, the problem can be expressed as follows. If we read the ἐγώ εἰμι passage as Matthew did ("I am the Christ"), we achieve a satisfactory parallelism, as regards content, between the two texts, but the continuation of 2 Ths 2 speaks of the man of lawlessness in such a way that it seems to presuppose exactly the interpretation of ἐγώ εἰμι as a blasphemous formula of revelation which we have to suppress (with Matthew), in order to achieve the parallelism as regards content. Parallelism as regards θροεῖσθαι is almost inevitable.

The following seems to be a possible solution. Paul regards ἐγώ εἰμι, and the abomination of desolation and the prophets with the false signs and wonders as expressions of one and the same phenomenon. Now when he has to exhort the Thessalonians to calmness, his main argument is that this phenomenon has not yet been revealed. But he derives the knowledge that it will happen from the tradition which he has already passed on to the Thessalonians. When his thoughts go to this tradition and the exhortations not to be alarmed by false rumours of the Parousia are to be formulated, they are coloured by the mode in which this tradition is expressed, in the context of the ἐγώ εἰμι passage used. This must have been so much easier as the θροεῖσθαι in both the texts is used in similar senses: "Be not alarmed, the end is not yet" and "the day of the Lord has not yet come", respectively. If this proposed solution is correct, the parallelism as regards content between the Matthaean version ("I am the Christ") and 2 Ths 2,2 ("the day of the Lord has come") is not due to any direct or indirect dependence of 2 Ths on Matthew in this respect.

In giving a brief summary of the results yielded by the analyses in this chapter, it is possible to make the following observations, first with regard to 1 and 2 Ths. In both 1 and 2 Ths Paul bases his eschatological teaching on a form of the eschatological discourse which he regards as an authoritative παράδοσις, originating from the Lord. He presumes that it is known to those he is addressing, since he has passed it on to them in his previous teaching. He shows that he is probably aware of the "midrashic" basis of this tradition, in that he supplements it with more OT material, with which it may very well have been associated via the texts which are used in the "midrash" adopted (Dn 12,2 on the resurrection; Ez 28 on the blasphemies of the lawless one; perhaps also κατέχων).

As regards the eschatological discourse, the following observations may be made. A form of it constitutes an authoritative παράδοσις, a λόγος κυρίου, which Paul in his previous teaching has transmitted to those he is addressing. It consists not only of a parenetic "midrash" but also of added words of Jesus on watchfulness and on the unexpected occurrence of the end. The discourse existed in this form at the latest a few years before 50 A.D., for Paul must have come into contact with it before his arrival in Thessalonica. Those parts of the discourse which are instanced at this date by 1 and 2 Ths or which have parallels therein may be indicated by the following key-words: "let no one lead you astray" (13,5), "I am" (v. 6), "be not alarmed" (v. 7), the abomination (v. 14), troubles (Mt 24,9; Mk 13,19), false prophets (v. 22), the Parousia according to Dn 7 (v. 26), the angels at the Parousia (Mt 24,31), the gathering (v. 27), the carelessness of "the world" (Mt 24,37 ff., Lk 21,34), the thief in the night (24,43), ἀπάντησις (25,6), the sudden arrival (Lk 21,34), and the travail/snare (Lk 21,35).

On the other hand, the following sections of the discourse have not clear equivalents in 1,2 Ths: war and catastrophes (vv. 7 f.), the persecutions,[59] the family divisions, the hatred (vv. 9–13), the flight from the abomination (vv. 14b–18), the shortening of the days (v. 20), and the heavenly phenomena at the Parousia (v. 24 f.). For work on the history of the tradition of the discourse, these latter statements can only serve as *argumenta e silentio*.

Finally, we have established that Paul describes as a single phenomenon what in the discourse are more or less separate phenomena— "I am", the abomination and the prophets with the false signs. This also must be discussed in connection with the attempts to trace the history of the tradition of the discourse.

---

[59] Cf. however 1 Ths 2,15.

CHAPTER VII

Phases in the Development of the Eschatological Discourse

1. *Introduction*

Now we enter an area in which the ground is undermined by the intense debates between NT scholars in the last hundred years concerning eschatology, apocalyptic, *Parusieverzögerung* and related themes. Moreover there is at almost every step a danger of falling into one of the traps unwittingly laid by the labours of the scholars of the last few generations and especially by the strenuous discussions concerning the original character of the Gospel material and its history prior to its being written down. The participants in these discussions often take sides for and against the opinions of certain "schools".

Nevertheless one of the main purposes of this entire investigation is to try and contribute to our understanding of how Mk 13 par. acquired its present form and to get some idea of what happened to the material before it was written down. Perhaps some reasons for the changes in the material may also be discerned.[1] As in the previous chapter, the investigation here will also be on the literary plane. There will be few glances at the history of the ideas and problems of the early Church, there will, on the whole, be no attempts to trace the theology of the individual evangelist, as it may be read from the way in which his Gospel was edited, and the thorough exegesis of the text will have to be deferred.

The procedure in this chapter will be as follows. First of all, I present the elements which may be of importance in the endeavour to reconstruct the history of the tradition (section 2). I gather together the conclusions which have emerged in Chaps. V and VI (A) and then discuss the persecution logia in the discourse (13,9–13 par.) (B), after which I try and determine how the discourse was fitted into the context (C) and define my opinion of the Lucan version of it (D). As regards Did. 16 and Apc. Petri 1–2, other scholars have expressed views which would seem to give reason for thinking that an analysis of these texts would also contribute to our understanding of the history

---

[1] Though the inquiry concerning the *ipsissima verba Iesu* may be included in this context, it is not my purpose here. Cf. JOACH. JEREMIAS, Kennzeichen der ipsissima vox Jesu, in *Synoptische Studien A. Wikenhauser dargebracht* (1953), 86–93, and id., *Die Gleichnisse Jesu* (6th ed. 1962), 19 ff.

of the tradition of Mk 13 par.[2] However, a closer examination will show that this is not the case.[3] Against this background and with the help of the material produced by these analyses, I attempt in section 3 to outline the history of the tradition of the discourse. Finally, I give some indications of the consequences which follow from the results of these analyses and of the problems into which they lead us (section 4).

2. Elements in the Evaluation of the History of the Tradition

A. Elements from Chaps. V and VI

(a) The "midrashic" substrate. An important element in work on the historical development of the eschatological discourse is the "midrashic" substrate revealed by the analyses in Chap. V. There, against the background of the results obtained in Part I, it was possible to see how large parts of the discourse could be explained, step by step, as something resembling a midrash based on some portions of the Book of Daniel. To all appearances, this "midrash" included from the beginning at least a proportion of the present parenetic details.[4] This provides us a more objective basis for arguments on the history of the tradition than those available in previous discussions, whether based on the hypothesis that the discourse has as its nucleus a borrowed Jewish apocalypse or broadsheet[5] or a Jewish–Christian apocalypse or on the assumption that the whole thing is a mosaic of many small elements which were originally disparate. In these cases the process of evaluating the history of the tradition has to some extent

---

[2] For Did. 16, see H. Köster, Synoptische Überlieferung bei den apostolischen Vätern (1957), 173 ff., and R. Glover, The Didache's Quotations and the Synoptic Gospels, NT Stud. 5 (1958/59), 22 ff.; for Apc. Petri see A. Loisy, Les origines du NT (1936), 320, and cf. M. Dibelius, Geschichte der urchristlichen Literatur I (1926), 94 ff.

[3] I hope to be able to give a more detailed account of this in a later article. Cf. for Did. 16 also E. Massaux, Influence de l'Évangile de saint Matthieu (1950), 631 ff.; E. Stommel, Σημεῖον ἐκπετάσεως (Didache 16,6), Röm. Quartalschr. 48 (1953), 21–42; J.-P. Audet, La Didachè (1958), 176 ff., 468 ff.; E. Bammel, Schema und Vorlage von Didache 16, Stud. Patr. 4 (1961), 253–62; Vielhauer, in Hennecke, Apokryphen II, 442 ff.; for Apc. Petri, see also Beasley-Murray, Future, 240 ff.

[4] See Chap. V, section 6.

[5] This broadsheet theory seems a strange one to me. If we assume that it is a matter of manifold copies of a pamphlet or a brochure, is there a single example of such a phenomenon in antiquity? Has a copy been preserved or mentioned in literature? Cf. Hölscher, Theol. Blätter 12 (1933), 193 ff., and recently A. Suhl, Die Funktion der alttestamentlichen Zitate und Anspielungen im Markusevangelium (1965), 18, 152.

moved in a circle: the conclusions were based on assumptions which were formulated from the conclusions. The above-mentioned "midrash" gives us somewhat firmer ground beneath our feet, owing to the fact that, from the analogies given in Chaps. III and IV, we can determine with some certainty when the OT material is "carrying" the text and when the text deviates from it. The result is that we have a fairly solid initial position, from which the structure of the text may be derived, independently of our opinions as to its content and character.

I found traces of this "midrash" in the following verses in Mk 13: 5b–8, 12–16, 19–22, 24–27 (8b and 15a are somewhat less certain). We may compare this with one of the many suggestions as to the extent of the "basic text",[6] namely, Professor Bultmann's, which includes vv. 7 f., 12, 14–22, and 24–27.[7] He considers that vv. 5 f., 9–11, 13a, and 23 are Christian additions. My analysis showed that an earlier form of v. 5 f. constituted one of the main points in the "midrash" and v. 13a proved to be directly derivable from the passage used in v. 12.

This "midrashic" basis may also yield indications as to the passages in which the tradition grew. The position is not so simple as to permit us, for example, to boldly cut off certain verses and then regard what is left as the original "midrash". The material may also have been edited by making small changes in the wording. We may suspect this in the passages in which there seems to be a "gap" between the existing discourse and the text expounded.[8] Such passages are v. 6, in which "I am" is said by "many" who will come "in my name", v. 13, where the Apostles will be hated of all men "for my name's sake", v. 14, where neither Gn 19 nor the actual Daniel passages give reason for the introduction of the name "Judaea", and vv. 21 f., where it is not possible to regard false Messiahs as being by any means implied in Dt 13, the text expounded.

We may compare these views of the extent of the early parenetic "midrash" with that of the "midrash" for which evidence was given from 1 and 2 Ths (Chap. VI). There we found equivalents for vv. 5–7, 14, 22, and 26 f. (together with Mt 24,31 and Lk 21,34 f.). We also found that here the three phenomena were kept together, as referring to a single occurrence, while in the discourse they were more or less kept separate: the "I am", the abomination of desolation, and the prophets giving false signs and wonders.[9]

---

[6] See on this point BEASLEY-MURRAY, *Future*.

[7] BULTMANN, *Geschichte*, 129. HÖLSCHER, op. cit., 195 f., reaches the same conclusion, though he leaves out vv. 21 f.

[8] Though in principle the "gap" may have been original.

[9] See, above, 202.

We furthermore established that certain "additions" incorporated in Matthew's version of the discourse could be explained, as regarded their origin, in the same "midrashic", associative way as the "basic midrash" (24,20, 30 f.).[10]

Another feature of importance in evaluating the history of the tradition is that this "midrash" was, to all appearances, combined from the beginning with parenesis. The parenetic details may have been increased in number during the process which ended with the writing down of the Gospels, but at least part of the parenetic material is itself "midrashic".[11]

It is sometimes asserted so forcefully that the discourse is parenetic that its apocalyptic aspect is obscured.[12] It is undeniable that behind this "midrash" there *also* lies an examination and an exegesis of the Scriptures which debouches in predictions of what is to happen in the last days. The parenesis is occasioned by and combined with eschatological teaching of a type reminiscent of the Jewish apocalypses studied in Part I above.

(b) *Sitz im Leben*. The analyses in Chap. V thus revealed an underlying parenetic "midrash". In Chap. VI we encountered a form of this "midrash", so to speak, in action: it formed a basis for parenesis and detailed teaching on eschatological matters in 1 and 2 Ths. This is of some interest, now that we are to summarize what the content of previous chapters has yielded in the way of an evaluation of the tradition's *Sitz im Leben*. Asking the question about the *Sitz im Leben* implies inquiring in what context or in what milieu and activity of the early Church this text had a place before it was written down. This might also become an inquiry as to why, where and how a tradition arose, but it seems to me to be essential to keep the two questions separate.[13] In the same way we should keep separate a tradition and its form.[14]

---

[10] See above, 163 ff.

[11] See above, Chap. V, section 6.

[12] Cf. above, 16, and BEASLEY-MURRAY, *Future*, 212 ff.

[13] Cf. BULTMANN, *Geschichte*, 40 (on certain "pronouncement stories"): "die methodisch zuerst zu beantwortende Frage ist die nach der literarischen Art des Streitgesprächs und seinem Ursprung als literarischer Grösse. Das ist die Frage nach dem 'Sitz im Leben'; denn diese fragt … nach dem Ursprung und der Zugehörigkeit einer bestimmten Gattung in und zu typischen Situationen und Verhaltungen einer Gemeinschaft" (with a negative reference to E. FASCHER, *Die formgeschichtliche Methode*, 1924, 221); G. IBER, Zur Formgeschichte der Evangelien, *Theol. Rundschau* 24 (1957–58), 308 ff.

[14] Cf. BULTMANN, op. cit., 4, 48; DIBELIUS, *Formgeschichte*, 287 ff.; W. MANSON, *Jesus the Messiah* (1943), 29 f., 39 ff. (traditions which change their form).

At the beginning of his *Geschichte der synoptischen Tradition* Bultmann speaks of the circle in which form-critical argumentation moves: from the literary forms of traditions conclusions are drawn referring back to motifs in the life of the community, and these forms are to be explained by the life of the community.[15] A prerequisite condition is that it is the community which creates the forms (and often their content also).[16] These forms are assumed to be those of a *Kleinliteratur*,[17] a simple, popular literature, whose parallels are to be found in folk tales and folk songs.[18]

The eschatological discourse offers a certain resistance to these patterns. In its earlier form it was a kind of midrash, a form whose *Sitz im Leben* is incompatible with that of a *Kleinliteratur*, and its presumptive original milieu does not seem to conform with that of a *Kleinliteratur* either. This means that one of the two common hypotheses (sic!) as to the form and structure of the discourse must be abandoned at once; the discourse is certainly a composed speech *now* but its groundwork is not. There remains the view held by Bultmann and quoted above. It is consistent with the requirements of form history: a coherent form such as this is not created by the milieu of a *Kleinliteratur* and thus the groundwork is assumed to be a borrowed Jewish apocalypse.[19] If this view is to be maintained, it must be re-

[15] BULTMANN, *Geschichte*, 5. It would please several scholars who do not belong to the Bultmann school if, following the master, the members of it would show themselves more willing to accept this fact. The reservation in Bultmann (ibid.) that this circle applies "grundsätzlich bei aller historischen Arbeit" leaves room for an imperceptible shift in the argument. It is true that all historical research works *grundsätzlich* in a certain circle, i.e. that the scholar is always conditioned by his environment and his personality in collecting, evaluating and preparing his material, all of which influences his conclusions. But there is a certain difference between this "circle" and the degree to which the results and the presuppositions are made to support each other in the case of the form criticism. The situation is not made more rational when these hypothetical results are taken over as the assured "results of a critical analysis" (cf. H. CONZELMANN, *Die Mitte der Zeit*, 3rd ed. 1960, 4). For the principles of historical science, see L.-E. HALKIN, *Eléments de critique historique* (1960), 25 ff., 101 ff.

[16] BULTMANN, op. cit., 4 f.; DIBELIUS, *Formgeschichte*, 7 f.; IBER, op. cit., 322 f.

[17] DIBELIUS, op. cit., 1 f., 7, 31, 36, 90.

[18] BULTMANN, op. cit., 7 f., and IBER, *Theol. Rundschau* 24 (1957–58), 322.

[19] Of course, this is not the whole truth about Bultmann's attitude to Mk 13. Considerations as regards content might have played no small part here: Bultmann's view of Jesus presupposes that Jesus was not an *Apokalyptiker* (cf. R. BULTMANN, *Jesus*, 1929, 37 ff.). In addition there is the research tradition of the "Synoptic apocalypse" (BEASLEY-MURRAY, *Future*). Dibelius' wording is somewhat more indefinite, but his view seems to be close to Bultmann's; see DIBELIUS, *Geschichte der urchristlichen Literatur* I, 93 f., and id., *The Sermon on the Mount* (1940), 32 f.

vised, if my analysis is correct: several of the "Christian insertions" were present from the beginning and furthermore we have also to take into account the fact that, unlike the Jewish parallels, this Jewish apocalypse was parenetic. On the other hand, the fact that it was "midrashic" need not trouble us: Part I above provides certain analogies for this.

If now, after this rapid and superficial comparison of two suggested solutions, we inquire about a possible milieu in which a tradition such as this might have been preserved and used, Dibelius' thesis on *die Predigt* (sermon and preaching) with a parenetic purpose seems too narrow.[20] I would instead remind the reader of K. Stendahl's inquiry, in which he found a "school of St. Matthew"[21] underlying the way in which the OT was used in Matthew's Gospel. B. Gerhardsson made an advance in a similar direction, in finding indications for assuming that the Gospel tradition was largely preserved and used in separate traditionist circles in the early Church, in a way which was more reminiscent of the collegia of Jewish scribes (and moreover of the teaching in another (Hellenistic) milieu) than of the way in which folk tales are handed down.[22] If we now assume that the basic "midrash" was a borrowed Jewish parenetic (!) apocalypse, this "midrash" is evidenced by the examinations of 1 and 2 Ths as having been christianized a few years before 50 A.D., i.e. it must at any rate have had a Christian *Sitz im Leben* for at least two decades before Mark's Gospel was written down. The further argumentation in this chapter will serve to confirm the assumption of a *Sitz im Leben* in keeping with those suggested by Stendahl and Gerhardsson.

1 and 2 Ths show that at least Paul used this tradition not only for teaching on the truly Christian life and for parenesis but also for teaching on Christian eschatology. He both gave this teaching in Thessalonica and repeated it in his Letters. In this teaching Paul

---

[20] M. DIBELIUS, Die alttestamentlichen Motive in der Leidensgeschichte des Petrus- und des Johannes-Evangeliums, *Zschr. At. Wiss.*, *Beih.* 33 (1918), 146; id., *Formgeschichte*, 234 ff., 260. BULTMANN makes a reservation against this restriction in his *Geschichte* (64), where he is willing to supplement it with "schriftgelehrte Arbeit". Cf. also G. SCHILLE, Bemerkungen zur Formgeschichte des Evangeliums, *NT Stud.* 4 (1957/58), 11 ff.

[21] STENDAHL, *School*. And cf. BULTMANN, the preceding note.

[22] GERHARDSSON, *Memory*. The technique of the rabbinic school which Gerhardsson has examined in detail and presented in this book was brought forward as a component of an alternative theory to radical form criticism by H. RIESENFELD in The Gospel Tradition and its Beginnings, *Studia Evangelica* 1 (1959), 43–65. Gerhardsson has defined the issues in the discussion of his work more precisely in *Tradition and Transmission in Early Christianity* (1964).

211

applies the tradition to the actual situation of those he is addressing and makes it shed light on their situation. The two components of the early "midrash", both the parenetic and the eschatological, thus recur in its use.

The tradition shares this "usage" with other *paradoseis,* for example, those in 1 Co 11 or 15. The expression *paradoseis,* which presumably denoted an early form of the discourse in 2 Ths 2,15, also tells us something about the form in which the tradition existed, at least as Paul knew it.[23] It is something which he himself has received and which he has passed on to the Thessalonians. In 1 Ths 4,15 he seems to attribute the first link in the chain of transmission to the Lord Himself (cf. 1 Co 11,23 ἀπὸ τοῦ κυρίου). When the tradition was to be used to provide guidance in an actual situation, Paul may have modified and re-worded it. Thus it was scarcely so carefully cultivated a tradition as the *halakah* Paul had to work on in Beth Hillel. The similarities between the version of the discourse in 1 and 2 Ths and that in the Gospels, which were written down two or three decades later, are, however, so great that Stendahl's and Gerhardsson's assumptions as to the "school", the circle of men learned in the Scriptures and working on them in a "scribal" way and the teaching given in the early Church, seem applicable to the discourse. This also agrees with the transition from "midrash" to "mishna" pointed out in Chap. V: the form was adapted for the purposes of teaching[24].

If we then ask where the form or rather the forms of the discourse originated, it may be replied that the investigations so far lead to the following considerations. The present form is a more or less comprehensive combination, partly of the parenetic "midrash" transformed into a "mishna" and partly of other material of sayings. This combination is in part possibly the work of the evangelist[25] but some of it is older; thus 1 and 2 Ths reveal that the logia on watchfulness were linked with the "midrash" when these letters were written.[26] The combination would seem to reflect the need of teaching in the early Church, a need which was decided by its history. The question of the original *Sitz im Leben* of the parenetic "midrash" is more difficult.

---

[23] See, for example, F. V. FILSON, The Christian Teacher in the First Century, *J. Bibl. Lit.* 60 (1941), 326 f.; O. CULLMANN, Paradosis et Kyrios, *Rev. Hist. Phil. Rel.* 30 (1950), 12–30; CERFAUX, La tradition selon saint Paul, in *Recueil L. Cerfaux* II, 253–63, particularly 260 f.; STAUFFER; *NT Theology,* 235 ff.; GERHARDSSON, *Memory,* 288 ff. and passim; R. P. C. HANSON, *Tradition in the Early Church* (1962), 9 ff.

[24] See above, Chap. V, section 6.

[25] Se below, 222 ff.

[26] Se above, Chap. VI, section 3.

Must not a "midrash" as coherent as this be at bottom the work of one man, although it may have been expanded later by others? In what milieu, then, are we to seek this "midrashist", inside or outside the early Church? Was this "midrashist"—as Paul seems to think—Jesus Himself? We shall return to these questions later in this chapter (section 3, B).

B. The section on persecutions

In Chap. V, section 4, it was shown that Mk 13,9–11 did not have the same close relation to the OT as the surrounding verses and indeed that, if they were omitted, a clear link between the motifs of Is 19,2 (brother against brother) and Mi 7,2 ff. (children/parents) could be revealed. Furthermore the analysis in Chap. V showed that the Matthaean variant was surprisingly close to the passage in Daniel which deals with the persecutions of "those who are wise". This is generally held to have been written by the evangelist, to replace the verses in Mk 13,9–13 already used in Mt 10.[27]

In endeavouring to grasp the history of the tradition of this section, we may begin by determining the literary structure of the Marcan and Matthaean versions and then try to trace the development of the tradition backwards. We will begin with what seems to be the latest layer of text and work backwards from there.

(a) *The literary structure.* We have already touched upon the literary structure of *Mk 13,9–13* in Chap. V (section 4). A main word is παρα-διδόναι, which is to be found in vv. 9, 11 and 12. It may be regarded as the key-word which holds these three logia together.[28] The preceding analysis, which linked v. 12 with the "midrash", now results in its being possible to regard vv. 9 and 11 as being associated with v. 12 via the key-word.[29] A variant of v. 11 occurs as a separate logion in Lk 12,11 f. This also indicates that this grouping is not original and that at all events v. 11 is a logion which was associated with this passage afterwards[30] and which gives a parenesis with reference to the prophecy in v. 9. As regards v. 9, the situation is somewhat more difficult. The logion could be regarded as an exposition of "deliver up"

---

[27] See, for example, BULTMANN, *Geschichte*, 124; ALLEN, KLOSTERMANN, and SCHMID, *Comm. Mt*, ad loc.

[28] BEASLEY-MURRAY, *Mark 13*, ad loc.

[29] Similarly WENDLING, *Die Entstehung des Marcus-Evangeliums*, 157; J. SUNDWALL, *Die Zusammensetzung des Markusevangeliums* (1934), 78; LOHMEYER, *Comm. Mk*, ad loc. KLOSTERMANN (*Comm. Mk*, ad loc.) suggests the possibility. Cf. TAYLOR, *Comm. Mk*, ad loc.

[30] Thus also D. BOSCH, *Die Heidenmission in der Zukunftsschau Jesu* (1959), 154. Cf. WENDLING, op. cit., 157.

in Dn 7,25 and in that case would form a "siding" for the "main line" from v. 8 to v. 12 (from Is 19,2 to Mi 7,2 ff.). With some hesitation I find it more likely, however, that both v. 9 and v. 11 were incorporated later by means of key-words, breaking the originally close connection between vv. 8 and 12, which was established by the "midrashic" association. Mk 13,10 is an inserted logion, regarded from the point of view of the composition. It shows features of specifically Marcan idiom, *inter alia*, the absolute use of εὐαγγέλιον.[31]

We then investigate the literary structure of *Mt 24,9–14*. It is likely that there is a connection between Mk 13,9–13, and Mt 24,9–14. Thus παραδώσουσιν ὑμᾶς εἰς θλῖψιν (Mt 24,9 a) seems to refer to the handing over to courts and to punishment in Mk 13,9. The continuation καὶ ἀποκτενοῦσιν ὑμᾶς καὶ ἔσεσθε μισούμενοι κτλ. reproduces the similar sentences in Mk 13,12 about children killing their parents and the disciples being hated. Of the three main words παραδιδόναι, ἀποκτενεῖν and μισεῖσθαι, which are used in Mt 24,9 about persecutions, two recur in 24,10 b: καὶ ἀλλήλους παραδώσουσιν καὶ μισήσουσιν ἀλλήλους, i.e. the evils are regarded as coming not only from outside but also from within their own ranks.[32] It seems as if here Mk 13,12 f. (brother betrays brother to death, the disciples will be hated) has been re-interpreted so that ἀδελφός has the sense of "comrade" etc. and the reciprocal ἀδελφὸς ἀδελφόν has become ἀλλήλους.[33]

This re-interpretation of the Marcan version is introduced in Mt 24 by τότε σκανδαλισθήσονται πολλοί, which marks the transition to a description of the coming θλῖψις, which is to prevail within the Church. At this point the text passes from the second person plural to the third person plural and the word "many", presumably taken over from Daniel, comes to the fore. After this re-interpreted Marcan quotation, the text continues with variations on the same theme: false prophets, love waxing cold and apostasy. In Chap. V we found that the elements which at this point are peculiar to Matthew in relation to Mark are for the most part so close to Dn 11,32 ff. that a connection seems probable. Mt 24,9–13 may therefore be said to be composed of partly re-interpreted Marcan elements and of a Daniel exposition. Taken together, they describe the increasing moral and religious corruption.

The excellent coherence of Mt 24,9–12, as regards content, explains why the next connection with Mk 13, that with v. 13, does not occur until after the saying on degradation: "He who endures to the end

---

[31] See TAYLOR, *Comm. Mk*, ad loc.

[32] See, for example, WEISS, and M'NEILE, *Comm. Mt*, ad loc.

[33] Cf. how איש אחיו is usually rendered in the LXX by ἀλλήλων (for example Gn 42,28; Ex 26,3) but can also be rendered by ἀδελφὸς ἀδελφόν in Lv 26,37.

will be saved". It also explains why the variant of Mk 13,10 (the mission logion) does not occur until v. 14: the persecutions, the apostasy and the afflictions are all forms of suffering which the Christians must endure. Thus Mt 24,9–13 also forms a unit, as regards content.

The fairly free and re-interpretative fashion in which Matthew here uses Marcan material throws some light on the relation of Mt 24,14 to Mk 13,10. It is not a question of the mechanical adoption of fragments but of the interpretative use of a material. A problem which has been discussed in this connection is the striking similarity between, on the one hand, Mk 13,9 b f. (σταθήσεσθε ...) εἰς μαρτύριον αὐτοῖς. καὶ εἰς πάντα τὰ ἔθνη (πρῶτον δεῖ κηρυχθῆναι) and, on the other, Mt 24,14 (κηρυχθήσεται τοῦτο τὸ εὐαγγέλιον ...) εἰς μαρτύριον πᾶσιν τοῖς ἔθνεσιν. If we avoid regarding the words as isolated units and instead look more at the contents of the clauses, in comparison with how Matthew re-interprets παραδώσει ἀδελφὸς ἀδελφόν, it is fairly clear that Matthew was inspired by Mark 13,10 but was also influenced by the context of this logion (μαρτύριον!).[34] However, in addition, there are the points of contact between Mt 24,14 and Dn 11 which we discovered in Chap. V. Dn 11,33 speaks of the wise ones who shall make many understand, and perhaps even εἰς μαρτύριον had an equivalent in a לְמוֹעֵד.[35]

In so far as it was not directly influenced by Mk 13 or Daniel, the choice of words in Mt 24,9–14 is at times strikingly similar to the phraseology in other logia and to some extent is specifically Matthaean. Thus v. 11 is reminiscent of Mt 24,5 (πολλοὶ ... πολλοὺς πλανήσουσιν) and Mt 24,24 (ἐγερθήσονται ... ψευδοπροφῆται), ἀνομία occurs in the Gospels only in Matthew's,[36] the wording τοῦτο τὸ εὐαγγέλιον is to be found elsewhere in the NT only in Mt 26,13 (though slightly varied; in both these passages moreover along with a form of κηρυχθῆναι), and the construction εὐαγγέλιον τῆς βασιλείας is likewise a speciality of Matthew's.[37]

(b) *The development of the tradition.* Against the background of the

---

[34] See A. FARRER, An Examination of Mark xiii. 10, *J. Theol. Stud.* 7 (1956), 75–79, where Farrer opposes G. D. KILPATRICK (The Gentile Mission in Mark and Mark 13,9–11, in *Studies ... in mem. R. H. Lightfoot*, 1955, 145–58), who in conjunction with F. C. BURKITT (in *Christian Beginnings*, 1924, 145 ff.) would read 13,10 as εἰς μαρτύριον αὐτοῖς καὶ εἰς τὰ ἔθνη. The support consists primarily of the δέ which a number of textual authorities insert after πρῶτον. See on this point FARRER (op. cit.). KILPATRICK defended his view in his article entitled Mark xiii.9–10 in *J. Theol. Stud.* 9 (1958), 81–86. Cf. BEASLEY-MURRAY, *Mark 13*, ad loc., and JOACH. JEREMIAS, *Jesus' Promise to the Nations* (1958), 22 f.

[35] See above, 169 ff.

[36] Mt 7,23; 13,41; 23,28; 24,12.

[37] Mt 4,23; 9,35; 24,14.

foregoing literary analyses, I shall now try and follow the development of the tradition backwards. Mt 24,9–14 must be the latest layer of text. In another context I concluded, from analyses of certain linguistic phenomena in Matthew's Gospel, that the traditions of that Gospel were transmitted in Greek in a relatively fixed oral form for some time before it was written down and furthermore that for at least a part of this time Mark's Gospel was known in a written form to those who transmitted the Matthaean material.[38] It seems to me reasonable to assume that it was at this time that the Matthaean variant of the persecution logia was conceived in the Matthew circle on the basis of Dn 11,32 ff. and Mk 13,9 ff. Earlier in this chapter I suggested that the tradition's *Sitz im Leben* was the "school", the circle of teachers and traditionists and their teaching in the Church. It is also more natural to assign the origin of these verses of Matthew's to the "school" than to the work of the person who set down the Gospel.[39] This harmonizes with the fact that the phraseology is coloured by the existing Gospel tradition.[40] The procedure reveals, on the one hand, a desire to find new meanings in existing tradition and, on the other, a tendency to expand the adopted "midrash" (cf. Paul in 1 Ths 4[41]). We may almost take it for granted that this usage and further development of an adopted tradition was related to the actual situation of the Church.[42] Here we get a glimpse of the problem of apostates and heretics, as well as persecutions and missionary thinking. Everything is set in an eschatological perspective: it has its place in the progress of the world towards the ultimate crisis.[43]

---

[38] L. HARTMAN, Participial Constructions in the Synoptic Gospels, in *Testimonium linguae* (1963), 51 ff.

[39] Cf. BULTMANN, *Geschichte*, 129: as regards vv. 10–12, Bultmann finds it impossible to decide whether Matthew himself wrote these verses or whether he took them over from Jewish or Christian tradition.

[40] Cf. HARTMAN, op. cit., 53 f.

[41] See above, Chap. VI, section 2.

[42] See, for example, G. BORNKAMM, Enderwartung und Kirche im Matthäusevangelium, in *The Background ... in hon. C. H. Dodd* (1956), 222 f., and SCHMID, *Comm. Mt*, ad loc. Cf. BULTMANN, op. cit., 134, and E. HIRSCH, *Frühgeschichte des Evangeliums* II (1941), 312 f.

[43] For the false prophets in Matthew, see Mt 7,15 (see J. DUPONT, *Les béatitudes*, 2nd ed. 1958, 44 ff.) and cf. Ac 20,29; 2 Pt 2,1 ff.; 1 Jn 4,1 ff. Also E. KÄSEMANN, Die Anfänge christlicher Theologie, *Zschr. Theol. Ki.* 57 (1960), 162 ff.

For the apostasy, cf. Mt 13,21, and see also 2 Tm 3,1 ff. Cf. K. W. CLARK, The Gentile Bias in Matthew, *J. Bibl. Lit.* 66 (1947), 165 ff.

For the mission, cf. Mt 10,5 ff.; 28,18 ff. And see B. SUNDKLER, Jésus et les païens, *Rev. Hist. Phil. Rel.* 16 (1936), 472; R. LIECHTENHAN, *Die urchristliche Mission* (1946), 31 f.; JEREMIAS, *Jesus' Promise*, 55 ff.; O. CULLMANN, Eschatology and Missions in the NT, in *The Background ... in hon. C. H. Dodd* (1956), 409–21; H. SCHLIER,

The next latest layer of text in this context would seem to be Mk 13,10 (the mission logion). The choice of words is specifically Marcan but is nevertheless not of such a nature as to enable us to decide whether or not it derives from the evangelist or from the tradition he adopted, and so we cannot be certain either as to who introduced it here, the evangelist or a traditionist before him. The fact that the connection between v. 9 and v. 11 is broken by v. 10 is not a sufficient criterion to decide this question either.[44]

The insertion of the logion here—and perhaps also its origin—may be explained as follows.[45] The preceding logion (v. 9) states that those addressed will be handed over to councils (συνέδρια), will be beaten in the synagogues, and stand before governors and kings for Christ's sake "for a testimony against them" (AV, εἰς μαρτύριον αὐτοῖς). It is probable that μαρτύριον here, as in all other places in the NT, has the meaning of "testimony" as recorded fact, an objective quantity as distinguished from the nomen actionis μαρτυρία.[46] Here it also has the primary meaning of a negative testimony, consisting of the persecutions, and given in God's court.[47]

Now, however, the person who inserted v. 10 may have allowed his thoughts to wander from this original significance, which is still to be found in the parallels Mt 10,18 and Lk 21,13. The witness to Christ before the world seems to have been associated here with μαρτύριον. This has obviously occurred in other passages in the NT in which μαρτύριον is used almost as an alternative to εὐαγγέλιον.[48] We may add that 13,11 deals with "speaking" (λαλεῖν) with the help of the Holy Spirit before these fora. These associations do not mean that μαρτύριον came to be equated with μαρτυρία, but the context (v. 11) may have provided the stimulus for them and the Church's mission and its reflections on it seem to underlie v. 10 and to have influenced its insertion at this point.[49]

Die Entscheidung für die Heidenmission in der Urchristenheit, in *Die Zeit der Kirche* (3rd ed. 1962), 90–107; M. MEINERTZ, Zum Ursprung der Heidenmission, *Bibl.* 40 (1959), 762–77; W. TRILLING, *Das wahre Israel* (1959), 13 f.

For the persecutions, cf. Mt 5,11 f.; 10,17 ff.; 23,34. See also 2 Tm 3,12 f. For Jewish parallels, se above, 30.

[44] W. MARXSEN, *Der Evangelist Markus* (1956), 120.

[45] Similarly MARXSEN, op. cit., 119.

[46] See H. STRATHMANN, μάρτυς κτλ., *Theol. Wörterb.* IV (1942), 508 ff. See on this and the following point HARTMAN, A Linguistic Examination of Luke 21,13, in *Testimonium linguae*, 64 ff. Cf. RSV: "to bear testimony before them".

[47] See note 46 and LOHMEYER, *Comm. Mk*, ad loc.; HARDER, *Theol. Viat.* 4 (1952), 78.

[48] See Ac 4,33; 1 Co 1,6; 2,1; 2 Ths 1,10; 2 Tm 1,8.

[49] Cf. CULLMANN, op. cit., 417 ff.; CRANFIELD, *Scot. J. Theol.* 6 (1953), 291 ff.;

That I should choose to take the next step backwards to Lk 21 will probably surprise some readers, since there is a very widespread opinion that in ch. 21 Luke personally revised Mk 13 *ex eventu* and, in doing so, also allowed his personal theology to colour this portion of the text.[50] I shall discuss Lk 21 in more detail below (subsection D) and give the reasons which may be adduced for thinking that in this chapter Luke used a variant of the discourse, which he combined with Marcan material. One reason which has led several scholars to assume that it was the evangelist in particular who revised Mark's text is that Lk 21,12–19 show the same order of the different logia as does the Marcan parallel.[51] However, it is possible to reconcile this fact with the view that the Lucan version of the persecution section goes back to an early variant of that form of the discourse which was later to be found in Mark's Gospel, a form which, however, had not yet been expanded by the insertion of v. 10 (the mission logion) but which possessed, on the other hand, the three combined παραδιδόναι logia.[52]

The next step backwards is then to this Marcan triad of persecution logia, but without v. 10. This verse indicates that the evangelist did not compose this triad, as he was the last who could have interpolated v. 10. Then the context into which v. 10 is interpolated would be older than v. 10. This addition of logia to the key-word παραδιδόναι may reveal a knowledge of an existing association with παραδιδόναι

---

id., and GRUNDMANN, *Comm. Mk*, ad loc. Also JEREMIAS, *Jesus' Promise*, 23. The LXX and 1 En use μαρτύριον (and its Ethiopic equivalents) in an "eschatological" secondary sense: the testimony is given before God's throne on the last day. (See Ho 2,14; Si 36,14; 1 En 67,12; 89,63, 76; 96,4; 97,3 f.; 99,3. See further HARTMAN, op. cit., 67 f.) This associational field is also present in Mk 6,11 (cf. Ac 18,6). This may shed light on πρῶτον in 13,10: to the question as to when this session is to take place, in which the testimony is to be given, the answer is "first the gospel must be preached to all nations".

[50] Thus CONZELMANN, *Mitte*, 107 ff., 113 ff.; MARXSEN, *Markus*, 130 ff.; E. GRÄSSER, *Das Problem der Parusieverzögerung* (1957), 160 ff. Cf. Conzelmann's argument against V. TAYLOR (*Behind the Third Gospel*, 1926, 109): "Wenn nicht positiv weitere Quellenstoffe über Mc hinaus nachgewiesen werden können, dann ergibt sich aus der Textanalyse gerade: die Tatsache dass das Nicht-Marcinische den 'Rahmen' bildet, erweist, dass der *Verfasser* den Mc-Stoff 'gerahmt', also übernommen und nach seiner eigenen Vorstellung gestaltet hat" (op. cit., 107). At the same time Conzelmann asserts on the following page that Mark gives "eine Korrektur der (jüdischen?) apokalyptischen Überlieferung". When were in this matter "positiv weitere Quellenstoffe nachgewiesen"? Not at any rate only because BULTMANN in his *Geschichte* (129) declares that this is the case! See further below, section D.

[51] For example, SCHMID, *Comm. Lk*, ad loc.

[52] Cf. W. L. KNOX, *The Sources of the Synoptic Gospels* I (1953), 106 f., and HARDER, *Theol. Viat.* 4 (1952), 79.

(or its equivalent) in Dn 7,25 or a desire to establish one.[53] In the triad v. 12 is probably original and v. 11 the latest addition to the context. With some hesitation I assumed above that v. 9 was also later associated with v. 12. We have no reason in this case either to think that associations by key-words were made only quite mechanically. On the contrary, it is probable that the Church's experience and thinking are reflected in it.

In this retrograde examination we have not yet discussed the occurrence of the triad in Mt 10,17–22. It seems likely to me that this section was incorporated here from the written form of Mark's Gospel at the same time as Mt 24,9–13 were conceived and composed.[54] Other possible comparisons in detail, such as the difference in the kinds of *fora* in 13,9 par. and the "Gentiles" in Mt 10,18 and 24,9, will not be considered here. They are relevant in a detailed exegesis and in the precise evaluation of the Church milieu behind the tradition but would not seem to affect the general evaluation of the history of the tradition, as regards this section of the eschatological discourse.[55]

C. The framework of the discourse

By "framework" I mean in this context the material surrounding the analysed parenetic "midrash" in the Gospels, i.e. on the one hand, Mk 13,1–4 par. (*inter alia,* the fall of the Temple) and, on the other, Mk 13,28–32 par., viz. the parable of the fig tree and the following logia. For each framework I first analyse the material and then take a sight of the problems concerning the tradition.

(a) *Mk 13,1–4 par.* Mk 13,1 f. is a unit,[1] forming a "pronouncement story" (Bultmann's *Apophthegma*),[2] the nucleus of which is the saying in v. 2*b*, οὐ μὴ ἀφεθῇ λίθος ἐπὶ λίθον ὃς οὐ μὴ καταλυθῇ. The scene in which the logion is set reveals the hand of the evangelist (ἐκπορευομένου αὐτοῦ, the phrasing of the disciples' words).[3] This logion exists in

---

[53] A variant such as that in the Targ. to Mi 7,2 may also have been the origin: גבר ית אחוהי מסרין, "a man delivers up his brother".

[54] See, for example, SCHMID, *Comm. Mt*, ad loc. For a *redaktionsgeschichtlich* assessment of the passage, see BORNKAMM, *Enderwartung*, 226 f. (cf. MARXSEN, *Markus*, 138 f.); G. STRECKER, *Der Weg der Gerechtigkeit* (1962), 44. Cf. B. REICKE, Den primära israelsmissionen och hednamissionen enligt synoptikerna, *Svensk Teol. Kvartalskrift* 26 (1950), 77–100.

[55] See the commentaries and the works of BORNKAMM, CONZELMANN, HARDER, MARXSEN, STRECKER, and TRILLING.

[1] K. L. SCHMIDT, *Der Rahmen der Geschichte Jesu* (1919), 290.

[2] BULTMANN, *Geschichte*, 36.

[3] BULTMANN, ibid.; cf. 58 f., 64; TAYLOR, *Comm. Mk*, ad loc.; HARTMAN, *Testimonium linguae*, 21 f.

several versions, both in the Gospels and elsewhere in the NT.[4] These passages fall into two groups, the first of which includes Mk 13,2 par. and Lk 19,44, containing a saying of Jesus only on the destruction of the Temple. The second group consists of sayings which certainly deal with the destruction of the Temple but also state that a new Temple will be built.[5] The shorter form used in Mk 13 need be regarded neither as an abbreviation of a longer logion[6] nor as the original form from which the others have grown:[7] the two variants may in themselves have existed side by side from the beginning.[8]

Vv. 3 f. constitute the framework which introduces the actual discourse. It is Marcan in style,[9] but there is a possibility that the detail of the four named disciples putting the question was adopted from an older tradition.[10] Their question[11] runs: πότε ταῦτα ἔσται, καὶ τί τὸ σημεῖον ὅταν μέλλῃ ταῦτα συντελεῖσθαι πάντα. As we have already seen, the wording at the end resembles Dn 12,7: Daniel asks (12,6) "How long shall it be till the end of these wonders?" and receives the reply that "when the shattering of the holy people comes to an end, all

---

[4] See further P. VIELHAUER, *Oikodome* (1940), 62 ff., and KÜMMEL, *Promise*, 99 ff. The passages are Mk 14,58 par.; 15,29 par.; Lk 19,44; Jn 2,19; Ac 6,14; 2 Co 5,1. For 2 Co 5,1, see SELWYN, *Comm. 1 Pt*, 290, and A. FEUILLET, La demeure céleste et la destinée des chrétiens, *Rech. Sci. Rel.* 44 (1956), 361 ff.

[5] DW it Cypr have this longer form also in Mk 13,2. A. T. CADOUX (*The Sources of the Second Gospel*, 1935, 177) alleges the uncertain hypothesis that this is the original reading. It is more natural to assume that it represents a secondary combination. Thus, for example, LAGRANGE, *Comm. Mk*, and BEASLEY-MURRAY, *Mark 13*, ad loc. This phenomenon is not uncommon in D; see, for example, C. H. TURNER, Western Readings in the Second Half of St Mark's Gospel, *J. Theol. Stud.* 29 (1928), 8 f.

[6] LOISY and LOHMEYER, *Comm. Mk*, ad loc.; VIELHAUER, op. cit., 69; MARXSEN, *Markus*, 113.

[7] Cf. BULTMANN, *Geschichte*, 126 f.

[8] BEASLEY-MURRAY, *Mark 13*, ad loc. A more detailed assessment of the matter would have to enter into some delicate problems, especially those concerning Jesus' possible teaching about a new Temple and His own personal connection with it and the early Church's thought of itself. See on this point B. GÄRTNER, *The Temple and the Community in Qumran and the NT* (1965), 105 ff. (and references given there), and also K. BALTZER, The Meaning of the Temple in the Lukan Writings, *Harv. Theol. Rev.* 58 (1965), 263–77. Cf., for example, MARXSEN, loc. cit.

[9] See J. C. HAWKINS, *Horae synopticae* (2nd ed. 1909), 10 ff.; F. C. GRANT, *The Gospels: Their Origin and their Growth* (1957), 110; TAYLOR, *Comm. Mk*, ad loc.

[10] BULTMANN, op. cit., 370; TAYLOR and GRUNDMANN, *Comm. Mk*, ad loc. Cf. the Papias tradition of Mark as Peter's ἑρμηνευτής (Eusebius, *Hist. eccl.* III.39,15).

[11] A question from the disciples is often the introductory framework to a teaching pericope. See Mk 4,10 ff.; 7,17 ff.; 9,28 f.; 10,10 ff. (BULTMANN, op. cit., 356). Also Mk 9,22 f.; Mt 15,12; 21,20 f.

these things will be accomplished" (LXX συντελεσθήσεται πάντα ταῦτα; TM תכלינה כל אלה).

This question in 13,4 joins the saying about the fall of the Temple with the eschatological discourse: ταῦτα ... πάντα clearly alludes, linguistically speaking, to the preceding prophecy.[12] Does the question apply to the eschatology at the same time? It consists of two parallel clauses.[13] This parallelism means that it cannot be divided up into two separate questions, one on the Temple and one on the consummation, but it also means that the two clauses do not necessarily express exactly the same things. The second clause may be expansive or explanatory.[14] The decisive factor is then the nuance of meaning which is to be read in συντελεῖσθαι. If it has no eschatological reference, the sentence means that the first step has been taken towards "de-eschatologizing" the discourse, which in that case is made to deal with the fall of Jerusalem as a divine punishment.[15] However, this particular phraseological similarity to Dn 12,7 indicates that συντελεῖσθαι here really alludes to "the close of the age".[16] This means that the destruction of the Temple and the events of the last days are linked by this framework and that the eschatology then also includes sayings about this catastrophe.[17] On the other hand, Matthew's re-wording leaves no room for any doubt: "When will this be, and what will be the sign of your Parousia and of the close of the age?" (συντέλεια τοῦ αἰῶνος).[18]

While the Matthaean variant of these verses does not contain any

---

[12] WEISS and E. P. GOULD (1896), *Comm. Mk*, ad loc. Cf. KLOSTERMANN, LAGRANGE, and TAYLOR, *Comm. Mk*, ad loc.

[13] M. BLACK, *An Aramaic Approach to the Gospels and Acts* (2nd ed. 1954), 117, and BEASLEY-MURRAY, *Mark 13*, ad loc.

[14] C. F. BURNEY, *The Poetry of our Lord* (1925), 16, 20 f.; BLACK, op cit., 105. Cf. SCHMID, *Comm. Mk*, ad loc., and WENDLING, *Entstehung*, 163.

[15] Thus FEUILLET, *Rev. Bibl.* 55 (1948), 481–502, 56 (1949), 61–92. Cf. LAGRANGE, *Comm. Mk*, ad loc.

[16] LOHMEYER (*Comm. Mk*, ad loc.) speaks (without quoting any instances) of this verb as a technical term, and is followed by SCHNIEWIND, *Comm. Mt*, ad loc., BEASLEY-MURRAY, *Mark 13*, ad loc., and MARXSEN, *Markus*, 114.

[17] See, for example, A. SCHLATTER, *Comm. Mk* (1935), ad loc. Here we are faced by a complex of problems, in which the terminology (and the thinking) of some exegetes creates confusion. Thus an outsider may feel a little dubious about HARDER's statement that Mark here "das Drohwort eschatologisch versteht, nicht als die Vorhersage einer politischen Katastrophe" (*Theol. Viat.* 4, 1952, 74). Political catastrophes may certainly be included among the last things, τὰ ἔσχατα; it is only that the word "eschatological" no longer means "eschatological" in its accepted sense. Cf. above, 16, and O. CULLMANN, *Heil als Geschichte* (1965), Chap. 3 and p. 60 f.

[18] See, for example, MARXSEN, *Markus*, 136.

changes which we need discuss in any detail here,[19] the Lucan parallel shows substantial differences. We may either interpret this as meaning that Luke altered the Marcan wording (he concentrated the disciples' replies on the fall of the Temple and also omitted the change of scene in the Gospels of Matthew and Mark from the Temple to the Mount of Olives, so that the discourse is given in the Temple)[20] or possibly that Luke here followed another source.[21] Bearing in mind Luke's habit of abbreviating Marcan framework material in other passages,[22] I prefer the former solution.

The connection brought about in Mark's Gospel between the fate of the Temple and the eschatology marks an important phase in the history of the discourse. To be sure, the part played by the Temple in the eschatology is not a novelty in the history of Jewish ideas. We may find parallels in Jewish texts both for the ideas of the destruction of the Temple and the City, regarded as a judgement, and for the combination of these ideas with the eschatology, including the expectation of the building of a new Temple.[23] But in the history of this tradition the combination involves a re-interpretation. (It is possible, however, that a similar re-interpretation took place previously in the material peculiar to Luke; see below.)

The question whether it was Mark who made this re-interpretation[24] or whether it already existed in a tradition which he adopted is a difficult one to answer. The typical Marcan language in several places in 13,1–4 is a sign that the former may be the true answer but is hardly a proof of it.[25]

If, on the other hand, Luke's version of the discourse, which in v· 20 ff. definitely refers to the fall of Jerusalem (!), contains an older separate tradition, which Luke adopted and combined with his Marcan material, then this separate tradition bears witness to the fact that the tradition underlying the discourse was linked with the fall of the Temple and Jerusalem also in other quarters, presumably before Mark's Gospel was written down.[26]

[19] See the commentaries and STRECKER, Der Weg der Gerechtigkeit, 191 ff., 237 f.

[20] Thus most of the commentaries.

[21] W. BUSSMANN, Synoptische Studien I (1925), 184. Similarly BEASLEY-MURRAY, Future, 227. Cf. TAYLOR, Behind, 102 f., and id., Comm. Mk, ad loc.

[22] See, for example, Lk 6,17 f.; 9,10 f.; 18,35 f. See H. J. CADBURY, The Style and Literary Method of Luke (1920), 79 ff.

[23] See KÜMMEL, Promise, 101, and GÄRTNER, Temple, 16 ff. (and the references given in these two works).

[24] Thus MARXSEN, Markus, 113, and H. CONZELMANN, Geschichte und Eschaton nach Mc 13, Zschr. Nt. Wiss. 50 (1959), 212 f.

[25] Cf. below, 240.

[26] See further subsection D in this section.

(b) *Mk 13,28–32 par.* I would now direct the reader's attention to the other end of the discourse, in order to see what has happened there. I first establish the analytical data, and then go on to grapple with the problems of the tradition.

With Mk 13,28 par. all the three writers of the Synoptic Gospels begin a conclusion of the discourse which runs parallel for a few verses and then branches out, so that Mark and Luke each have their own short ending, while Matthew continues and expands his version into a larger composition on the current Matthaean pattern.[27]

It is generally recognized by scholars that 13,28–32 par. is a logia composition, secondarily joined to the discourse.[28] It has also proved to be outside the compass of the parenetic "midrash" reconstructed in Chap. V. It consists of a parable with an application (vv. 28 f.) and three separate logia (vv. 30–32). The key-words between the parable and the first logion are ταῦτα γενόμενα (v. 29) and ταῦτα πάντα γένηται (v. 30).[29] In its turn v. 30 is combined via the word παρέλθῃ with v. 31, which has παρελεύσονται.[30]

It is probable that in the beginning the parable referred to the fact that the kingdom of God was near in the work of Jesus:[31] this is indicated by the metaphorical function of the fig tree and the summer.[32] The application of the parable in v. 29 is perhaps secondary. One indication of this is that, apart from the discrepancy between the parable and its application,[33] the locution[34] that something is "at the doors" is used in isolation about the judge in Jc 5,9, with reference to the Parousia,[35] and about Christ in Ap 3,20 in a similar sense.[36]

---

[27] Cf. on this point A. FEUILLET, La synthèse eschatologique de saint Matthieu (XXIV–XXV), *Rev. Bibl.* 56 (1949), 340–64, 57 (1950), 62–91, 180–211; BORNKAMM, *Enderwartung*, 229 ff.; MARXSEN, *Markus*, 135 ff.

[28] For example, TAYLOR and SCHMID, *Comm. Mk*, ad loc.

[29] KÜMMEL, *Promise*, 60, and TAYLOR, *Comm.*, ad loc.

[30] TAYLOR, ibid.; SUNDWALL, *Zusammensetzung*, 77. Whether θύρα (v. 29), θυρωρός (v. 34) (thus TAYLOR, ibid.) and οὐρανός (vv. 31 f.) (thus SUNDWALL, op. cit., 78) act as key-words is more dubious.

[31] C. H. DODD, *The Parables of the Kingdom* (2nd ed. 1936), 137; JEREMIAS, *Gleichnisse*, 119 f.; R. SCHNACKENBURG, *Gottes Herrschaft und Reich* (1959), 145; N. A. DAHL, The Parables of Growth, *Stud. Theol.* 5 (1951), 145.

[32] JEREMIAS, loc. cit.; cf. Is 16,9; Jr 8,20; 48,32; Mi 7,1. See also Herm. *Sim.* IV, 2–5. It is not certain that on that account originally there was only the aspect of "realized eschatology" to be found in the parable. Cf. the possible play upon the words קַיִץ—קֵץ pointed out by I. Löw in Zum Feigengleichnis, *Zschr. Nt. Wiss.* 11 (1910), 167 f.

[33] See BULTMANN, *Geschichte*, 187.

[34] This is a widespread locution: see, for example, Demosth. 140,17.

[35] See F. MUSSNER, *Comm. Jc* (1964), ad loc.

[36] See W. HADORN (1928) and A. WIKENHAUSER (3rd ed. 1959), *Comm. Ap*, ad loc.

The logion in v. 30 reads: οὐ μὴ παρέλθῃ ἡ γενεὰ αὕτη μέχρις οὗ ταῦτα πάντα γένηται. It contains one link with the rear (ταῦτα ... γένηται) and one with the van (παρέλθῃ). The saying accordingly acts as a pivot in this combination of logia: if it is removed from the composition, the linkage which holds the composition together disappears. From the point of view of its content, the logion is a *crux interpretum*. Scholarly investigations have been concentrated on the expression ἡ γενεὰ αὕτη: has it a purely temporal meaning ("generation"), a purely qualitative meaning ("this evil type of men") or are the two combined?[37] As regards its content, the logion has a certain parallel in Mk 9,1 par.,[38] but there are two further parallels which may give us a hint as to its origin, namely, Mt 23,36[39] and Mt 5,18. The parallelism is best shown in tabular form:

Mt 23,36	Mt 5,18	Mk 13,30	Mk 13,31
ἀμὴν λέγω	ἀμὴν γὰρ λέγω	ἀμὴν λέγω	
ὑμῖν	ὑμῖν	ὑμῖν ὅτι οὐ μὴ	
	ἔως ἂν παρέλθῃ ὁ	παρέλθῃ	ὁ οὐρανὸς καὶ ἡ γῆ
	οὐρανὸς καὶ ἡ γῆ		παρελεύσονται,
	ἰῶτα ἓν ἢ μία		οἱ δὲ λόγοι μου
	κεραία οὐ μὴ		οὐ
	παρέλθῃ ἀπὸ τοῦ		παρελεύσονται.
ἥξει	νόμου		
ταῦτα πάντα[40]	ἔως ἂν	ἡ γενεὰ αὕτη	
ἐπὶ τὴν γενεὰν		μέχρις οὗ ταῦτα	
ταύτην.	πάντα γένηται.	πάντα γένηται.	

Mt 23,36 forms part of the punishment discourse against the Jews in ch. 23. Mt 5,18 and 23,36 both belong to the Q material, but the Lucan variants (Lk 16,17 and 11,50 f.) are far from showing these similarities with Mk 13,30 f. Thus the comparison also leads to the ques-

---

[37] See F. Büchsel, γενεά, *Theol. Wörterb.* I (1933), 660 f.; J. Guillet, "Cette génération infidèle et dévoyée", *Rech. Sci. Rel.* 35 (1948), 276 f.; M. Meinertz, "Dieses Geschlecht" im NT, *Bibl. Zschr.* 1 (1957), 287 f.; Schnackenburg, *Herrschaft*, 143 f.; E. Lövestam, En problematisk eskatologisk utsaga: Mark. 13:30 par., *Svensk Exeg. Årsbok* 28–29 (1963–64), 64–80. Cf. Weiss, *Comm. Mt*, ad loc.; Harder, *Theol. Viat.* 4 (1952), 94. On the verse as an Amen logion, cf. Jeremias, *Kennzeichen*, 89 ff.

[38] Bultmann (*Geschichte*, 130) admits the possibility of 13,30 being a variant of 9,1. Similarly G. Lindeskog, Logia-Studien, *Stud. Theol.* 4 (1950), 181. Cf. Kümmel, *Promise*, 60.

[39] Zahn, Schniewind, and Gaechter, *Comm. Mt*, ad loc.

[40] B ℵ W Δ λ *157 700 892 pm* read πάντα ταῦτα, in all probability under the influence of Mt 24,34. Also the MS. tradition combined the passages!

tion of the relationship between the Marcan tradition and Q. It is probable that there was such a relationship.[41] On the basis of the above table one may venture to surmise that Mk 13,30 f. is a variant combining the Marcan tradition with the two Matthew sayings from the Q material, conceived at a stage of oral tradition or at any rate on the basis of material preserved in the memory, as is indicated by the interweaving of key-words.[42] A logion of judgement uttered by Jesus against the Jews was interpreted as referring to the imminent fall of Jerusalem and was combined with a saying on the validity of Jesus' words. Here too it is difficult to decide whether it was the evangelist or the tradition he represented which was responsible for the combination.[43]

Finally, the content of v. 32 in this group of sayings is closely related to v. 30 but may perhaps be linked with v. 33 via key-words (οὐδεὶς οἶδεν–οὐκ οἴδατε). The omission of 13,32 by Luke in his parallel would seem to have been due to causes connected with its content.[44]

If we now consider these two portions of framework, Mk 13,1 ff. and 13,28 ff., we shall see the connection at once. V. 4 asks πότε ταῦτα ἔσται (i.e. the fall of the Temple), καὶ τί τὸ σημεῖον ὅταν μέλλῃ ταῦτα συντελεῖσθαι πάντα. The discourse forms a "reply" to this,[45] Jesus principally replying perhaps to the second element in the question. But the reply to πότε is given in vv. 28–32 and the wording in v. 4 has in all probability its counterpart in ταῦτα γενόμενα and ταῦτα πάντα γένηται in vv. 29 f.[46] This indicates that the portions of framework (vv. 4 and 28 ff.) are contemporary but also that the meaning of vv. 28 ff. is to be regarded in the light of vv. 1 ff. especially.[47] However, we

[41] See further B. H. Streeter, St. Mark's Knowledge and Use of Q, in *Studies in the Synoptic Problem* (1911), 165–83; id., *The Four Gospels*, 186 ff.; Grundmann, *Comm. Mk*, 9; A. H. McNeile, *An Introduction to the Study of the NT* (2nd ed. 1953), 83 f.; S. McLoughlin, *The Synoptic Theory of Xavier Léon-Dufour. An Analysis and Evaluation* (1965), passim.

[42] Cf. Marxsen, *Markus*, 127, note 5.

[43] Cf. above, 222.

[44] Thus Cranfield, *Comm. Mk*, Creed, *Comm. Lk* (with a certain hesitation), Schmid, *Comm. Lk*, ad loc.; Conzelmann, *Mitte*, 112; Harder, op. cit., 95. The fact that this logion was "difficult" is reflected in the MS. tradition in Matthew, in which οὐδὲ ὁ υἱός is missing in ℵ^corr 𝔏 L W Δ λ 69 *pm* lat syr^sin. pesh sa bo codd graeci apud Hier. et Amb. Hirsch (*Frühgeschichte* I, 141) thinks that the logion was missing in the version of Mark used by Luke.

[45] Cf. the often quoted catena: "They asked one thing and he answers another" (Klostermann, *Comm. Mk*, ad loc.).

[46] For example, Lohmeyer, and Schmid, *Comm. Mk*, ad loc.; Marxsen, op. cit., 127.

[47] We certainly isolated vv. 1 f. from vv. 3 f. above, but this does not *per se* mean that these two verses entered the composition at different times.

cannot conclude that vv. 28 ff. (including v. 30 on ἡ γενεὰ αὕτη) deal only with the fall of the Temple, although it is regarded in the light of a "realized eschatology".[48] For, since vv. 1 ff. associated the last things and the fall of the Temple, vv. 28 ff. should also do so. That is to say, this *composition* becomes an expression of a kind of *Naher-wartung*, which is possibly modified by v. 32.[49]

Now that we have established these consequences, as regards the content of the discourse, by means of the added framework, we may take up for consideration a couple of details from the discourse itself which may be related to these consequences. We observed that some expressions seemed to he more remote from the OT texts used than those that were directly "midrashic". This was the case as regarded the fact that it was the inhabitants of *Judaea* in particular who were to flee.[50] This detail fits well into a picture in which an eschatological "midrash" has come to be combined with predictions as to the literal destruction of the Temple (and the City). It is also quite conceivable that it was in connection with this actualization of the flight that this portion of text was expanded by the logia in 13,15–17, which, as we found above, may have been separate at the beginning (take nothing from the house; alas for those with child).[51]

After this point the three versions go separate ways. The common motif of watching, as we found above in Chap. V, may be related to Dn 12,12: "Blessed is he who waits". We found clear parallels to the end of the Lucan version (21,34 ff.) in 1 Ths 5, which thereby provided evidence that these logia were combined with the discourse before 50 A.D.[52]

D. Luke's version of the discourse

The Lucan parallel with Mk 13,1–32 poses several problems, but here I shall only discuss those which are relevant in evaluating the history of the tradition of the eschatological discourse in the narrow sense

---

[48] Thus FEUILLET, *Rev. Bibl.* 56 (1949), 82 ff., and Parousie, *Dict. de la Bible, Suppl.* VI (1960), 1347 ff. Cf. SCHNACKENBURG, *Herrschaft*, 144. The vital point in Feuillet's line of thought is that he interprets the eschatological expressions to so great an extent as symbols of judgement. His view merits serious discussion (against KÜMMEL, *Promise*, 97) on the basis of an investigation as to the extent to which the apocalyptic terminology is meant to be a symbolic language by the Biblical authors, and, if so, what meaning it has. Cf. above, 141, and below, 249.

[49] CONZELMANN, *Zschr. Nt. Wiss.* 50 (1959), 220; HARDER, op. cit., 95; MARXSEN, op. cit., 127. Cf. GRÄSSER, *Parusieverzögerung*, 164 ff.

[50] See above, 177.

[51] Se above, 162.

[52] See above, Chap. VI, section 3.

(in the broad sense this history includes all the aspects of the redactional history of Lk 21). With a certain amount of simplification we may say that the relation between Lk 21 and Mk 13 has so far been assessed in accordance with one of the following two alternatives. Either Luke gave a free rendering of Mk 13, partly *ex eventu*, and then revised it[1] or he combined Mk 13 with other material that was available to him.[2] I shall now consider the most important arguments which have been adduced to support the assumption of the use of other sources, oral or written, for Lk 21,5 ff., apart from Mk 13.

(a) *Luke's usual fidelity to Mark's text.* Luke is usually quite faithful to his source (Mark), though he sometimes "improves" the idiom and now and then contracts the narrative, especially in the framework.[3] All the differences in 21,12–14, 18, 20, 22, 24–26a and 28 can only with some difficulty be explained as editorial changes, i.e. as rewordings *ex eventu* or on the basis of the evangelist's theological views.[4]

(b) *The uneven parallelism.* If we compare Mk 13 and Lk 21, the parallelism is surprisingly uneven. In some passages it is, as usual, very close or at least fairly close (vv. 7–11a, 16 f., 21a, 26b–27, 29–33), and in others it is much less close or almost non-existent (vv. 12–15, 18–20, 22, 24–26a, 28).[5] However, these two observations must be compared with another phenomenon in Luke's Gospel: the evangelist

---

[1] F. C. BURKITT, The Use of Mark in the Gospel according to Luke, in *The Beginnings of Christianity* II (1922), 106 ff.; BULTMANN, *Geschichte*, 129; T. F. GLASSON, *The Second Advent* (2nd ed. 1947), 191 f.; CONZELMANN, *Mitte*, 107; GRÄSSER, *Parusieverzögerung*, 154 ff.; HARDER, *Theol. Viat.* 4 (1952), 81 ff.; MARXSEN, *Markus*, 129 ff.; A. LOISY (1924), E. KLOSTERMANN (2nd ed. 1929), CREED, SCHMID, and A. R. C. LEANEY (1958), *Comm. Lk*, ad loc.

[2] WEISS, *Comm. Lk*, 620 f.; BACON, *Gospel of Mark*, 113 ff.; A. SCHLATTER, *Comm. Lk* (1931), 412 ff.; BUSCH, *Verständnis*, 61 f.; C. H. DODD, The Fall of Jerusalem and the 'Abomination of Desolation', *J. Rom. Stud.* 37 (1947), 47–54; T. W. MANSON, *The Sayings of Jesus* (1949), 329 f.; J. A. T. ROBINSON, *Jesus and His Coming* (1957), 122; TAYLOR, *Behind*, 101 ff.; id., *Comm. Mk*, 512; id., The Proto-Luke Hypothesis, *Exp. Times* 67 (1955/56), 12–16; BEASLEY-MURRAY, *Future*, 226 f.; P. WINTER, The Treatment of His Sources by the Third Evangelist in Luke xxi–xxiv, *Stud. Theol.* 8 (1954), 141 ff.; L. GASTON, Sondergut und Markusstoff in Luk. 21, *Theol. Zschr.* 16 (1960), 161–72; K. H. RENGSTORF, *Comm. Lk* (9th ed. 1962), ad loc.

W. GRUNDMANN (*Comm. Lk*, 1961, ad loc.) admits it as a possibility. Cf. moreover F. REHKOPF, *Die lukanische Sonderquelle* (1959), and the examination of Rehkopf's book by H. SCHÜRMANN, Protolukanische Spracheigentümlichkeiten?, *Bibl. Zschr.* 5 (1961), 266–86.

[3] See CADBURY, *Style*, 73 ff.; HARTMAN, *Testimonium linguae*, 50 f. (and the references given there).

[4] CONZELMANN (*Mitte*, 109 ff.) passes lightly over some and is not entirely successful with others.

[5] See TAYLOR, *Behind*, 102 ff.; WINTER, op. cit., 144 f.; GASTON, op. cit., 164.

does not "patch together" his material but instead follows Mark for whole blocks of text, block for block.[6] If this uneven parallelism could be shown to derive from some separate material unknown to Mark, Lk 21 would be an exception from Luke's usual method of dealing with Mark's Gospel.[7]

(c) *The homogeneity of the separate material.* If we put together the passages which differ from Mark's Gospel, one after the other, they form a coherent literary unit and not, as might have been expected, a collection of loose fragments.[8] This method of analysing and arguing has been applied in source criticism in the OT field and, after seeing the somewhat unsatisfactory results which it has led to, one is inclined to attach a secondary value to this line of argument.[9]

(d) *Some details.* The fact that Luke, in his introductory narrative framework, describes the discourse as being given in the Temple and in public (vv. 5 f.) has been regarded as so radical a change as to indicate the use of a separate source.[10] Above I adduced reasons arguing that this was an editorial change on the part of the evangelist.[11]

Mk 13,11 speaks of the assistance of the Holy Spirit being given to persecuted Christians at their trials; in the Lucan parallel, on the other hand, there is no mention of the Holy Spirit. It has been remarked that this can hardly have been a change on Luke's part, for he shows great interest in the Holy Spirit.[12] This argument is questionable, since several factors make the evaluation of the passage a complicated matter.[13] Thus Lk 21,15 alludes to Ex 4,12, 15;[14] the closest Lucan parallel to Mk 13,11 is Lk 12,11 f. and thus we have one of the many doublets in Luke's Gospel;[15] another version of the logion is to

[6] See, for example, STREETER, *Four Gospels*, 167; JOACH. JEREMIAS, Perikopen-Umstellungen bei Lukas?, *NT Stud.* 4 (1957/58), 115–19.

[7] Thus GASTON, op. cit., 163 f.

[8] TAYLOR, op. cit., 113 f.; WINTER, op. cit., 145 f.; GASTON, op. cit., 166.

[9] A. BENTZEN, *Introduction to the OT* II (2nd ed. 1952), 24 ff. And cf. P. VOLZ and W. RUDOLPH, *Der Elohist als Erzähler* (1933), for example, 177 ff.

[10] BEASLEY-MURRAY, *Future*, 227. Cf. GASTON, *Theol. Zschr.* 16 (1960), 168.

[11] See above, 222, and note 22 there.

[12] Thus C. K. BARRETT, *The Holy Spirit and the Gospel Tradition* (1947), 131 f. Also J. WELLHAGEN, *Anden och riket* (1941), 16 ff.

[13] See, for example, BEASLEY-MURRAY, *Mark 13*, and CRANFIELD and TAYLOR, *Comm. Mk*, ad loc.

[14] J. W. H. LAMPE, The Holy Spirit in the Writings of St. Luke, in *Studies ... in mem. R. H. Lightfoot* (1955), 192. See also Jr 1,9 (A. PLUMMER, *Comm. Lk*, 4th ed. 1901, ad loc.); Ez 3,27; Dn 2,23; and cf. Jo 1,5; Is 41,11.

[15] See SCHMID, *Comm. Lk*, and cf. M.-J. LAGRANGE, *Comm. Lk* (3rd ed. 1927), ad loc. Also H. SCHÜRMANN, Die Dubletten im Lukasevangelium, *Zschr. Kath. Theol.* 75 (1953), 338–45 (on the present passage at 340 f.); id., Die Dubletten-vermeidungen im Lukasevangelium, ibid. 76 (1954), 83–93.

be found in Ac 6,10.[16] Taken by itself, therefore, this verse can hardly provide a clear answer either one way or the other.

Among these details we may finally adduce a stylistic observation. As a rule, when Luke uses Mark's Gospel, he changes Marcan examples of complex-sentence construction with the asyndeton so as to eliminate the asyndeton. On the whole, asyndeta are rare in Luke's Gospel.[17] Now we meet with asyndeton in two passages in Lk 21, in both of which Mark has parataxis! Moreover in both cases we find ourselves at possible transitions between separate Lucan tradition and Marcan material. The passages are Mk 13,13 ὁ δὲ ὑπομείνας (Lk 21,19 ἐν τῇ ὑπομονῇ...) and Mk 13,17 οὐαὶ δὲ ταῖς ἐν γαστρὶ ἐχούσαις (Lk 21,23 οὐαὶ ταῖς ἐν γ.ἐ.).[18] The asyndeton may indicate an Aramaic substrate,[19] but there is also the possibility that here it was used to avoid making the sentence so introduced stand out markedly in the narrative. It merges better with the preceding text and the connection between Lk 21,22 and 24 is not broken; the effect is almost that of a parenthesis.[20] However, in this case we ought not to expect anything more than possibilities and weak indications.[21]

(e) *The connection with the OT*. The portions of text that differ from Mark show a connection with the OT which would be strange if the differences were only editorial alterations of Mark's Gospel on Luke's part.[22] Here I shall discuss vv. 12 ff., vv. 20 ff. and vv. 25 ff. separately.

Lk 21,12–18 contains some expressions from the Septuagint:[23] one of them is ἐπιβαλοῦσιν ἐφ' ὑμᾶς τὰς χεῖρας αὐτῶν,[24] with which we may

---

[16] See on this point BEASLEY-MURRAY, loc. cit., and SCHMID, loc. cit.

[17] C. H. TURNER, Marcan Usage, *J. Theol. Stud.* 28 (1927), 18; HAWKINS, *Horae*, 138; CADBURY, *Style*, 147.

[18] The asyndeton is supported by B D L *pc* it. It must be regarded as the *lectio difficilior* in comparison with the Marcan and Matthaean parataxis with δέ. A δέ is to be found in ℵ C 𝔐 A W Γ Δ Θ λ φ *pl*.

[19] Thus BLACK, *Approach*, 38 ff. He finds that Lk 21,25 may also have an Aramaic background (196 f.).

[20] There may also be a similar case in Lk 14,26 ff., where v. 27 is asyndetic and v. 28, a γάρ clause, explains *both* the preceding clauses.

[21] Thus the fact that 21,23 is an exclamation may have some influence. For asyndeton in classical times, see R. KÜHNER and B. GERTH, *Ausführliche Grammatik* II (3rd ed. 1904), § 546, and J. D. DENNISTON, *The Greek Particles* (2nd ed. 1954), xliii ff. For the use of particles in later Greek, see M. E. THRALL, *Greek Particles in the NT* (1962), 1 ff.

[22] BEASLEY-MURRAY, *Future*, 227; cf. SCHMID, *Comm. Lk*, 309.

[23] See for the following paragraph HARTMAN, *Testimonium linguae*, 74.

[24] See also Gn 22,12; 46,4; Ex 7,4; Dt 12,7; 15,10; Est 6,2; Is 25,11, rendering various Hebrew expressions. Yet the phrase is to be found in extra-Biblical Greek too; see, for example, Polybius, 3,2,8.

compare 1 Rg 21,6 (LXX) ἐφ' ἃ ἂν ἐπιβάλωσι τὰς χεῖρας αὐτῶν. Ἕνεκεν τοῦ ὀνόματός μου instead of Mark's ἕνεκεν ἐμοῦ is an obvious "Semitizing" feature, of which there are several instances in the LXX, especially in the Psalms.[25] With v. 14 (θέτε οὖν ἐν ταῖς καρδίαις ὑμῶν) we may compare, for example, 1 Sm 21,13 (LXX) ἔθετο ... ἐν τῇ καρδίᾳ.[26] For v. 15 "I will give you a mouth and wisdom" I have already quoted the parallel from Ex 4,12, 15. There the TM reads: "I will be with your mouth", which is paraphrased both in the LXX and in the Targums. The LXX reads: "I will open (ἀνοίξω) your mouth" and both Targ. Jon. and Targ. Onk. have "my word (מימרי) will be with your mouth". Thus here the OT echoes are loud and clear but are not in harmony with the LXX. V. 18 ("not a hair of your head will perish") is, presumably, proverbial and has several OT parallels.[27] This accumulation of differences from Mark which are connected with OT idioms (not always Septuagintal) is noteworthy.

As regards *Lk 21,20–24*, C. H. Dodd has asserted that, while in Mk 13,14 ff. the defilement of the Temple by Antiochus lent colour to the pericope, the prototype in Lk 21,20 ff. was the sack of Jerusalem by Nebuchadnezzar in 586 B.C. Dodd advances parallels from the LXX for every point in the description and finds it probable that Luke was dependent on earlier sources, either written or oral.[28] However, a detailed examination shows, on the one hand, that the choice of words is scarcely typical of the Septuagint and, on the other, that the commensurable OT texts are not only those which relate the sack of Jerusalem in 586 B.C. or other sieges but also those which deal with "days of vengeance" (cf. Lk 21,22 ἡμέραι ἐκδικήσεως) and similar motifs.[29]

---

[25] See Ps 22,3; 24,11; 30,3; 43,26; Is 48,9; Bar 2,14 (A). For a similar extra-Biblical use, see STEPHANUS, *Thesaurus* V (1842–46), sub ὄνομα.

[26] See also Dt 11,18; Hg 2,15; Ml 1,1; Ez 14,3; Si 50,28.

[27] See 1 Sm 14,45; 2 Sm 14,11; 1 Rg 1,52; Dn 3,27.

[28] DODD, *J. Rom. Stud.* 37 (1947), 47–54.

[29] Thus στρατόπεδον occurs only once in the LXX with a Hebrew original (חיל), viz. in the short announcement of Nebuchadnezzar's attack (Jr 41,1, TM 34,1). But in the more detailed descriptions of the same event חיל is rendered by δύναμις (Jr 39,2, TM 32,2; 46,1, TM 39,1; 52,4).

There is a striking parallel for the flight from the city and the explanation of it in Jr 51,6: "Flee (נסו) from the midst of Babylon ... for this is the time of Yahweh's vengeance" (עת נקמה); LXX (28,6) φεύγετε ἐκ μέσου B. .... ὅτι καιρὸς ἐκδικήσεως αὐτῆς ἐστιν παρὰ κυρίου. Luke does not use the same expression as the LXX.

The phrase πίπτειν στόματι μαχαίρης is not to be found in the LXX, but renders the Hebrew נפל לפי חרב, which occurs in Jo 8,24 and Jdc 4,16. On the other hand, both (ἐν) στόματι μαχαίρης and πίπτειν (ἐν) μαχαίρᾳ are not uncommon in the LXX; see, for example, Gn 34,26; Jo 19,47, and Lv 26,8; Nu 14,43; Jr 16,4, respectively.

For the encirclement, see not only 2 Rg 25,1, 4, Jr 52,4, 7, and Ez 4,2 (on the

The manner of using OT motifs here shows that the stress was placed not on the fact that Jerusalem will be destroyed but on the assertion that the destruction will be a divine punishment. As in most of the Jeremiah texts in which the destruction is announced, the account is not in the first place a description of how a city is captured but of the divine visitation which strikes an apostate city. Thus it comes about that most of the motifs in this section are to be found in texts on the day of Yahweh, the day of vengeance, etc.[30] A couple of examples may make this clear.

Is 10 contains a judgement on Israel:

(3) what will you do on *the day of punishment*[31] (יום פקדה, ἡμέρα τῆς ἐπισκοπῆς)...
to whom will you *flee* (תנוסו, καταφεύξεσθε) for help,
and where will you leave your wealth (כבודכם, δόξα)?
(4) Nothing remains but to crouch among the *prisoners* (אסיר, ἐπαγωγήν[32]) or fall among the *slain* (הרוגים).
For all this his anger (אפו, θυμός[33]) is not turned away,
and his hand is stretched out still.
(5) Ah, Assyria, the rod of my *anger* (אפי, θυμοῦ)...
(6) Against a godless nation I send him,
and against the *people of my wrath* (עם עברתי) I command him,

---

events of 586 B.C.), but also Jr 1,15, Ez 23,24 (which stresses the significance of this event as a punishment), Jr 50,14, 29, and Ez 26,8 (which prophesy how Babylon and Tyrus will be punished by being conquered).

For the flight, see (apart from Jr 51,6 above) Is 10,3; 13,14; 37,32; Jr 46,6; 48,19; Mi 4,10.

For the day of vengeance (the LXX renders both (נקמה) and פקדה by ἐκδίκησις), see Dt 32,35 (LXX); Is 10,3; 34,8; 61,2; 63,4; Jr 46,10 (LXX 26,10); 50,27, 31 (LXX 27,27, 31); 51,6 (LXX 28,6); Ho 9,7. For נקם, פקד see also Is 47,3; Jr 50,15; 51,36, and Is 13,11; 24,21; Zph 1,8 ff. respectively.

For the tribulation, see Dt 28,52, 55, 57; Is 8,22; 30,6; Am 3,11; Zph 1,15.

For the wrath of God, see Is 10,4, 6; 13,9, 13; Zph 1,15.

For "falling by the sword", see Is 3,25; 13,15; 37,7; Jr 15,12 f.; 16,4; 20,4; Ez 11,10; 21,9; 26,6; Am 9,10.

For the captivity, see Dt 28,41, (64); 2 Rg 24,14; Is 5,13; 24,21 f.; 46,2; Jr 15,2; 20,4; Am 9,4; Zch 14,2.

For the treading down, see Is 5,5; 10,6; 22,5; Ez 26,11; Dn 7,19, 23 f.; 8,10, 13. Lk 21,24 is often cited as a free quotation from Zch 12,3 (LXX): θήσομαι τὴν Ἰερουσαλὴμ λίθον καταπατούμενον πᾶσι τοῖς ἔθνεσιν. In view of the fact that the motif is so common and the similarity between Lk 21,24 and Zch 12,3 not striking, it seems somewhat doubtful whether Zch 12,3 in particular should be preferred to other OT parallels. Cf. Ps Sal 17,25; 1 Mcc 3,45, 51; 4,60; 2 Mcc 8,2 (Cod. Venetus).

[30] DODD (op. cit.) also cites passages from these texts but concentrates on the siege and fall of Jerusalem.

[31] For "day of punishment" and "day of vengeance", see note 29 above.

[32] *v.l.* ἀπ-.

[33] *v.l.* ὀργή.

to take spoil and seize plunder,
and to *tread* them *down* (מרמס, καταπατεῖν) like the mire of the streets.

Is 13 contains a judgement on Babylon:

(4) Hark, a tumult on the mountains
as of a great multitude!
Hark, an uproar of kingdoms,
of nations gathering together! ...
(6) Wail for the *day of Yahweh* (יום יהוה, ἡμέρα κ.) is near;
as *destruction* (שד, συντριβή) from Shaddai it will come!
(8) Pangs and agony will seize them; ...
(9) Behold, the *day of Yahweh* comes,
cruel, with *wrath* (עברה, θυμοῦ) and fierce *anger* (אף, ὀργῆς),
to make the earth (or the land) a *desolation* (שמה, ἔρημον),
and to destroy its sinners from it.
(10) For the stars of the heavens and their constellations
will not give their light; ...
(11) I will *punish* (פקדתי, ἐντελοῦμαι) the world for its evil ...
(13) I will make the heavens tremble ...
(14) every man will turn to his own people
and every man will *flee* (ינוסו, διῶξαι[34]) to his own land ...
(15) Whoever is caught will *fall by the sword* (יפול בחרב, μαχαίρᾳ πεσοῦνται).

Finally, Zph 1 deals with the day of Yahweh:

(7) The *day of Yahweh* is at hand ...
(12) At that time I will search Jerusalem with lamps,
and I will *punish* (פקדתי, ἐκδικήσω) the men ...
(13) Their goods shall be plundered,
and their houses laid *waste* (שממה, εἰς ἀφανισμόν) ...
(15) A day of *wrath* (עברה, ὀργή) is that day,
a day of *distress and anguish* (יום צרה ומצוקה, ἡμ. θλίψεως καὶ ἀνάγκης),
a day of *ruin and devastation* (שאה ומשואה, ἡμ. ἀωρίας καὶ ἀφανισμοῦ),
a day of trumpet blast and battle cry
against the fortified cities ...

It is now apparent that this widening of the OT background to Lk
21,20–24 makes the difference between these verses and *Lk 21,25–28*
much less than is sometimes stated,[35] in that both portions of text
have the same OT framework of associations. Thus Lk 21,25 first
gives: καὶ ἔσονται σημεῖα ἐν ἡλίῳ καὶ σελήνῃ καὶ ἄστροις. This may be a
summary of Jl 3,3: "I will give portents (מופתים, τέρατα; Targ. Jon.
"signs", (אתין)) in the heavens"[36] and Jl 2,10: "The sun and moon are
darkened, and the stars withdraw their shining". We may also recall

---

[34] *v.l.* διώξεται.

[35] Cf. how CONZELMANN (*Mitte*, 109) calls vv. 20–24 a polemical excursus on
things which were wrongly included in the eschatological events.

[36] Ac 2,19 has the same wording as the LXX. Note, however, the following words
in Ac 2,19; καὶ σημεῖα ἐπὶ τῆς γῆς.

Is 13,10 just quoted: "The stars ... will not give their light, the sun will be dark at its rising, and the moon will not shed its light".

Lk 21,25 continues: ἐπὶ τῆς γῆς συνοχὴ ἐθνῶν. For a close parallel we need only turn to Is 13 again. Is 13,4 reads: "Hark, a tumult (המון, φωνή) on the mountains as of a great multitude! Hark, an uproar (שאון, φωνή) of kingdoms, of nations (גוים, ἔθνη) gathering together".[37] The המון and שאון pair also turn up in Ps 65,8, which is responsible for the next passage in Lk 21,25 ((συνοχὴ ἐθνῶν) ἐν ἀπωρίᾳ ἤχους θαλάσσης καὶ σάλου). Thus Ps 65,8 f. reads:

(God) who dost still the roaring of the seas (שאון ימים, τὸ κύτος τῆς θαλάσσης),
the roaring of their waves (שאון גליהם, ἤχους κυμάτων αὐτῆς),
the tumult of the peoples (המון לאמים, ταραχθήσονται τὰ ἔθνη),
(9) so that those who dwell at earth's farthest bounds
are afraid at thy signs (מאותתיך, ἀπὸ τῶν σημείων σου).

If these motifs from Is 13 and Ps 65 were associated with Lk 21 via key-words,[38] as seems likely, it must have been on the basis of the TM and not of the LXX.

After this digression from Is 13 to Ps 65, the text of Lk 21 is again associated with Is 13 in the continuation. Thus Lk 21,26 reads: ἀποψυχόντων[39] ἀνθρώπων ἀπὸ φόβου καὶ προσδοκίας τῶν ἐπερχομένων τῇ οἰκουμένῃ. We may compare this with Is 13,6 ff.:

Wail, for the day of Yahweh is near; ...
(7) every man's heart will melt (ימס, δειλιάσει),
(8) and they will be dismayed (נבהלו, ταραχθήσονται).
Pangs and agony will seize them; ...
(9) Behold, the day of Yahweh comes, ...
to make the earth (or the land) a desolation
and to destroy its sinners from it ...
(11) I will punish the world (פקדתי על תבל, ἐντελοῦμαι τῇ οἰκουμένῃ ὅλῃ) for its evil.

We may also cite Is 13,5: "They come from a distant land ... Yahweh and the weapons of His indignation, to destroy the whole earth (or land)". From v. 26b ("for the powers of the heavens will be shaken") Luke's text again forms a close parallel with that of Mark.

These relations of Luke's with the OT seem to me to constitute a serious argument in favour of assuming that Luke also used a different version of the eschatological discourse, in addition to Mk 13. For the

---

[37] See also Is 17,12.

[38] Cf. also σημεῖα in 21,25, Jl 3,3 (Targ. Jon.), and Ps 65,9.

[39] I prefer the translations "faint" or "swoon" (with RSV; LIDDELL & SCOTT, Lexicon, sub voce; PLUMMER, LEANEY, and W. F. ARNDT (1956), Comm. Lk, ad loc.) to "breath out life" (thus WEISS, LOISY, SCHMID, and RENGSTORF, Comm. Lk, ad loc.).

connection with the LXX, which is otherwise typical of Luke,[40] is slight here; indeed in some passages it is almost non-existent. The fact that the OT motifs were, to all appearances, linked together in the narrative on the basis of the TM and not of the LXX is surely an analytical result that is worthy of serious consideration.

(*f*) *The prooem*. Finally, we may recall the prooem to Luke's Gospel, in which the evangelist refers to οἱ ἀπ᾽ ἀρχῆς αὐτόπται καὶ ὑπηρέται γενόμενοι τοῦ λόγου as traditionists (παρέδοσαν). This passage has been used to support the hypothesis of a Proto–Luke,[41] but we can at most glimpse behind it a desire to attribute the contents of the Gospel to reliable witnesses.[42]

In conclusion, not all the arguments which I have just presented carry the same weight, but especially those concerning the relationship of Luke's Gospel to the OT seem to me, when taken together with other arguments, to place such facts before us as to make the most natural solution to assume that in ch. 21 Luke based his text to some extent on a separate tradition.

This separate tradition must in that case have had a place in the development which the Daniel "midrash" underwent. If we compare it with the "midrash" analysed in Chap. V, it appears to be secondary.[43] If this separate tradition underlay both the persecution section (21, 12–19) and the remainder, it must consequently have come into existence after the παραδιδόναι triad which we find in Mk 13 and Mt 10 had been drawn up but probably before the Marcan tradition had been supplemented by v. 10 (the mission logion).[44] It is, however, not a necessary pre-condition that 21,12–19 and the remainder shall be treated as an organic whole; a separate tradition may also undergo development.

However, it is essential that this separate tradition should witness that the eschatological discourse was combined with the prediction of the fall of Jerusalem in a tradition which may have been independent

---

[40] See H. F. D. SPARKS, The Semitisms of St. Luke's Gospel, *J. Theol. Stud.* 44 (1943), 133 f.; A. WIFSTRAND, Lukas och Septuaginta, *Svensk Teol. Kvartalskrift* 16 (1940), 243 ff.; T. HOLTZ, *Untersuchungen über die alttestamentlichen Zitate bei Lukas* (typed MS.; see the summary in *Theol. Lit.-Zeit.* 90, 1965, 863 f.). Also STENDAHL, *School*, 143, 149 f.

[41] TAYLOR, *Behind*, 197 f.

[42] See, for example, SCHMID, *Comm. Lk*, ad loc. Cf. STENDAHL, op. cit., 32 f., and GERHARDSSON, *Memory*, 243.

[43] Cf. BUSSMANN, *Synoptische Studien* I, 187 f.; DODD, *J. Rom. Stud.* 37 (1947), 52; MANSON, *Sayings*, 328 ff.; ROBINSON, *Coming*, 122 f.; TAYLOR, *Comm. Mk*, 512.

[44] Cf. HARDER, *Theol. Viat.* 4 (1952), 79: Luke has "die Geschichtsquelle noch ohne den V. 10 benutzt".

234

in relation to the written form of Mark's Gospel. We have already considered the possibility that Mark or his tradition produced through his composition this combination of eschatology and a prophecy of an actual catastrophe. We now have indications that there were precedents for thus combining eschatology and history.

3. An Attempt to Reconstruct the History of the Tradition of the Eschatological Discourse

A. From the Daniel "midrash" to the Synoptic Gospels

To be quite honest, I must first of all emphasize that what is presented here is only an attempt at such a reconstruction. Many of the facts brought to light by the analyses in the preceding pages and the suggested solutions they have resulted in can be interpreted and combined in different ways. The solutions which I shall now present are those which I regard as the most probable of those I have found to be possible.

(a) *The "midrashic" nucleus.* The analyses above in Chap. V, supported by the analogies in Part I, made it probable that the nucleus of the eschatological discourse consisted of a "midrash" on Dn (2,31–45), 7,7–27, 8,9–26, 9,24–27 and 11,21–12,4(13). In Mk 13 this "midrash" has its equivalent in vv. 5b–8, 12–16, 19–22 and 24–27, although there may be some doubt about vv. 8b and 15a. This "midrash" is interwoven with OT associations which derive from the text interpreted. It contains partly apocalyptic and eschatological material and partly parenesis. One pole of the apocalyptic and eschatological field consists of the activity of "Antichrist", viz. the "I am", the abomination of desolation and the false prophets giving signs and wonders. In 2 Ths 2 we found all three of these elements intimately related, and they had a common origin in Daniel's blasphemous king (the horn).[1] This makes it seem probable that the present wording of Mk 13,6 (*"many* will come *in my name*, saying 'I am'"') is later than a text which was more clearly related to the blasphemy of "Antichrist" and which contained neither "many" or "in my name".[2] On the other hand, it is quite possible that the plural number of the false prophets (13,22) is original but that it too is bound up with the revelation of "Antichrist". In connection with this "Antichrist" phase of the tribulations, with all its temptations to apostasy, we find the nations falling into conflicts and families into dissension.

---

[1] See above, 199 f.

[2] The interpretation seems to be represented in Did. 16,4: "then the deceiver of the world will appear as the son of God". Cf. above, 207, note 3. And cf. Asc. Is. 4,2–13; Apc. Petri 2.

The other pole of the apocalyptic and eschatological field consists of a description of the Parousia of the Son of Man, in order to gather the faithful into the eternal kingdom. This Parousia is painted in the colours of a theophany, such as those used in the OT in connection with the day of Yahweh.

At the same time, however, this "midrash" is also parenetic. The disciples are informed of the temptation that is to come but are also exhorted not to be led astray. They learn that war will be part of the sufferings at the end of time, but they are not to be alarmed. They are told that tribulation will come, but that they must endure. The faithful are to shun the blasphemous revelation which is hidden in the abomination of desolation.[3] The fact that this apocalyptic and eschatological teaching is so parenetic distinguishes it from the current Jewish apocalyptic which has an otherwise similar content.

It seems as if the mode of expression in this "midrash" was "mythical", in that the last things were described in imagery taken over from the OT and understood, at least to some extent, as a symbolic language. This applies particularly to the "Antichrist" phenomena and the Parousia.

This "midrash" had its *Sitz im Leben* in early Christian teaching.[4] Thus, we encounter it with this function in 1 and 2 Ths, where, together with other material, it is assigned to the παραδόσεις which the Apostle administered and passed on. But it is not a stereotyped tradition, comparable, let us say, with museum objects, which must not be touched. It is *used* to give teaching on eschatology and exhortation in an eschatological perspective. This usage, this fresh application to new problems, means that Paul can expand the "midrash" with additional material taken from its basic text, Daniel.

(b) *The logia on watchfulness.* At an early stage this original "midrash" was supplemented by some sayings of Jesus which compare "that day" with a thief and with a snare (and/or a travail, חבל) and which emphasize the necessity of watchfulness at the prospect of the sudden occurrence of the end. This exhortation to watchfulness recurs later in all three Synoptic versions, but Luke presents material which may lay claim to belong to the oldest layers of text, since it is evidenced in combination with a form of the "midrash" in 1 Ths.[5]

This combination should also be assigned to the sphere of Church teach-

---

[3] Cf. JEREMIAS, *Unbekannte Jesusworte*, 75 ff. on an agraphon which is interpreted as referring to "die eschatologische Flucht".

[4] Cf. the teaching scene in Mk 13,3 f. par. Cf. T. W. MANSON, *The Teaching of Jesus* (1931), 17 ff.

[5] See above, Chap. VI, section 3.

ing, as well as the elements here combined.[6] At this point we are also reminded of the linguistic change from Hebrew (Aramaic) to Greek, since two variants of one logion may be explained by a common Semitic basis. Such a phenomenon may also be easily assigned to the sphere of the "school", the traditionist circle of teachers.

(c) *Incipient "historicization"?* I assumed above under (a) that the "I am" passage was from the beginning intimately connected with the two other "Antichrist" motifs—the abomination of desolation and the prophets with the false signs. Somewhere between the stage of development which is reflected in 1 and 2 Ths and another stage which shows greater similarity to the Synoptic Gospels, it seems as if a differentiation took place, which meant that the discourse was more closely linked with the Church's experience.

Although the texts are considerably later than the Synoptic ones, 1 Jn 2,18 ff., 4,1 ff. and 2 Jn 7 may serve as examples of a way of thinking which must resemble those which provoked this differentiation and "historicization".[7]

1 Jn 2,18 ff.

Children, it is the last hour; and as you have heard that Antichrist is coming, so now many Antichrists have come; ... (21) I write to you not because you do not know the truth, but because you know it, and know that no lie (ψεῦδος) is of the truth. (22) Who is the liar (ψεύστης) but he who denies that Jesus is the Christ? This is the Antichrist, he who denies the Father and the Son.

1 Jn 4,1 ff.

... many false prophets (ψευδοπροφῆται) have gone out into the world ... (3) every spirit which does not confess Jesus is not of God. This is the spirit of Antichrist, of which you heard that it was coming, and now it is in the world already.

2 Jn 7

Many deceivers (πολλοὶ πλάνοι) have gone out into the world, men who will not acknowledge the coming of Jesus Christ in the flesh; this (οὗτος) is the deceiver (πλάνος) and the Antichrist.

Thus, the writer of the Letters saw in the activity of the false prophets in the Church a manifestation of the great resistance to God, of Antichrist's own work. Antichrist accordingly takes on the shapes of different individuals and his spirit is active in many. The shift in

---

[6] For the wakefulness as a motif in the early Christian parenesis, see above, 193, note 10.

[7] See SCHNACKENBURG, *Johannesbriefe*, ad loc., and the excursus on 127 ff.

2 Jn 7 from πολλοί to οὗτος is a typical feature. Similar experiences and ways of thought may also underlie Mk 13,6: "Many will come in my name, saying 'I am', and will lead many astray"[8] and Mk 13,21 f.: "And then if anyone says to you, 'Look, here is the Christ!' or 'Look, there he is!', do not believe it. (22) False Christs and false prophets will arise ...". If the argument is correct, we have here encountered yet another use of the "midrash", a use also related to problems which had arisen in the Church and been inserted in an eschatological perspective.

(d) *The persecution logia.* The eschatological discourse acquires a further and quite remarkable root in the Church's experience owing to its being supplemented by the logia on being handed over to the courts. We concluded above that 13,11 was just such a parenetic supplement and, with some hesitation, assumed that v. 9 was also incorporated at a later date.[9] The question whether these logia are to be regarded as sayings of Jesus or as *Gemeindetradition* has, of course, nothing to do with their place in the composition. Nevertheless it seems probable to me that these incorporated logia are based on Jesus' prediction that His followers would be persecuted for His sake but would have no need to be afraid during this persecution.[10] When the persecution of the faithful is explicitly inserted among the tribulations at the end of time in this way, this *may* have been related to the Church's strained relations with the outside world, while it also expresses a reflection on the prospect of the torment.

At this stage of the development of the eschatological discourse, I would remind the reader of the patterns of thought analysed in Chap. II above. I referred there to *A*, the preliminary time of evil, *B*, the divine intervention, *C*, the judgement, *D*, the punishment of the wicked, and *E*, the felicity of the righteous. These main themes were combined in different ways. If we look for a corresponding pattern of thought in the eschatological discourse at this stage of its development, we find the following state of affairs:

---

[8] It is noteworthy that, besides this similarity of motif between 1, 2 Jn and Mk 13 par., there is also a point of contact in the "I am", which is so typical as a formula of revelation on Jesus' lips, according to John (see above, 159, note 45), compared with the "I am" with which these impostors will come "in my name". For the phrase "in my name", see the discussions in the commentaries.

[9] See above, 214.

[10] See Mt 5,11 f., 44; 23,34; Lk 6,22, 27; 12,4; Jn 15,18 f.; 17,14. DUPONT, *Béatitudes*, 223 ff. Cf. D. W. RIDDLE, Die Verfolgungslogien in formgeschichtlicher und soziologischer Beleuchtung, *Zschr. Nt. Wiss.* 33 (1934), 271–89; S. G. F. BRANDON, *The Fall of Jerusalem and the Christian Church* (1951), 94; E. DINKLER, Jesu Wort vom Kreuztragen, *Zschr. Nt. Wiss., Beih.* 21 (1954), 110–29.

A: Many misleading "Antichrist" phenomena, war, natural catastrophes, persecutions, family dissension, the abomination of desolation and false prophets.

B: The Parousia of the Son of Man.

E: The gathering together of the elect.

This gives rise to the following observations. *C* and *D* are missing
(as yet; cf. Mt 25); there is no mention of any last great assault by
the heathen.[11] It is *A* that has grown during the development of the
discourse up to this point. The pattern bears some resemblances to
that in 4 Ez and 2 Bar,[12] where the evil times with their signs fore-
bode the intervention of the Messiah, judgement, the destruction of
the enemies and of Antichrist, and the joy of the righteous during the
limited reign of the Messiah. It is possible that such ways of thought
as underlay 4 Ez and 2 Bar, which were not very remote in time from
the eschatological discourse, also exercised an influence on this discourse. 4 Ez and 2 Bar also place the main emphasis on the *A* part
of the pattern.

These persecutions are narrated with a specifically Christian stress
by the use of the expression ἕνεκεν ἐμοῦ in v. 9. This suggests ideas of
a communion of suffering between Jesus and His disciples, ideas
which are also expressed in the circumstance that these persecution
logia have turns of phrase which also recur in Mk 14 f. on the Passion
of Jesus.[13]

(e) *The connection with Jerusalem's fate in Luke's source*. Above I
adopted the view that in the present ch. 21 Luke also used, apart
from Mk 13, another version of the discourse,[14] which was, however,
related to Mk 13, in so far as this variant also contained the persecution logia. For the sake of simplicity, I shall now treat this variant
as being uniform, though in actual fact it may also have undergone
a development. But what we are concerned with at present is that
this variant shows that with reference to the Hebrew OT the author
continued to associate the original eschatological "midrash" with
history.

In this case also the sayings of Jesus probably provided the material.
The principal objection to the assumption that Jesus predicted the
fall of Jerusalem[15] is, of course, that this fall in fact took place later.

---

[11] Cf. CONZELMANN, *Zschr. Nt. Wiss.* 50 (1959), 217.

[12] See above, 68 f.

[13] See R. H. LIGHTFOOT, *The Gospel Message of St. Mark* (1950), 48 ff., and E.
LARSSON, *Christus als Vorbild* (1962), for example, 39 ff.

[14] See above, 234.

[15] Lk 19,41 ff. except Mk 13,2 par. Cf. Mk 14,58 par.; Jn 2,19; Mk 15,29.

However, these warnings bear hardly any traces of having come into existence *ex eventu*.[16] The terminology is that of the OT and the details are such as to reproduce only the events that usually took place during the conquest of cities in antiquity.[17] But these logia are not neutral; they imply judgement. It now seems as if these logia were placed in a more definite connection with the last things, with the possible support of Jeremiah[18] and the contemporary apocalyptic and eschatological expectations.[19] The שממ/ἐρήμωσις of the original "midrash" *may* have been a contributory cause.[20] The result was that the section on the flight from the abomination of desolation became a section of sayings on the flight from the judgement on Jerusalem, which is depicted in colours which seem to have been taken from the same "eschatological" texts in the OT as supplied motifs for the section on the Parousia.

The re-interpretation no doubt reflects a situation in which the Church was clearly demarcated from Judaism and in which Jerusalem and the Jewish people were regarded as having incurred the wrath of God by their rejection of the Messiah.[21] This judgement on God's old people forms part of the events at the end of time, which are thus again anchored in the Church's experience or in what the Church expected to experience.[22]

(*f*) *The framework in Mk 13,1–4, 28–32*. If the above assumptions as to the Lucan tradition hold good, there was no great novelty in the eschatological discourse being associated with the destruction of the Temple, as happens in Mk 13,1 ff. Yet this framework—whether it was written by Mark or not[23]—forms a borderline in the history of the tradition.

By being introduced by the question "When will this be?", the discourse forms an answer to a question on the fall of the Temple, while at the same time this fall is brought into the events at the end of time. The corresponding framework in 13,28 ff. is also connected with this question. This second framework is thus inserted between the

---

[16] See BEASLEY-MURRAY, *Mark 13*, GRUNDMANN and TAYLOR, *Comm. Mk,* ad 13,2; KÜMMEL, *Promise*, 100; SCHMID and GRUNDMANN, *Comm. Lk*, ad 19,41 ff. Cf. BULTMANN, *Geschichte*, 37, 126 f.; LOISY, *Comm. Lk*, ad 19,41 ff.

[17] DODD, *J. Rom. Stud.* 37 (1947), 49 ff.

[18] Cf., for example, Jr 4–6; 9–13; 19.

[19] See above, 222, note 23.

[20] Cf. LOISY and WEISS, *Comm. Lk*, ad loc.

[21] Cf. CONZELMANN, *Mitte*, 113 ff., and G. BRAUMANN, Die lukanische Interpretation der Zerstörung Jerusalems, *Nov. Test.* 6 (1963), 120–27.

[22] Cf. below, 245, note 41.

[23] Cf. above, 222 ff.

description of the Parousia and the "watch" parenesis, which, according to my analysis, was linked with it earlier. The parable of the fig tree then means that part of what is said in the discourse is characterized as a sign of the Parousia. We found above that the logion on "this generation" may have been rooted in warnings to the people belonging to the Q tradition. This logion, together with other components of the framework, is connected with the question on when the fall of the Temple will occur. But since, on the one hand, the discourse, including the description of the Parousia, forms a preliminary answer to this question and, on the other, the fall of the Temple is brought into the series of eschatological events, the logion on "this generation" cannot be restricted to apply only to the conquest of the City. The composition must reflect thinking in which the fall of Jerusalem is a phase in the eschatology and the Parousia is also expected to occur soon.[24]

When the discourse had been modified by these additions, so that it answered the question on the fall of the Temple, it must have been fairly easy to proceed to the point of clarifying the section on the abomination of desolation to the extent of saying that, whatever the "abomination" might be, it was still a "desolation" from which the inhabitants of *Judaea* in particular must flee. It is not impossible that here we have reminiscences of 1 Mcc 2, in which, after the abomination of desolation has been set up, Mattathias and his sons offer resistance and flee to the mountains (ἔφυγον ... εἰς τὰ ὄρη), leaving their property in the City (1 Mcc 2,28). It is conceivable that the separate (?) logia in 13,15–17 were also inserted at this point in the development.

(g) *Mk 13,10 and a retrospect.* A further link between the life of the Church and the eschatological discourse was forged when Mk 13,10 was inserted in the persecution logia in one of the closing stages of the development of the tradition. This was occasioned by the Church's experience of missionary work amongst Jews and heathens, which was of such a nature as to make it natural to insert this verse amongst logia on persecutions.[25] At the same time the missionary work was also fitted into the eschatological picture.

We have now established how, step by step, the original eschatological "midrash" was expanded and linked more closely with the Church's experience.[26] To all appearances, "mythical" elements were

---

[24] See, for example, KÜMMEL, op. cit. 99 f., and MARXSEN, *Markus*, 113 ff.

[25] See HARDER, *Theol. Viat.* 4 (1952), 79, and cf. MARXSEN, op. cit., 119.

[26] Cf. CARRINGTON, *Comm. Mk*, 273 f., on developing earlier prophecies, and J. M. ROBINSON, *Das Geschichtsverständnis des Markusevangeliums* (1956), 92 ff.

transposed into indications of more tangible things, inasmuch as the Church desired to find its own situation predicted in the eschatological discourse. It is clear that this situation was thought to be concealed there; it was only a matter of bringing it to light and of making what was implicit explicit. Thus, for instance, we may imagine that behind the development leading to the wording in 13,6 (many saying "I am") there was a reflection on a prophecy about a blasphemous "Antichrist" revelation, in which the name of God ("I am") was used in self-exaltation. In this the Church saw the appearance of false Christs, who certainly said "I am" in the sense of "I am the returned Jesus" but who thereby also appeared with the same claims to be divine as the Church believed only her Lord could make.

In its progress to this point the original "midrash" lost many of its once probably explicit associations with the OT text. Instead it became something of a prophetic tract on the last things, used and interpreted in Christian teaching. I have tried to point out some landmarks in this progress and, in doing so, have not found it necessary to discuss all the details in the discourse.[27] As regards some of those discussed, it is an open question how they are to be placed in the history of the discourse.

Finally, we may only note that the end product of this development, as it is now to be found in the written form of Mark's Gospel, has become a relatively coherent compositional unit. Other scholars have devoted their attention to its structure[28] and I shall not discuss it here. Instead I now pass on to consider the further history of this tradition, as it appears in the Gospels of Matthew and Luke.

(h) *The version of St. Matthew.* There are several indications that the milieu in which Matthew's Gospel was used and transmitted was comparable with that of the collegia of Jewish scribes.[29] This also

---

[27] For example, the beginnings of the travail (v. 8), the exhortation "take heed to yourselves" (v. 9), the verse on the women with child and the flight in the winter (v. 17), and the saying on the shortening of the days, which may have originated in a midrashic interpretation (v. 20; see above, 164).

[28] In 1965 J. LAMBRECHT publicly defended in Rome a thesis entitled *Die Redaktion der synoptischen Apokalypse. Literarische Analyse und Strukturuntersuchung* (*Mk 13; Lk 21*); see *Bibl.* 46 (1965), 259. He has summarized his results in Redactio Sermonis Eschatologici, *Verb. Dom.* 43 (1965), 278–87.

[29] See further J. HOH, Der christliche γραμματεύς (Mt. 13,52), *Bibl. Zschr.* 17 (1925/26), 256–69; E. VON DOBSCHÜTZ, Matthäus als Rabbi und Katechet, *Zschr. Nt. Wiss.* 27 (1928), 338–48; G. D. KILPATRICK, *The Origins of the Gospel according to St. Matthew* (2nd ed. 1950), 103 ff., 137 ff.; STENDAHL, *School,* 30 ff., and passim; HARTMAN, *Testimonium,* 52 f. See also a forthcoming monograph by B. GERHARDSSON on the Temptation Story. And cf. C. H. LOHR, Oral Techniques in the Gospel of Matthew, *Cath. Bibl. Quart.* 23 (1961), 403–35.

means that this Gospel, as a literary product, did not come into existence as one man's work, during a short concentrated period of writing and editorial work, but that there existed what we may call a Matthew tradition for some time before the Gospel was written down. A scribal milieu such as that indicated is a natural *Sitz im Leben* for several of the details in the eschatological discourse which are specifically Matthaean.

Thus, by means of key-words (Hebrew or Greek), the description of the Parousia was expanded by further details from the OT (the sign of the Son of Man, the mourning of the tribes, the loud trumpet).[30] 1 Ths 4,16 gives an indication that this expansion may have taken place relatively early.[31]

In addition, it seems possible to give a place in the development of the discourse that is anything like clear only to the wording in Mt 24,14. It must belong to the latest textual layers in the Gospel, since it has a specific Matthaean terminology and is dependent on the written form of Mark's Gospel.[32]

Other data are more difficult to place. At any rate some of them are of such a character as to make it natural to imagine that they arose in a circle of Christian "scribes". Thus we find a variant of the persecution logia in the Marcan tradition (and in Mt 10,17 ff.). Mk 13,9 ff. is interpreted in this variant, possibly in view of the Church's own experience, but at the same time it is combined with sayings which, to all appearance, use the section on the persecutions of "those who are wise" in Dn 11.[33] This makes one think that the author (or group of authors) was aware of the tradition's original connection with Daniel and simply drew additional material from the same source.

My suggested solution as to how the Sabbath entered the picture of the flight from the abomination of desolation[34] clearly points to a "scribal" work on the contemporary Jewish pattern. In addition there was a problem which leads one's thoughts in the same direction—the application of the Sabbath commandment to the Christians.[35]

---

[30] See above, Chap. V, section 3. On the detail that the Son of Man sends out "his" angels (24,31), see the commentaries, and already Apollinaris, *Fragm. 127* (ed. J. REUSS).

[31] See above, Chap. VI, section 2.

[32] See above, 215.

[33] See above, 170 f., 214 ff.

[34] See above, 163.

[35] Cf. how Mt 12,12 becomes a halakic statement on what is permitted on the Sabbath, while the parallels (Mk 3,4; Lk 6,9; 14,3) have instead a captious question. And cf. also how in Mk 1,21 ff. Peter's mother-in-law is healed on the Sabbath, but not in Mt 8,14 ff. See LINDESKOG, *Stud. Theol.* 4 (1950), 179; E. LOHSE, Jesu Worte

When Matthew makes the "I am" more specific by writing ἐγώ εἰμι ὁ χριστός, this marks the final point in the development which we assumed began with a more precise definition of a picture of Satanic blasphemy, painted on general lines, so that it came to deal with the "many" who will appear with blasphemous claims.

We should also note here that Matthew expands the discourse with a number of parables about the Parousia, and so produces a comprehensive eschatological tract, which, together with ch. 23, forms the second part of the fifth teaching section in the Gospel, concluding with the current Matthaean formula which with slight variations concludes the discourses in Matthew's Gospel: "And it came to pass, when Jesus had finished all these words, He said to His disciples ..." (26,1).[36] This tendency to collect material in large blocks that are relatively homogeneous as regards content also underlies Matthew's insertion of vv. 26–28 in ch. 24; the last two verses of these are Q material (the parallels in Lk 17,24 and 37b).

Also the Matthaean form of the eschatological discourse is obviously, so to speak, addressed to the Church. It came into existence in connection with the needs of Church teaching and so came to be a comprehensive teaching tract on the end and on the demands which the prospect of the end made on Christians. It is "a pure Parousia discourse".[37]

(i) *The version of St. Luke.* In the previous pages I found it probable that the author of the Lucan version of the eschatological discourse used not only the written form of Mark's Gospel but also other material.[38] In the tradition whose history we have tried to follow, the Lucan version constitutes the final stage in a development characterized by constantly renewed associations with the Church's situation. I need

---

über den Sabbat, *Zschr. Nt. Wiss.*, *Beih.* 26 (1960), 86 ff. Cf. H. BIETENHARDT, Sabbatvorschriften von Qumrān im Lichte des rabbinischen Rechts und der Evangelien, in *Qumran-Probleme* (1963), 53–74.

[36] Cf. Mt 7,28 f.; 11,1; 13,53; 19,1; see, for example, STENDAHL, *School*, 24 ff.

[37] MARXSEN, *Markus*, 139. For further analyses of the *Redaktionsgeschichte*, see the literature, quoted above, 219, note 55.

For the tradition of the parables in Mt 25, cf., apart from the commentaries, FEUILLET, *Rev. Bibl.* 57 (1950), 66 ff., 86 f.; G. BORNKAMM, Die Verzögerung der Parusie, in *In mem. E. Lohmeyer* (1951), 119 ff.; M. MEINERTZ, Die Tragweite des Gleichnisses von den zehn Jungfrauen, in *Synoptische Studien A. Wikenhauser dargebracht* (1953), 94–106; W. MICHAELIS, *Die Gleichnisse Jesu* (3rd ed. 1956), ad loc.; C. W. F. SMITH, The Mixed State of the Church in Matthew's Gospel, *J. Bibl. Lit.* 82 (1963), 158 ff., 225–37; J. A. T. ROBINSON, The 'Parable' of the Sheep and the Goats, *NT Stud.* 2 (1955/56), 225–37; JEREMIAS, *Gleichnisse*, ad loc.; SCHNACKENBURG, *Herrschaft*, 168 ff. (literature); LÖVESTAM, *Wakefulness*, 92 ff.

[38] Above, 234.

not enter upon any detailed analyses here, but may content myself with describing some of the main features.

By using the non-Marcan material, the evangelist eliminates the remainder of the obscurity about the abomination of desolation: the section deals only with the fall of Jerusalem, interpreted as a judgement on the Jewish people. Some small changes in relation to Mark produce quite large differences:[39] the disciples' question in the introduction refers unambiguously to the Temple alone (Mark's συντελεῖσθαι is replaced by γίνεσθαι); the persecutions are moved back in time to "before" the great signs in v. 10; the consolatory *Mahnwort* which concludes the sayings on persecution (that on endurance εἰς τέλος) is reworded so that no τέλος is mentioned; the parable on the fig tree (v. 29) is separated from the immediately preceding description of the Parousia by the insertion of a "framework" as an introduction. The result of these and other changes in the Lucan redaction is that the end is pushed further into the future: the unknown factor as regards the question of the date of the Parousia is the καιροὶ ἐθνῶν (v. 24) which precede it.[40] On the other hand, the evangelist obviously saw other elements of the discourse as prophecies which had been fulfilled in his own time, and there are reasons for assuming that he wrote at a date close to the fall of Jerusalem—just before or just after.[41]

B. The question of authenticity

I hardly need point out that, as a composition, the discourse does not reproduce a speech by Jesus, but it can hardly be doubted that a good deal of what came to be included in this discourse during the history of its tradition consists of *verba Christi* or derives from them.[42] But what about the parenetic eschatological "midrash" found at the first stage in the history of the tradition?

---

[39] See for the following exposition WELLHAGEN, *Anden och riket*, 32 ff.; SCHMID, *Comm. Lk*, ad loc.; MARXSEN, *Markus*, 129 ff.; CONZELMANN, *Mitte*, 107 ff.; SCHNACKENBURG, op. cit., 192.

[40] It is true that Luke lacks the phrase in Mk "but in those days, after that tribulation" (13,24) which introduces the Marcan verses on the Parousia, and thus in Luke the Parousia is not connected with any possibly identifiable period of tribulation via an adverbial phrase of time. But Luke passes abruptly from the fate of Jerusalem and the times of the Gentiles to the Parousia (cf. M. GOGUEL, Luke and Mark, *Harv. Theol. Rev.* 26 (1933), 28 f. We should remember that the first readers of Luke's Gospel did not read it in either Huck-Lietzmann's or Aland's synopsis!

[41] Thus most of the authorities, for example, E. HOSKYNS and N. DAVEY, *The Riddle of the NT* (rev. ed. 1936), 244; SCHMID, *Comm. Lk*, 303; RENGSTORF, *Comm. Lk*, 11.

[42] See, for example, GLASSON, *Advent*, 77, and GRUNDMANN, *Comm. Mk*, 260.

Let me first extract a few points from the preceding analyses. We found it probable that in 1 and 2 Ths Paul used an early form of the eschatological discourse, a form which appeared to be closely related to the oldest form. He calls it a λόγος κυρίου and this expression need by no means denote an isolated saying of the Lord; it could equally well refer to a "teaching", an "instruction", etc. of the Lord. The content of this *logos* was presumed to be known to the readers, since Paul had passed it on to them during his visit. This permits of the conclusion that Paul, writing about 15 years after the death of Jesus, attributes the beginning of this tradition to Him.

If Paul is right, Jesus must be assumed to have based much of His teaching on the OT. We have no reason to doubt that Jesus did in fact act as a teacher[43] or that, in doing so, He used the teaching methods of His time.[44] To some extent the Qumran texts, and especially, it seems to me, some of the texts analysed above in Part I, bear witness to the fact that "midrashic" teaching from the OT was not restricted to the rabbinic circles with their specialized methods. As far as Jesus is concerned, other texts in the Gospels indicate that sometimes at least He based His teaching on the Scriptures:[45] this applies to His teaching in the synagogues and to the controversy stories (*Streitgespräche*).

If it was given by Jesus, this original "midrash" can hardly have been given in the public part of His work. In both the Marcan and the Matthaean framework the discourse is also assigned to the teaching given to the disciples in private. (If we accept that there is any significance at all in the facts that Jesus is addressed as a teacher and that his followers are called disciples or pupils, we have no reason to doubt that Jesus taught κατ' ἰδίαν.)[46]

We can hardly bring the eschatological discourse and Jesus much closer together than this, even though the gap could be imagined as being filled by the traditions handed down by His disciples.[47] But for all that the last steps towards a certainty as regards the relation between Jesus and our original "midrash" can only be taken on the

---

[43] See BULTMANN, *Jesus*, 52 ff.; id., *Geschichte*, 52; R. O. P. TAYLOR, *The Groundwork of the Gospels* (1946), 46 ff.; MANSON, *Sayings*, 11 f.; E. FASCHER, Jesus der Lehrer, *Theol. Lit.-Zeit.* 79 (1954), 325–42.

[44] See MANSON, *Teaching*, 45 ff., and GERHARDSSON, *Memory*, 326 ff.

[45] See MANSON, op. cit., 48, and GERHARDSSON, op. cit., 327 f. Cf. E. KÄSEMANN, Das Problem des historischen Jesus, *Zschr. Theol. Ki.* 51 (1954), 147.

[46] Cf. A. W. MOSLEY, Jesus' Audiences in the Gospels of St Mark and St Luke, *NT Stud.* 10 (1963/64), 139–49.

[47] See GERHARDSSON, op. cit., 329.

basis of less defensible indications, and this applies whether we affirm or deny its authenticity.

These indications are concerned with the image the scholar has of Jesus and His work. If, for example, he finds the nucleus of the eschatological discourse to be "apocalyptic" and is at the same time definitely of the opinion that Jesus was not an "apocalyptic",[48] the conclusion is obvious. With less simplified reasoning, others may find that the eschatological discourse is so isolated from what has otherwise been handed down to us about the teaching of Jesus that it must be assumed to have had, let us say, a Jewish–Christian origin.[49] Again, other and more "conservative" scholars have ideas about Jesus and His teaching that do not prevent them from ascribing the content of the discourse to Him.[50]

As far as I am concerned, what inclines me to assume that the original "midrash" originated in the teaching of Jesus is as follows. The form of the parenetic "midrash" is that of a teacher and not that of a community, nor that of an inspired prophet, who, as it is sometimes assumed, was interpreted as being the mouthpiece of the risen Lord.[51] The concept of "the kingdom of God" is fundamental in Jesus' preaching and teaching; this kingdom of God was in one way or another bound up with Jesus' person and work, and His followers are in a positive relation to this kingdom. The basic theme in the original "midrash" is not so remote from this as one might think: the Satanic, blasphemous resistance to God is depicted with reference to Daniel and the author describes how, in spite of this resistance, the kingdom of God (Dn 2,44!) will be set up at the coming of the Son of Man. Furthermore Jesus probably regarded His work as in some way the struggle of the kingdom of God against evil powers.[52] Now the "midrash" not

---

[48] For exemple, BULTMANN, *Geschichte*, 113; GLASSON, *Advent*, 63 ff., 135 ff.; H. CONZELMANN, Gegenwart und Zukunft in der synoptischen Tradition, *Zschr. Theol. Ki.* 54 (1957), 287 ff.; VIELHAUER, in HENNECKE, *Apokryphen* II, 428 f. Cf., for example, J. W. BOWMAN, *The Intention of Jesus* (1945), 55 ff.; id., *The Religion of Maturity* (1948), 235 ff.

[49] Thus, for example, KÜMMEL, *Promise*, 103 f., and N. PERRIN, *The Kingdom of God in the Teaching of Jesus* (1963), 134.

[50] For example, BUSCH, *Verständnis*; BEASLEY-MURRAY, *Mark 13*; R. A. COLE, *Comm. Mk* (1961).

[51] See, for example, BULTMANN, *Geschichte*, 135 (where he cites H. GUNKEL, Die Oden Salomos, in *Reden und Aufsätze*, 1913, 173); E. KÄSEMANN, Sätze heiligen Rechtes im NT, *NT Stud.* 1 (1954/55), 256 ff.; P. VIELHAUER, Propheten III A, *Rel. in Gesch. u. Geg.* V (1961), 633 f.; id. in HENNECKE, *Apokryphen* II, 425 f. Also DAVIES, *J. Theol. Stud.* 14 (1963), 104–07.

[52] See, for example, A. FRIDRICHSEN, Jesu kamp mot de urene ånder, *Svensk Teol. Kvartalskrift* 5 (1929), 299–314; RIGAUX, *Antéchrist*, 205 ff.; B. NOACK, *Satanás und Soteria* (1948), 65 ff.; SCHNACKENBURG, *Herrschaft*, 84.

only deals with a similar struggle but is also parenetic from the beginning. It is intended to warn and to prepare the disciples—the sons of the kingdom (Mt 13,38)—before the struggle which, according to the Scriptures, is to precede the setting up of God's kingdom. That is to say, the situation of the disciples is determined in the "midrash" by the same struggle as Jesus was involved in.

In the last resort, however, this leads to the question of the relationship of the NT eschatological sayings to the person of Jesus and to the difficult question of Jesus' consciousness of His own role. The scholars who think they can trace some form of Messianic consciousness in Jesus naturally adopt a different basic attitude as regards Jesus' relationship to the eschatological expectations than those who deny the existence of such a consciousness. Whether, in that case, Jesus really was the person He believed Himself to be is a question which falls outside the domain of historical criticism.

4. *Some Final Remarks*

If the results of the analyses in this part of my work hold good, they both provide fresh viewpoints on the exegesis of the eschatological discourse and open up several other themes in Gospel research. Here I want to make a few suggestions as regards both these fields.

In so far as it is of value to reconstruct the original meaning of a discourse, an exegesis of Mk 13 par. may establish that the original "midrash" dealt with the great distress of the last days in connection with the appearance of an idolatrous "Antichrist". The faithful must shun or flee from this blasphemous revelation. However, the torments will come to an end, the Son of Man will come and God's kingdom will be established. Among the details which appear in a different light, we find v. 6 on the many who will say "I am". We may certainly still doubt whether the present Marcan text is intended to render a blasphemous appellation by the paraphrase of the Name of God or whether it is correctly paraphrased in Matthew's "I am the Christ", but it is clear that in any case a blasphemous revelation formula underlies Mark's "I am" and this increases the possibility of this being the case in the present text as well.[53] The wars which are referred to in what follows were also related from the beginning with this activity of the "Antichrist" and are therefore not isolated elements in a general description of the troubles before the end.

According to the outline of the history of the tradition which I have

---

[53] See above, 159, note 45.

given above, the flight of the inhabitants of Judaea from the abomination of desolation (13,14 ff.) originally meant a flight like that of Lot from the abomination which God was soon to punish, a flight which was not originally locally limited, as it is now.

I would like to mention one final detail for the exegesis. The activity of the false prophets (13,22) is also from the beginning a manifestation of the blasphemous Satanic resistance to God. It is not impossible that this bond between "Antichrist" and the false prophets survives in Mark's Gospel and in this case the false Christs are drawn into the same sphere—they really become Antichrists. We then also have an early manifestation of the same way of thinking as we later encounter in 1 Jn 2,18 ff.

One very important question which is intimately concerned with the exegesis of this chapter but which opens onto other parts of the Gospels and elsewhere in the NT is, to what extent were the OT motifs of which the text is composed used as a symbolic language? In the concluding reflections on Part I, I touched upon similar questions as regarded the Jewish apocalyptical and eschatological texts. To what extent, for example, were the celestial phenomena at the Parousia or the Son of Man on the clouds consciously used as symbols? It is important to try and answer these questions by using the methods of historical criticism and by careful analyses of the Jewish and early Christian material.[54] Such inquiries could also provide new points of departure, as regards evaluating Jesus' relationship to apocalyptic ideas.[55]

---

[54] I am anxious to stress the necessity of using the methods of historical criticism for this purpose. The reason why a critical exegete should give a "demythologized" interpretation of apocalyptic sayings is scarcely that the idea of the world assumed in the texts cannot be shared by twentieth-century man, but that the authors of these texts and their contemporaries perhaps intended them to be components of a symbolic language. (Cf. R. BULTMANN, NT und Mythologie, in *Kerygma und Mythos*, 4th ed. 1960, 15 ff.) If it can be established that a text uses a symbolic language which was intended as such from the beginning, it is a necessary condition for the understanding of the text that the meaning of this symbolic language should be elucidated. (I use the word "understanding" with none of the overtones which it may have in terminology influenced by Heidegger's philosophy; cf., for example, J. MACQUARRIE, *An Existentialist Theology* (1955), 54 ff.; O. SCHNÜBBE, *Der Existenzbegriff in der Theologie R. Bultmanns* (1959), 30 f., 129 ff.; F. HOHMEIER, *Das Schriftverständnis in der Theologie R. Bultmanns* (1964), 68 f.) See GOULD, *Comm. Mk*, 250 ff.; CARRINGTON, *Comm. Mk*, 281 ff.; A. N. WILDER, Eschatological Imagery and Earthly Circumstance, *NT Stud.* 5 (1958/59), 229–45. And cf. C. C. McCown, Symbolic Interpretation, *J. Bibl. Lit.* 63 (1944), 329–38.

[55] See J. A. T. ROBINSON, *Coming*, passim, and T. F. GLASSON, *His Appearing and His Kingdom* (1953), 1 ff., 113 ff. Cf. R. BULTMANN, *Theologie des NT* (1953), 3 f.; KÜMMEL, *Promise*, 88 ff.; G. BORNKAMM, *Jesus von Nazareth* (4/5th ed. 1960), 60 f., 85 f.

We have thereby already passed over to the other themes in NT exegesis for the evaluation of which these results may be relevant. Thus, a comparison between my analyses and certain parts of the Revelation of St. John would perhaps be informative as regards the germination of the Revelation (consider, for example, how Ap 13 exhibits several similarities to our "midrash"). Similarly a certain light may be shed on the intensive use the writer of the Revelation made of the Book of Daniel.

The fact that Daniel is at the centre of our "midrash" may also illustrate other passages in the Gospels. Indeed, perhaps the apocalyptic ideas in Daniel played a more important part in Jesus' thinking than modern, non-apocalyptic, sober-minded western scholars may imagine at first glance. Concepts such as the kingdom of God and the Son of Man are fundamental to it and it is, as I suggested above, far from evident that the gulf is so very wide between Mk 13 par. (which explains Daniel) and other Gospel material.[56]

As regards the history of the early Church, my inquiries may yield some knowledge of the place occupied by "apocalyptic" in the early Church. The Second Coming of Jesus was included as a *topos* in the *kerygma* (the missionary preaching),[57] but the long history of the discourse indicates that the teaching of the Church also went into eschatological questions in detail, on the basis of what was thought to be the Jesus tradition (and in my opinion with some justification). But in this eschatological tradition the Church also found its own situation described more or less—it was living in the phase of realized eschatology.

The stages in the history of the tradition also indicate that aspect of the relation of the early Church to the eschatology which is expressed in the antithesis between the catchwords *Naherwartung* and *Parusieverzögerung*.[58] The earliest stages slide out of this simple grip.

---

[56] Cf. A. FARRER, *A Study in St. Mark* (1951), 165, 265 ff.; J. DUPONT, Le logion des douze trônes (Mt 19,28; Lc 22,28–30), *Bibl.* 45 (1964), 355–92.

[57] See DODD, *Apostolic Preaching*.

[58] A selection from an immense literature: M. WERNER, *Die Entstehung des christlichen Dogmas* (1941); W. MICHAELIS, *Der Herr verzieht nicht die Verheissung* (1942); id., Kennen die Synoptiker eine Verzögerung der Parusie?, in *Synoptische Studien A. Wikenhauser dargebracht* (1954), 107–23; O. CULLMANN, Das wahre durch die ausgebliebene Parusie gestellte neutestamentliche Problem, *Theol. Zschr.* 3 (1947), 177–91; id., Parusieverzögerung und Urchristentum, *Theol. Lit.-Zeit.* 83 (1958), 1–12; id., *Heil als Geschichte*; BORNKAMM, *Die Verzögerung der Parusie*; GRÄSSER, *Problem der Parusieverzögerung*; H.-W. BARTSCH, Zum Problem der Parusieverzögerung bei den Synoptikern, *Evang. Theol.* 19 (1959), 116–31; J. GNILKA, "Parusieverzögerung" und Naherwartung, *Cath.* 13 (1959), 277–90; W. G. KÜMMEL, Futurische und präsentische Eschatologie im ältesten Urchristentum, *NT*

On the other hand, the view which is expressed in the combination between the sayings on the (approaching) fall of Jerusalem, the eschatological discourse and the parable of the fig tree, with the following logia, seem to mark an increased *Naherwartung*. This increased expectation is later removed in various ways in the Gospels of Matthew and Luke. These sketchy outlines of a view of this hotly debated problem may perhaps be filled out by a closer investigation to give an ampler and more detailed picture.[59]

Then we come to the problem of the Gospel tradition. The analysis of the history of this tradition has given us some insight into the function of a Jesus tradition in the early Church. Even though my view of the origin of this tradition may be erroneous, we are on safer ground for a period of about 20 years before the first written version available to us. It would hardly be historically sound to deny that the early Church regarded different forms of the eschatological discourse as a Jesus tradition, when we have the evidence of 1 and 2 Ths. This Jesus tradition was regarded as authoritative. It was a tradition that was *used* the whole time; it was re-formed, re-interpreted and expanded.[60] But the analyses have also indicated that this use, these reformations and these expansions had their *Sitz im Leben* in the Church's teaching and were undertaken by persons who knew how to deal with "midrashic" material and how to use the "midrashic" technique. But they also had other Jesus material at their disposal, *inter alia*, logia which were combined with the original eschatological "midrash", so as to produce new viewpoints, new significances and new applications of the tradition. Here it is worth noting the combination of solidity and plasticity which we have observed in the tradition during its transmission.[61]

This also brings us close to the questions of the nature of the Gospel tradition and its early history. It may be sufficient to observe that the results of the analyses have led us to put a question mark in the margin as regards a good deal of the dogma of form criticism. The

Stud. 5 (1958/59), 113–26; H. P. OWEN, The Parousia of Christ in the Synoptic Gospels, *Scot. J. Theol.* 12 (1959), 171–92; E. KÄSEMANN, Die Anfänge christlicher Theologie, *Zschr. Theol. Ki.* 57 (1960), 162–85; id., Zum Thema der urchristlichen Apokalyptik, ibid. 59 (1962), 257–84; STROBEL, *Untersuchungen zum eschatologischen Verzögerungsproblem*; J. W. DOEVE, Parousieverzögerung, *Nederl. Theol. Tijdschr.* 17 (1962/63), 32–38; G. LUNDSTRÖM, *The Kingdom of God in the Teaching of Jesus* (1963), 69 ff., 241 ff.; SINT, *Zschr. Kath. Theol.* 86 (1964), 47–79; S. S. SMALLEY, The Delay of the Parousia, *J. Bibl. Lit.* 83 (1964), 41–54.

[59] Cf. CULLMANN, *Heil als Geschichte*, 173 ff.

[60] See also GERHARDSSON, *Memory*, for example, 309 ff., and id., *Tradition*, 37 ff.

[61] Cf. GERHARDSSON, *Memory*, 332 ff.

form of the tradition, its mode of development and the *Sitz im Leben* which these factors lead us to assume do not agree very well with the pre-conditions of form criticism. Though perhaps scholars who are conscious of their scholarly traditions and are justifiably proud of them may return a ringing *Nein* to these remarks, it is still conceivable that the analyses which I have presented here contain some measure of truth.

As I remarked before, only suggestions have been adduced in this section. To investigate them in detail lies outside the framework of the present investigation. But if this investigation, with its limited aims, can be shown to have shed some light on this text, "one of the unsolved problems of New Testament exegesis",[62] it will have fulfilled its purpose.

[62] V. TAYLOR, The Apocalyptic Discourse of Mark xiii, *Exp. Times* 60 (1948/49), 94.

Bibliography

A. Texts and Translations

Biblia hebraica ..., ed. R. KITTEL. 12th ed. by P. KAHLE, A. ALT, O. EISS-
FELDT. Stuttgart 1961.
Die Weisheit des Jesus Sirach, hebräisch und deutsch, ed. R. SMEND. Berlin
1906.
Targum Onkelos I–II, ed. A. BERLINER. Berlin, Frankfurt, London 1884.
The Bible in Aramaic I–III, ed. A. SPERBER. Leiden 1959–62.
The Targum of Isaiah, ed. J. F. STENNING. Oxford 1949.
SS. Biblia polyglotta I–IV, ed. B. WALTON. London 1657.
Septuaginta. Vetus Testamentum Graecum auctoritate Societatis Littera-
rum Gottingensis editum:
    IX: 1. Maccabaeorum liber 1, ed. W. KAPPLER. Göttingen 1936.
    X. Psalmi cum Odis, ed. A. RAHLFS. Göttingen 1931.
    XIII. Duodecim prophetae, ed. J. ZIEGLER. Göttingen 1943.
    XIV. Isaias, ed. J. ZIEGLER. Göttingen 1939.
    XV. Ieremias, Baruch, Threni, Epistula Ieremiae, ed. J. ZIEGLER.
    Göttingen 1954.
    XVI: 1. Ezechiel, ed. J. ZIEGLER. Göttingen 1954.
    XVI: 2. Susanna, Daniel, Bel et Draco, ed. J. ZIEGLER. Göttingen 1954.
Septuaginta ... I–II, ed. A. RAHLFS. 7th ed. Stuttgart 1962.
The Old Testament in Greek ... I–III, ed. H. B. SWETE. 2nd ed. Cambridge
1895–99.
Origenis Hexaplorum quae supersunt ... I–II, ed. F. FIELD. Oxford 1875.
The Syriac Old and New Testament, ed. S. LEE. London 1823–26.
Biblia Sacra Vulgatae editionis ..., ed. M. HETZENAUER. 2nd ed. Regensburg,
Roma 1922.
Novum Testamentum Graece, ed. E. NESTLE, K. ALAND. 25th ed. Stuttgart
1963.
Synopse der drei ersten Evangelien, ed. A. HUCK. 9th ed. by H. LIETZMANN.
Tübingen 1936.
Synopsis Quattuor Evangeliorum ..., ed. K. ALAND. Stuttgart 1964.

Die Apokryphen und Pseudepigraphen des Alten Testaments ... I–II, ed.
E. KAUTZSCH. Tübingen 1900.
The Apocrypha and Pseudepigrapha of the Old Testament in English I–II,
ed. R. H. CHARLES. Oxford 1913.
Altjüdisches Schrifttum ausserhalb der Bibel ..., ed. P. RIESSLER. Augsburg
1928.
La Bible Apocryphe en marge de l'Ancien Testament ..., ed. J. BONSIRVEN.
(Textes pour l'hist. sacrée.) Paris 1953.
De Gammeltestamentlige Pseudepigrafer [trans. into Danish] ... I–IV, ed.
E. HAMMERSHAIMB, J. MUNCK, B. NOACK, P. SEIDELIN. Copenhagen,
Oslo, Lund 1953–63.

Monumenta sacra et profana ..., ed. A. M. CERIANI: I, Milano 1861–66; V, Milano 1868–71.

HILGENFELD, A., *Messias Judaeorum,* libris eorum paulo ante et paulo post Christum natum conscriptis illustratus. Leipzig 1869.

Apocrypha anecdota. Second series, ed. M. R. JAMES. (Texts and Studies 5: 1.) Cambridge 1897.

The Ethiopic Version of the Book of Enoch, ed. R. H. CHARLES. (Analecta Oxon. Sem. Ser. 11.) Oxford 1906.

The Last Chapters of Enoch in Greek, ed. C. BONNER, H. C. YOUTIE. (Stud. and Docum. 8.) London 1937.

Das Buch Henoch übersetzt und erklärt von A. DILLMANN. Leipzig 1853.

Das Buch Henoch ..., ed. J. FLEMMING, L. RADEMACHER. (Griech. christl. Schriftst.) Leipzig 1901.

Le livre d'Hénoch traduit ..., ed. F. MARTIN. (Docum. pour l'ét. de la Bible.) Paris 1906.

The Book of Enoch or 1 Enoch, translated ..., ed. R. H. CHARLES. Rev. ed. Oxford 1912.

Les Psaumes de Salomon ..., ed. J. VITEAU. (Docum. pour l'ét. de la Bible.) Paris 1911.

The Odes and Psalms of Solomon I–II, ed. R. HARRIS, A. MINGANA. Manchester, London, New York, etc. 1916–20.

BAARS, W., A New Fragment of the Greek Version of the Psalms of Solomon, *Vet. Test.* 11 (1961), 441–44.

The Greek Versions of the Testaments of the Twelve Patriarchs ..., ed. R. H. CHARLES. Oxford, Hildesheim 1908/1960.

Testamenta XII Patriacharum, ed. ... M. DE JONGE. (Pseudepigr. Vet. Test. Graeca 1.) Leiden 1964.

The Assumption of Moses ..., ed. R. H. CHARLES. London 1897.

Die Himmelfahrt des Mose, ed. C. CLEMEN. (Kleine Texte ..., ed. H. Lietzmann, 10.) Bonn 1904.

Die Esra-Apokalypse I–II, ed. B. VIOLET. (Griech. christl. Schriftst.) Leipzig 1910–24.

The Ezra-Apocalypse ..., ed. G. H. Box. London 1912.

Liber apocalypseos Baruch filii Neriae ... ed. M. KMOSKO. (Patrol. syriaca I: 2, p. 1055–1206.) Paris 1907.

The Apocalypse of Abraham, ed. G. H. BOX, J. I. LANDSMAN. (Trans. of Early Docum. Ser. 1.) London, New York 1919.

The Ascension of Isaiah, ed. R. H. CHARLES. (Trans. of Early Docum. Ser. 1.) London, New York 1919.

Die Oracula Sibyllina ..., ed. J. GEFFCKEN. (Griech. christl. Schriftst.) Leipzig 1902.

Sibyllinische Weissagungen, ed. A. KURFESS. München 1951.

The Sibylline Oracles, Books III–V, ed. H. N. BATE. (Trans. of Early Docum. Ser. 2.) London, New York 1918.

Neutestamentliche Apokryphen in deutscher Übersetzung I–II, ed. E.
HENNECKE. 3rd ed. by W. SCHNEEMELCHER. Tübingen 1959–64.

Documents of Jewish Sectaries I. Fragment of a Zadokite Work ..., ed.
S. SCHECHTER. Cambridge 1910.

The Zadokite Documents. I: The Admonition, II: The Laws, ed. C. RABIN.
2nd ed. Oxford 1958.

The Dead Sea Scrolls of St. Mark's Monastery. I: The Isaiah Manuscript
and the Habakkuk Commentary; II: 2: Plates and Transcription of the
Manual of Discipline, ed. M. BURROWS, J. C. TREVER, W. H. BROWN-
LEE. New Haven 1950–51.

Discoveries in the Judaean Desert I. Qumran Cave I, ed. D. BARTHÉLEMY,
J. T. MILIK, etc. Oxford 1955.

Discoveries in the Judaean Desert of Jordan III. Les 'Petites Grottes' de
Qumrân ..., ed. M. BAILLET, J. T. MILIK, R. DE VAUX. Oxford 1962.

Die Texte aus Qumran, hebräisch und deutsch ..., ed. E. LOHSE. München
1964.

La Règle de la Guerre des Fils de Lumière contre les Fils de Ténèbres, ed.
J. CARMIGNAC. (Autour de la Bible.) Paris 1958.

The Scroll of the War of the Sons of Light Against the Sons of Darkness ...,
ed. Y. YADIN. Oxford 1962.

J. M. ALLEGRO, Further Messianic References in Qumran Literature, J.
Bibl. Lit. 75 (1956), 174–87. (4 QpIs^a.)

—— More Isaiah Commentaries from Qumran's Fourth Cave, J. Bibl. Lit.
77 (1958), 215–21. (4 QpIs^b.)

J. A. FITZMYER, The Aramaic "Elect of God" Text from Qumran Cave IV,
Cath. Bibl. Quart. 27 (1965), 348–72.

Dødehavsteksterne [trans. into Danish] ..., ed. E. NIELSEN, B. OTZEN.
2nd ed. Copenhagen 1959.

Die Texte vom Toten Meer I–II, ed. J. MAIER. München, Basel 1960.

The Thanksgiving Hymns ..., ed. M. MANSOOR. (Stud. in the Texts of the
Desert of Judah 3.) Leiden 1961.

Philonis Alexandrini opera quae supersunt I–VII, ed. L. COHN, P. WEND-
LAND. Berlin 1896–1930.

Flavii Josephi opera omnia I–IV, ed. S. A. NABER. Leipzig 1888–96.

Die sechs Ordnungen der Mischna ... I–VI, ed. E. BANETH, J. COHN, etc.
(I, IV 2nd ed.) Wiesbaden 1924–33.

Die Mischna. Text, Übersetzung und ausführliche Erklärung ..., ed. G.
BEER, D. HOLTZMANN, etc. Giessen, Berlin 1912–.

The Mishnah. Translated ... by H. DANBY. Oxford 1933.

Tosephta, ed. M. S. ZUCKERMANDEL. Pasewalk, Trier 1879–82.

Der babylonische Talmud ... I–IX, ed. L. GOLDSCHMIDT. Berlin, Leipzig,
Haag 1897–1934.

The Babylonian Talmud translated into English I–XXXV, ed. I. EPSTEIN.
London 1935–48.

Der Jerusalemische Talmud ... Krotoschin 1886.

Le Talmud de Jérusalem traduit ... par M. SCHWAB, I–XI. Paris 1878–90.
(Nouv. éd. photomec. Paris 1932–33.)

Mechilta, der älteste halachische und haggadische Commentar zum zweiten Buche Moses ..., ed. I. H. WEISS. Wien 1865.

Sifra. Commentar zu Leviticus ..., ed. I. H. WEISS, J. SCHLOSSBERG. Wien 1862.

Sifra. Halachische Midrasch zu Leviticus, übers. von J. WINTER. (Schr. d. Gesellsch. z. Förd. d. Wiss. d. Judent. 42.) Breslau 1938.

Pesikta, die älteste Hagada, redigiert in Palästina von Rab Kahana, ed. S. BUBER. Lyck 1868.

Pesikta des Rab Kahana ... ins Deutsche übertragen, ed. A. WÜNSCHE. Leipzig 1885.

Midrash Tanchuma I–III (Title in Hebrew), ed. S. BUBER. Wilna 1885.

Midrash Rabbah translated into English ... I–IX, ed. H. FREEDMAN, M. SIMON. London 1939.

The Midrash on Psalms I–II, translated by W. G. BRAUDE. (Yale Jud. Ser. 13.) New Haven 1959.

Bibliotheca Rabbinica I–XII, ed. A. WÜNSCHE. Leipzig 1880–85.

Haggada für Pessach ..., ed. J. BRONNER. Wien [1931].

The Apostolic Fathers ... I–II, ed. K. LAKE. (Loeb Class. Libr.) Cambridge, Mass. 1950–52.

Die apostolischen Väter. Neubearb. d. Funkschen Ausgabe I, ed. K. BIHLMEYER, W. SCHNEEMELCHER. (Samml. ausgew. kirchen- u. dogmengesch. Quellenschr. II: 1: 1.) 2nd ed. Tübingen 1956.

Origenes Werke III ..., ed. E. KLOSTERMANN. (Griech. christl. Schriftst.) Leipzig 1901.

Eusebius Werke II: 1–3, ed. E. SCHWARTZ, T. MOMMSEN. (Griech. christl. Schriftst.) Leipzig 1903–09.

Matthäus-Kommentare aus der griechischen Kirche, aus Katenenhandschriften gesammelt ..., ed. J. REUSS. (Texte u. Unters. 61.) Berlin 1957.

Aristotelis De sensu et De memoria libri, ed. A. FÖRSTER. (Ed. crit. script. gr. et rom.) Budapest 1942.

Demosthenis Orationes I–II, ed. C. FUHR, I. SYKUTRIS. Leipzig 1914–37.

Epicteti dissertationes ab Arriano digestae ..., ed. H. SCHENKL. Leipzig 1916.

Polybius, Historiae I–V, ed. TH. BÜTTNER-WOBST. (I: 2nd ed.) Leipzig 1889–1905.

B. Literature

AALEN, S., Die Begriffe 'Licht' und 'Finsternis' im Alten Testament, im Spätjudentum und im Rabbinismus. Diss. Oslo. (Skrifter, D. Norske Vidensk.-Akad., Oslo, II. Hist.-Filos. kl. 1951: 1.) Oslo 1951.

ADAMI, F., De poetis scaenicis Graecis hymnorum sacrorum imitatoribus, Jahrbücher f. class. Philol., Suppl. 26 (1901), 213–62.

AHLSTRÖM, G. W., Psalm 89. Eine Liturgie aus dem Ritual des leidenden Königs. Diss. Uppsala. Lund 1959.

AICHER, G., Das Alte Testament in der Mischna. (Bibl. Stud. XI: 4.) Freiburg i. B. 1906.

ALLEN, W. C., A Critical and Exegetical Commentary on the Gospel according to S. Matthew. (Int. Crit. Comm.) 3rd ed. Edinburgh 1912.

ALTHAUS, P., *Die letzten Dinge*. Entwurf einer christlichen Eschatologie. (Studapol-Sem. 9.) 4th ed. Gütersloh 1933.

ANDEL, C. P. VAN, *De Structuur van de Henoch-traditie en het Nieuwe Testament*. Diss. Utrecht 1955.

ANDERSON, B. W., Exodus Typology in Second Isaiah, in *Israel's Prophetic Heritage*: Essays in hon. J. Muilenburg, ed. B. W. Anderson, W. Harrelson, New York 1962, 177–95.

ANDRÆ, T., *Mystikens psykologi*. Besatthet och inspiration. (Modern religionspsykol. 4.) Stockholm 1926.

APTOWITZER, V., *Parteipolitik der Hasmonäerzeit* im rabbinischen und pseudepigraphischen Schrifttum. (Veröffentl. d. A. Kohut Memor. Found. 5.) Wien, New York 1927.

ARNDT, W. F., *The Gospel according to St. Luke*. (Bible Comm.) Saint Louis, Missouri 1956.

ARNDT, W. F., GINGRICH, F. W., *A Greek-English Lexicon of the New Testament* and Other Early Christian Literature ... Chicago, Cambridge 1957.

AUBERT, L., Une première apocalypse (Esaie 24–27), *Ét. Théol. Rel.* 11 (1936), 280–96, 12 (1937), 54–67.

AUDET, J.-P., *La Didachè*. Instruction des apôtres. (Ét. bibl.) Paris 1958.

AULÉN, G., *Den allmänneliga kristna tron*. 5th ed. Stockholm 1957. (Eng. trans.: *The Faith of the Christian Church*. Philadelphia 1960.)

BACHER, W., *Die älteste Terminologie der jüdischen Schriftauslegung* ... Leipzig 1899.

BACON, B. W., *The Gospel of Mark*: its Composition and Date. New Haven, London, Oxford 1925.

BALTZER, K., The Meaning of the Temple in the Lukan Writings, *Harv. Theol. Rev.* 58 (1965), 263–77.

BAMMEL, E., Herkunft und Funktion der Traditionselemente in 1. Kor. 15, 1–11, *Theol. Zschr.* 11 (1955), 401–19.

—— Schema und Vorlage von *Didache* 16, in *Studia Patristica* 4 (Texte u. Unters. 79), Berlin 1961, 253–62.

BARRETT, C. K., *The Holy Spirit and the Gospel Tradition*. London, New York 1947.

—— The Old Testament in the Fourth Gospel, *J. Theol. Stud.* 48 (1947), 155–69.

—— New Testament Eschatology, *Scot. J. Theol.* 6 (1953), 136–55, 225–43.

—— *The Gospel according to St. John*. 2nd impr. London 1956/1960.

BARTH, K., *Der Römerbrief*. 3. Abdruck d. neuen Bearb. 1922. München 1924.

—— *Die kirchliche Dogmatik*. II: 1, 2nd ed., Zollikon, Zürich 1946; IV: 1 Zürich 1960.

BARTSCH, H.-W., Zum Problem der Parusieverzögerung bei den Synoptikern, *Evang. Theol.* 19 (1959), 116–31.

—— Die Argumentation des Paulus in I Cor 15, 3–11, *Zschr. Nt. Wiss.* 55 (1964), 261–74.

BEASLEY-MURRAY, G. R., The Two Messiahs in the Testaments of the Twelve Patriarchs, *J. Theol. Stud.* 48 (1947), 1–12.

—— A Century of Eschatological Discussion, *Exp. Times* 64 (1952/53), 312–16.

—— The Rise and Fall of the Little Apocalypse Theory, *Exp. Times* 64 (1952/53), 346–49.

—— *Jesus and the Future.* An Examination of the Criticism of the Eschatological Discourse, Mark 13, with Special Reference to the Little Apocalypse Theory. London, New York 1954.

—— *A Commentary on Mark Thirteen.* London 1957.

BEEK, M. A., *Nationale en Transcendente Motieven in de Joodse Apokalyptiek van de laatste Eeuwen voor Christus.* Assen 1941.

—— *Inleiding in de Joodse Apocalyptiek van het Oud- en Nieuw-Testamentisch Tijdvak.* (Theologia 6.) Haarlem 1950.

BEGRICH, J., Der Text der Psalmen Salomos, *Zschr. Nt. Wiss.* 38 (1939), 131–64.

—— Berit. Ein Beitrag zur Erfassung einer alttestamentlichen Denkform, *Zschr. At. Wiss.* 60 (1944), 1–11.

BENGEL, J. A., *Gnomon Novi Testamenti.* Ed. tertia cur. M. E. Bengel, ed. J. Steudel. London 1862.

BENTZEN, A., *Daniel.* (Handb. z. AT 19.) Tübingen 1952.

—— *Introduction to the Old Testament* I–II. 2nd. Copenhagen 1952.

—— *King and Messiah.* (Lutterworth Stud. in Church and Bible.) London 1955.

BERGSON, H., *Matière et mémoire* ... 15th ed. Paris 1919.

BETZ, O. *Offenbarung und Schriftforschung in der Qumransekte.* (Wiss. Unters. z. NT 6.) Tübingen 1960.

—— Der Katechon, *NT Stud.* 9 (1962/63), 276–91.

BICKERMAN, E. J., The Date of the Testaments of the Twelve Patriarchs, *J. Bibl. Lit.* 69 (1950), 245–60.

BIETENHARD(T), H., *Die himmlische Welt im Urchristentum und Spätjudentum.* (Wiss. Unters. z. NT 2.) Tübingen 1951.

—— Sabbatvorschriften von Qumrān im Lichte des rabbinischen Rechts und der Evangelien, in *Qumran-Probleme* ..., ed. H. Bardtke (Deutsche Akad. d. Wiss. z. Berlin. Sekt. f. Altert.-Wiss. 42), Berlin 1963, 53–74.

BILLERBECK, P., see STRACK, H. L.

BILLING, E., *De etiska tankarne i urkristendomen* i samband med dess religiösa tro I–II. Uppsala 1907.

BLACK, M., The Eschatology of the Similitudes of Enoch, *J. Theol. Stud. N.S.* 3 (1952), 1–10.

—— *An Aramaic Approach to the Gospels and Acts.* 2nd ed. Oxford 1954.

BLOCH, J., *On the Apocalyptic in Judaism.* (Jew. Quart. Rev. Monogr. Ser. 2.) Philadelphia 1952.

—— Some Christological Interpolations in the Ezra-Apocalypse, *Harv. Theol. Rev.* 51 (1958), 87–94.

BLOCH, R., Écriture et tradition dans le Judaïsme. Aperçus sur l'origine du Midrash, *Cah. Sion.* 8 (1954), 9–34.

—— Midrash, *Dict. de la Bible, Suppl.* V (1957), 1263–81.

BOEHMER, J., *Die neutestamentliche Gottesscheu und die ersten drei Bitten des Vaterunsers.* Halle (Saale) 1917.

BONNARD, P., *L'Évangile selon Saint Matthieu.* (Comm. du NT 1.) Neuchâtel 1963.

BONSIRVEN, J., *Le judaïsme palestinien au temps de Jésus-Christ.* Sa théologie I–II. (Biblioth. théol. hist.) Paris 1934–35.

BOOTH, O., The Semantic Development of the Term מִשְׁפָּט in the Old Testament. *J. Bibl. Lit.* 61 (1942), 105–10.

BORNKAMM, G., Die Verzögerung der Parusie. Exegetische Bemerkungen zu zwei synoptischen Texten, in *In memoriam E. Lohmeyer*, ed. W. Schmauch, Stuttgart 1951, 116–26.

—— Enderwartung und Kirche im Matthäusevangelium, in *The Background of the New Testament and its Eschatology*, ed. W. D. Davies, D. Daube in hon. C. H. Dodd, Cambridge 1956, 222–60. (Also in *Überlieferung und Auslegung im Matthäusevangelium* (Wiss. Monogr. z. A u. NT 1), Neukirchen, Kr. Moers 1960, 13–47.)

—— *Jesus von Nazareth.* (Urban-Bücher 19.) 4th and 5th ed. Stuttgart 1960.

—— Paulus, *Rel. in Gesch. u. Geg.* V (3rd ed. 1961), 166–90.

BOSCH, D., *Die Heidenmission in der Zukunftsschau Jesu.* Eine Untersuchung zur Eschatologie der synoptischen Evangelien. (Abh. z. Theol. d. A u. NT 36.) Zürich 1959.

BOSTRÖM, G., *Paronomasi i den äldre hebreiska maschallitteraturen* med särskild hänsyn till Proverbia. Diss. Lund. (Lunds Univ. Årsskrift, N.F., I: 23, 8.) Lund, Leipzig 1928.

BOUSSET, W., *Der Antichrist* in der Überlieferung des Judentums, des Neuen Testaments und der alten Kirche. Göttingen 1895.

—— *Die Offenbarung Johannis.* (Krit.-exeg. Komm. ü. d. NT 16, 6th ed.) Göttingen 1906.

—— *Hauptprobleme der Gnosis.* (Forsch. z. Rel. u. Lit. d. A u. NT 10.) Göttingen 1907.

—— *Die Religion des Judentums im neutestamentlichen Zeitalter.* 2nd ed. Berlin 1906. 3rd ed. by H. Gressmann, entitled *Die Religion des Judentums im späthellenistischen Zeitalter.* (Handb. z. NT 21.) Tübingen 1926.

BOWMAN, J., The Background of the Term 'Son of Man', *Exp. Times* 59 (1947/48), 283–88.

—— Early Samaritan Eschatology, *J. Jew. Stud.* 6 (1955), 63–72.

—— *The Gospel of Mark.* The New Christian Jewish Passover Haggadah. (Studia post-bibl. 8.) Leiden 1965.

BOWMAN, J. W., *The Intention of Jesus.* London 1945.

—— *The Religion of Maturity.* New York, Nashville 1948.

BRANDON, S. G. F., *The Fall of Jerusalem and the Christian Church.* A Study of the Effects of the Jewish Overthrow of A.D. 70 on Christianity. London 1951.

BRAUMANN, G., Die lukanische Interpretation der Zerstörung Jerusalems, *Nov. Test.* 6 (1963), 120–27.

BRAUN, F. M., *Neues Licht auf die Kirche.* Die protestantische Kirchendogmatik in ihrer neuesten Entfaltung. Köln 1946.

BRAUN, H., *Spätjüdisch-häretischer und frühchristlicher Radikalismus.* Jesus von Nazareth und die essenische Qumransekte I–II. (Beitr. z. hist. Theol. 24: 1–2.) Tübingen 1957.

BRIGHT, J., The Date of the Prose Sermons of Jeremiah, *J. Bibl. Lit.* 70 (1951), 15–35.

BRISTOL, L. O., Mark's Little Apocalypse: A Hypothesis, *Exp. Times* 51 (1939/40), 301–03.

BROWN, J. P., Synoptic Parallels in the Epistles and Form-History, *NT Stud.* 10 (1963/64), 27–48.

BROWNLEE, W. H., Biblical Interpretation among the Sectaries of the Dead
Sea Scrolls, *Bibl. Archaeol.* 14 (1951), 54–76.
—— *The Text of Habakkuk in the Ancient Commentary from Qumran.* (J.
Bibl. Lit. Monogr. Ser. 11.) Philadelphia 1959.
BRUCE, F. F., *Biblical Exegesis in the Qumran Texts.* (Exegetica 3: 1.) Den
Haag 1959.
—— Christianity under Claudius, *Bull. J. Ryl. Libr.* 44 (1961/62), 309–26.
BRUNEC, M., De "Homine peccati" in 2 Thess. 2, 1–12, *Verb. Dom.* 35 (1957),
3–33.
BUCHANAN, G. W., Midrashim prétannaites, *Rev. Bibl.* 72 (1965), 227–39.
BÜCHSEL, F., γενεά κτλ., *Theol. Wörterb.*, ed. G. Kittel, I (1933), 660–63.
BÜCHSEL, F., HERNTRICH, V., κρίνω κτλ., *Theol. Wörterb.*, ed. G. Kittel,
III (1938), 920–55.
BUHL, F., *Wilhelm Gesenius' hebräisches und aramäisches Handwörterbuch
über das Alte Testament.* 16th ed. Leipzig 1915.
BULTMANN, R., Die Bedeutung des geschichtlichen Jesus für die Theologie
des Paulus, *Theol. Blätter* 8 (1929), 137–51. (Also in *Glauben und Ver-
stehen* ... I, Tübingen 1933, 188–213.)
—— *Jesus.* (Die Unsterblichen 1.) Berlin 1929.
—— *Die Geschichte der synoptischen Tradition.* (Forsch. z. Rel. u. Lit. d.
A u. NT 29.) 2nd ed. Göttingen 1931.
—— *Geschichte der synoptischen Tradition. Ergänzungsheft.* 2nd ed. Göt-
tingen 1962.
—— Weissagung und Erfüllung, *Zschr. Theol. Ki.* 47 (1950), 360–83.
—— Das Problem der Hermeneutik, in *Glauben und Verstehen* ... II,
Tübingen 1952, 211–35.
—— *Theologie des Neuen Testaments.* Tübingen 1953.
—— History and Eschatology in the New Testament, *NT Stud.* 1 (1954/
55), 5–16.
—— Neues Testament und Mythologie, in *Kerygma und Mythos* ..., ed.
H.-W. Bartsch (Theol. Forsch. 1), 4th ed., Hamburg-Bergstedt 1960,
15–48.
—— *Das Verhältnis der urchristlichen Christusbotschaft zum historischen
Jesus.* (Sitz.-ber. d. Heidelb. Akad. d. Wiss., Phil.-hist. Kl. 1960: 3.)
Heidelberg 1960.
—— Wissenschaft und Existenz, in *Glauben und Verstehen* ... III, Tü-
bingen 1960, 107–21.
—— Ist voraussetzungslose Exegese möglich?, in *Glauben und Verstehen* ...
III, Tübingen 1960, 142–50.
—— Ist die Apokalyptik die Mutter der urchristlichen Theologie? Eine
Auseinandersetzung mit Ernst Käsemann, in *Apophoreta, Festschr.
f. E. Haenchen*, ed. W. Eltester, F. H. Kettler (Zschr. Nt. Wiss., Beih.
30), Berlin 1964, 64–69.
BURI, F., *Die Bedeutung der neutestamentlichen Eschatologie für die neuere
protestantische Theologie.* Zürich, Leipzig 1935.
BURKITT, F. C., *Jewish and Christian Apocalypses.* (Schweich Lect. 1913.)
London 1914.
—— The Use of Mark in the Gospel according to Luke, in *The Beginnings
of Christianity* I, ed. F. J. F. Jackson, K. Lake, vol. II, London 1922,
106–20.

—— *Christian Beginnings*. Three Lectures. London 1924.

BURNEY, C. F., *The Poetry of our Lord*. Oxford 1925.

BURROWS, M., *The Literary Relations of Ezekiel*. Diss. Yale. Philadelphia 1925.

—— Ancient Israel, in *The Idea of History in the Ancient Near East* (Amer. Orient. Ser. 38), New Haven, London 1955, 99–131.

BUSCH, F., *Zum Verständnis der synoptischen Eschatologie*. Markus 13 neu untersucht. (Neutest. Forsch. IV: 2.) Gütersloh 1938.

BUSSMANN, W., *Synoptische Studien* I–III. Halle (Saale) 1925–31.

BUTTENWIESER, M., *The Psalms*, chronologically treated ... Chicago 1938.

BUZY, D., Saint Paul et Saint Matthieu, *Rech. Sci. Rel.* 28 (1938), 473–78.

CADBURY, H. J., *The Style and Literary Method of Luke*. (Harv. Theol. Stud. 6.) Cambridge, Mass., London 1920.

CADOUX, A. T., *The Sources of the Second Gospel*. London 1935.

CAIRD, G. B., Do Computers Count?, *Exp. Times* 76 (1964/65), 176.

CAMBIER, J., Les images de l'Ancien Testament dans l'Apocalypse de S. Jean, *Nouv. Rev. Théol.* 87 (1955), 113–22.

CAMPENHAUSEN, H., FRHR VON, Die Begründung kirchlicher Entscheidungen beim Apostel Paulus, in *Aus der Frühzeit des Christentums*, Tübingen 1963, 30–80.

CARLSON, R. A., *David, the Chosen King*. A Traditio-historical Approach to the Second Book of Samuel. Diss. Uppsala 1964.

CARMIGNAC, J., Les citations de l'Ancien Testament dans "la Guerre des Fils de la Lumière contre les Fils de Ténèbres", *Rev. Bibl.* 63 (1956), 234–60, 375–90.

—— Les citations de l'Ancien Testament, et spécialement des Poèmes du Serviteur, dans les Hymnes de Qumrân, *Rev. Qumr.* 2 (1959/60), 357–94.

—— Un Qumrânien converti au Christianisme: l'auteur des Odes de Salomon, in *Qumran-Probleme* ..., ed. H. Bardtke (Deutsche Akad. d. Wiss. z. Berlin. Sekt. f. Altert.-Wiss. 42), Berlin 1963, 75–108.

CARRINGTON, PH., *The Primitive Christian Catechism*. A Study in the Epistles. Cambridge 1940.

—— *According to Mark*. A Running Commentary on the Oldest Gospel. Cambridge 1960.

CERFAUX, L., La tradition selon saint Paul, in *Receuil L. Cerfaux* II (Biblioth. Ephem. Theol. Lovan. 7), Gembloux 1954, 253–63.

CERFAUX, L., CAMBIER, J., *L'Apocalypse de saint Jean* lue aux chrétiens. (Lectio divina 17.) Paris 1955.

ČERNÝ, L., *The Day of Yahweh* and Some Relevant Problems. (Práce z Vědeckých Ústavů ... 53.) Prague 1948.

CHAMBERLAIN, J. V., Another Qumran Thanksgiving Psalm, *J. Near East. Stud.* 14 (1955), 32–41.

—— Further Elucidation of a Messianic Thanksgiving Psalm from Qumran, *J. Near East. Stud.* 14 (1955), 181–82.

CHARLES, R. H., *A Critical History of the Doctrine of a Future Life* ... (Jowett Lect. 1898–99.) London 1899.

CLARK, K. W., The Gentile Bias in Matthew, *J. Bibl. Lit.* 66 (1947), 165–72.

COHEN, N. G., Josephus and Scripture: Is Josephus' Treatment of the Scriptural Narrative Similar throughout the Antiquities I–XI?, *Jew. Quart. Rev.* 54 (1963/64), 311–32.

COLANI, T., *Jésus Christ et les croyances messianiques de son temps*. 2nd ed. Strasbourg 1864.

COLE, (R.) A., *The New Temple* ... (Tyndale NT Lect. 1950.) London 1950.

—— *The Gospel according to St. Mark*. (Tyndale NT Comm.) London 1961.

CONZELMANN, H., Gegenwart und Zukunft in der synoptischen Tradition, *Zschr. Theol. Ki.* 54 (1957), 277–96.

—— Geschichte und Eschaton nach Mc 13, *Zschr. Nt. Wiss.* 50 (1959), 210–21.

—— *Die Mitte der Zeit*. Studien zur Theologie des Lukas. (Beitr. z. hist. Theol. 17.) 3rd ed. Tübingen 1960.

—— Jesu självmedvetande, *Svensk Exeg. Årsbok* 28–29 (1963–64), 39–53.

COPPENS, J., Les apports du Psaume CX (Vulg. CIX) à l'idéologie royale israélite, *Studies in the History of Religions* 4 (1959), 333–48.

—— Le Fils d'homme daniélique et les relectures de Dan., VII, 13, dans les apocryphes et les écrits du Nouveau Testament, *Ephem. Theol. Lovan.* 37 (1961), 5–42.

COTHENET, E., La IIe Épître aux Thessaloniciens et l'Apocalypse synoptique, *Rech. Sci. Rel.* 42 (1954), 5–39.

CRANFIELD, C. E. B., St. Mark 13, *Scot. J. Theol.* 6 (1953), 189–96, 287–303, 7 (1954), 284–303.

—— *The Gospel according to St. Mark*. (Cambr. Gr. Test. Comm. 2.) Cambridge 1959.

CREED, J. M., *The Gospel according to St. Luke*. London 1930.

CROSS, F. M., *The Ancient Library of Qumrân and Modern Biblical Studies*. London 1958.

CULLMANN, O., Das wahre durch die ausgebliebene Parusie gestellte neutestamentliche Problem, *Theol. Zschr.* 3 (1947), 177–91.

—— Paradosis et Kyrios. Le problème de la tradition dans le paulinisme, *Rev. Hist. Phil. Rel.* 30 (1950), 12–30.

—— Eschatology and Missions in the New Testament, in *The Background of the NT and its Eschatology*, ed. W. D. Davies, D. Daube, in hon. C. H. Dodd, Cambridge 1956, 409–21.

—— *Die Christologie des Neuen Testaments*. 2nd ed. Tübingen 1958.

—— Parusieverzögerung und Urchristentum. Der gegenwärtige Stand der Diskussion, *Theol. Lit.-Zeit.* 83 (1958), 1–12.

—— *Christ and Time*. The Primitive Christian Conception of Time and History. 3rd ed. London 1962.

—— *Heil als Geschichte*. Heilsgeschichtliche Existenz im Neuen Testament. Tübingen 1965.

DAHL, M. E., *The Resurrection of the Body*. A Study of I Corinthians 15. (Stud. in Bibl. Theol. 36.) London 1962.

DAHL, N. A., The Parables of Growth, *Stud. Theol.* 5 (1951), 132–66.

—— Eschatologie und Geschichte im Lichte der Qumrantexte, in *Zeit und Geschichte*: Dankesgabe an R. Bultmann ..., ed. E. Dinkler, Tübingen 1964, 3–18.

DALMAN, G., *Die Worte Jesu* I ... 2nd ed. Leipzig 1930.

DANIÉLOU, J., *Sacramentum futuri*. Études sur les origines de la typologie biblique. (Ét. de Théol. hist.) Paris 1950.

DAUBE, D., the following two articles in *The New Testament and Rabbinic Judaism* (Lond. Univ. School Orient. and Afr. Stud. Jordan Lect. 2), London 1956: The 'I Am' of the Messianic Presence, 325–29; The Abomination of Desolation, 418–37.

—— *The Exodus Pattern in the Bible*. (All Souls Stud. 2.) London 1963.

DAVIES, J. G., The Genesis of Belief in an Imminent Parousia, *J. Theol. Stud. N.S.* 14 (1963), 104–07.

DAVIES, W. D., *Torah in the Messianic Age and/or the Age to Come*. (J. Bibl. Lit. Monogr. Ser. 7.) Philadelphia 1952.

—— *Paul and Rabbinic Judaism*. Some Rabbinic Elements in Pauline Theology. 2nd ed. London 1955.

DEESE, J., *The Psychology of Learning*. (McGraw-Hill Ser. in Psychol.) 2nd ed. New York, Toronto, London 1958.

DEISSMANN, A., *Licht vom Osten*. Das Neue Testament und die neuentdeckten Texte der hellenistisch-römischen Welt. 4th ed. Tübingen 1923.

DELACROIX, H., L'invention et le génie, in G. Dumas, *Nouveau traité de Psychologie* VI, Paris 1939, 447–544.

DELCOR, M., Contribution à l'étude de la législation des sectaires de Damas et de Qumrân IV. Le Meḥoqeq du document de Damas et Taxo dans l' "Assomption de Moïse" IX, *Rev. Bibl.* 62 (1955), 60–66.

DELLING, G., χολοβόω, *Theol. Wörterb.*, ed. G. Kittel, III (1938), 823.

DENNISTON, J. D., *The Greek Particles*. 2nd ed. Oxford 1954.

DHANIS, E., De Filio hominis in Vetere Testamento et in Iudaïsmo, *Gregor.* 45 (1964), 1–59.

DIBELIUS, M., Die alttestamentlichen Motive in der Leidensgeschichte des Petrus- und des Johannes-Evangeliums, in *Abhandlungen ... W. W. von Baudissin ... überreicht* (Zschr. At. Wiss., Beih. 33), Giessen 1918, 125–50.

—— *Geschichte der urchristlichen Literatur* I–II. (Samml. Göschen 934 f.) Berlin, Leipzig 1926.

—— *An die Thessalonicher I, II. An die Philipper*. (Handb. z. NT 11.) 3rd ed. Tübingen 1937.

—— *The Sermon on the Mount*. New York 1940.

—— *Die Formgeschichte des Evangeliums*. Dritte, durchges. Aufl. mit einem Nachtrag von G. Iber, ed. G. Bornkamm. Tübingen 1959.

DIEHL, E., *Inscriptiones latinae Christianae veteres* I. Berlin 1961.

DINKLER, E., Jesu Wort vom Kreuztragen, in *Neutestamentliche Studien f. R. Bultmann*, ed. W. Eltester (Zschr. Nt. Wiss., Beih. 21), Berlin 1954, 110–29.

DIX, G. H., The Enochic Pentateuch, *J. Theol. Stud.* 27 (1926), 29–42.

DOBSCHÜTZ, E. VON, *Die Thessalonicher-Briefe*. (Krit.-exeg. Komm. ü. d. NT 10, 7th ed.) Göttingen 1909.

—— Matthäus als Rabbi und Katechet, *Zschr. Nt. Wiss.* 27 (1928), 338–48.

DODD, C. H., *The Apostolic Preaching and its Developments*. London 1936/1944.

—— *The Parables of the Kingdom*. 2nd ed. London 1936.

—— *History and the Gospel*. London 1938.

—— The Fall of Jerusalem and the 'Abomination of Desolation', *J. Rom. Stud.* 37 (1947), 47–54.

—— *According to the Scriptures*. The Substructure of New Testament Theology. London 1952.

—— Matthew and Paul, in *New Testament Studies*, Manchester 1953, 53–66.

—— *The Interpretation of the Fourth Gospel*. Cambridge 1953.

—— The Primitive Catechism and the Sayings of Jesus, in *New Testament Essays*. Studies in mem. T. W. Manson, ed. A. J. B. Higgins, Manchester 1959, 106–18.

DOEVE, J. W., *Jewish Hermeneutics in the Synoptic Gospels and Acts*. Diss. Leiden. Assen 1953.

—— Parousieverzögerung, *Nederl. Theol. Tijdschr.* 17 (1962/63), 32–38.

DUPONT, J., Σὺν Χριστῷ. *L'Union avec le Christ suivant saint Paul.* I: "Avec le Christ" dans la vie future. Bruges, Louvain, Paris 1952.

—— L'utilisation apologétique de l'Ancien Testament dans les discours des Actes, *Ephem. Theol. Lovan.* 29 (1953), 289–327.

—— *Les Béatitudes.* Le problème littéraire. Les deux versions du Sermon sur la montagne et les Béatitudes. 2nd ed. Bruges, Louvain 1958.

—— Le logion des douze trônes (Mt 19, 28; Lc 22, 28–30), *Bibl.* 45 (1964), 355–92.

DUPONT-SOMMER, A., *Aperçus préliminaires sur les manuscrits de la Mer Morte.* (L'Orient ancien illustré 4.) Paris 1950.

—— *Les écrits esséniens découverts près de la mer Morte.* (Biblioth. hist.) Paris 1959.

DÜRR, L., *Die Stellung des Propheten Ezechiel in der israelitisch-jüdischen Apokalyptik* ... (Alttest. Abhandl. IX: 1.) Münster i. W. 1923.

EBBINGHAUS, H., *Grundzüge der Psychologie* I–II. 4th ed. Leipzig 1919.

EBELING, G., Der Grund christlicher Theologie. Zum Aufsatz Ernst Käsemanns über „Die Anfänge christlicher Theologie", *Zschr. Theol. Ki.* 58 (1961), 227–44.

ECKART, K. G., Der zweite echte Brief des Apostels Paulus an die Thessalonicher, *Zschr. Theol. Ki.* 58 (1961), 30–44.

EDGAR, S. L., Respect for Context in Quotations from the Old Testament, *NT Stud.* 9 (1962/63), 55–62.

EDSMAN, C.-M., Eschatologie I, *Rel. in Gesch. u. Geg.* II (3rd ed. 1958), 650–55.

EDWARDS, G., The Exodus and Apocalyptic, in *A Stubborn Faith*, Papers ... in hon. W. A. Irwin, ed. E. C. Hobbs, Dallas 1956, 27–38.

EICHRODT, W., *Theologie des Alten Testaments* I. 5th ed. Stuttgart, Göttingen 1957.

EISSFELDT, O., *Einleitung in das Alte Testament.* (Neue Theol. Grundrisse.) 3rd ed. Tübingen 1964.

ELLIGER, K., *Studien zum Habakuk-Kommentar vom Toten Meer.* (Beitr. z. hist. Theol. 15.) Tübingen 1953.

ELLIS, E. E., *Paul's Use of the Old Testament.* Edinburgh, London 1957.

—— Jesus, the Sadducees and Qumran, *NT Stud.* 10 (1963/64), 274–79.

ELMGREN, H., *Philon av Alexandria.* Med särskild hänsyn till hans eskatologiska föreställningar. Diss. Lund. Stockholm 1939.

ENGNELL, I., *Gamla Testamentet*. En traditionshistorisk inledning I. Stockholm 1945.

—— [a review of] E. Sjöberg, Der Menschensohn im äthiopischen Henochbuch, 1946, *Biblioth. Orient.* 8 (1951), 187–92.

—— The following articles in I. Engnell (ed.) *Svenskt Bibl. Uppslagsverk* I–II, 2nd ed., Stockholm 1962–63: Dom, I, 426–28; Historieskrivning, I, 970 f.; Jesajas bok, I, 1143–47; Messias, II, 77–92; Motståndare, II, 169–71; Människosonen, II, 229–32; Profeter, profetism, II, 562–603; Psaltaren, II, 618–57; Traditionshistorisk metod, II, 1254–61; Yttersta dagen, II, 1449–52.

ENZ, J. J., The Book of Exodus as a Literary Type for the Gospel of John, *J. Bibl. Lit.*, 76 (1957), 208–15.

EPPEL, R., *Le piétisme juif dans les Testaments des Douze Patriarches*. (Ét. Hist. Phil. Rel. 22.) Diss. Strasbourg 1930.

FARRER, A., *A Study in St Mark*. London 1951.

—— An Examination of Mark xiii.10, *J. Theol. Stud. N.S.* 7 (1956), 75–79.

—— *The Revelation of St. John the Divine*. Commentary on the English Text. Oxford 1964.

FASCHER, E., *Die formgeschichtliche Methode*. Eine Darstellung und Kritik. Zugleich ein Beitrag zur Geschichte des synoptischen Problems. (Zschr. Nt. Wiss., Beih. 2.) Giessen 1924.

—— Antike Geschichtsschreibung als Beitrag zum Verständnis der Geschichte, *Theol. Lit.-Zeit.* 77 (1952), 641–52.

—— Jesus der Lehrer. Ein Beitrag zur Frage nach dem „Quellort der Kirchenidee", *Theol. Lit.-Zeit.* 79 (1954), 325–42.

FAW, C. E., On the Writing of First Thessalonians, *J. Bibl. Lit.* 71 (1952), 217–25.

FELDMAN, L., *Scholarship on Philo and Josephus (1937–1962)*. (Stud. in Judaica [1].) New York [1963].

FENTON, J. C., Paul and Mark, in *Studies in the Gospels* … in mem. R. H. Lightfoot, ed. D. E. Nineham, Oxford 1955, 89–112.

FEUILLET, A., Le discours de Jésus sur la ruine du temple d'après Marc XIII et Luc XXI, 5–36, *Rev. Bibl.* 55 (1948), 481–502, 56 (1949), 61–92.

—— La synthèse eschatologique de saint Matthieu (XXIV–XXV), *Rev. Bibl.* 56 (1949), 340–64, 57 (1950), 62–91, 180–211.

—— Le Fils de l'homme de Daniel et la tradition biblique, *Rev. Bibl.* 60 (1953), 170–202, 321–46.

—— La demeure céleste et la destinée des chrétiens. Exegèse de II Cor., V, 1–10 et contribution à l'étude des fondements de l'eschatologie paulinienne, *Rech. Sci. Rel.* 44 (1956), 161–92, 360–402.

—— Le sens du mot Parousie dans l'Evangile de Matthieu. Comparaison entre Matth. xxiv et Jac. v, 1–11, in *The Background of the New Testament and its Eschatology*, ed. W. D. Davies, D. Daube in hon. C. H. Dodd, Cambridge 1956, 261–80.

—— Parousie, *Dict. de la Bible, Suppl.* VI (1960), 1331–1419.

—— *L'Apocalypse*. État de la question. (Studia neotest. subsidia 3.) Paris, Bruges 1963.

FILSON, F. V., The Christian Teacher in the First Century, *J. Bibl. Lit.* 60 (1941), 317–28.

—— *A Commentary on the Gospel according to St. Matthew*. (Black's NT Comm.) London 1960.

FITZMYER, J. A., The Use of Explicit Old Testament Quotations in Qumran Literature and in the New Testament, *NT Stud.* 7 (1960/61), 297–333.

FLUSSER, D., Two Notes on the Midrash on 2 Sam. VII. I. The Temple 'Not Made with Hands' in the Qumran Doctrine, *Isr. Explor. J.* 9 (1959), 99–104.

FOERSTER, W., σῴζω κτλ., *Theol. Wörterb.*, ed. G. Kittel, VII (1964), 966–1024.

FOHRER, G., Die Struktur der alttestamentlichen Eschatologie, *Theol. Lit.-Zeit.* 85 (1960), 401–20.

FRAME, J. E., *A Critical and Exegetical Commentary on the Epistles of St. Paul to the Thessalonians*. (Int. Crit. Comm.) Edinburgh 1912.

FREY, J.-B., Apocalyptique, *Dict. de la Bible, Suppl.* I (1928), 326–54.

FRIDRICHSEN, A., Jesu kamp mot de urene ånder, *Svensk Teol. Kvartalskrift* 5 (1929), 299–314.

—— Non laudo. Note sur I. Cor. 11,17, 22, *Horae Soederbl.* 1 (1944), 28–32.

—— Antikrist, *Oikodomé* 1 (1949), 43–57.

FROST, S. B., *Old Testament Apocalyptic*. Its Origin and Growth. London 1952.

FUCHS, E., Über die Aufgabe einer christlichen Theologie. Zum Aufsatz Ernst Käsemanns über „Die Anfänge christlicher Theologie", *Zschr. Theol. Ki.* 58 (1961), 245–67.

GAECHTER, P., *Maria im Erdenleben*. Neutestamentliche Marienstudien. Innsbruck 1953.

—— *Das Matthäusevangelium*. Innsbruck, Wien, München 1964.

GÄRTNER, B., The Habakkuk Commentary (DSH) and the Gospel of Matthew, *Stud. Theol.* 8 (1954), 1–24.

—— Bakgrunden till Qumranförsamlingens krig, *Rel. o. Bibel* 19 (1960), 35–72.

—— *The Temple and the Community in Qumran and the New Testament*. A Comparative Study in the Temple Symbolism of the Qumran Texts and the New Testament. (Soc. NT Stud. Monogr. Ser. 1.) Cambridge 1965.

GASTER, M., *Samaritan Eschatology*. (The Samaritan Oral Law and Ancient Trad. 1.) Leicester 1932.

GASTER, TH. H., *The Scriptures of the Dead Sea Sect*. London 1957.

GASTON, L., Sondergut und Markusstoff in Luk. 21, *Theol. Zschr.* 16 (1960), 161–72.

GERHARDSSON, B., *The Good Samaritan—the Good Shepherd?* (Coniect. neotest. 16.) Lund, Copenhagen 1958.

—— *Memory and Manuscript*. Oral Tradition and Written Transmission in Rabbinic Judaism and Early Christianity. Diss. Uppsala. (Acta Sem. Neotest. Upsal. 22.) Uppsala, Lund, Copenhagen 1961.

—— Die Boten Gottes und die Apostel Christi, *Svensk Exeg. Årsbok* 27 (1962), 89–131.

—— *Tradition and Transmission in Early Christianity*. (Coniect. neotest. 20.) Lund, Copenhagen 1964.

GERLEMAN, G., Hesekielsbokens Gog, *Svensk Exeg. Årsbok* 12 (1947), 148–62.

GERTNER, M., Midrashim in the New Testament, *J. Sem. Stud.* 7 (1962), 267–92.

GESE, H., Geschichtliches Denken im Alten Orient und im Alten Testament, *Zschr. Theol. Ki.* 55 (1958), 127–45.

GESENIUS, W., see BUHL, F.

GHISELIN, B., (ed.) *The Creative Process.* A Symposium. Berkeley, Los Angeles 1952.

GILS, F., *Jésus prophète d'après les évangiles synoptiques.* (Orient. et bibl. Lovan. 2.) Diss. Louvain 1957.

GINSBERG, H. L., The Oldest Interpretation of the Suffering Servant, *Vet. Test.* 3 (1953), 400–04.

GLASSON, T. F., *The Second Advent.* The Origin of the New Testament Doctrine. 2nd ed. London 1947.

—— *His Appearing and His Kingdom.* The Christian Hope in the Light of its History. London 1953.

—— Mark xiii. and the Greek Old Testament, *Exp. Times* 69 (1957/58), 213–15.

—— *Greek Influence in Jewish Eschatology.* With Special Reference to the Apocalypses and Pseudepigraphs. London 1961.

—— The Ensign of the Son of Man (Matt. xxiv. 30), *J. Theol. Stud. N.S.* 15 (1964), 299–300.

GLATZER, N. N., *Untersuchungen zur Geschichtslehre der Tannaiten.* Ein Beitrag zur Religionsgeschichte. Berlin 1933.

GLOVER, R., The Didache's Quotations and the Synoptic Gospels, *NT Stud.* 5 (1958/59), 12–29.

GNILKA, J., „Parusieverzögerung" und Naherwartung in den synoptischen Evangelien und in der Apostelgeschichte, *Cath.* 13 (1959), 277–90.

GOGUEL, M., Luke and Mark: with a Discussion of Streeter's Theory, *Harv. Theol. Rev.* 26 (1933), 1–55.

GOULD, E. P., *A Critical and Exegetical Commentary on the Gospel according to St. Mark.* (Int. Crit. Comm.) Edinburgh 1896.

GOULDER, M. D., SANDERSON, M. L., St. Luke's Genesis, *J. Theol. Stud. N. S.* 8 (1957), 12–30.

GRANT, F. C., *The Gospels: their Origin and their Growth.* New York 1957.

GRÄSSER, E., *Das Problem der Parusieverzögerung in den synoptischen Evangelien und in der Apostelgeschichte.* (Zschr. Nt. Wiss., Beih. 22.) Berlin 1957.

GRAY, G. B., *Sacrifice in the Old Testament.* Its Theory and Practice. Oxford 1925.

GRELOT, P., L'eschatologie des Esséniens et le livre d'Hénoch, *Rev. Qumr.* 1 (1958/59), 113–31.

—— La géographie mythique d'Hénoch et ses sources orientales, *Rev. Bibl.* 65 (1958), 33–69.

—— La légende d'Hénoch dans les apocryphes et dans la Bible. Origine et signification, *Rech. Sci. Rel.* 46 (1958), 5–26, 181–210.

GRESSMANN, H., *Der Ursprung der israelitisch-jüdischen Eschatologie.* (Forsch. z. Rel. u. Lit. d. A u. NT 6.) Göttingen 1905.

—— *Der Messias.* (Forsch. z. Rel. u. Lit. d. A u. NT 43.) Göttingen 1929.

GRUBER, H. E., TERRELL, G., WERTHEIMER, M., *Contemporary Approaches to Creative Thinking.* A Symposion held at the University of Colorado. New York 1962.

267

GRUNDMANN, W., *Das Evangelium nach Markus*. (Theol. Handkomm. z. NT 2.) 2nd ed. Berlin 1959.

—— *Das Evangelium nach Lukas*. (Theol. Handkomm. z. NT 3.) 2nd ed. Berlin 1961.

—— Überlieferung und Eigenaussage im eschatologischen Denken des Apostels Paulus, *NT Stud.* 8 (1961/62), 12–26.

GRY, L., Essai sur la plus ancienne teneur et la fortune du Catalogue de Signes de la Fin (IV Esdras, V 1–14, VI 18–29, VII 26–38[15]), *Rev. Sci. Phil. Théol.* 29 (1940), 264–77.

—— La « mort du Messie » en IV Esdras, VII, 29 [III, V, 4], in *Mémorial Lagrange*, ed. L.-H. Vincent, Paris 1940, 133–39.

GUILLET, J., « Cette génération infidèle et dévoyée », *Rech. Sci. Rel.* 35 (1948), 275–281.

GUNKEL, H., *Schöpfung und Chaos in Urzeit und Endzeit*. Eine religionsgeschichtliche Untersuchung über Gen. 1 und Ap. Joh. 12. Göttingen 1895.

—— Die Oden Salomos, in *Reden und Aufsätze*, Göttingen 1913, 163–92.

GUNTERMANN, F., *Die Eschatologie des hl. Paulus*. (Neutest. Abhandl. 13: 4–5.) Münster i. W. 1932.

HADORN, W., *Die Offenbarung des Johannes*. (Theol. Handkomm. z. NT 18.) Leipzig 1928.

HAEKEL, J., Mythos und Mythologie II, *Rel. in Gesch. u. Geg.* IV (3rd ed. 1960), 1268–74.

HAENCHEN, E., *Die Apostelgeschichte*. (Krit.-exeg. Komm. ü. d. NT 3, 12th ed.) Göttingen 1959.

HAHN, I., Josephus und die Eschatologie von Qumrān, in *Qumran-Probleme* ..., ed. H. Bardtke (Deutsche Akad. d. Wiss. z. Berlin. Sekt. f. Altert.- Wiss. 42), Berlin 1963, 167–91.

HAIDUK, A., „Ego eimi" bei Jesus und seine Messianität, *Communio Viat.* 6 (1963), 55–60.

HALKIN, L.-E., *Éléments de critique historique*. Liège 1960.

HAMILTON, N. Q., The Last Things in the Last Decade. The Significance of Recent Study in the Field of Eschatology, *Interpr.* 14 (1960), 131–42.

[HAMMILL, L. R., *Biblical Interpretation in the Apocrypha and Pseudepigrapha*. Diss. Chicago 1951. In typescript.]

HANSON, R. P. C., *Tradition in the Early Church*. (Libr. of Hist. and Doctr.) London 1962.

HARDER, G., Das eschatologische Geschichtsbild der sogenannten kleinen Apokalypse Markus 13, *Theol. Viat.* 4 (1952), 71–107.

HARRIS, J. R., A Study in Letter-Writing, *Expositor Ser. 5* 8 (1898), 161–80.

HARTMAN, L., *Testimonium linguae*. Participial Constructions in the Synoptic Gospels; A Linguistic Examination of Luke 21,13. (Coniect. neotest. 19.) Lund, Copenhagen 1963.

HAWKINS, J. C., *Horae Synopticae*. Contributions to the Study of the Synoptic Problem. 2nd ed. Oxford 1909.

HEATON, E. W., *The Book of Daniel*. (Torch Bible Comm.) London 1956.

HEIDEL, W. A., *The Day of Yahweh*. A Study of Sacred Days and Ritual Forms in the Ancient Near East. New York, London 1929.

HEITMÜLLER, W., Zum Problem Paulus und Jesus, *Zschr. Nt. Wiss.* 13 (1912), 320–37. (Also in *Das Paulusbild in der neueren deutschen Forschung*, ed. K. H. Rengstorf (Wege der Forsch. 24), Darmstadt 1964, 124–43.)

HEMPEL, J., Bund II, *Rel. in Gesch. u. Geg.* I (3rd ed. 1957), 1513–16.

—— Königtum Gottes im Alten Testament, *Rel. in Gesch. u. Geg.* III (3rd ed. 1959), 1706–09.

HENGEL, M., *Die Zeloten.* (Arb. z. Gesch. d. Spätjud. und Urchrist. 1.) Leiden, Köln 1961.

HERFORD, R. T., *Talmud and Apocrypha.* A Comparative Study of the Jewish Ethical Teaching in the Rabbinical and Non-Rabbinical Sources in the Early Centuries. London 1933.

HERMANN, I., *Begegnung mit der Bibel.* Eine Einübung. Düsseldorf 1962.

HERNTRICH, V., κρίνω κτλ. B., *Theol. Wörterb.*, ed. G. Kittel, III (1938), 922–33.

HERR, M. D., The Problem of War on the Sabbath in the Second Temple and the Talmudic Periods (Hebrew), *Tarbiz* 30 (1960/61), 242–56, 341–56. (Eng. summary, p. vii–ix.)

HERRMANN, J., *Ezechiel*, übersetzt und erklärt. (Komm. z. AT 11.) Leipzig, Erlangen 1924.

HERRMANN, S., *Die prophetischen Heilserwartungen im Alten Testament.* Ursprung und Gestaltwandel. (Beitr. z. Wiss. v. A u. NT V: 5.) Stuttgart 1965.

HERTZBERG, H. W., Die Nachgeschichte alttestamentlicher Texte innerhalb des Alten Testaments, in *Werden und Wesen des Alten Testaments ...*, ed. P. Volz, etc. (Zschr. At. Wiss., Beih. 66), Berlin 1936, 110–21.

HIGGINS, A. J. B., The Sign of the Son of Man (Matt. xxiv. 30), *NT Stud.* 9 (1962/63), 380–82.

HINSON, G., Hodayoth III, 6–18; in what Sense Messianic?, *Rev. Qumr.* 2 (1959/60), 183–204.

HIRSCH, E., *Frühgeschichte des Evangeliums* I–II. Tübingen 1941.

HOENIG, S. B., *The Great Sanhedrin.* A Study of the origin, development, composition and functions of the *Bet Din ha-Gadol* during the Second Jewish Commonwealth. Philadelphia, New York 1953.

HØFFDING, H., *Psykologi i Omrids paa Grundlag af Erfaring.* 6th ed. Copenhagen, Kristiania (Oslo) 1911.

HOH, J., Der christliche γραμματεύς (Mt. 13, 52), *Bibl. Zschr.* 17 (1925/26), 256–69.

HOHMEIER, F., *Das Schriftverständnis in der Theologie Rudolf Bultmanns.* (Arb. z. Gesch. u. Theol. d. Luthert. 13.) Berlin, Hamburg 1964.

HOLLADAY, W. L., Prototype and Copies: a New Approach to the Poetry–Prose Problem in the Book of Jeremiah, *J. Bibl. Lit.* 79 (1960), 351–67.

HOLMSTRÖM, F., *Das eschatologische Denken der Gegenwart.* Drei Etappen der theologischen Entwicklung des zwanzigsten Jahrhunderts. Gütersloh 1936.

HÖLSCHER, G., *Die Ursprünge der jüdischen Eschatologie.* (Vorträge d. theol. Konf. z. Giessen 41.) Giessen 1925.

—— Problèmes de la littérature apocalyptique juive, *Rev. Hist. Phil. Rel.* 9 (1929), 101–14.

—— Der Ursprung der Apokalypse Mrk 13, *Theol. Blätter* 12 (1933), 193–202.

269

—— *Geschichtsschreibung in Israel.* Untersuchungen zu Jahvisten und Elohisten. (Skrifter, Kungl. Humanist. Vetenskapssamfundet, Lund, 50.) Lund 1952.

[HOLTZ, T., *Untersuchungen über die alttestamentlichen Zitate bei Lukas.* Habil.-schr. Halle 1964.] Summary in *Theol. Lit.-Zeit.* 90 (1965), 863–64.

HOOKE, S. H., The Myth and Ritual Pattern in Jewish and Christian Apocalyptic, in *The Labyrinth* ..., ed. S. H. Hooke, London, New York 1935, 211–33.

HOSKYNS, E., DAVEY, N., *The Riddle of the New Testament.* Rev. ed. London 1936.

HYATT, J. PH., The Peril from the North in Jeremiah, *J. Bibl. Lit.* 59 (1940), 499–513.

IBER, G., Zur Formgeschichte der Evangelien, *Theol. Rundschau N.F.* 24 (1957–58), 283–338.

JANSEN, H. L., *Die spätjüdische Psalmendichtung*, ihr Entstehungskreis und ihr „Sitz im Leben". Eine literaturgeschichtlich-soziologische Untersuchung. (Skrifter, D. Norske Vidensk.-Akad., Oslo, II. Hist.-Filos. Kl. 1937: 3.) Oslo 1937.

JANSSEN, E., *Juda in der Exilszeit.* Ein Beitrag zur Frage der Entstehung des Judentums. (Forsch. z. Rel. u. Lit. d. A u. NT 69.) Göttingen 1956.

JANZON, P., Nikolaiterna i Nya Testamentet och i fornkyrkan, *Svensk Exeg. Årsbok* 21 (1956), 82–108.

JASTROW, J., Automatic Writing, *Dict. of Philosophy and Psychol.*, ed. J. M. Baldwin, I (1928), 94–95.

JASTROW, M., *A Dictionary of the Targumim, the Talmud Babli and Yerushalmi, and the Midrashic Literature* I–II. New York, Berlin, London 1926.

JAUBERT, A., *La notion d'alliance dans le Judaïsme aux abords de l'ère chrétienne.* Diss. Paris 1963.

JEFFERY, A., The Book of Daniel, in *The Interpreter's Bible* VI, New York, Nashville 1956, 341–549.

JELSKI-COLDIN, I., *Die innere Einrichtung des grossen Synedrions zu Jerusalem* ... Diss. Leipzig. Breslau [1893].

JENNI, E., Das Wort ʿōlām im Alten Testament, *Zschr. At. Wiss.* 64 (1952), 197–248, 65 (1953), 1–35.

JEREMIAS, JOACH., Erlöser und Erlösung im Spätjudentum und Urchristentum, *Deutsche Theol.* 2 (1929), 106–19.

—— Zum Problem der Deutung von Jes. 53 im palästinischen Spätjudentum, in *Aux Sources de la tradition chrétienne*: Mélanges ... M. Goguel, ed. O. Cullmann, P. Menoud, Neuchâtel, Paris 1950, 113–19.

—— Kennzeichen der ipsissima vox Jesu, in *Synoptische Studien ... A. Wikenhauser dargebracht*, ed. J. Schmid, A. Vögtle, München 1953, 86–93.

—— παῖς θεοῦ, *Theol. Wörterb.*, ed. G. Kittel, V (1954), 653–713.

—— Perikopen-Umstellungen bei Lukas?, *NT Stud.* 4 (1957/58), 115–19.

—— *Jesus' Promise to the Nations.* (Stud. in Bibl. Theol. 24.) London 1958.

—— πολλοί, *Theol. Wörterb.*, ed. G. Kittel, VI (1959), 536–45.

—— *Die Gleichnisse Jesu.* 6th ed. Göttingen 1962.

—— *Unbekannte Jesusworte.* 3rd ed. Gütersloh 1963.

JEREMIAS, JÖRG, *Theophanie.* Die Geschichte einer alttestamentlichen Gattung. (Wiss. Monogr. z. A u. NT 10.) Neukirchen–Vluyn 1965.

JOHANSSON, N., *Parakletoi.* Vorstellungen von Fürsprechern für die Menschen vor Gott in der alttestamentlichen Religion, im Spätjudentum und Urchristentum. Diss. Lund 1940.

—— *Det urkristna nattvardsfirandet.* Dess religionshistoriska bakgrund, dess ursprung och innebörd. Lund 1944.

JOHNSON, A. R., *Sacral Kingship in Ancient Israel.* Cardiff 1955.

JONGE, M. DE, *The Testaments of the Twelve Patriarchs.* A Study of their Text, Composition and Origin. Diss. Leiden. Assen 1953.

—— The Testaments of the Twelve Patriarchs and the New Testament, in *Studia Evangelica*, ed. K. Aland etc. (Texte u. Unters. 73), Berlin 1959, 546–56.

—— Christian Influence in the Testaments of the Twelve Patriarchs, *Nov. Test.* 4 (1960), 182–235.

—— Once More: Christian Influence in the Testaments of the Twelve Patriarchs, *Nov. Test.* 5 (1962), 311–19.

JUNG, L., *Fallen Angels in Jewish, Christian and Mohammedan Literature.* Diss. London. Philadelphia 1926.

JUNKER, H., *Untersuchungen über literarische und exegetische Probleme des Buches Daniel.* Bonn 1932.

KADUSHIN, M., *The Rabbinic Mind.* New York 1952.

KAHLE, P. E., *The Cairo Genizah.* 2nd ed. Oxford 1959.

KAMINKA, A., Beiträge zur Erklärung der Ezra-Apokalypse und zur Rekonstruktion ihres hebräischen Urtextes, *Monatsschr. f. Gesch. u. Wiss. d. Judent.* 76 (1932), 121–38, 206–12, 494–511, 604–07, 77 (1933), 339–55.

KAPELRUD, A. S., *Joel Studies.* (Diss.) (Uppsala Univ. Årsskrift 1948: 4.) Uppsala, Leipzig 1948.

—— Die aktuellen und die eschatologischen Behörden der Qumrangemeinde, in *Qumran-Probleme ...*, ed. H. Bardtke (Deutsche Akad. d. Wiss. z. Berlin. Sekt. f. Altert.-Wiss. 42), Berlin 1963, 259–68.

KAPLAN, C., The Pharisaic Character and the Date of the Book of Enoch, *Angl. Theol. Rev.* 12 (1929–30), 531–37.

KÄSEMANN, E., Das Problem des historischen Jesus, *Zschr. Theol. Ki.* 51 (1954), 125–53.

—— Sätze heiligen Rechtes im Neuen Testament, *NT Stud.* 1 (1954/55), 248–60.

—— Die Anfänge christlicher Theologie, *Zschr. Theol. Ki.* 57 (1960), 162–85.

—— Zum Thema der urchristlichen Apokalyptik, *Zschr. Theol. Ki.* 59 (1962), 257–84.

KAUFMANN, J., Apokalyptik, *Enc. Jud.* II (1928), 1142–61.

KELLER, C. A., *Das Wort OTH als „Offenbarungszeichen Gottes".* Eine philologisch-theologische Begriffsuntersuchung zum Alten Testament. Diss. Basel 1946.

KEULERS, J., *Die eschatologische Lehre des vierten Esrabuches*. (Bibl. Stud. 20: 2–3.) Freiburg i. Br. 1922.

KEYSSNER, K., *Gottesvorstellung und Lebensauffassung im griechischen Hymnus*. (Würzb. Stud. z. Altertumswiss. 2.) Stuttgart 1932.

KILPATRICK, G. D., *The Origins of the Gospel according to St. Matthew*. 2nd. ed. Oxford 1950.

—— The Gentile Mission in Mark and Mark 13, 9–11, in *Studies in the Gospels* ... in mem. R. H. Lightfoot, ed. D. E. Nineham, Oxford 1955, 145–58.

—— Mark xiii. 9–10, *J. Theol. Stud. N.S.* 9 (1958), 81–86.

KISSANE, E. J., *The Book of Isaiah* I–II. Dublin 1941–43.

KLAUSNER, J., *The Messianic Idea in Israel*. From Its Beginning to the Completion of the Mishnah. New York 1955.

KLOSTERMANN, E., *Das Matthäusevangelium*. (Handb. z. NT 4.) 2nd ed. Tübingen 1927.

—— *Das Lukasevangelium*. (Handb. z. NT 5.) 2nd ed. Tübingen 1929.

—— *Das Markusevangelium*. (Handb. z. NT 3.) 4th ed. Tübingen 1950.

KNABENBAUER, J., *Commentarius in evangelium secundum Matthaeum* I–II. (Cursus Script. Sacr. III: 1: 1–2.) 3rd ed. Paris 1922.

KNOCH, O., Die eschatologische Frage, ihre Entwicklung und ihr gegenwärtiger Stand. Versuch einer knappen Übersicht, *Bibl. Zschr. N.F.* 6 (1962), 112–20.

KNOX, T. M., The Computer and the New Testament, *Svensk Exeg. Årsbok* 28–29 (1963–64), 111–16.

KNOX, W. L., *The Sources of the Synoptic Gospels* I–II, ed. H. Chadwick. Cambridge 1953–57.

KOCH, K., *Was ist Formgeschichte?* Neue Wege der Bibelexegese. Neukirchen–Vluyn 1964.

KOEP, L., Buch IV (himmlisch), *Reallex. f. Ant. u. Christ.* II (1954), 725–31.

KOHLER, K., The Essenes and the Apocalyptic Literature, *Jew. Quart. Rev.* 11 (1920), 145–68.

KÖHLER, W., *Psychologische Probleme*. Berlin 1933.

KON, I. S., *Die Geschichtsphilosophie des 20. Jahrhunderts*. Kritischer Abriss II. Berlin 1964.

KÖSTER, H., *Synoptische Überlieferung bei den apostolischen Vätern*. (Texte u. Unters. 65.) Berlin 1957.

KRAUS, H.-J., *Psalmen* I–II. (Bibl. Komm. z. AT 15.) 2nd ed. Neukirchen Kr. Moers 1961.

KUHN, G., Beiträge zur Erklärung des Buches Henoch, *Zschr. At. Wiss.* 39 (1921), 240–75.

KUHN, K. G., Βαλαάμ, *Theol. Wörterb.*, ed. G. Kittel, I (1933), 521–23.

—— *Die älteste Textgestalt der Psalmen Salomos* ... (Beitr. z. Wiss. d. A u. NT IV: 21.) Stuttgart 1937.

—— Die in Palästina gefundenen hebräischen Texte und das Neue Testament, *Zschr. Theol. Ki.* 47 (1950), 192–211.

—— Die beiden Messias Aarons und Israels, *NT Stud.* 1 (1954/55), 168–79.

KÜHNER, R., GERTH, B., *Ausführliche Grammatik der griechischen Sprache* II: 1–2 Satzlehre. 3rd ed. Hannover, Leipzig 1898–1904.

KÜMMEL, W. G., *Promise and Fulfilment*. The Eschatological Message of Jesus. (Stud. in Bibl. Theol. 23.) London 1957.

—— Futurische und präsentische Eschatologie im ältesten Urchristentum, *NT Stud.* 5 (1958/59), 113–26.

—— Das literarische und geschichtliche Problem des ersten Thessalonicherbriefes, in *Neotestamentica et Patristica*, Freundesgabe ... O. Cullmann, ed. W. C. van Unnik (Suppl. Nov. Test. 6), Leiden 1962, 213–27.

—— Jesus und Paulus, *NT Stud.* 10 (1963/64), 163–81.

KÜPPERS, W., *Das Messiasbild der spätjüdischen Apokalyptik.* Diss. Bern 1933.

LADD, G. E., The Kingdom of God in the Jewish Apocryphal Literature, *Biblioth. Sacra* 109 (1952), 55–62, 164–74, 318–31, 110 (1953), 32–49.

—— Why Not Prophetic-Apocalyptic?, *J. Bibl. Lit.* 76 (1957), 192–200.

LAGRANGE, M.-J., *Évangile selon saint Luc.* (Ét. bibl.) 3rd ed. Paris 1927.

—— *Évangile selon saint Matthieu.* (Ét. bibl.) 3rd ed. Paris 1927.

—— *Évangile selon saint Marc.* (Ét. bibl.) 4th ed. Paris 1929.

—— *Le Judaïsme avant Jésus-Christ.* (Ét. bibl.) Paris 1931.

LAMARCHE, P., *Zacharie IX–XIV.* Structure littéraire et messianisme. (Ét. bibl.) Paris 1961.

[LAMBRECHT, J., *Die Redaktion der synoptischen Apokalypse.* Literarische Analyse und Strukturuntersuchung (Mk 13; Lk 21). Diss. Rom 1965.] In typescript.

—— Redactio Sermonis Eschatologici, *Verb. Dom.* 43 (1965), 278–87.

LAMPE, G. W. H., The Holy Spirit in the Writings of St. Luke, in *Studies in the Gospels* ... in mem. R. H. Lightfoot, ed. D. E. Nineham, Oxford 1955, 159–200.

LARSSON, E., Qumranlitteraturen och De tolv patriarkernas testamenten, *Svensk Exeg. Årsbok* 25 (1960), 109–18.

—— *Christus als Vorbild.* Eine Untersuchung zu den paulinischen Tauf- und Eikontexten. Diss. Uppsala. (Acta Sem. Neotest. Upsal. 23.) Uppsala, Lund, Copenhagen 1962.

—— Paulus och den hellenistiska församlingsteologin. Ett blad i den vetenskapliga dogmbildningens historia, *Svensk Exeg. Årsbok* 28–29 (1963–64), 81–110.

LASOR, W. S., The Messianic Idea in Qumran, in *Studies and Essays in honor of A. A. Neuman*, ed. M. Ben-Horin, B. D. Weinryb, S. Zeitlin, Leiden 1962, 343–64.

LAUHA, A., *Zaphon.* Der Norden und die Nordvölker im Alten Testament. (Annal. Acad. Sci. Fenn. B 49, 2.) Helsinki 1943.

LAURENTIN, R., Traces d'allusions étymologiques en Luc 1–2, *Bibl.* 37 (1956), 435–56, 38 (1957), 1–23.

LAUTERBACH, J. Z., Talmud Hermeneutics, *Jew. Enc.* XII (1906), 30–33.

—— Midrash and Mishna. A Study in the Early History of the Halakah, in *Rabbinic Essays*, Cincinnati 1951, 163–256.

LEANEY, A. R. C., *A Commentary on the Gospel according to St. Luke.* (Black's NT Comm.) London 1958.

LIDDELL, H. G., SCOTT, R., *A Greek-English Lexicon* I–II. Rev. ed. by H. S. Jones. Oxford 1925–40.

LIEBERMAN, S., *Hellenism in Jewish Palestine* ... (Texts and Stud. of the Jew. Theol. Sem. of Am. 18.) New York 1950.

LIECHTENHAN, R., *Die urchristliche Mission.* Voraussetzungen, Motive und Methoden. (Abhandl. z. Theol. d. A u. NT 9.) Zürich 1946.

LIETZMANN, H., *An die Korinther I. II.* (Handb. z. NT 9.) 4th ed. by W. G. Kümmel. Tübingen 1949.

LIGHTFOOT, R. H., *The Gospel Message of St. Mark.* Oxford 1950.

LINDARS, B., Books of Testimonies, *Exp. Times* 75 (1963/64), 173–75.

LINDBLOM, J., *Die Jesaia-Apokalypse, Jes. 24–27.* (Lunds Univ. Årsskrift N.F. I: 34: 3.) Lund, Leipzig 1938.

—— *Prophecy in Ancient Israel.* Oxford 1962.

LINDESKOG, G., Logia-Studien, *Stud. Theol.* 4 (1950), 128–89.

LINDROTH, HJ., *Tankar om kyrkan och sakramenten.* Stockholm 1948.

LINTON, O., *Pauli mindre brev.* (Tolkning av NT 9.) Stockholm 1964.

LODS, A., La chute des anges. Origine et portée de cette spéculation, *Rev. Hist. Phil. Rel.* 7 (1927), 301–15.

LOHMEYER, E., *Das Evangelium des Markus.* (Krit.-exeg. Komm. ü. d. NT 1: 2, 12th ed.) Göttingen 1953.

—— *Die Offenbarung des Johannes.* (Handb. z. NT 16.) 2nd ed. Tübingen 1953.

LOHR, C. H., Oral Techniques in the Gospel of Matthew, *Cath. Bibl. Quart.* 23 (1961), 403–35.

LOHSE, B., *Das Passafest der Quartadecimaner.* (Beitr. z. Förd. christl. Theol. II: 54.) Göttingen 1953.

LOHSE, E., Jesu Worte über den Sabbat, in *Judentum, Urchristentum, Kirche.* Festschrift für Joach. Jeremias, ed. W. Eltester (Zschr. Nt. Wiss., Beih. 26), Berlin 1960, 79–89.

—— Die alttestamentliche Sprache des Sehers Johannes, *Zschr. Nt. Wiss.* 52 (1961), 122–26.

LOISY, A., *Les évangiles synoptiques* I–II. Ceffonds 1907–08.

—— *L'Évangile selon Marc.* Paris 1912.

—— *L'Évangile selon Luc.* Paris 1924.

—— *Les origines du Nouveau Testament.* Paris 1936.

LÖVESTAM, E., *Son and Saviour.* A Study of Acts 13,32–37. With an Appendix: 'Son of God' in the Synoptic Gospels. (Coniect. neotest. 18.) Lund, Copenhagen 1961.

—— *Spiritual Wakefulness in the New Testament.* (Lunds Univ. Årsskrift N.F. I:55:3.) Lund 1963.

—— En problematisk eskatologisk utsaga: Mark. 13:30 par., *Svensk Exeg. Årsbok* 28–29 (1963–64), 64–80.

Löw, I., Zum Feigengleichnis, *Zschr. Nt. Wiss.* 11 (1910), 167–68.

LUND, N. W., *Chiasmus in the New Testament.* Diss. Chicago 1941. Chapel Hill, N.C. 1942.

LUNDSTRÖM, G., *The Kingdom of God in the Teaching of Jesus.* A History of Interpretation from the Last Decades of the Nineteenth Century to the Present Day. Edinburgh, London 1963.

MAAG, V., Der Antichrist als Symbol des Bösen, in *Das Böse* (Stud. aus d. C. G. Jung-Inst. Zürich, 13), Zürich, Stuttgart 1961, 63–89.

—— Beʾlijaʿal im Alten Testament, *Theol. Zschr.* 21 (1965), 287–99.

MAASS, F., Von den Ursprüngen der rabbinischen Schriftauslegung, *Zschr. Theol. Ki.* 52 (1955), 129–61.

McArthur, H. H., Computer Criticism, *Exp. Times* 76 (1964/65), 367–70.

McCown, C. C., Hebrew and Egyptian Apocalyptic Literature, *Harv. Theol. Rev.* 18 (1925), 357–411.

—— Symbolic Interpretation, *J. Bibl. Lit.* 63 (1944), 329–38.

McLoughlin, S., *The Synoptic Theory of Xavier Léon-Dufour.* An Analysis and Evaluation. Diss. Louvain 1965. In typescript.

McNeile, A. H., Τότε in St Matthew, *J. Theol. Stud.* 12 (1910/11), 127–28.

—— *The Gospel according to St. Matthew.* London 1915.

—— *An Introduction to the Study of the New Testament.* 2nd ed. rev. by C. S. G. Williams. Oxford 1953.

Macquarrie, J., *An Existentialist Theology.* A Comparison of Heidegger and Bultmann. London 1955.

Mach, R., *Der Zaddik in Talmud und Midrasch.* Diss. Basel. Leiden 1957.

Manson, T. W., *The Teaching of Jesus.* Studies in its Form and Content. Cambridge 1931.

—— Miscellanea apocalyptica, *J. Theol. Stud.* 46 (1945), 41–45.

—— *The Sayings of Jesus* as Recorded in the Gospels according to St. Matthew and St. Luke ... London 1949/1950.

—— Some Reflections on Apocalyptic, in *Aux Sources de le tradition chrétienne*: Mélanges ... M. Goguel, ed. O. Cullmann, P. Menoud (Biblioth. théol.), Neuchâtel, Paris 1950, 139–45.

—— The Son of Man in Daniel, Enoch and the Gospels, *Bull. J. Ryl. Libr.* 32 (1949/50), 171–93.

—— The Old Testament in the Teaching of Jesus, *Bull. J. Ryl. Libr.* 34 (1951/52), 312–32.

—— The Letters to the Thessalonians, in *Studies in the Gospels and Epistles,* Manchester 1962, 259–78.

Manson, W., *Jesus the Messiah.* The Synoptic Tradition of the Revelation of God in Christ with Special Reference to Form-Criticism. London 1943/1952.

—— The ΕΓΩ ΕΙΜΙ of the Messianic Presence in the New Testament, *J. Theol. Stud.* 48 (1947), 137–45.

—— Eschatology in the New Testament, *Scot. J. Theol., Occ. Pap.* 2 [1953], 1–16.

Marmorstein, A., *The Old Rabbinic Doctrine of God* I. (Jews' Coll. Publ. 10.) London 1927.

—— Agada, *Enc. Jud.* I (1928), 951–79.

Marshall, J. T., Did St. Paul Use a Semitic Gospel?, *Expositor Ser. 4* 2 (1890), 69–80.

Marxsen, W., *Der Evangelist Markus.* Studien zur Redaktionsgeschichte des Evangeliums. (Forsch. z. Rel. u. Lit. d. A u. NT 67.) Göttingen 1956.

Massaux, É., *Influence de l'Évangile de saint Matthieu sur la littérature chrétienne avant saint Irénée.* (Univ. Cath. Lovan. Diss. ad grad. mag. Facult. Theol. II: 42.) Louvain, Gembloux 1950.

Masson, C., *Les deux épîtres de saint Paul aux Thessaloniciens.* (Comm. du NT 11a.) Neuchâtel, Paris 1957.

Mayer, R., *Die biblische Vorstellung vom Weltenbrand.* Eine Untersuchung über die Beziehungen zwischen Parsismus und Judentum. (Bonn. Orient. Stud. N.S. 4.) Bonn 1956.

MEAD, R. T., A Dissenting Opinion about Respect for Context in Old Testament Quotations, *NT Stud.* 10 (1963/64), 279–89.

MEINERTZ, M., Die Tragweite des Gleichnisses von den zehn Jungfrauen, in *Synoptische Studien* ... *A. Wikenhauser dargebracht*, ed. J. Schmid, A. Vögtle, München 1953, 94–106.

—— „Dieses Geschlecht" im Neuen Testament, *Bibl. Zschr. N.F.* 1 (1957), 283–89.

—— Zum Ursprung der Heidenmission, *Bibl.* 40 (1959), 762–77.

MESSEL, N., *Die Einheitlichkeit der jüdischen Eschatologie.* (Zschr. Nt. Wiss., Beih. 30.) Giessen 1915.

—— *Der Menschensohn in den Bilderreden des Henoch.* (Zschr. Nt. Wiss., Beih. 35.) Giessen 1922.

METZGER, B. M., *The Text of the New Testament.* Its Transmission, Corruption, and Restoration. Oxford 1964.

MEYER, R., Abraham-Apokalypse, *Rel. in Gesch. u. Geg.* I (3rd ed. 1957), 72.

MICHAELIS, W., *Täufer, Jesus, Urgemeinde.* Die Predigt vom Reiche Gottes vor und nach Pfingsten. (Neutest. Forsch. II: 3.) Gütersloh 1928.

—— *Der Herr verzieht nicht die Verheissung.* Die Aussagen Jesu über die Nähe des jüngsten Tages. Bern 1942.

—— λέων, *Theol. Wörterb.*, ed. G. Kittel, IV (1942), 256–59.

—— Kennen die Synoptiker eine Verzögerung der Parusie?, in *Synoptische Studien* ... *A. Wikenhauser dargebracht*, ed. J. Schmid, A. Vögtle, München 1954, 107–23.

—— *Die Gleichnisse Jesu.* Eine Einführung. (Die urchristl. Botschaft 32.) 3rd ed. Hamburg 1956.

MILIK, J. T., [a communication in] Le travail d'édition des fragments manuscrits de Qumrân, *Rev. Bibl.* 63 (1956), 60–62.

—— *Ten Years of Discovery in the Wilderness of Judaea.* (Stud. in Bibl. Theol. 26.) London 1959.

MILLIGAN, G., *St Paul's Epistles to the Thessalonians.* London 1908.

MÓCSY, E., De gratiarum actione in epistolis paulinis, *Verb. Dom.* 21 (1941), 193–201, 225–32.

MOE, P. O., *Paulus und die evangelische Geschichte.* Zugleich ein Beitrag zur Vorgeschichte der Evangelien. Leipzig 1912.

MONTGOMERY, J. A., *A Critical and Exegetical Commentary on The Book of Daniel.* (Int. Crit. Comm.) Edinburgh 1927.

MOORE, G. F., *Judaism in the First Centuries of the Christian Era, the Age of the Tannaim* I–II. Cambridge, Mass. 1927.

MORTON, A. Q., McLEMAN, J., *Christianity and the Computer.* London 1964.

MOSLEY, A. W., Jesus' Audiences in the Gospels of St Mark and St Luke, *NT Stud.* 10 (1963/64), 139–49.

MOULTON, J. H., MILLIGAN, G., *The Vocabulary of the Greek Testament* I–VIII. London, New York, Toronto 1914–29.

MOWINCKEL, S., *Psalmenstudien* I–VI. Kristiania (Oslo) 1921–24.

—— Opphavet til den senjødiske forestilling om Menneskesønnen, *Norsk Teol. Tidsskrift* 45 (1944), 189–244.

—— Urmensch und „Königsideologie", *Stud. Theol.* 2 (1948), 71–89.

—— The Hebrew Equivalent of Taxo in Ass. Mos. IX, *Suppl. Vet. Test.* 1 (1953), 88–96.

—— *He That Cometh.* Oxford 1956.

—— The Psalms in Israel's Worship I–II. Oxford 1962.

MULDER, E. S., Die Teologie van die Jesaja-Apocalipse (Jesaja 24–27). Diss. Groningen 1954.

MUNCK, J., Discours d'adieu dans le Nouveau Testament et dans la littérature biblique, in Aux Sources de la tradition chrétienne: Mélanges ... M. Goguel, ed. O. Cullmann, P. Menoud (Biblioth. théol.), Neuchâtel, Paris 1950, 155–70.

—— I Thess. i. 9–10 and the Missionary Preaching of Paul. Textual Exegesis and Hermeneutic Reflections, NT Stud. 9 (1962/63), 95–110.

MUNDLE, W., Das religiöse Problem des IV. Esrabuches, Zschr. At. Wiss. 47 (1929), 222–49.

MUSSNER, F., Der Jakobusbrief. (Herders Theol. Handkomm. z. NT 13: 1.) Freiburg, Basel, Wien 1964.

NESTLE, E., Der Greuel der Verwüstung, Zschr. At. Wiss. 4 (1884), 248.

NOACK, B., Satanás und Soteria. Untersuchungen zur neutestamentlichen Dämonologie. Diss. Aarhus. Copenhagen 1948.

NORTH, C. R., The Old Testament Interpretation of History. London 1946.

NOTH, M., Überlieferungsgeschichtliche Studien I. (Schr. d. Königsb. Gel. Ges., Geisteswiss. Kl. 18: 2.) Halle (Saale) 1943.

—— Das Geschichtsverständnis der alttestamentlichen Apokalyptik, in Gesammelte Studien (Theol. Bücherei 6), München 1957, 248–73.

—— „Die Heiligen des Höchsten", in Gesammelte Studien (Theol. Bücherei 6), München 1957, 274–90.

NÖTSCHER, F., Zur theologischen Terminologie der Qumran-Texte. (Bonner Bibl. Beitr. 10.) Bonn 1956.

—— Himmlische Bücher und Schicksalsglaube in Qumran, Rev. Qumr. 1 (1958/59), 405–11.

NYGREN, A., Commentary on Romans. London 1952.

ODEBERG, H., 3 Henoch or the Hebrew Book of Henoch. Cambridge 1928.

—— Fragen von Metatron, Schekina und Memra, in Kungl. Humanist. Vetenskapssamf. i Lund, Årsberättelse 1941/42, Lund 1942, 31–46.

—— Pauli brev till korintierna. (Tolkning av NT 7.) 2nd ed. Stockholm 1953.

OEPKE, A., ἀνίστημι κτλ., Theol. Wörterb., ed. G. Kittel, I (1933), 368–72.

—— ἐγείρω κτλ., Theol. Wörterb., ed. G. Kittel, II (1935), 332–37.

—— Die Briefe an die Thessalonicher, in Die kleineren Briefe des Apostels Paulus (Das NT Deutsch 8), 6th ed., Göttingen 1953, 127–58.

OESTERLEY, W. O. E., Le Sabbat. Textes de la Mishnah relatifs au repos du Sabbat avec commentaires. (Biblioth. hist.) Paris 1935.

—— The Apocalyptic Literature: a Seer among His People, in The Age of Transition (Judaism and Christianity I), ed. W. O. E. Oesterley, London, New York 1937, 83–101.

OLRIK, A., Om Ragnarok I–II. Copenhagen 1902–14.

ORCHARD, J. B., Thessalonians and the Synoptic Gospels, Bibl. 19 (1938), 19–42.

—— St Paul and the Book of Daniel, Bibl. 20 (1939), 172–79.

ORLINSKY, H. M., Qumran and the Present State of Old Testament Text Studies: The Septuagint Text, J. Bibl. Lit. 78 (1959), 26–33.

Östborn, G., *Yahweh's Words and Deeds*. A Preliminary Study into the Old
Testament Presentation of History. (Uppsala Univ. Årsskrift 1951: 7.)
Uppsala, Wiesbaden 1951.

Otto, R., *Reich Gottes und Menschensohn*. Ein religionsgeschichtlicher
Versuch. München 1934.

Otzen, B., *Studien über Deuterosacharja*. (Acta Theol. Danica VI.) Copenhagen 1964.

Owen, H. P., The Parousia of Christ in the Synoptic Gospels, *Scot. J. Theol.*
12 (1959), 171–92.

Pape, W., *Griechisch-Deutsches Handwörterbuch* I–II. Dritte Aufl. bearb.
von M. Sengebusch. 2nd ed. Braunschweig 1888.

Passow, F., *Handwörterbuch der griechischen Sprache* I: 1–II: 2. Neubearb.
... von V. C. F. Rost, F. Palm, etc. Leipzig 1841–57.

Patrick, C., *Creative Thought in Poets*. Diss. Columbia. New York 1935.

—— Creative Thought in Artists, *J. Psychol.* 4 (1937), 35–73.

—— *What is Creative Thinking?* New York 1955.

Pedersen, J., *Der Eid bei den Semiten* ... (Stud. z. Gesch. u. Kult. d. islam.
Orient 3.) Strasbourg 1914.

—— Zur Erklärung der eschatologischen Visionen Henochs, *Islamica*
2 (1926), 416–29.

—— *Israel*. Its Life and Culture I–IV. London, Copenhagen 1926–40.

Perrin, N., *The Kingdom of God in the Teaching of Jesus*. (NT Libr.) London
1963.

Peterson, E., Die Einholung des Kyrios, *Zschr. System. Theol.* 7 (1929/30),
682–702.

Pfeiffer, R. H., *History of New Testament Times*. With an Introduction to
the Apocrypha. New York 1949.

Philonenko, M., *Les interpolations chrétiennes des Testaments des Douze
Patriarches et les manuscrits de Qoumrân*. (Cah. Rev. Hist. Phil. Rel.
35.) Paris 1960.

Ploeg, J. van der, La guerre sainte dans la « Règle de la guerre » de Qumran,
in *Mélanges Bibliques ... in hon. A. Robert* (Trav. Inst. Cath. Paris 4),
Paris 1957, 326–33.

Plöger, O., Geschichte und Geschichtsauffassung, *Rel. in Gesch. u. Geg.* II
(3rd ed. 1958), 1473–76.

—— *Theokratie und Eschatologie*. (Wiss. Monogr. z. A u. NT 2.) Neukirchen
Kr. Moers 1959.

—— *Das Buch Daniel*. (Komm. z. AT 18.) Gütersloh 1965.

Plummer, A., *A Critical and Exegetical Commentary on the Gospel according
to S. Luke*. (Int. Crit. Comm.) 4th ed. Edinburgh 1901.

Porteous, N. M., *Das Danielbuch*. (Das AT Deutsch 23.) Göttingen 1962.

Porter, F. C., *The Messages of the Apocalyptic Writers*. (The Messages of the
Bible.) London 1916.

Preisigke, F., *Wörterbuch der griechischen Papyrusurkunden* I–II, ed.
E. Kiessling. Berlin 1925–27.

Rad, G. von, Theologische Geschichtsschreibung im Alten Testament, *Theol.
Zschr.* 4 (1948), 161–74.

—— The Origin of the Concept of the Day of Yahweh, *J. Sem. Stud.* 4
(1959), 97–108.

Rehkopf, F., *Die lukanische Sonderquelle*. Ihr Umfang und Sprachgebrauch. (Wiss. Unters. z. NT 5.) Tübingen 1959.

Reicke, B., Den primära israelsmissionen och hednamissionen enligt synoptikerna, *Svensk Teol. Kvartalskrift* 26 (1950), 77–100.

Rengstorf, K. H., ἀποστέλλω κτλ., *Theol. Wörterb.*, ed. G. Kittel, I (1933), 397–448.

—— *Das Evangelium nach Lukas*. (Das NT Deutsch 3.) 9th ed. Göttingen 1962.

—— Old and New Testament Traces of a Formula of the Judaean Royal Ritual, *Nov. Test.* 5 (1962), 229–44.

Resch, A., *Der Paulinismus und die Logia Jesu* in ihrem gegenseitigen Verhältnis untersucht. (Texte u. Unters. N.F. 12.) Leipzig 1904.

Rese, M., Überprüfung einiger Thesen von Joachim Jeremias zum Thema des Gottesknechtes im Judentum, *Zschr. Theol. Ki.* 60 (1963), 21–41.

Richter, G., *Textstudien zum Buche Hiob*. (Beitr. z. Wiss. v. A u. NT. III: 7.) Stuttgart 1927.

Richter, J., Die „konsequente Eschatologie" im Feuer der Kritik, *Zschr. Rel. u. Geistesgesch.* 12 (1960), 147–66.

Riddle, D. W., Die Verfolgungslogien in formgeschichtlicher und soziologischer Beleuchtung, *Zschr. Nt. Wiss.* 33 (1934), 271–89.

Riesenfeld, H., *Jésus transfiguré*. L'arrière-plan du récit évangélique de la transfiguration de Notre-Seigneur. Diss. Uppsala. (Acta Sem. Neotest. Upsal. 16.) Lund, Copenhagen 1947.

—— The Gospel Tradition and its Beginnings, in *Studia Evangelica*, ed. K. Aland etc. (Texte u. Unters. 73), Berlin 1959, 43–65.

—— Das Bildwort vom Weizenkorn bei Paulus. (Zu I Cor 15), in *Studien zum Neuen Testament … E. Klostermann … dargebracht*, ed. G. Delling (Texte u. Unters. 77), Berlin 1961, 43–55.

Rigaux, B., *L'Antéchrist* et l'Opposition au Royaume Messianique dans l'Ancien et le Nouveau Testament. (Univ. Cath. Lovan. Diss. ad grad. mag. Facult. Theol. II: 24.) Gembloux, Paris 1932.

—— *Saint Paul. Les épîtres aux Thessaloniciens*. (Ét. bibl.) Paris, Gembloux 1956.

—— Βδέλυγμα τῆς ἐρημώσεως Mc 13,14; Mt 24,15, *Bibl.* 40 (1959), 675–83.

—— Vocabulaire chrétien antérieur à la première épître aux Thessaloniciens, in *Sacra Pagina* II (Biblioth. Ephem. Theol. Lovan. 13), Paris Gembloux 1959, 380–89.

—— *Saint Paul et ses lettres*. État de la question. (Studia Neotest. Subsidia 2.) Paris, Bruges 1962.

Ringgren, H., *The Messiah in the Old Testament*. (Stud. in Bibl. Theol. 18.) London 1956.

—— Apokalyptik I, II, *Rel. in Gesch. u. Geg.* I (3rd ed. 1957), 463–66.

—— *Tro och liv enligt Döda-havsrullarna*. Stockholm 1961.

Roberts, B. J., The Dead Sea Scrolls and the Old Testament Scriptures, *Bull. J. Ryl. Libr.* 36 (1953/54), 75–96.

Robinson, D. W. B., II Thess. 2, 6: "That which restrains" or "That which holds sway"?, *Studia evangelica* 2 (Texte u. Unters. 87), Berlin 1964, 635–38.

Robinson, J. A. T., The 'Parable' of the Sheep and the Goats, *NT Stud.* 2 (1955/56), 225–37.

—— *Jesus and his Coming.* The Emergence of a Doctrine. London 1957.

ROBINSON, J. M., *Das Geschichtsverständnis des Markus-Evangeliums.* (Abhandl. z. Theol. d. A u. NT 30.) Zürich 1956.

ROBINSON, TH. H., *The Gospel of Matthew.* (The Moffat NT Comm.) London 1928.

ROLOFF, J., *Apostolat–Verkündigung–Kirche.* Ursprung, Inhalt und Funktion des kirchlichen Apostelamtes nach Paulus, Lukas und den Pastoralbriefen. Gütersloh 1965.

ROSENZWEIG, A., Die Al-tikri-Deutungen. Ein Beitrag zur talmudischen Schriftdeutung, in *Festschrift z. I. Lewy* ..., ed. M. Brann, J. Elbogen, Breslau 1911, 204–53.

RÖSSLER, D., *Gesetz und Geschichte.* Untersuchungen zur Theologie der jüdischen Apokalyptik und der pharisäischen Orthodoxie. (Wiss. Monogr. z. A u. NT 3.) Neukirchen Kr. Moers 1960.

ROWLEY, H. H., The Figure of "Taxo" in The Assumption of Moses, *J. Bibl. Lit.* 64 (1945), 141–43.

—— The Prophet Jeremiah and the Book of Deuteronomy, in *Studies in Old Testament Prophecy*, presented to ... Th. H. Robinson, ed. H. H. Rowley, Edinburgh 1950, 157–74.

—— *The Relevance of Apocalyptic.* A Study of Jewish and Christian Apocalypses from Daniel to the Revelation. 3rd ed. London 1963.

RUSSELL, D. S., *The Method and Message of Jewish Apocalyptic 200 BC–AD 100.* (The OT Libr.) London 1964.

RUST, E. C., *The Christian Understanding of History.* (Lutterworth Libr. 30.) London, Redhill 1947.

SAHLIN, H., Das Exodus-Schema als Kompositions-Prinzip, in *Zur Typologie des Johannesevangeliums* (Uppsala Univ. Årsskrift 1950: 4), Uppsala, Leipzig 1950, 74–78.

SCHILLE, G., Bemerkungen zur Formgeschichte des Evangeliums, Rahmen und Aufbau des Markus-Evangeliums, *NT Stud.* 4 (1957/58), 1–24.

SCHLATTER, A., *Das Alte Testament in der johanneischen Apokalypse.* (Beitr. z. Förd. christl. Theol. 16: 6.) Gütersloh 1912.

—— *Der Evangelist Matthäus.* Seine Sprache, sein Ziel, seine Selbständigkeit. Stuttgart 1929.

—— *Das Evangelium des Lukas aus seinen Quellen erklärt.* Stuttgart 1931.

—— *Markus, der Evangelist für die Griechen.* Stuttgart 1935.

SCHLIER, H., the following articles in *Die Zeit der Kirche*, 3rd ed. Freiburg, Basel, Wien 1962: Die Entscheidung für die Heidenmission in der Urchristenheit, 90–107; Die Verkündigung im Gottesdienst der Kirche, 244–64; Zum Verständnis der Geschichte nach der Offenbarung Johannis, 265–74.

SCHMAUS, M., *Katholische Dogmatik* IV: 2: Von den letzten Dingen. 3rd & 4th ed. München 1953.

SCHMID, J., *Das Evangelium nach Lukas.* (Regensb. NT 3.) 3rd ed. Regensburg 1955.

—— *Das Evangelium nach Matthäus.* (Regensb. NT 1.) 3rd ed. Regensburg 1956.

—— *Das Evangelium nach Markus.* (Regensb. NT 2.) 4th ed. Regensburg 1958.

SCHMIDT, K. L., *Der Rahmen der Geschichte Jesu.* Literarkritische Untersuchungen zur ältesten Jesusüberlieferung. Berlin 1919.

SCHMITHALS, W., Paulus und der historische Jesus, *Zschr. Nt. Wiss.* 53 (1962), 145–60.

SCHNACKENBURG, R., *Die Johannesbriefe.* (Herders Theol. Handkomm. z. NT 13: 3.) Freiburg 1953.

—— *Gottes Herrschaft und Reich.* Eine biblisch-theologische Studie. Freiburg 1959.

SCHNEIDER, C., *Die Erlebnisechtheit der Apokalypse des Johannes.* Leipzig 1930.

SCHNIEWIND, J., *Das Evangelium nach Matthäus.* (Das NT Deutsch 2.) 5th ed. Göttingen 1950.

SCHNÜBBE, O., *Der Existenzbegriff in der Theologie Rudolf Bultmanns.* Ein Beitrag zur Interpretation der theologischen Systematik Bultmanns. (Forsch. z. Syst. Theol. u. Rel.-philos. 4.) Göttingen 1959.

SCHOEPS, H.-J., *Paulus.* Die Theologie des Apostels im Lichte der jüdischen Religionsgeschichte. Tübingen 1959.

SCHOLEM, G. G., *Jewish Gnosticism, Merkabah Mysticism, and Talmud Tradition.* (Jew. Theol. Sem. of Am. 7.) New York 1960.

SCHOONHEIM, P. L., *Een semasiologisch Onderzoek van Parousia* met Betrekking tot het Gebruik in Mattheüs 24. Diss. Utrecht. Aalten 1953.

SCHUBERT, K., Die Entwicklung der eschatologischen Naherwartung im Frühjudentum, in *Vom Messias zu Christus* ..., ed. K. Schubert, Wien, Freiburg, Basel 1964, 1–54.

SCHUBERT, P., *Form and Function of the Pauline Thanksgivings.* (Zschr. Nt. Wiss., Beih. 20.) Giessen 1939.

SCHÜRER, E., *Geschichte des jüdischen Volkes im Zeitalter Jesu Christi* I–III. (3rd &) 4th ed. Leipzig 1901–09. (II: 2nd ed. 1886.)

SCHÜRMANN, H., Die Dubletten im Lukasevangelium. Ein Beitrag zur Verdeutlichung des lukanischen Redaktionsverfahrens, *Zschr. Kath. Theol.* 75 (1953), 338–45.

—— Die Dublettenvermeidungen im Lukasevangelium. Ein Beitrag zur Verdeutlichung des lukanischen Redaktionsverfahrens, *Zschr. Kath. Theol.* 76 (1954), 83–93.

—— Protolukanische Spracheigentümlichkeiten? Zu Fr. Rehkopf, Die lukanische Sonderquelle ..., *Bibl. Zschr. N.F.* 5 (1961), 266–86.

SCHWEITZER, A., *Geschichte der Leben-Jesu-Forschung.* 2nd ed. Tübingen 1913.

SCHWYZER, E., *Griechische Grammatik* auf der Grundlage von Karl Brugmanns griechischer Grammatik I–III. (Handb. d. Altert.-wiss. II:1:1–3.) München 1939–53.

SCOTT, R. B. Y., 'Behold, He cometh with Clouds', *NT Stud.* 5 (1958/59), 127–32.

SEELIGMANN, I. L., *Phasen uit de Geschiedenis van het Joodsch Historische Bewustzijn* ..., Mededeel. en Verhandel. van het vooraz.-egypt. Gezelsch. "Ex Oriente Lux", Leiden, 7 (1947), 49–73.

—— *The Septuagint Version of Isaiah.* A Discussion of its Problems. (Mededeel. en Verhandel. van het vooraz.-egypt. Genootschap "Ex Oriente Lux", Leiden, 9 (1948).)

—— Voraussetzungen der Midraschexegese, *Suppl. Vet. Test.* 1 (1953), 150–81.

Selwyn, E. G., *The First Epistle of St. Peter.* 2nd ed. London, New York 1947/1955.

Simon, M., *Verus Israel.* Étude sur les relations entre chrétiens et juifs dans l'empire romain (135–425). (Biblioth. des écoles franç. d'Athènes et de Rome 166.) Paris 1948.

—— Retour du Christ et reconstruction du Temple dans la pensée chrétienne primitive, in *Aux Sources de la tradition chrétienne*: Mélanges ... M. Goguel, ed. O. Cullmann, P. Menoud (Biblioth. théol.), Neuchâtel, Paris 1950, 247–57.

Simonsen, D., Ein Midrasch im IV. Buch Esra, in *Festschrift z. I. Lewy* ..., ed. M. Brann, J. Elbogen, Breslau 1911, 270–78.

Sint, J. A., Parusie-Erwartung und Parusie-Verzögerung im paulinischen Briefcorpus, *Zschr. Kath. Theol.* 86 (1964), 47–79.

Sirard, L., La parousie de l'Antéchrist, 2 Thess. 2, 3–9, in *Analecta Bibl.* 18 (Stud. Paul. Congr. Int. Cath. 1961, 2), Roma 1963, 89–100.

Sjöberg, E., *Gott und die Sünder im palästinischen Judentum* nach dem Zeugnis der Tannaiten und der apokryphisch-pseudepigraphischen Literatur. Diss. Lund. (Beitr. z. Wiss. v. A u. NT, IV: 27.) Stuttgart 1938.

—— Känna 1 Henok och 4 Esra tanken på den lidande Människosonen?, *Svensk Exeg. Årsbok* 5 (1940), 163–83.

—— *Der Menschensohn im äthiopischen Henochbuch.* (Skrifter, Kungl. Humanist. Vetenskapssamf., Lund, 41.) Lund 1946.

—— *Der verborgene Menschensohn in den Evangelien.* (Skrifter, Kungl. Humanist. Vetenskapssamf., Lund, 53.) Lund 1955.

Skehan, P. W., Qumran and the Present State of Old Testament Text Studies: The Masoretic Text, *J. Bibl. Lit.* 78 (1959), 21–25.

Sløk, J., Mythos und Mythologie I, *Rel. in Gesch. u. Geg.* IV (3rd ed. 1960), 1263–68.

Smalley, S. S., The Delay of the Parousia, *J. Bibl. Lit.* 83 (1964), 41–54.

Smith, C. W. F., The Mixed State of the Church in Matthew's Gospel, *J. Bibl. Lit.* 82 (1963), 149–68.

Smith, M., What is Implied by the Variety of Messianic Figures?, *J. Bibl. Lit.* 78 (1959), 66–72.

Sowers, S. G., *The Hermeneutics of Philo and Hebrews.* A Comparison of the Interpretation of the Old Testament in Philo Judaeus and the Epistle to the Hebrews. (Basel Stud. of Theol. 1.) Zürich 1965.

Sparks, H. F. D., The Semitisms of St. Luke's Gospel, *J. Theol. Stud.* 44 (1943), 129–38.

Spender, S., The Making of a Poem, in B. Ghiselin (ed.), *The Creative Process*, Berkeley, Los Angeles 1952, 113–26.

Staab, K., *Die Thessalonicherbriefe*, in Regensburger NT 7, 3rd ed., Regensburg 1959, 7–63.

Staerk, W., *Soter.* Die biblische Erlösererwartung als religionsgeschichtliches Problem. Eine biblisch-theologische Untersuchung. (Beitr. z. Förd. christl. Theol. II: 31.) Gütersloh 1933.

—— *Die Erlösererwartung in den östlichen Religionen.* Untersuchungen zu den Ausdrucksformen der biblischen Christologie. (Soter II.) Stuttgart, Berlin 1938.

Stanley, D. M., Pauline Allusions to the Sayings of Jesus, *Cath. Bibl. Quart.* 23 (1961), 26–39.

STARFELT, E., *Studier i rabbinsk och nytestamentlig skrifttolkning*. Diss. Lund. (Studia Theol. Lund. 17.) Lund 1959.

STAUFFER, E., Das theologische Weltbild der Apokalyptik, *Zschr. System. Theol.* 8 (1930/31), 203–15.

—— *New Testament Theology*. London 1955.

—— *Jesus, Gestalt und Geschichte*. (Dalp Taschenb. 332.) Bern 1957.

STEFANIAK, L., Messianische oder eschatologische Erwartungen in der Qumransekte?, in *Neutestamentliche Aufsätze*: Festschrift für J. Schmid ..., ed. J. Blinzler, O. Kuss, F. Mussner, Regensburg 1963, 294–302.

STEINMANN, A., *Die Briefe an die Thessalonicher und Galater*. (Die hl. Schrift d. NT 23.) Bonn 1918.

STENDAHL, K., *The School of St. Matthew and its Use of the Old Testament*. Diss. Uppsala. (Acta Sem. Neotest. Upsal. 20.) Uppsala, Lund, Copenhagen 1954.

STEPHANUS, H., *Thesaurus Graecae Linguae* I–VIII. Paris 1831–65.

STEUERNAGEL, C., Die Strukturlinien der Entwicklung der jüdischen Eschatologie, in *Festschrift A. Bertholet* ..., ed. W. Baumgartner, O. Eissfeldt, K. Elliger, L. Rost, Tübingen 1950, 477–87.

STOMMEL, E., Σημεῖον ἐκπετάσεως (Didache 16,6), *Röm. Quartalschr.* 48 (1953), 21–42.

[STONE, M., *Features of the Eschatology of IV Ezra*. Diss. Harvard (1965?).] Summary in *Harv. Theol. Rev.* 58 (1965), 463.

STRACK, H., *Introduction to the Talmud and Midrash*. New York, Philadelphia 1959.

STRACK, H. L., BILLERBECK, P., *Kommentar zum Neuen Testament aus Talmud und Midrasch* I–IV (VI). München 1922–28 (1959).

STRATHMANN, H., μάρτυς κτλ., *Theol. Wörterb.*, ed. G. Kittel, IV (1942), 477–520.

STRECKER, G., *Der Weg der Gerechtigkeit*. Untersuchung zur Theologie des Matthäus. (Forsch. z. Rel. u. Lit. d. A u. NT 82.) Göttingen 1962.

STREETER, B. H., St. Mark's Knowledge and Use of Q, in *Studies in the Synoptic Problem* ..., ed. W. Sanday, Oxford 1911, 165–83.

—— *The Four Gospels*. A Study of Origins. London 1924/1926.

STROBEL, A., Die Passa-Erwartung als urchristliches Problem in Lc 17,20 f., *Zschr. Nt. Wiss.* 49 (1958), 164–96.

—— *Untersuchungen zum eschatologischen Verzögerungsproblem* auf Grund der spätjüdisch-urchristlichen Geschichte von Habakuk 2, 2 ff. (Suppl. Nov. Test. 2.) Leiden, Köln 1961.

—— *Die apokalyptische Sendung Jesu*. Gedanken zur Neuorientierung in der kerygmatischen Frage. Rothenburg ob der Tauber 1962.

STRÖM, Å. V., *Der Hirt des Hermas. Allegorie oder Wirklichkeit*. (Arb. u. Mitteil. aus d. neutest. Sem. z. Uppsala 3.) Uppsala 1936.

SUHL, A., *Die Funktion der alttestamentlichen Zitate und Anspielungen im Markusevangelium*. Gütersloh 1965.

SUNDKLER, B., Jésus et les païens, *Rev. Hist. Phil. Rel.* 16 (1936), 462–99.

SUNDWALL, J., *Die Zusammensetzung des Markusevangeliums*. (Acta Acad. Aboens. Human. 9: 2.) Åbo 1934.

SUTCLIFFE, E. F., *The Monks of Qumran as depicted in the Dead Sea Scrolls*. London 1960.

SWETE, H. B., *The Parables of the Kingdom*. A Course of Lectures. London 1921.

TAYLOR, R. O. P., *The Groundwork of the Gospels* with some collected papers. Oxford 1946.

TAYLOR, V., *Behind the Third Gospel*. A Study of the Proto-Luke Hypothesis. Oxford 1926.

—— The Apocalyptic Discourse of Mark xiii, *Exp. Times* 60 (1948/49), 94–98.

—— *The Gospel according to St. Mark*. London 1952.

—— The Proto-Luke Hypothesis, *Exp. Times* 67 (1955/56), 12–16.

TESTUZ, M., *Les idées religieuses du Livre des Jubilés*. Genève, Paris 1960.

THEODOR, J., Midrash Haggadah, *Jew. Enc.* VIII (1904), 550–69.

THIERING, B., The Poetic Forms of the Hodayot, *J. Sem. Stud.* 8 (1963), 189–209.

THOMSON, R., *Tänkandets psykologi*. Stockholm 1963.

THORNDIKE, J. P., The Apocalypse of Weeks and the Qumran Sect, *Rev. Qumr.* 3 (1961/62), 163–84.

THRALL, M. E., *Greek Particles in the New Testament*. Linguistic and Exegetical Studies. (NT Tools and Stud. 3.) Leiden 1962.

TILLMANN, F., *Die Wiederkunft Christi nach den paulinischen Briefen*. (Bibl. Stud. 14: 1–2.) Freiburg i. Br. 1909.

TORREY, C. C., *Documents of the Primitive Church*. New York, London 1941.

—— Notes on the Greek Texts of Enoch, *J. Amer. Orient. Soc.* 62 (1942), 52–60.

—— "Taxo" in the Assumption of Moses, *J. Bibl. Lit.* 62 (1943), 1–7.

—— "Taxo" once More, *J. Bibl. Lit.* 64 (1945), 395–97.

TRILLING, W., *Das wahre Israel*. Studien zur Theologie des Matthäusevangeliums. (Erfurt. Theol. Stud. 7.) Leipzig 1959.

TURNER, C. H., Marcan Usage: Notes, Critical and Exegetical, on the Second Gospel, *J. Theol. Stud.* 28 (1927), 9–30, 349–62.

—— Western Readings in the Second Half of St Mark's Gospel, *J. Theol. Stud.* 29 (1928), 1–16.

ULLENDORFF, E., An Aramaic "Vorlage" of the Ethiopic Text of Enoch, in *Atti del Convegno Intern. di Studi Etiop.*, *Roma 1958* (Quaderni ... Lincei 48), Roma 1960, 259–68.

VALÉRY, P., The Course in Poetics: First Lesson, in B. Ghiselin (ed.), *The Creative Process*, Berkeley, Los Angeles 1952, 92–105.

VANHOYE, A., L'utilisation du livre d'Ézéchiel dans l'Apocalypse, *Bibl.* 43 (1962), 436–76.

VAWTER, B., "And He Shall Come Again with Glory", *Analecta Bibl.* 17 (1963), 143–50.

VIELHAUER, P., *Oikodome*. Das Bild vom Bau in der christlichen Literatur vom Neuen Testament bis Clemens Alexandrinus. Diss. Heidelberg. (Printed at) Karlsruhe-Durlach 1940.

—— Propheten III A., *Rel. in Gesch. u. Geg.* V (3rd ed. 1961), 633–34.

—— In E. Hennecke, W. Schneemelcher (ed.), *Neutestamentliche Apokryphen* ... II, 3rd ed., Tübingen 1964: 407–27: Apokalypsen und Verwandtes, Einleitung; 428–54: Apokalyptik des Urchristentums, Einleitung.

Volz, P., *Jesaia II.* (Komm. z. AT 9: 2.) Leipzig 1932.

—— *Die Eschatologie der jüdischen Gemeinde* im neutestamentlichen Zeitalter, nach den Quellen der rabbinischen, apokalyptischen und apokryphen Literatur. Zweite Auflage des Werkes „Jüdische Eschatologie von Daniel bis Akiba" [1903]. Tübingen 1934.

Volz, P., Rudolph, W., *Der Elohist als Erzähler, ein Irrweg der Pentateuchkritik?* An der Genesis erläutert. (Zschr. At. Wiss., Beih. 63.) Giessen 1933.

Vos, G., *The Pauline Eschatology.* Grand Rapids 1953.

Wallace, D. H., The Semitic Origin of the Assumption of Moses, *Theol. Zschr.* 11 (1955), 321–28.

Weber, F., *Jüdische Theologie* auf Grund des Talmud und verwandter Schriften. 2nd ed. Leipzig 1897.

Wegenast, K., *Das Verständnis der Tradition bei Paulus und in den Deuteropaulinen.* (Wiss. Monogr. z. A u. NT 8.) Neukirchen Kr. Moers 1962.

Weiss, B., *Die Evangelien des Markus und Lukas.* (Krit.-exeg. Komm. ü. d. NT I: 2, 9th ed.) Göttingen 1901.

—— *Das Matthäus-Evangelium.* (Krit.-exeg. Komm. ü. d. NT I: 1, 10th ed.) Göttingen 1910.

Weiss, J., *Die Predigt Jesu vom Reiche Gottes.* Göttingen 1892.

Welch, A. C., A Zealot Pamphlet, *Expositor Ser.* 8 25 (1923), 273–87.

Wellhagen, J., *Anden och riket.* Lukas religiösa åskådning med särskild hänsyn till eskatologien. Diss. Uppsala. (Nytestam. avhandl. 1.) Stockholm 1941.

Wellhausen, J., *Das Evangelium Marci.* 2nd ed. Berlin 1909.

Wendland, H. D., *Die Eschatologie des Reiches Gottes bei Jesus.* Eine Studie über den Zusammenhang von Eschatologie, Ethik und Kirchenproblem. Gütersloh 1931.

Wendling, E., *Die Entstehung des Marcus-Evangeliums.* Philologische Untersuchungen. Tübingen 1908.

Wernberg-Møller, P., Observations on the Interchange of ע and ה in the Manual of Discipline (DSD), *Vet. Test.* 3 (1953), 104–07.

—— Some Reflections on the Biblical Material in the Manual of Discipline, *Stud. Theol.* 9 (1955), 40–66.

—— Waw and Yod in the "Rule of Community" (1 QS), *Rev. Qumr.* 2 (1959/60), 223–36.

Werner, M., *Die Entstehung des christlichen Dogmas* problemgeschichtlich dargestellt. Bern, Leipzig 1941.

Wichmann, W., *Die Leidenstheologie.* Eine Form der Leidendeutung im Spätjudentum. (Beitr. z. Wiss. v. A u. NT IV: 2.) Stuttgart 1930.

Widengren, G., *Psalm 110 och det sakrala kungadömet i Israel.* (Uppsala Univ. Årsskrift 1941: 7: 1.) Uppsala, Leipzig 1941.

—— *Till det sakrala kungadömets historia i Israel.* (Horae Soederbl. I: 3.) Stockholm 1947.

—— *Literary and Psychological Aspects of the Hebrew Prophets.* (Uppsala Univ. Årsskrift 1948: 10.) Uppsala, Leipzig 1948.

—— *The Ascension of the Apostle and the Heavenly Book* (King and Saviour III). (Uppsala Univ. Årsskrift 1950: 7.) Uppsala, Leipzig 1950.

—— *Religionens värld.* Religionsfenomenologiska studier och översikter. 2nd ed. Stockholm 1953.

—— *Sakrales Königtum im Alten Testament und im Judentum.* (Franz Delitzsch-Vorles. 1952.) Stuttgart 1955.

—— Quelques rapports entre Juifs et Iraniens à l'époque des Parthes, *Suppl. Vet. Test.* 4 (1957), 197–241.

—— *Iranisch-semitische Kulturbegegnung in parthischer Zeit.* (Arbeitsgemeinsch. f. Forsch. d. Landes Nordrhein-Westf., Geisteswiss. 70.) Köln, Opladen 1960.

—— [a review article on] E. S. Drower, The Canonical Prayerbook of the Mandaeans, *J. Royal As. Soc.* (1961), 124–26.

WIFSTRAND, A., Lukas och Septuaginta, *Svensk Teol. Kvartalskrift* 16 (1940), 243–62.

WIKENHAUSER, A., *Einleitung in das Neue Testament.* 2nd ed. Freiburg 1956.

—— *Die Offenbarung des Johannes.* (Regensb. NT 9.) 3rd ed. Regensburg 1959.

WILDER, A. N., The Eschatology of Jesus in Recent Criticism and Interpretation, *J. Rel.* 28 (1948), 177–87.

—— Eschatological Imagery and Earthly Circumstance, *NT Stud.* 5 (1958/59), 229–45.

WIMMER, A., Trostworte des Apostels Paulus an Hinterbliebene in Thessalonich (1 Th 4, 13–17), *Bibl.* 36 (1955), 273–86.

WINDISCH, H., *Die Orakel des Hystaspes.* (Verhandel. d. Koninkl. Akad. van Wetensch., Amsterdam, Letterkunde, N.R. 28: 3.) Amsterdam 1929.

WINTER, P., The Treatment of His Sources by the Third Evangelist in Luke xxi–xxiv, *Stud. Theol.* 8 (1954), 138–72.

WOHLENBERG, G., *Der erste und zweite Thessalonicherbrief.* (Komm. z. NT 12.) 2nd ed. Leipzig 1909.

WOLFSON, H. A., *Philo.* Foundations of Religious Philosophy in Judaism, Christianity, and Islam I–II. 2nd ed. Cambridge, Mass. 1948.

WOUDE, A. S. VAN DER, *Die messianischen Vorstellungen der Gemeinde von Qumrân.* Diss. Assen. (Stud. Sem. Neerland. 3.) Assen 1957.

WRIGHT, L. E., *Alterations of the Words of Jesus as Quoted in the Literature of the Second Century.* (Harv. Hist. Monogr. 25.) Cambridge, Mass. 1952.

ZAHN, TH., *Das Evangelium des Matthäus.* (Komm. z. NT 1.) 2nd ed. Leipzig 1905.

ZEITLIN, S., The Apocrypha, *Jew. Quart. Rev.* 37 (1946/47), 219–48.

ZIMMERLI, W., *Ezechiel.* (Bibl. Komm. AT 13.) Neukirchen–Vluyn 1962–63.

ZIMMERMANN, F., Textual Observations on the Apocalypse of Baruch, *J. Theol. Stud.* 40 (1939), 151–56.

—— Underlying Documents of IV Ezra, *Jew. Quart. Rev.* 51 (1960/61), 107–34.

ZIMMERMANN, H., Das absolute Ἐγώ εἰμι als die neutestamentliche Offenbarungsformel, *Bibl. Zschr.* N.F. 4 (1960), 54–69, 226–76.

—— Das absolute „Ich bin" in der Redeweise Jesu, *Trier. Theol. Zschr.* 69 (1960), 1–20.

ZUNTZ, G., Notes on the Greek Enoch, *J. Bibl. Lit.* 61 (1942), 193–204.

—— Enoch on the Last Judgement, *J. Theol. Stud.* 45 (1944), 161–70.

—— The Greek Text of Enoch 102, 1–3, *J. Bibl. Lit.* 63 (1944), 53–54.

Index of Authors

289

Index of Passages

Old Testament and Apocrypha (selection)

GENESIS

3_{15}: 48, 16: 48, 17 ff.: 48, 23 f.: 48
6_5: 32
7_{21} ff.: 115
19_{12}: *163*, 14: 163, 17: *151*, 173, 177
30_{20}: 111
49: 105, 8: 138

EXODUS

1–15: 67 f.
3_5: *133*, 14: 147
4_{11} ff.: 168, 12: 228, 230, 15: 238, 230
7–12: 75
7_{20}: 77
14_8 f.: 125, 13: 67, 14: 113, 28: ff.: 67
15_7: 67, 10: 67, 12: 87
16_{29}: *163*, 173
19_5: 116, 11: 72, 114, 16: 115, 135, 18: 115, 20: 72, *114*
20_{18}: 115

LEVITICUS

26: 33

NUMBERS

6_{24-26}: *116*
10_{35}: 129 f.
16_{30}: *88*, 30 ff.: 73, *86*
24_3: *113 f.*, 4: *113*, 7: *113*, 8: 138

DEUTERONOMY

4_{28}: 124
13_2: *155*, 173, 2 f.: 77, *199*, 4: *155*, 177, 6: *199*, 6 f.: *155*, 7: 173, 9: 177, 11: 199, 14: 77, 155, *199*
26_8: 77
28: 33, 46: 76, 50: *81*
29_{16}: 152, 19–22: 152
30_3 f.: *156*, 174
31_{17}: 151, 21: 151
32_{39}: 147, 43: 127
33: 105, 1: *113*, 2: 72, *114*, 117, 29: *130*

JUDGES

5_5: 115
6_1 ff.: 33
13_6: 118

1 SAMUEL

16_{10} ff.: 119
21_{13}: 230
29_9: 118

2 SAMUEL

22_8: 133

1 KINGS

21_6: 230

1 CHRONICLES

29_{23}: 35, 39

2 CHRONICLES

15_5 f.: *79 f.*, 6: *148*, 151, 173, 176

NEHEMIAH

10_{34}: 192
13_{31}: 192

JOB

8_{22}: 122
15_{25}: *124*
17_{13} ff.: *122*
40_{11} ff.: 122

PSALMS

1_3: 116
2: 65, 108 f., 1 f.: 80, 2: 90, *92*, 2 f.: *121*, 5: *92*, 8 f.: 120, 9: *99*
3_8: *121*
7_9: 115
8_4: 116, 5: 158
9_7: *88*, 8 f.: 42
12_6: 129
16_5 f.: 120
17_{25} ff.: 46, 28: 45, 47
18_5 f.: 192, 14 f.: 73, 16 f.: 130, 28: 113, 122, 39 f.: *100*
24_5: 116
33_8: 135
37_{34}: *130 f.*
41_9: 122
49_7: *124*
50_{23}: 135
52_9: *124*
58_7: 121
59_6: 130
63_{10} f.: *87*
64_8 f. (Lxx): 78
65_8 f.: 233
67_2: 116, 5: 26, 8: 115
68_1: 129, 2 f.: 95, 2–4: 60, 3: 115
69_{27}: 125
72: 68
74_{10}: 125
75_5 f.: 162
76_{10}: 129 f.
78: 75, 4 ff.: *113 f.*
79_1: 100, 3: *81*
82_5: 133
83_{17}: 122
85_9: 116, 12: *136*
91_8: 131, 16: *135*
92_{12}: 131

9_6: 72, $_{13}$: 115, 117, 130
9_7: 72 f., $_5$: 36, *115*, $_{11}$: 116
98_9: 115
102_{17}: 127, $_{27}$: *133*
106_{41}: 168 f., $_{47}$: 156
109_{16}: 125
110_1: 39, $_{1-6}$: 65 f.
114_4: 36, $_6$: 36
118_7: 131
119_{46}: 168, $_{86}$: 125

Proverbs
11_{28}: 124
14_8: 161

Isaiah
1_{24}: 127
2_4: 42, $_8$: 124, $_{11}$: 122, $_{12}$ ff.: 129, $_{19}$: 129 f., $_{21}$: 130
3_{13}: 130
4_2 f.: 135
5_{14}: *88*, 91, $_{25}$: 129
6_4: *133*, $_6$: 119
9_2: 116, $_6$ f.: 119
9_8-10_{34}: 33
10_{3-6}: 231 f., $_5$: 86, $_{20}$: 113, $_{22}$: 135
11_{1-9}: 66, $_3$ ff.: 119, $_4$: 42, *86, 96, 99*, 199, $_6$ ff.: 48, $_{10}$ f.: 156, $_{10}$ ff.: *165* f., 174
13_4: 233, $_{4-15}$: 232, $_5$ ff.: 233, $_{10}$: 73, 129, *156*, 174, 233, $_{11}$: 122, *134*, $_{13}$: 73, 129, 133, $_{19}$: *129*
14_9: *121*, $_{11}$: 122, $_{13}$: *124*, 172, $_{13}$ f.: 34, *160 f.*, 199, $_{15}$: 87, $_{22}$: 129 f.
18_3: 135
19_2: *80, 88, 135, 148*, 168 f., 173, 213, $_5$: 130, $_{12}$: 176
24-27: 27
24_{18}: 133, $_{19}$: 115
26_5: 122, $_{21}$: 73, *114*, *129* f., *134*
27_{13}: 135, *156, 166*, 174
28_{21}: 129
30_{10}: 170, $_{30}$ f.: 74
32_{16}: 119
33_2 f.: *85*

34_4: 48, *156*, 174, $_7$: 94
35_{10}: *127*
37_{22}: 135
38_{18}: 122
40_2: *130, 134*, $_4$: *115*, 129, $_5$: *127, 134*, $_9$: *127*, $_{10}$: 134, $_{31}$: *130*
41_4: 147
42_1: *119*
43_5 ff.: 156, $_6$: *158*, 174, $_{10}$: *119*
45_3: *119*, $_4$: 113, $_{18}$: 160
47_8: 147, 160, 172, $_{10}$: 147, 160
49_7: *119*, 121, $_{13}$: 116, $_{23}$: 138
51_{11}: *127*
52_2: 121
56_8: 156
59_{1-21}: 58
60_1 f.: 116, $_2$: 127, $_{5-14}$: 138, $_{14}$ f.: 138
64_1: 36, 115, 129, $_2$: *115*, $_3$: 115, 129
65_9: 113, $_{15}$: 113, $_{22}$: 113
66_{14}: 131, $_{15}$ ff.: *117*, $_{24}$: 131

Jeremiah
1_{11} f.: 111, $_{15}$: *92*
2_{18}: 155
5_{12}: 125, $_{31}$: 155
6_{22} f.: *81*
13_{22} ff.: 33
16_{10} ff.: 33, $_{19}$: 113
23_{1-8}: 62, $_5$ f.: *119*, $_{13}$: 147, $_{15}$ f.: 155, $_{32}$: 147
25_{31}: 115, *117*
29_8 f.: 147, $_{14}$: 156
30_7: 152, $_9$: *100*, $_{22}$: 116
31_1: 116, $_8$ ff.: 156
32_{26} ff.: 33, $_{37}$: 156, $_{38}$ f.: 116
33_{1-15}: 68, $_{15}$ f.: *119*
50_{44}: 90
51_6: 230, $_{11}$: *88 ff.*, $_{29}$: 135

Lamentations
4_6: 152 f., $_{13}$: 33

Ezekiel
1_{22} ff.: *134*, $_{24}$: *133*, $_{26}$: 39

2_1 f.: *133*
3_{24}: *133*
7_{16}: 151, $_{19}$: 36
11_{19}: 136, $_{20}$: 116
12_{24}: 170
14_{22}: 135
20_{48}: 134
21_{26}: 122, $_{29}$: *124*
22_{27}: *88*
28_2 ff.: 199 f., $_{25}$: 156
30_{12} f.: 130
32_7: 156, $_9$ f.: 156
34: 62, *83 f.*, $_{12}$ f.: 156
35: 33, $_8$: *93*
36_{26}: 136
37 ff.: *92 ff.*
37_{21}: 156
38 f.: 47, 59, 81
38_7 ff.: 85, $_9$: 139, $_{16}$: 139, $_{19}$ ff.: 86
39_{21}: 134
43_2: *133*

Daniel
2_{21}: 192, $_{27-45}$: 146, $_{28}$ f.: *148*, 173, $_{31-35}$: *97*, $_{31-45}$: 234, $_{34}$: 146, $_{38-43}$: 97, $_{40}$: 146, *148*, $_{44}$: 146, 247, $_{44}$ f.: 97, $_{45}$: 146, *148*, 173
4_{22}: *122*, $_{23}$: 192, $_{27}$: *122*, $_{29}$: *122*, $_{34}$: *122*
5_{20} f.: *122*, $_{28}$: 88
6_{13} ff.: 168
7_{2-14}: 97, $_{2-27}$: 146, $_7$: 146, $_{7-27}$: 235, $_8$: *160*, 172, $_9$: 118, $_9$ ff.: 35, *63, 86*, 157, $_{10}$: 114 f., *117, 134*, $_{10}$ ff.: 117, $_{11}$: *160*, 172, $_{12}$: 192, $_{13}$: 38, 96 f., 118, *166, 186 f.*, 190 f., $_{13}$ f.: 40, *156*, 174, $_{14}$: 166, $_{16}$: *119*, $_{19}$: *124*, 146, $_{20}$: *160*, 172, $_{20}$ f.: 161, 173, $_{21}$: *148*, $_{23}$: *124*, 146, $_{23-27}$: *57 f.*, $_{25}$: 117, 146, 150, 160, 168 f., 173, 214, $_{26}$: 40, 117
8_4: 146, $_{8-11}$: 146, $_{9-26}$: 235, $_{10}$: 146, 162, $_{10}$ f.: *160 f.*, 172, $_{11}$: 34, 153, $_{12}$ f.: 146,

13: *119*, 13 f.: 100, 15 ff.: 113, 17 ff.: 133, 19: *148*, 173, 176, 23 ff.: 173, 24: *155*, 24 f.: 146, 150, 25: *160 f.*, 172, 176, 27: 146
922–27: 146, 24–27: 235, 26: *148*, 173, 26 f.: 146, 27: *151*, *162*, 173, 200
106: *133*, 9: *133*, 11 ff.: *133*, 13 f.: 84, 20: *88 f.*

11 f.: 95
113: 171, 4–27: *148*, 25 ff.: 173, 30 ff.: 150, 31: 146, *151*, 31 f.: 173, 32: 150, 168, 32 ff.: 214, 216, 32–35: *169 ff.*, 35: 150, 168, 173, 36: 146, *160*, 172, *198 f.*, 36 f.: 146, 36–45: *155*, 37 f.: 173, 41: *169*, 41 ff.: *83 f.*
1121–1213: 235
121: *84 f.*, 95, 113, *127*, *151 f.*, *164*, 168 f., 173, 2 f.: *189*, 2–4: 110, 3: 170 f., 4: 52, *169 f.*, 7: *145 f.*, *159*, 220 f., 9 f.: 52, 11: 146, *151*, 173, 12: *167* ff.

HOSEA
19 f.: 116
214: 218

JOEL
120: 130
21: *135*, 10: 73, *129*, *156*, 173, 232, 10 f.: 74
33: 77, 156, 232, 3 f.: *76*, 4: 73, *129*, 5: 135, 12: 78
42: 115, 15: *129*, *156*

AMOS
36: *135*
413: *114*
515: 116

OBADIAH
14: 113

MICAH
13: 73, *114*, *129*, 3 f.: 72, 4: 36, *115*, 7: 73, *130*

51–9: 69
72: *168*, 219, 2 ff.: 173, 213 f., 6: 91, *168*, 6 f.: 173, 7: 168 f.

NAHUM
12: 113, 127, 4: 73, *129 f.*, 5: 115, 5 f.: 73, 129, 7: 113
33: *88*

HABAKKUK
216: 122, 18: 36
33 f.: *114*, 6: 72, *115*, 129, 9: *115*, 16: 113, 152

ZEPHANIAH
15 ff.: 152, 7–15: 232, 15: 113, 18: 36
215: 160
33: 90

ZECHARIAH
22: 119, 10: 156, 174, 13 (17): 114, 129
99: 119
121–9: 82, 2 f.: 85, 2–4: *89*, 3: 231, 8: 118 f., 9: 91, 10 ff.: 94, 12: *156*, *165 f.*, 174, 14: 156, 165 f., 174
145: 156, 6: 129, 13: *88*, 135

MALACHI
35: 117, 134
46: *136*

WISDOM
88: 34, 77

SIRACH
720: 69
1511 ff.: 25
3310 ff.: 25
3614: 218

1 MACCABEES
137 f.: 100, 54: 200, 59: 200
228: 151, 162, 241, 34: 163
345: 100, 231, 51: 100, 231
436 ff.: 100, 60: 231

---

2 MACCABEES
62: 200, 7: 200, 18: 100
52 ff.: 34
515 f.: 100
7: 49
910: 160
82: 100, 231
103 ff.: 100
115 f.: 85
116–8: 84

Pseudepigrapha

1 ENOCH
11–2: *113 f.*, 1–3a: 112, 2a: 112 f., 2: 118, 3 ff.: 35, 40, 3–9: 53, *60*, *71 ff.*, *112–18*, 125, 4: 141, 5: 79 7: 42 f., 7 f.: 44, 7 ff.: 40, 8: 47, 9: 41 ff., 46
21: 113 f.
10: 32, 42, 9: 115, 15: 115, 16: 47 f., 17: 47 f., 18 ff.: 48, 21: 48
1016–112: 53, 55 f.
111: 48, 2: 47
1222 ff.: 115
1310: 115
149 ff.: 39
253: 35, 3 f.: 42, 45, 3–6: 53, *59 f.*, 4: 40, 42, 44, 4 f.: 48, 6: 47 f.
381: 44, 1 ff.: 166, 1–6: 53, 63, 2: 37, 47, 2 ff.: 39, 3: 46, 4: 46 f., 5: 89
395: 47, 6 f.: 37
451–6: 53, 118, 3: 39, 47, 4: 47, 4 ff.: 63 f., 5: 48, 6: 42, 44, 47, 166
461–8: 53, 63, *118–26*, 1 ff.: 141, 3 ff.: 39, 4: 89 f., 4 f.: 89, 4 ff.: 41, 46, 166, 7: 34, 160, 7 f.: 29, 8: 52
472: 29, 42, 3: 35
47–48: 118
471–4810: 53, *63*, 65
481: 47, 2 ff.: 37, 39, 3: 141, 3 ff.: 39, 4: 47, 4 f.: 48, 6: 38, 6 f.: 35, 7: 30, 37, 41, 47, 8: 46, 89, 166, 9: 46, 67, 9 f.: 46

49$_1$ ff.: 96, 1–4: 53
50$_1$: 47, 3: 41, 47, 4: 42, 44, 46
50$_1$–51$_5$: 53, 63
51$_1$: 45, 1 ff.: 39, 2: 41, 3 ff.: 39, 47, 4: *36*, 74, 5: 47
52$_1$–53$_7$: 53, 63
52$_2$ ff.: 36, 7–9: *36*, 9: 37 f.
53$_1$: 44, 46, 2 f.: 46, 5: 46, 89, 6: 52
54$_2$: 89
55$_3$: 88, 4: 89
55$_3$–57$_3$: 64 f.
56: 84, 1 ff.: 45, 5–8: *88–91*, 6 ff.: 47, 7: 31
56$_1$–57$_3$: 53
57$_1$: 88, 1 f.: 47, 3: 48
58$_{1-6}$: 53 f., 2 f.: 47, 2 ff.: 39, 3: 48
61$_{1-13}$: 53, 4 f.: 39, 8: 39 f., 42, 8 f.: 44
62$_1$ ff.: 166, 1–16: 53, 63, 2: 39, 42, 46, 2 f.: 44, 2 ff.: 41, 3: 89 f., 4 f.: 46, 7: 37 f., 8: 47, 9: 89, 9 f.: 46, 48, 10 f.: 46, 11 f.: 46, 14 f.: 47
63: 55, 1: 89, 1–12: 53, 63. 8: 42, 11: 46
67$_{12}$: 218
69$_{26}$: 37, 26–29: 53, 63, *64*, 27: 39 f., 42, 28: 46
71$_5$ ff.: 39, 14 ff.: 39, 14–17: 53, 16 f.: 47
80$_2$ f.: 31, 2–8: 53, 55 f., 4 ff.: 31, 7: 30, 8: 46
81$_1$ f.: 24
82$_1$ ff.: 52
84 ff.: 104
89$_{16}$: 85, 141, 20: 85, 141, 59: 65, 63: 218, 70 f.: 86, 76: 218, 76 f.: 86
90: 94, 1 ff.: 84, 11–42: *61 f.*, 12 ff.: 95, 13–19: 53, 62, *81–88*, 13 ff.: 90, 137, 141, 15: 35, 141, 18: 35, 71, 73, 141, 20 ff.: 40, 42 f., 62, 20–27: 83, 20–42: 53, 21 ff.: 45, 24 ff.: 46, 25 f.: 44, 26: 41, 28 f.: 48, 28–38: 83, 30:

48, 33: 47, 33 ff.: 47, 37: 47 f., 37 f.: 38
91$_{1-11}$: 105, 5 ff.: 32, 6: 32, 6 f.: 30, 6–11: 53, 55 f., 7: 35, 40, 43, 9: 45 f., 10: 47, 49, 11: 46, 48, 12: 42, 44, 12–17: 53, 87, 13 f.: 48, 14: 44, 14 f.: 43, 15: 42, 45, 16 f.: 48, 18 f.: 105
92$_{1-5}$: 105, 2: 24, 2–5: 53, 3: 49, 4: 47, 5: 48
93: 87, 2: 24, 2–15: 35, 4 ff.: 32, 9: 30, 9 f.: 53, 10: 52
96$_4$: 218
97$_3$ f.: 218
99$_1$: 46, 1 f.: 78, 1 ff.: 30, 1–16: 53, 55 f., 2: 46, 3: 218, 4: 30, *78 f.*, 5: 30, 7: 30, 8: 46, 8 ff.: 30, 9: 46, 10: 41, 47, 12 f.: 46, 13 ff.: 47, 15: 30, 15 f.: 44, 16: 46
100$_1$ f.: 80, 1–9: 53, *55 f.*, 4: 35, 44, 46, 5: 48, 6: 52, 7 ff.: 46
102: 35, 1: 46, 1 f.: *73 f.*, 1–11: 53, 55 ff., 3: 79, 5: 42
103$_{1-15}$: 53, 55 f., 2: 24, 3 f.: 47, 6: 42, 8: 46
104$_2$: 47, 13: 52
104$_1$–105$_2$: 53, 55 f., *61*
105$_2$: 47, 61
106$_{13}$ ff.: 32, 19: 24, 32
106$_{18}$–107$_1$: 53
106$_{19}$–107$_1$: 30

2 ENOCH
201–215: 39

JUBILEES
5$_9$ ff.: 32, 13: 24 f., 30 f., 14: 45
23$_{11}$ ff.: 32, 11–31: 53, 55 f., 12 f.: 30, 14: 30, 16: 52, 17 ff.: 30, 18: 31, 19: 30, 23: 31, *80 f.*, 23 ff.: 30, 27 f.: 48, 28: 47, 28 f.: 46, 30: 46 f., 30 f.: 42 f.
41$_{24}$ ff: 25

PSALMS OF SOLOMON
2: 31, 81, 1 ff.: 33, 100, 20: 100
3$_{16}$: 49
9$_7$: 25
11$_1$: 167
14$_5$: 25
17$_5$ ff.: 100, 5–51: 53, *66 f.*, 15 ff.: 30, 20: 31, 20 f.: 31, 34, 21: 32, 22: 30, 23: 35 f., 23 ff.: 27, 47, 23–27: *99 f.*, 24 ff.: 39, 25: 231, 27: 45, 199, 28: 33, 40, 42 f., 28 f.: 48, 31: 42 f., 45, 31 ff.: 48, 33: 99, 35 f.: 44, 45 f.: 65, 48: 40, 42 f., 51: 41, 47

TESTAMENTS OF THE XII PATRIARCHS
Levi
3$_9$: 74
4: 52, 1: 30 f., 42 ff., *74 f.*, 1–4: 53, 55, 6: 46
5$_2$: 47
14$_1$: 30
14$_1$–16$_5$: 53, 55
15$_2$: 43 f.
17$_{11}$: 30
17$_{11}$–18$_{14}$: 53, 67
18$_1$ f.: 67, 2: 36, 40, 42 ff., 2 ff.: 39, 4 f.: 47, 7: 52, 9: 47 f., 10 f.: 48, 12: 41, 46, 13 f.: 47

Judah
21$_8$ f.: 30
21$_6$–22$_3$: 32, 53, 55 f.
22$_2$: 31, 35, 47, 81
23$_1$: 30, 3: 31, 81, 3 f.: 31, 5: 33
23$_1$–25 5: *53*, 67
23$_5$–24$_1$: 67
24$_1$: 39, 3: 47, 4: 48, 6: 43
25$_1$ ff.: 49, 3: 46, 48, 4: 49, 5: 47

Issachar
6$_1$: 30, 1–2: 53, 4: 33

Other Texts

Did. 7₁: 191
  9₁: 191
  11₃: 191
  16: 206 f., 4: 235
Herm. *Sim.* IV 2–5: 223

Orig. *Hom. in Jer.* IV. 3:
  202
Eus. *Hist. eccl.* III. 39, 15:
  220
Apollinaris *Fragm. 127*: 243
Theod. Heracl. *Fragm. 122*:
  152

Apc. Petri 1–2: 206 f.
  2: 235
Asc. Is. 4₂₋₁₃: 235
Aristotle *De mem.* 2: 109
Demosth. 140,17: 223
Polyb. 3, 2, 8: 229